ROMANTIC WOMEN POETS

1770 – 1838

Romantic women poets 1770-1838

Volume 1 (revised edition)

edited by
Andrew Ashfield

Manchester University Press
Manchester and New York

distributed exclusively in the USA and Canada
by St. Martin's Press

First edition published 1995 by Manchester University Press

This edition published 1997 by
Manchester University Press
Oxford Road, Manchester M13 9NR, UK
and Room 400, 175 Fifth Avenue, New York, NY 10010, USA

Distributed exclusively in the USA by
St. Martin's Press, Inc., 175 Fifth Avenue, New York,
NY 10010, USA

Distributed exclusively in Canada by
UBC Press, University of British Columbia, 6344 Memorial Road,
Vancouver, BC, Canada V6T 1Z2

British Library Cataloguing-in-Publication Data

A catalogue record for this book is available from the British Library

Library of Congress Cataloging-in-Publication Data

Women romantic poets. 1770–1838: an anthology / edited by Andrew Ashfield.

p. cm.

ISBN 0-7190-3788-3 (hardback). -- ISBN 0-7190-3789-1 (paperback)

1. English poetry--Women authors. 2. English poetry--19th century. 3. English poetry--18th century. 4. Romanticism--Great Britain.

PR1177.W65 1994
821'.6080145'082--dc20 93-37288

ISBN 0 7190 5308 0 *paperback*

First published 1997

01 00 99 98 97 10 9 8 7 6 5 4 3 2 1

Typeset by Bryan Williamson, Frome, Somerset
Printed in Great Britain
by Bell & Bain Ltd, Glasgow

Contents

Note to the revised edition

For the revised edition I have corrected a few errors, updated a few references and omitted one poem previously attributed to Anna Barbauld by a nineteenth-century editor which now seems to me to be doubtful.

Editorial principles remain the same. Texts have been lightly modernised, mostly involving the expansion of contractions, the modernisation of some archaic spellings and, in the case of Mary Robinson, a reduction of extensive capitalisation. Since the arrangement of texts is, by and large, chronological, I have generally preferred first printings. In a few cases I have preferred a later printing, if a text was more generally known in this form, and have supplied information on the earlier printing in the notes.

The book offers a fairly thick description of women's relationship to modes of transcendence and power in the period and attempts to chart the possibilities of a female sublime or counter sublime. This is certainly not the whole story of women's poetry in the period and I shall, at some stage, present evidence of other concerns and other dimensions.

Introduction

In the eighteenth century the idea of a canon of English poetry emerged, culminating in vast historical collections of English verse.[1] This legislative activity which prescribes best texts is accompanied by a profoundly unstable and transgressive technical vocabulary together with new technologies designed to heighten the affective power of texts. These two activities—the advent of a national canon and the advent of a type of highly subjective and emotionally involved reading—are bound together and create a cluster of complications for our understanding of women's poetry.

The first complication concerns the absence of any woman poet in the national collections. The earliest national collections, appearing in the early 1770s, quickly canonised recently deceased poets such as Akenside (d.1770), Chatterton (d.1770), Gray (d.1771) and Smart (d.1771) together with many other poets who had died in the 1750s and 1760s. The booksellers, in an attempt to avoid payments to living authors, simply collected the works of the recently deceased poets and incorporated them into the existing canon. As a result, the canon becomes skewed at this point—a generation of minor dead poets is canonised and the modern is made classic—and as we know from the mechanics of other canons, once you're in, you're in. Living poets had a much harder time of it and few scholars have ever unravelled the complications of having a plethora of minor figures of the 1770s in the canon and a wide range of poets in the 1780s and 1790s excluded. By the time the major women candidates printed in this volume became available for canonical inclusion, other forces operated to exclude them. Some figures such as Barbauld, Williams, More, Baillie and Alderson simply outlived the major period of the national collections (1773–1810). This left only Robinson (d.1800), Smith (d.1806) and Seward (d.1809) available for inclusion. Marital difficulties, liberal connections and political verse in the 1790s probably required Smith's and Robinson's exclusion, leaving only Seward as a safe choice. Yet she too was excluded. After 1810, the canon of English verse veers away from a concern to promote mid-eighteenth-century poets and is more concerned with the reputations of those male poets we now call 'the Romantics'. At first Byron and Scott eclipse all other poets. In the 1820s and 1830s a dual mythology emerges, centring on the healing power of Wordsworth and the fate of the poet as exemplified by the deaths of Keats (1821), Shelley (1822) and Byron (1824), and Coleridge's loss of power. The fate of the poet and the reader's recovery through poetry prove a delicious blend of weakness and robustness which will resonate throughout the Victorian period. The healing power of Wordsworth for De Quincey, Hazlitt, Mill, Newman, Arnold, and many others, stands in stark contrast to the idea of the fated and isolated poet which Galignani's *The Poetical Works of Coleridge, Shelley, and Keats* (Paris, 1829) had begun to promote. In 1833, when Wordsworth looked at the problem of the omission of the women poets from the canon, it was too late. The radical women poets of the 1790s—Barbauld, Smith, Williams, Robinson, Alderson—had largely been forgotten.

Attention to women poets in the 1830s was centred not on the contribution they had made in the 1790s to the development of Romanticism but on the specifically feminine characteristics of a new generation of women poets whose figureheads were Hemans and Landon. In the space of less than thirty years two distinct generations of women poets had been firmly characterised according to how they matched up to established and accepted gender characteristics. The first generation mostly consisted of dissenting radicals or sympathisers: Barbauld, Williams, Smith, Robinson, Hays, Alderson and, although she was not a poet, Wollstonecraft. Under threat of invasion, at a time of national crisis, these women were perceived as 'unsex'd females', their perverse politics firmly linked to gender perversity.[2] The second generation, with the exception of Jewsbury and Roberts, who still retained certain 'masculine' intellectual traits of the dissenting radicals, embraced the notion of the 'poetess' and were widely admired for their feminine concerns. Yet just as the generation of the 1790s had largely been forgotten by the 1830s, so too the generation of the 1820s and 1830s was largely disparaged and forgotten in the second half of the century. (Certain figures, such as Hemans, survived in popular taste, but were not canonical. Other figures such as Landon, Abdy, Browne and Jewsbury were simply forgotten.) The suspicion must be that it is a complicated law of literary history that the characterisation of women's literature—be it as perversely masculine, 'unsex'd', or sweetly feminine—ensures that it can never be canonical and survive as a persistent object of attention.

This erasure of the radical unsex'd females from literary history and the promotion of the exquisitely female 'poetess' in the 1830s leads us back to a second set of complications which accompanied the formation of the English canon. In the eighteenth century literature became no longer the best vehicle for moral precepts, it became the actual site of moral activity itself. The key terms most eighteenth-century writers used to describe the intense passions generated by exposure to great authors were 'ravishment' and 'transport' (which also meant the taking away of a woman by force).[3] Readers were ravished into a more refined being and transported to the site of romance. Literature became both virtual reality and the source of new virtues. The reading of imaginative literature became a 'waking dream' where author, reader and the figures of the text fused and the reader emerged morally enhanced with ego aggrandised by commerce with the author and his figures. This was particularly true in the reading of the central canonical figures of Shakespeare, Spenser and Milton. When Joseph Warton read Shakespeare, the text seemed not only to describe moments in the drama but also to describe what was happening to the reader as he was reading. Similarly, when Thomas Warton read Spenser, he was sometimes unsure who was speaking: the poet, the poet for the reader, or the reader himself. Readers became authors and texts became deeply-layered autobiographical performances. Towards the end of the century, William Godwin declared: 'When I read Thomson, I become Thomson; when I read Milton, I become Milton. I find myself a sort of intellectual camelion, assuming the colours of the substances on which I rest.'[4]

But beyond the blurring of the distinction between author and reader, eighteenth-century readers found themselves identifying with the heroes of antiquity in the reading scene. In reading the account of the battle between Scipio and Hannibal, Lord Kames noted how he 'was insensibly transformed into a spectator' losing consciousness of the self and of reading.[5] Again by the end of the century, literature's ability to turn us into eye-witnesses had turned by degrees into an identification with the heroes themselves. In the reading scene, Godwin sometimes imagined himself 'the occupier of palaces, or the ruler of nations'. When reading Roman history, Sir James Mackintosh fancied himself the Emperor of Constantinople. Thomas Holcroft highlighted the central crux of eighteenth-century theory when he confessed that 'From the glow of poetry I learnt many noble precepts; but from the same source I derived the pernicious supposition that to conquer countries and exterminate men are the act of heroes.'[6] In short, the ravishment of literature might lead to a higher morality beyond maxims and rules, but it could also lead to levels of male fantasy located at the opposite pole of social virtues. Ancient authors might still inspire imitation but their heroes might also incite emulation. Most significantly, however, this male fantasy permeated the idea of the canon itself. Later, when Wordsworth and Arnold consider the high destinies of poetry and the English canon they will invoke the figures of Hannibal and Napoleon. The figures which haunted private reading experiences resurfaced in critical discrimination.[7]

If, as I have argued, the construction of the English canon was partly a memorial to a mid-century male coterie and partly, in the cases of Shakespeare, Spenser and Milton, the elevation of private bewilderment to national monuments, the position of women's poetry in such a canon becomes problematic. Further, when we factor in the sexed terminology of ravishment and transport, the gendered aesthetic of the sublime and the beautiful, and the figure of the conquering hero in both private reading and canonical theory, a much darker picture of the eighteenth century's commitment to imaginative literature emerges. For men, ravishment and transport reveal the mystery of being. Initially lost in the scene of romance, the eighteenth-century male reader would eventually emerge from ravishment refined with new moral prospects before him. This was not the case with women. Although they experienced similar levels of fantasy and moral awakening in the reading experience, this provoked a sustained and severe reaction from the male establishment. In an elegant and unjustly neglected piece of scholarship some years ago, John Tinnon Taylor documented male hostility to the acts of imagination and identification involved in women reading. When women experience ravishment and transport, waking dreams and 'ideal presences', these are viewed as acts of adulterous imagination.[8] When Emma Courtney discovers the pleasures of ravishment and transport, her books are taken away:

> In the course of my researches, the Heloise of Rousseau fell into my hands.—Ah! with what transport, with what enthusiasm, did I peruse this dangerous, enchanting work!—How shall I paint the sensations that were excited in my mind!—the pleasure I experienced approached the limits of pain—it was tumult—all the ardour of my character was excited. Mr. Courtney, one day, surprised me weeping over the sorrows of the tender St. Preux. He hastily snatched the book from my hand, and, carefully collecting the remaining volumes, carried them in silence to his chamber: but the impression made on my mind was never to be effaced—it was even productive of a long chain of consequences, that will continue to operate till the day of my death.[9]

Mary Wollstonecraft similarly noted how literature 'seemed to open up a new world to her—the only one worth inhabiting'. The literature of the period is littered with examples of women experiencing the same passions and complications when reading—sexed responses, blurred distinctions between author, reader and hero(ine), texts turning into autobiography, new worlds.[10] Yet while this set of complications led men to a concept of the 'imaginative self' at the heart of Romanticism, it created more complicated positions for women. For if acts of imagination were species of adultery, literature and its figures were closed to women.

For these reasons, women's Romantic poetry develops along different lines to those of the major male Romantics. In the early part of the period, the sonnet form is largely rehabilitated by three women, Anna Seward, Charlotte Smith and Helen Maria Williams, as the supreme vehicle for the expression of isolated dramatic thought in situations of loneliness before the landscape. This sense of loneliness was also shared by a number of male poets but became more acute in female experience as hostility to female literature, and to many women's radical politics, intensified. Unlike the major male Romantics who sustained long periods of friendship (Coleridge and Wordsworth, Byron and Shelley, Keats and Leigh Hunt), the female poets of the 1790s became a dispersed group, often silenced by hostile criticism. Anna Barbauld never printed many of her more radical poems of the 1790s. Charlotte Smith died alone after years of caring for a large family, Helen Maria Williams remained in exile, Mary Robinson died, crippled, ostracised and impoverished, Hannah More, Mary Hays and Amelia Alderson succumbed to religion.

By the time another cluster of women poets emerged in the 1820s and 1830s—Hemans, Landon, Jewsbury, Abdy and Browne—the memory of the talented group of the 1790s had faded. What remained, however, was a terrible anxiety concerning the status of the 'poetess', the cost of imaginative activity and the conflict between 'woman's heart' and the claims of art. For the later women poets woman's heart was hidden, its emblem a 'silent ocean cave' far 'from the tempest's power' (no. 151), yet poetic creation runs directly counter to this as 'thoughts chase thoughts, like the tumultuous billow' (no. 148). The lure of 'inspiration, vast, mighty and deep' (no. 150) threatens to open up the cave and take the poetess away from the 'household hearth' (no. 185). Again and again, these women embraced the sublime of nature and the pains of creativity but drew back, deeply worried that the exposure would endanger the cherished virtues of domesticity. In 'The Traveller at the Source of the Nile' (no. 130), Heman's explorer experiences the 'rapture of a conqueror's mood' only to find 'yearnings for his home' more powerful. Similarly, Landon in her elegy to Hemans posed the question whether female fame and creativity had been 'purchased all too dearly' (no. 148). At other times, Landon could view poetic activity as 'pearls amid the troubled waters' and 'an unknown curse' (see nos 144, 146). As with Hemans's explorer, Landon in 'Night at Sea' (no. 149) turns away from the sublimities of seas and stars to thoughts of absent friends. Elizabeth Barrett in her poem 'L.E.L.s Last Question' (no. 187) saw the ocean 'Dashing his mocking infinite round / The craver of a little love'. More complex and dramatic are the sacrifices made by women in sublime scenery. In Hemans's 'The Hebrew Mother' (no. 123) and 'Indian Woman's Death-Song' (no. 128), children are sacrificed on Mount Zion and the Mississippi. A still more complicated poem on female creativity, 'Proserpzia Rossi' (no. 127) links 'the power within me' to love and inevitable death.

The persistence of the iconography of the sea, and its ambiguity as emblem of tumultuous creativity above and the scene of peace in the depths, is radically different from the male iconography of sea and desert.[11] From Charlotte Smith at the beginning of the period to Elizabeth Barratt at the end, the sea remains central to female concerns. The women poets remain unique examples of how historical realities such as the invasion threats of the 1790s and the drama of the expanding empire in the 1830s (Landon, Jewsbury and Roberts were all to die in distant parts of the empire) combined with an intense and anxious dialogue on the nature and cost of art and its conflict with domestic virtue.

Anthologies, like national collections, always distort literary history, and this volume is no exception. At the expense of some variety, I have tried to demonstrate the remarkable coherence of women's concerns and to show that these concerns confront very fully central developments in eighteenth-century moral and aesthetic theory. At the very least this should allow us to reshape the period of Romanticism away from 'Wordsworth to Tennyson' and 1798–1830 and allow us to escape the hegemony of the central nineteenth-century myths of the fated and isolated poet and the reader's recovery through poetry. For those unhappy with my selection of texts, I draw their attention to Jackson's useful remark that between 1770 and 1835, 1,402 first editions by women were published, 'not too many, perhaps, for an individual to consider reading'.[12]

Notes

1 See Hugh Blair, *The British Poets*, 44v., 1773–76, *Bell's Edition*, 109v., 1776–83, Samuel Johnson, *The Works of the English Poets*, 68., 1779–81, Robert Anderson, *The Works of the British Poets*, 13v., 1792–95, *Cooke's Pocket Edition*, 48v. (?), 1794–1805, Samuel Bagster, *The Poets of Great Britain*, 124v., 1807, Thomas Park, *The Works of the British Poets*, 70v., 1805–12, Alexander Chalmers, *The Works of the English Poets*, 21v., 1810. There were, however, two major anthologies of women's poetry, only one of which covers the period after 1770; George Colman and Bonnell Thornton, *Poems by Eminent Ladies*, 2v., London, 1755, and Alexander Dyce, *Specimens of British Poetesses*, London, 1825. Other collections of women's poetry appeared in the nineteenth century: Frederic Rowton, *The Female Poets of Great Britain*, London, 1848, G. W. Bethune, *The British Female Poets*, Philadelphia, 1848, Jane Williams, *The Literary Women of England*, London, 1861, Eric S. Robertson, *English Poetesses*, London, 1883, Elizabeth Amelia Sharp, *Women's Voices*, London, 1887.

2 Richard Polwhele, *The Unsex'd Females: A Poem*, London, 1798.

3 'the Sublime does not so properly persuade us, as it Ravishes and Transports us, . . . it gives a noble Vigour to Discourse, an invincible force which commits a pleasing Rape upon the very Soul of the Reader', John Dennis, *The Grounds of Criticism in Poetry*, London, 1704, p.79. The same opposition of 'ravishment' and 'transport' to socially sanctioned morality was a significant element in the schematic canon produced by Joseph Warton. Pope, for instance, 'does not frequently ravish and transport his reader, yet he does not disgust him . . . The perusal of him affects not our minds with such strong emotions as we feel from *Homer* and *Milton*; so that no man of a true poetical spirit, *is master of himself while he reads them*.' Joseph Warton, *An Essay on the Genius and Writings of Pope*, fourth edition, corrected, 2v., London, 1782, i.xi–xiii, ii.409. As ravishment and transport gain hegemony as signs of authentic reading experiences, they are accompanied by technical developments in reading which further enhance their authority. With the proliferation of *Elegant Extracts, Select Passages, Speakers, Readers, Beauties*, and other anthologies, readers found new ways to move around texts to heighten their transport. The moral transport of reading is intensified by the enhanced technology of

transporting oneself around a text. Reading without the boring bits became a battery of intense lyrical experiences highly significant in the development of Romanticism.

For the gendered nature of eighteenth-century aesthetics, see Francis Hutcheson, *A System of Moral Philosophy*, 2vs., 1755, i.33, 87-8, David Hume, *Enquiries Concerning Human Understanding and the Principles of Morals*, ed. L. A. Selby-Bigge, Oxford, 1975, p.267, Edmund Burke, *A Philosophical Enquiry into the Origin of our Ideas of the Sublime and the Beautiful*, ed. James T. Boulton, London, 1958, pp.42-3, 91, 110, 113, 115, 157–8, William Hogarth, *The Analysis of Beauty*, London, 1753, Sections v, vii–x, Frances Reynolds, *An Enquiry Concerning the Principles of Taste, and the Origin of our Ideas of Beauty, &tc.*, London, 1785, p.29, Erasmus Darwin, *The Poetical Works*, 3v., London, 1806, i.324, Thomas De Quincey, *The Collected Writings*, ed. David Mason, 14v., Edinburgh, 1889–90, x.300n–301n. Hester Piozzi also noted how gendered distinctions also applied to such terms as fancy (feminine) and imagination (masculine), *British Synonymy*, 2v., London, 1794, i.221.

It is by no means clear what women's position is in this ideological network. What would it mean for a woman to be 'ravished and transported' in the reading scene? What would it mean for a woman to recover mastery in the moment of the sublime? This central feature of eighteenth-century ideology, the loss of mastery but subsequent aggrandised sense of self, would have involved complex gender transitions for women—from fallen woman to becoming a man. Given that literary history has succeeded in erasing the 1790s generation for being too masculine and the 1830s generation for being too feminine, we may be some years away from fully understanding eighteenth-century gender transitions and a whole range of other complications.

4 William Godwin, 'Of an early taste for reading', in *The Enquirer*, London, 1798, p.33. Compare Adam Smith, *The Theory of Moral Sentiments*, ed. D. D. Raphael and A. L. MacFie, Oxford, 1976, p.75: 'In imagination we become the very person whose actions are represented to us: we transport ourselves in fancy to the scenes of those distant and forgotten adventures, and imagine ourselves acting the part of a Scipio or a Camillus, a Timoleon or an Aristides.' The idea of the reader becoming an author is central to much eighteenth-century theory. See Joseph Addison, *The Spectator*, no.512, 17 October 1712. Thomas Warton, *Observations on the Fairy Queen of Spenser*, second edition, 2v., 1762, ii.269–70, Joseph Warton, *The Adventurer*, no.93, 25 September 1753.

5 Henry Home, Lord Kames, *The Elements of Criticism*, second edition, with additions and improvements, 3v., Edinburgh, 1763, i.113–17.

6 Thomas Holcroft, *The Adventures of Hugh Trevor*, ed. Seamus Deane, London, 1973, p.63. William Godwin, *Fleetwood: or, The New Man of Feeling*, 3v., London, 1805, i.9. Sir James Mackintosh, *Memoirs of the Life of Sir James Mackintosh*, ed. Robert James Mackintosh, 2v., London, 1835, i.5–6. Rousseau, with whom all these Dissenters have close spiritual affinities, had earlier noted, 'Je me croyais Grec ou Romain; je devenais le personnage dont je lisais la vie . . . Ce fut ici

mon premier mouvement de vanite bien marquée', *Les Confessions*, Paris: Pocket 1996, i.38, 56.

7 William Wordsworth, 'Essay supplementary to the preface', in *The Prose Works*, ed. W. J. B. Owen and Jane Worthington Smyser, 3v., Oxford, 1974, iii.62–4, 67, 80. Matthew Arnold, 'The study of poetry' in *Essays in Criticism*, Second Series, London, 1888, pp.1–2, 4.

8 John Tinnon Taylor, *Early Opposition to the English Novel: The Popular Reaction from 1760 to 1830*, New York, 1943. See also Gary Kelly, *The English Jacobin Novel, 1780–1805*, Oxford, 1976. 'Ideal Presence', Kames's term for the 'waking dream' effects of literature, haunted male reaction to female investigative activity, and many critics believed that intense involvement in the text would terminate in further acts of licentious imagination. By the nineteenth century, 'ideal presence' had modulated into the fictional other worlds created by the Taylor and Brontë sisters.

9 Mary Hays, *The Memoirs of Emma Courtney*, ed. Sally Cline, London, 1987, p.25.

10 Mary Wollstonecraft, 'The wrongs of woman', in *Mary and The Wrongs of Woman*, ed. James Kinsley and Gary Kelly, Oxford, 1980, p.88.

11 See W. H. Auden, *The Enchafèd Flood: or the Romantic Iconography of the Sea*, Charlottesville, 1950. The conflict between sublimity and repose in the women poets is acutely expressed by Felicia Hemans, 'Did you ever observe how strangely sounds and images of waters—rushing torrents, and troubled ocean waves, are mingled with the visionary distresses of dreams and delirium? To me there is no more perfect emblem of peace than that expressed by the scriptural phrase, "there shall be no more sea."' *The Works of Mrs Hemans: with a memoir of her life by her sister*, 7v., Edinburgh and London, 1839, i.86.

12 J. R. de J. Jackson, *Romantic Poetry by Women: A Bibliography, 1770–1835*, Oxford, 1993.

Romantic women poets

1770 – 1838

ANNA SEWARD (1742 – 1809)

She lived for most of her life with her father who was Canon of Lichfield Cathedral (1754 – 90). A childhood accident left her lame. She never married despite numerous suitors. Following the marriage in 1773 of Honora Sneyd, who had been adopted by her parents, she experienced a deep sense of loss. However, Sir Samuel Egerton Brydges, in his *Autobiography* (1834), i.57, believed, on the authority of the André family, that the Honora Sneyd episode was 'a nonsensical falsehood, of her own invention'. Her *Elegy on Captain Cook* (1780), *Monody on the Unfortunate Major André* (1781) and *Louisa, a Poetical Novel* (1784) established her reputation. She knew many of the figures of the Lunar Society, an important cluster of literary, scientific and industrial men, who constituted a sort of Midlands Enlightenment, although her reputation extended to London literary circles. In literary matters she was less than charitable to other women poets. Her contempt for Charlotte Smith (who rivalled her for prominence in the restoration of the sonnet) and aversion to the politics of Anna Laetitia Barbauld and Helen Maria Williams compare strangely with the coterie she formed with Whalley and Hayley for the purposes of mutual admiration, and her activity in Lady Miller's poetical competitions at Batheaston. She had looked after her father for many years, and after his death in 1790 she lived on an annuity of £400 a year but remained in Lichfield. She later published *Llangolen Vale* (1796), *Original Sonnets on Various Subjects* (1799) and *Memoirs of the Life of Dr Darwin* (1804), the last of which remains an important social document on the Midlands Enlightenment. The authenticity of the sonnets dating from the 1770s and 1780s is perhaps suspect and they may have been revised for publication. Sir Walter Scott edited *The Poetical Works*, 3 vols, Edinburgh 1810, the textual authority of which is unclear.

1 SONNET

By Derwent's rapid stream as oft I strayed,
With Infancy's light step and glances wild,
And saw vast rocks, on steepy mountains piled,
Frown o'er the umbrageous glen; or pleased surveyed
The cloudy moonshine in the shadowy glade,
Romantic Nature to the enthusiast Child
Grew dearer far than when serene she smiled,
In uncontrasted loveliness arrayed.
But O! in every Scene, with sacred sway,
Her graces fire me; from the bloom that spreads
Resplendent in the lucid morn of May,
To the green light the little Glow-worm sheds
On mossy banks, when midnight glooms prevail,
And softest Silence broods o'er all the dale.

(Wr. 1771 – 72, pub. 1799)

2 SONNET: AN EVENING IN NOVEMBER, WHICH HAD BEEN STORMY, GRADUALLY CLEARING UP, IN A MOUNTAINOUS COUNTRY

Ceased is the rain; but heavy drops yet fall
From the drenched roof;—yet murmurs the sunk wind
Round the dim hills; can yet a passage find
Whistling through yon cleft rock, and ruined wall.

The swollen and angry torrents heard, appal,
 Though distant.—A few stars, emerging kind,
 Shed their green, trembling beams.—With lustre small,
 The moon, her swiftly-passing clouds behind,
Glides o'er that shaded hill.—Now blasts remove
 The shadowing clouds, and on the mountain's brow,
 Full-orbed, she shines.—Half sunk within its cove
Heaves the lone boat, with gulphing sound;—and lo!
 Bright rolls the settling lake, and brimming rove
 The vale's blue rills, and glitter as they flow.

(Wr. 1775, pub. 1799)

3 SONNET: AUTUMN

Through changing Months a well-attempered Mind
 Welcomes their gentle or terrific pace.—
 When o'er retreating Autumn's golden grace
 Tempestuous Winter spreads in every wind
Naked asperity, our musings find
 Grandeur increasing, as the Glooms efface
 Variety and glow.—Each solemn trace
 Exalts the thoughts, from sensual joys refined.
Then blended in our rapt ideas rife
 The vanished charms, that summer-suns reveal,
 With all of desolation, that now lies
Dreary before us;—teach the Soul to feel
 Awe in the Present, pleasure in the Past,
 And to see vernal Morns in Hope's perspective cast.

(Wr. 1782, pub. 1799)

4 SONNET: TO COLEBROOKE DALE

Thy Genius, Coalbrooke, faithless to his charge,
 Amid thy woods and vales, thy rocks and streams,
 Formed for the Train that haunt poetic dreams,
 Naiads, and Nymphs,—now hears the toiling Barge.
And the swart Cyclops ever-clanging forge
 Din in thy dells;—permits the dark-red gleams,
 From umbered fires on all thy hills, the beams,
 Solar and pure, to shroud with columns large
Of black sulphureous smoke, that spread their veils
 Like funeral crape upon the sylvan robe
 Of thy romantic rocks, pollute thy gales,
And stain thy glassy floods;—while o'er the globe
 To spread thy stores metallic, this rude yell
 Drowns the wild woodland song, and breaks the Poet's spell.

(Wr. *c.*1785 – 87, pub. 1799)

5 SONNET: TO THE POPPY

While Summer Roses all their glory yield
To crown the Votary of Love and Joy,
Misfortune's Victim hails, with many a sigh,
Thee, scarlet Poppy of the pathless field,
Gaudy, yet wild and lone; no leaf to shield
Thy flaccid vest, that, as the gale blows high,
Flaps, and alternate folds around thy head.—
So stands in the long grass a love-crazed Maid,
Smiling aghast; while stream to every wind
Her garish ribbons, smeared with dust and rain;
But brain-sick visions cheat her tortured mind,
And bring false peace. Thus, lulling grief and pain,
Kind dreams oblivious from thy juice proceed,
Thou flimsy, showy, melancholy weed.

(Wr. 1789, pub. 1799)

6 SONNET: TO FRANCE ON HER PRESENT EXERTIONS

Thou, that where Freedom's sacred fountains play,
Which sprung effulgent, though with crimson stains,
On transatlantic shores, and widening plains,
Hast, in their living waters washed away
Those cankering spots, shed by tyrannic sway
On thy long drooping lilies, English veins
Swell with the tide of exultation gay,
To see thee spurn thy deep-galling chains.
Few of Britannia's free-born sons forbear
To bless thy Cause;—cold is the heart that breathes
No wish fraternal.—France, we bid thee share
The blessings twining with our civic wreaths,
While Victory's trophies, permanent as fair,
Crown the bright Sword that Liberty unsheaths.

(1789)

7 SONNET

On the damp margin of the sea-beat shore
Lonely at eve to wander;—or reclined
Beneath a rock, what time the rising wind
Mourns o'er the waters, and, with solemn roar,
Vast billows into caverns surging pour,
And back recede alternate; while combined
Loud shriek the sea-fowls, harbingers assigned,
Clamorous and fearful, of the stormy hour;
To listen with deep thought those awful sounds;
Gaze on the boiling, the tumultuous waste,

Or promontory rude, or craggy mounds
Staying the furious main, delight has cast
O'er my rapt spirit, and my thrilling heart,
Dear as the softer joys green vales impart.

(Wr. 1790, pub. 1799)

8 'O'ER THIS DEEP GLEN, DEPARTING AUTUMN THROWS'

O'er this deep Glen, departing Autumn throws,
With kind reverted glance, a short repose,
E'er yet she leaves her England's fading scene,
Where sickly yellow stains the vivid green,
And many an icy morn, and stormy gale
Embrown the pathway of the winding vale.

Now, while I seek the bosom of the Glade,
And the thin shelter of the impoverished Shade,
Unequal steps, and rising sighs, disclose
The thorny pressure of tyrannic woes;
And where the incumbent Rock, with awful face,
Bends o'er the fountain, gurgling from its base,
And marks the limit of the silent Dell,
Sadly I sit my bosomed griefs to tell;
Invoke thy Spirit, those fond griefs to sooth,
And bid, alas! their surging tide be smooth.

It will not be;—since here, with yearning thought,
By weak, involuntary impulse brought,
Where Love and Memory bear resistless sway,
And all the weakness of the Soul betray!

O ye known objects!—how ye strike my heart!
And vain regrets, with keener force, impart!
Slow, through the faded grove, past Pleasures glide,
Or sadly linger by the fountain's side.

Dear, awful witness of a broken vow,
Steep Rock, how sternly frowns thy rugged brow!
But, if the frequent blast shall bend thy pines,
Clear at thy foot the crystal water shines!
Though drizzling Clouds the misty Mountains veil,
Yet the mild Sun-beam gilds the narrow Dale!
Though vernal flowers this bank no more adorn,
Nor Summer's wild rose blushes on its thorn,
Yet sheltered, mossy, dry, and warm, it draws
The heedless roving step to quiet pause.

Thus the pale Year, though Nature's edicts urge
Her step to Winter's desolating verge,
Sedately passes to the drear domain,
And breathes, e'en yet, soft comforts o'er the plain;
But oh! for me, in Youth's luxuriant glow,
Hope's lovely florets wither as they blow!...

(Wr. 1779, pub. 1784)

9 'ONCE MORE THESE EYES, WITH SMILES OF PLEASURE HAIL'

Once more these eyes, with smiles of pleasure hail
The vernal beauties of my native Vale;
The plenteous dews, that in the early ray
Gem the light leaf, and tremble on the spray;
The fresh cool gales, that undulating pass,
With shadowy sweep, along the bending grass.—
Now throw the shrubs and trees the lengthened shade
On the smooth turf distinct!—and now they fade,
As sinks the Sun, behind a cloud withdrawn,
That late unveiled shone yellow on the lawn.
Soft o'er the Vale, from this my favourite seat,
Serene I mark the vagrant beauties fleet;
In different lights the changing features trace,
Catch the bright form, and paint the shadowy grace.
Where the light Ash, and browner Oak extend,
And high in Air their mingled branches bend,
The mossy bank, beneath their trembling bowers,
Arises, fragrant with uncultured flowers,
That stoop the sweet head o'er the latent spring,
And bear the pendant Bees, that humming cling.
Just gleams the Fount—for, curving o'er its brink,
The lengthened grass the shining Waters drink;
Their green arms half its glassy beauties hide,
As from beneath them steals the wandering tide,
And down the Valley careless winds away,
While in its streams the glancing Sun-beams play....

(Wr. 1781, pub. 1784)

10 'AS CONSCIOUS MEMORY, WITH REVERTED GLANCE'

As conscious Memory, with reverted glance,
Roves o'er the wild and mountainous expanse,
Her faithful traces to my sight restore
The long, long tracts of Tideswell's naked Moor;
Stretched on vast hills, that far and near prevail,
Bleak, stony, bare, monotonous, and pale.

Wide o'er the waste, in noon-tide's sultry rays,
The frequent lime-kiln darts her umbered blaze;
Her suffocating smoke incessant breathes,
And shrouds the sun in black convolving wreaths;
And here, with pallid ashes heaped around,
Oft sinks the mine, and blots the dreary ground.
In vain warm Spring demands her robe of green,
No sheltering hedge-rows vivify the scene;
O'er its grey breast no undulating trees
With lavish foliage court the lively breeze;
But from the Moor the rude stone walls disjoin,
With angle sharp, and long unvaried line,
The cheerless field,—where slowly wandering feed
The lonely cow, and melancholy steed,
Exposed abide the summer's ardent breath,
And wintery storm that yells along the heath.

At length benigner mountains meet the eyes;
Their shrubby heights in rounder grace arise;
And, from the first steep summit, pleased I throw
My eager glances on the depths below,
As sinks abrupt the sylvan Monsaldale
From the swart sun-beam and the howling gale.

Behold in front the lucid river spread
His bankless waters o'er the sunny mead;
As of his broad and sheety shallows proud,
Shine the clear mirror of the passing cloud:
Then to the left along the valley glide,
With smooth meander, and with narrower tide,
Through banks, where thick the spreading alders grow,
And deep calm waves reflect their pendent bough.
Refreshing sweets the breathing hay-cocks yield,
That richly tuft the long and narrow field,
As gently to the right it curves away
Round the green cliffs with scattered nut-trees gay;
Cliffs, whose smooth breast, above the silver stream,
Swells to the sun, and yellows in his beam,
While on the opposing shore dwarf foliage hides,
Sombrous, and soft, the mountain's lofty sides,
And throws its latest fringe upon the flood,
That laves the concave of the pensile wood;
Till down the rocks, rude, broken, mossy, steep,
In parted tides the foaming waters leap;
Then through the mazes of the rambling dale
With silent lapse they flow, or rush with tuneful wail....

(Wr. 1783, pub. 1785)

11 COLEBROOK DALE

Scene of superfluous grace, and wasted bloom,
O, violated Colebrook! in an hour,
To beauty unpropitious and to song,
The Genius of thy shades, by Plutus bribed,
Amid thy grassy lanes, thy woodwild glens,
Thy knolls and bubbling wells, thy rocks, and streams,
Slumbers!—while tribes fuliginous invade
The soft, romantic, consecrated scenes;
Haunt of the wood-nymph, who with airy step,
In times long vanished, through thy pathless groves
Ranged;—while the pearly-wristed Naiads leaned,
Braiding their light locks o'er thy crystal flood,
Shadowy and smooth. What, though to vulgar eye
Invisible, yet oft the lucid gaze
Of the rapt Bard, in every dell and glade
Beheld them wander;—saw, from the clear wave
Emerging, all the watery sisters rise,
Weaving the aqueous lily, and the flag,
In wreaths fantastic, for the tresses bright
Of amber-haired Sabrina.—Now we view
Their fresh, their fragrant, and their silent reign
Usurpt by Cyclops;—hear, in mingled tones,
Shout their thronged barge, their ponderous engines clang
Through thy coy dales; while red the countless fires,
With umbered flames, bicker on all thy hills,
Darkening the Summer's sun with columns large
Of thick, sulphureous smoke, which spread, like palls,
That screen the dead, upon the sylvan robe
Of thy aspiring rocks; pollute thy gales,
And stain thy glassy waters.—See, in troops,
The dusk artificers, with brazen throats,
Swarm on thy cliffs, and clamour in thy glens,
Steepy and wild, ill suited to such guests.

Ah! what avails it to the poet's sense,
That the large stores of thy metallic veins
Gleam over Europe; transatlantic shores
Illumine wide;—are changed in either Ind
For all they boast, hot Ceylon's breathing spice;
Peruvian gums; Brazilia's golden ore;
And odorous gums, which Persia's white-robed seer,
With warbled orisons, on Ganges' brink,
Kindles, when first his Mithra's living ray
Purples the Orient.—Ah! the traffic rich,
With equal 'vantage, might Britannia send
From regions better suited to such aims,
Than from her Coalbrook's muse-devoted vales,
To far resounding Birmingham, the boast,

The growing London of the Mercian realm;
Thence to be wafted o'er our subject seas
To every port;—yes, from that town, the mart
Of rich inventive Commerce. Science there
Leads her enlightened sons, to guide the hand
Of the prompt artist, and with great design
Plan the vast engine, whose extended arms,
Heavy and huge, on the soft-seeming breath
Of the hot steam, rise slowly;—till, by cold
Condensed, it leaves them soon, with clanging roar,
Down, down, to fall precipitant. Nor yet
Her famed Triumvirate, in every land
Known and revered, not they the only boast,
Of this our second London; the rapt sage,
Who traced the viewless Aura's subtle breath
Through all its various powers, there bending feeds
The lamp of Science with the richest oils
Which the arch-chemist, Genius, knows to draw
From Nature's stores, or latent, or revealed.

While neighbouring cities waste the fleeting hours,
Careless of art and knowledge, and the smile
Of every Muse, expanding Birmingham,
Illumed by intellect, as gay in wealth,
Commands her aye-accumulating walls,
From month to month, to climb the adjacent hills;
Creep on the circling plains, now here, now there,
Divergent—change the hedges, thickets, trees,
Upturned, disrooted, into mortared piles,
The street elongate, and the statelier square.

So, with intent transmutant, Chemists bruise
The shrinking leaves and flowers, whose steams saline,
Congealing swift on the recipient's sides,
Shoot into crystals;—and the night-frost thus
Insidious creeping on the watery plain,
Wave after wave incrusts, till liquid change
To solid, and support the volant foot.

Warned by the Muse, if Birmingham should draw
In future years, from more congenial climes
Her massy ore, her labouring sons recall,
And sylvan Colebrook's winding vales restore
To beauty and to song, content to draw
From unpoetic scenes her rattling stores,
Massy and dun; if, thence supplied, she fail,
Britain, to glut thy rage commercial, see
Grim Wolverhampton lights her smouldering fires,
And Sheffield, smoke-involved; dim where she stands

Circled by lofty mountains, which condense
Her dark and spiral wreaths to drizzling rains,
Frequent and sullied; as the neighbouring hills
Ope their deep veins, and feed her caverned flames;
While, to her dusky sister, Ketley yields,
From her long-desolate, and livid breast,
The ponderous metal. No aerial forms
On Sheffield's arid moor, or Ketley's heath,
E'er wove the floral crowns, or smiling stretched
The shelly sceptre;—there no Poet roved
To catch bright inspirations. Blush, ah, blush,
Thou venal Genius of these outraged groves,
And thy apostate head with thy soiled wings
Veil!—who hast thus thy beauteous charge resigned
To habitants ill-suited; hast allowed
Their rattling forges, and their hammer's din,
And hoarse, rude throats, to fright the gentle train,
Dryads, and fair haired Naiades;—the song,
Once loud as sweet, of the wild woodland choir
To silence;—disenchant the poet's spell,
And to a gloomy Erebus transform
The destined rival of Tempean vales.

(Wr. *c.*1785 – 90, pub. 1810)

ANNA LAETITIA BARBAULD (née AIKIN) (1743 – 1825)
She was born at Kibworth, an important Dissenting educational centre. John Jennings, the eminent Dissenter, was her father-in-law. The Jenningses and Aikins were also related to the Belshams, another distinguished Dissenting family. Her father became Tutor in Languages and Belles-Lettres at Warrington Academy in 1758. Her brother was Tutor in Divinity 1761 – 80. She early acquired Latin and Greek (after initial resistance from her father) and came to know other famous Dissenters, notably Joseph Priestley and William Enfield, to whom she wrote poems. She collaborated with her brother in *Miscellaneous Pieces in Prose* (1773). Charles James Fox complimented her brother on two pieces only to find they were written by her. She also published *Poems* (1773) which went through three editions that year. Having spiritedly escaped one suitor by leaping over a garden wall, she married Rochemont Barbauld, a Dissenting minister, in 1774 and later opened a school with him at Palgrave in Sussex where he was minister to the Dissenting congregation. Samuel Johnson thought both husband and school a waste of her talents, a view reiterated by Wordsworth in a letter to Alexander Dyce in 1830—her 'higher powers of mind was spoiled as a Poetess by being a Dissenter, and concerned with a Dissenting Academy' (WW *CL*, v.529). The school closed in 1785 but the educational writings, *Lessons for Children* (1778) and *Hymns in Prose for Children* (1781), which emerged from her teaching experiences at school and at home (where she took charge of the education of a nephew whom they had adopted), proved popular. Frank Sayers, a friend of Coleridge's and a neglected figure among

the romantics, attended the school and praised her teaching and Hazlitt learned to spell from the *Lessons for Children*. Although she declined a proposal from Mrs Montague to open a Literary Academy for young ladies, and expressed reservations about the education of women, she was well aware that any such knowledge gained, if displayed, would be 'punished with disgrace' and that her own 'situation has been peculiar, and would be no rule for others'. Following the closure of the school, the Barbaulds travelled in France and Switzerland 1785 – 86. In the 1790s she appears to have refrained from publishing her political poetry apart from her *Epistle to William Wilberforce* (1791), but she continued to write radical prose. When Coleridge and Wordsworth were about to publish *Lyrical Ballads*, Wordsworth wrote to Thomas Longman (15 Dec. 1800, WW *CL*, vi, L.368) suggesting that three or four copies be sent to eminent people, notably William Wilberforce and Anna Barbauld. The Barbaulds moved to Hampstead in 1787, and to Stoke Newington in 1802, where her husband became minister to the Dissenting congregation. Richard Price had earlier been minister there and it was one of the main centres of Dissenting radicalism in the 1790s. (In Stoke Newington she appears to have had some dealings with Hackney Academy.) Her husband had a long history of mental illness and was found drowned in 1808. She returned to poetry with *Eighteen Hundred and Eleven* (1812), a fierce attack on commerce and empire. The hostile reaction to the poem seems to have ensured another retreat from political poetry and she never ventured into the area again. However, the range of her activities is unparalleled by other women poets. She was equally distinguished as a defender of Dissenting interests, opponent of slavery, educational writer and editor of English classics, notably editions of Akenside (1794) and Collins (1797), which, according to Crabb Robinson, Wordsworth disliked for 'utterly forestalling the natural feeling and judgment of young and ingeuous readers'. She was also an energetic contributor to the *Monthly Magazine* on a variety of subjects. In contradistinction to Seward, she moved easily among highly talented men without the need for praise. She similarly formed intimate friendships with women, notably Joanna Baillie. She is perhaps unique in having formed friendships ranging from the Warrington tutors of the 1760s and 1770s to the Bluestockings of the 1770s, the radicals of the 1790s and the generation of writers after 1815. Mackintosh, Macaulay, Coleridge, Lamb, the Edgeworths, Bowring, Rogers, Scott, Crabb Robinson and the Baillie sisters were all visitors at Stoke Newington. She was, for many, one of the last remaining links with a rapidly disappearing radical Dissenting culture. Lucy Aikin edited *The Works*, 2 vols (1825), but by mid-century, however, according to De Quincey, she had largely been forgotten. See Appendix for an attribution of unestablished provenance.

12 *from* CORSICA

How raptured fancy burns, while warm in thought
I trace the pictured landscape; while I kiss
With pilgrim lips devout, the sacred soil
Stained with the blood of heroes. Cyrnus, hail!
Hail to thy rocky, deep indented shores,
And pointed cliffs, which hear the chafing deep
Incessant foaming round their shaggy sides.

Hail to thy winding bays, thy sheltering ports
And ample harbours, which inviting stretch
Their hospitable arms to every sail:
Thy numerous streams, that bursting from the cliffs
Down the steep channelled rock impetuous pour
With grateful murmur: on the fearful edge
Of the rude precipice, thy hamlets brown
And straw-roofed cots, which from the level vale
Scarce seen, amongst the craggy hanging cliffs
Seem like an eagle's nest aerial built.
Thy swelling mountains, brown with solemn shade
Of various trees, that wave their giant arms
O'er the rough sons of freedom; lofty pines,
And hardy fir, and ilex ever green,
And spreading chestnut, with each humbler plant,
And shrub of fragrant leaf, that clothes their sides
With living verdure; whence the clustering bee
Extracts her golden dews: the shining box,
And sweet-leaved myrtle, aromatic thyme,
The prickly juniper, and the green leaf
Which feeds the spinning worm; while glowing bright
Beneath the various foliage, wildly spreads
The arbutus, and rears his scarlet fruit
Luxuriant, mantling o'er the craggy steeps;
And thy own native laurel crowns the scene.
Hail to thy savage forests, awful, deep:
Thy tangled thickets, and thy crowded woods,
The haunt of herds untamed; which sullen bound
From rock to rock with fierce unsocial air,
And wilder gaze, as conscious of the power
That loves to reign amid the lonely scenes
Of unbroke nature: precipices huge,
And tumbling torrents; trackless desarts, plains
Fenced in with guardian rocks, whose quarries teem
With shining steel, that to the cultured fields
And sunny hills which wave with bearded grain
Defends their homely produce. Liberty,
The mountain Goddess, loves to range at large
Amid such scenes, and on the iron soil
Prints her majestic step. For these she scorns
The green enamelled vales, the velvet lap
Of smooth savannahs, where the pillowed head
Of luxury reposes; balmy gales,
And bowers that breathe of bliss. For these, when first
This isle emerging like a beauteous gem
From the dark bosom of the Tyrrhene main
Reared its fair front, she marked it for her own,
And with her spirit warmed....

(Wr. 1769, pub. 1773)

ANNA
LAETITIA
BARBAULD

13 ODE TO SPRING

Hope waits upon the flowery prime. [Waller]

Sweet daughter of a rough and stormy fire,
Hoar Winter's blooming child; delightful Spring!
Whose unshorn locks with leaves
And swelling buds are crowned;

From the green islands of eternal youth,
(Crowned with fresh blooms, and ever springing shade)
Turn, hither turn thy step,
O thou, whose powerful voice

More sweet that softest touch of Doric reed,
Or Lydian flute, can sooth the madding winds,
And through the stormy deep
Breathe thy own tender calm.

Thee, best beloved! the virgin train await
With songs and festal rites, and joy to rove
Thy blooming wilds among,
And vales and dewy lawns,

With untired feet; and cull thy earliest sweets
To weave fresh garlands for the glowing brow
Of him, the favoured youth
That prompts their whispered sigh.

Unlock thy copious stores; those tender showers
That drop their sweetness on the infant buds,
And silent dews that swell
The milky ear's green stem,

And feed the flowering osier's early shoots;
And call those winds which through the whispering boughs
With warm and pleasant breath
Salute the blowing flowers.

Now let me sit beneath the whitening thorn,
And mark thy spreading tints steal o'er the dale;
And watch with patient eye
Thy fair unfolding charms.

O nymph approach! while yet the temperate sun
With bashful forehead, through the cool moist air
Throws his young maiden beams,
And with chaste kisses wooes

The earth's fair bosom; while the streaming veil
Of lucid clouds with kind and frequent shade
Protects thy modest blooms
From his severer blaze.

Sweet is thy reign, but short: The red dog-star
Shall scorch thy tresses, and the mower's scythe
    Thy greens, thy flowerets all,
    Remorseless shall destroy.

Reluctant shall I bid thee then farewell;
For O, not all that Autumn's lap contains,
    Nor Summer's ruddiest fruits,
    Can aught for thee atone,

Fair Spring! whose simplest promise more delights
Than all their largest wealth, and through the heart
    Each joy and new-born hope
    With softest influence breathes.

(1773)

14 A SUMMER EVENING'S MEDITATION

One sun by day, by night ten thousand shine. Young

'Tis past! The sultry tyrant of the south
Has spent his short-lived rage; more grateful hours
Move silent on; the skies no more repel
The dazzled sight, but with mild maiden beams
Of tempered light, invite the cherished eye
To wander o'er their sphere; where hung aloft
Dian's bright crescent, like a silver bow
New strung in heaven, lifts high its beamy horns
Impatient for the night, and seems to push
Her brother down the sky. Fair Venus shines
Even in the eye of day; with sweetest beam
Propitious shines, and shakes a trembling flood
Of softened radiance from her dewy locks.
The shadows spread apace; while meekened Eve,
Her cheek yet warm with blushes, slow retires
Through the Hesperian gardens of the west,
And shuts the gates of day. 'Tis now the hour
When Contemplation, from her sunless haunts,
The cool damp grotto, or the lonely depth
Of unpierced woods, where wrapt in solid shade
She mused away the gaudy hours of noon,
And fed on thoughts unripened by the sun,
Moves forward; and with radiant finger points
To yon blue concave swelled by breath divine,
Where, one by one, the living eyes of heaven
Awake, quick kindling o'er the face of ether
One boundless blaze; ten thousand trembling fires,
And dancing lustres, where the unsteady eye,
Restless and dazzled, wanders unconfined
O'er all this field of glories: spacious field;

And worthy of the Master: he, whose hand
With hieroglyphics elder than the Nile,
Inscribed the mystic tablet; hung on high
To public gaze, and said, adore, O man!
The finger of thy God. From what pure wells
Of milky light, what soft o'erflowing urn,
Are all these lamps so filled? these friendly lamps,
For ever streaming o'er the azure deep
To point our path, and light us to our home.
How soft they slide along their lucid spheres!
And silent as the foot of time, fulfil
Their destined courses: Nature's self is hushed,
And, but a scattered leaf, which rustles through
The thick-wove foliage, not a sound is heard
To break the midnight air; though the raised ear,
Intensely listening, drinks in every breath.
How deep the silence, yet how loud the praise!
But are they silent all? or is there not
A tongue in every star that talks with man,
And woos him to be wife? Nor woos in vain:
This dead of midnight is the noon of thought,
And wisdom mounts her zenith with the stars.
At this still hour the self-collected soul
Turns inward, and beholds a stranger there
Of high descent, and more than mortal rank;
An embryo God; a spark of fire divine,
Which must burn on for ages, when the sun
(Fair transitory creature of a day!)
Has closed his golden eye, and wrapt in shades
Forgets his wonted journey through the east.

Ye citadels of light, and seats of Gods!
Perhaps my future home, from whence the soul
Revolving periods past, may oft look back,
With recollected tenderness, on all
The various busy scenes she left below,
Its deep laid projects and its strange events,
As on some fond and doting tale that soothed
Her infant hours; O be it lawful now
To tread the hallowed circle of your courts,
And with mute wonder and delighted awe
Approach your burning confines. Seized in thought,
On fancy's wild and roving wing I sail,
From the green borders of the peopled earth,
And the pale moon, her duteous fair attendant;
From solitary Mars; from the vast orb
Of Jupiter, whose huge gigantic bulk
Dances in ether like the lightest leaf;
To the dim verge, the suburbs of the system,

Where cheerless Saturn 'midst his watery moons
Girt with a lucid zone, in gloomy pomp,
Sits like an exiled monarch: fearless thence
I launch into the trackless deeps of space,
Where, burning round, ten thousands suns appear,
Of elder beam; which ask no leave to shine
Of our terrestrial star, nor borrow light
From the proud regent of our scanty day;
Sons of the morning, first-born of creation,
And only less than Him who marks their track,
And guides their fiery wheels. Here must I stop,
Or is there aught beyond? What hand unseen
Impels me onward through the glowing orbs
Of habitable nature, far remote,
To the dread confines of eternal night,
To solitudes of vast unpeopled space,
The desarts of creation, wide and wild;
Where embryo systems and unkindled suns
Sleep in the womb of chaos? fancy droops,
And thought astonished stops her bold career.
But oh thou mighty mind! whose powerful word
Said, thus let all things be, and thus they were,
Where shall I seek thy presence? how unblamed
Invoke thy dread perfection?
Have the broad eye-lids of the morn beheld thee?
Or does the beamy shoulder of Orion
Support thy throne? O look with pity down
On erring, guilty man; not in thy names
Of terror clad; not with those thunders armed
That conscious Sinai felt, when fear appalled
The scattered tribes; thou hast a gentler voice,
That whispers comfort to the swelling heart,
Abashed, yet longing to behold her Maker.

But now my soul unused to stretch her powers
In flight so daring, drops her weary wing,
And seeks again the known accustomed spot,
Drest up with sun, and shade, and lawns, and streams,
A mansion fair and spacious for its guest,
And full replete with wonders. Let me here,
Content and grateful, wait the appointed time
And ripen for the skies: the hour will come
When all these splendours bursting on my sight
Shall stand unveiled, and to my ravished sense
Unlock the glories of the world unknown.

(1773)

ANNA LAETITIA BARBAULD

15 AUTUMN, A FRAGMENT

Farewell the softer hours, Spring's opening blush
And Summer's deeper glow, the shepherd's pipe
Tuned to the murmurs of a weeping spring,
And song of birds, and gay enamelled fields,—
Farewell! 'Tis now the sickness of the year,
Not to be medicined by the skilful hand.
Pale suns arise that like weak kings behold
Their predecessor's empire moulder from them;
While swift-increasing spreads the black domain
Of melancholy Night;—no more content
With equal sway, her stretching shadows gain
On the bright morn, and cloud the evening sky.
Farewell the careless lingering walk at eve,
Sweet with the breath of kine and new-spread hay;
And slumber on a bank, where the lulled youth,
His head on flowers, delicious languor feels
Creep in the blood. A different season now
Invites a different song. The naked trees
Admit the tempest; rent is Nature's robe;
Fast, fast, the blush of Summer fades away
From her wan cheek, and scarce a flower remains
To deck her bosom; Winter follows close,
Pressing impatient on, and with rude breath
Fans her discoloured tresses. Yet not all
Of grace and beauty from the falling year
Is torn ungenial. Still the taper fir
Lifts its green spire, and the dark holly edged
With gold, and many a strong perennial plant,
Yet cheer the waste: nor does yon knot of oaks
Resign its honours to the infant blast.
This is the time, and these the solemn walks,
When inspiration rushes o'er the soul
Sudden, as through the grove the rustling breeze.

(Wr. *c.* 1780, pub. 1825)

16 ON THE EXPECTED GENERAL RISING OF THE FRENCH NATION, IN 1792

Rise, mighty nation, in thy strength,
And deal thy dreadful vengeance round;
Let thy great spirit, roused at length,
Strike hordes of despots to the ground!

Devoted land! thy mangled breast
Eager the royal vultures tear;
By friends betrayed, by foes oppressed,—
And Virtue struggles with Despair.

The tocsin sounds! arise, arise!
Stern o'er each breast let Country reign;
Nor virgin's plighted hand nor sighs
Must now the ardent youth detain:

Nor must the hind who tills thy soil
The ripened vintage stay to press,
Till Rapture crown the flowing bowl,
And Freedom boast of full success.

Briareus-like extend thy hands,
That every hand may crush a foe;
In millions pour thy generous bands,
And end a warfare by a blow!

Then wash with sad repentant tears
Each deed that clouds thy glory's page;
Each frenzied start impelled by fears,
Each transient burst of headlong rage:

Then fold in thy relenting arms
Thy wretched outcasts where they roam;
From pining want and war's alarms,
O call the child of misery home!

Then build the tomb—O not alone
Of him who bled in Freedom's cause;
With equal eye the martyr own
Of faith revered and ancient laws.

Then be thy tide of glory staid;
Then be thy conquering banners furled;
Obey the laws thyself hast made,
And rise the model of the world!

(Wr. 1792, pub. 1825)

17 THE RIGHTS OF WOMAN

Yes, injured Woman! rise, assert thy right!
Woman! too long degraded, scorned, oppressed;
O born to rule in partial Law's despite,
Resume thy native empire o'er the breast!

Go forth arrayed in panoply divine;
That angel pureness which admits no stain;
Go, bid proud Man his boasted rule resign,
And kiss the golden sceptre of thy reign.

Go, gird thyself with grace; collect thy store
Of bright artillery glancing from afar;
Soft melting tones thy thundering cannon's roar,
Blushes and fears thy magazine of war.

Thy rights are empire: urge no meaner claim,—
Felt, not defined, and if debated, lost;
Like sacred mysteries, which withheld from fame,
Shunning discussion, are revered the most.

Try all that wit and art suggest to bend
Of thy imperial foe the stubborn knee;
Make treacherous Man thy subject, not thy friend;
Thou mayst command, but never canst be free.

Awe the licentious, and restrain the rude;
Soften the sullen, clear the cloudy brow:
Be, more than princes' gifts, thy favours sued;—
She hazards all, who will the least allow.

But hope not, courted idol of mankind,
On this proud eminence secure to stay;
Subduing and subdued, thou soon shalt find
Thy coldness soften, and thy pride give way.

Then, then, abandon each ambitious thought,
Conquest or rule thy heart shall feebly move,
In Nature's school, by her soft maxims taught,
That separate rights are lost in mutual love.

(Wr. *c.* 1792, pub. 1825)

18 INSCRIPTION FOR AN ICE-HOUSE

Stranger, approach! within this iron door
Thrice locked and bolted, this rude arch beneath
That vaults with ponderous stone the cell; confined
By man, the great magician, who controls
Fire, earth and air, and genii of the storm,
And bends the most remote and opposite things
To do him service and perform his will,—
A giant sits; stern Winter; here he piles,
While summer glows around, and southern gales
Dissolve the fainting world, his treasured snows
Within the rugged cave.—Stranger, approach!
He will not cramp thy limbs with sudden age,
Nor wither with his touch the coyest flower
That decks thy scented hair. Indignant here,
Like fettered Sampson when his might was spent

In puny feats to glad the festive halls
Of Gaza's wealthy sons; or he who sat
Midst laughing girls submiss, and patient twirled
The slender spindle in his sinewy grasp;
The rugged power, fair Pleasure's minister,
Exerts his art to deck the genial board;
Congeals the melting peach, the nectarine smooth,
Burnished and glowing from the sunny wall:
Darts sudden frost into the crimson veins
Of the moist berry; moulds the sugared hail:
Cools with his icy breath our flowing cups;
Or gives to the fresh dairy's nectared bowls
A quicker zest. Sullen he plies his task,
And on his shaking fingers counts the weeks
Of lingering Summer, mindful of his hour
To rush in whirlwinds forth, and rule the year.

(Wr. 1795, pub. 1825)

19 WASHING-DAY

————And their voice,
Turning again towards childish treble, pipes
And whistles in its sound—— [Shakespeare]

The Muses are turned gossips; they have lost
The buskined step, and clear high-sounding phrase,
Language of gods. Come, then, domestic Muse,
In slip-shod measure loosely prattling on
Of farm or orchard, pleasant curds and cream,
Or drowning flies, or shoe lost in the mire
By little whimpering boy, with rueful face;
Come, Muse, and sing the dreaded *Washing-Day*.
—Ye who beneath the yoke of wedlock bend,
With bowed soul, full well ye ken the day
Which week, smooth sliding after week, brings on
Too soon; for to that day nor peace belongs
Nor comfort; e'er the first grey streak of dawn,
The red-armed washers come and chase repose.
Nor pleasant smile, nor quaint device of mirth,
E'er visited that day; the very cat,
From the wet kitchen scared, and reeking hearth,
Visits the parlour, an unwonted guest.
The silent breakfast-meal is soon dispatched
Uninterrupted, save by anxious looks
Cast at the lowering sky, if sky should lower.
From that last evil, oh preserve us, heavens!
For should the skies pour down, adieu to all
Remains of quiet; then expect to hear

Of sad disasters—dirt and gravel stains
Hard to efface, and loaded lines at once
Snapped short—and linen-horse by dog thrown down,
And all the petty miseries of life.
Saints have been calm while stretched upon the rack,
And Montezuma smiled on burning coals;
But never yet did housewife notable
Greet with a smile a rainy washing-day.
—But grant the welkin fair, require not thou
Who call'st thyself perchance the master there,
Or study swept, or nicely dusted coat,
Or usual 'tendance; ask not, indiscreet,
Thy stockings mended, though the yawning rents
Gape wide as Erebus, nor hope to find
Some snug recess impervious; should'st thou try
The customed garden walks, thine eye shall rue
The budding fragrance of thy tender shrubs,
Myrtle or rose, all crushed beneath the weight
Of coarse checked apron, with impatient hand
Twitched off when showers impend: or crossing lines
Shall mar thy musings, as the wet cold sheet
Flaps in thy face abrupt. Woe to the friend
Whose evil stars have urged him forth to claim
On such a day the hospitable rites;
Looks, blank at best, and stinted courtesy,
Shall he receive; vainly he feeds his hopes
With dinner of roast chicken, savoury pie,
Or tart or pudding:—pudding he nor tart
That day shall eat: nor though the husband try,
Mending what can't be helped, to kindle mirth
From cheer deficient, shall his consort's brow
Clear up propitious; the unlucky guest
In silence dines, and early slinks away.
I well remember, when a child, the awe
This day struck into me; for then the maids,
I scarce knew why, looked cross, and drove me from them;
Nor soft caress could I obtain, nor hope
Usual indulgencies; jelly or creams,
Relic of costly suppers, and set by
For me their petted one; or buttered toast,
When butter was forbid; or thrilling tale
Of ghost, or witch, or murder—so I went
And sheltered me beside the parlour fire,
There my dear grandmother, eldest of forms,
Tended the little ones, and watched from harm,
Anxiously fond, though oft her spectacles
With elfin cunning hid, and oft the pins
Drawn from her ravelled stocking, might have soured
One less indulgent.—

At intervals my mother's voice was heard,
Urging dispatch; briskly the work went on,
All hands employed to wash, to rinse, to wring,
To fold, and starch, and clap, and iron, and plait.
Then would I sit me down, and ponder much
Why washings were. Sometimes through hollow bole
Of pipe amused we blew, and sent aloft
The floating bubbles, little dreaming then
To see, Montgolfier, thy silken ball
Ride buoyant through the clouds—so near approach
The sports of children and the toils of men.
Earth, air, and sky, and ocean, hath its bubbles,
And verse is one of them——this most of all.

(1797)

20 TO MR C[OLERID]GE

Midway the hill of science, after steep
And rugged paths that tire the unpractised feet,
A *grove* extends; in tangled mazes wrought,
And filled with strange enchantment:—dubious shapes
Flit through dim glades, and lure the eager foot
Of youthful ardour to eternal chase.
Dreams hang on every leaf: unearthly forms
Glide through the gloom; and mystic visions swim
Before the cheated sense. Athwart the mists,
Far into vacant space, huge shadows stretch
And seem realities; while things of life,
Obvious to sight and touch, all glowing round,
Fade to the hue of shadows——*Scruples* here,
With filmy net, most like the autumnal webs
Of floating gossamer, arrest the foot
Of generous enterprise; and palsy hope
And fair ambition with the chilling touch
Of sickly hesitation and blank fear.
Nor seldom *Indolence*, these lawns among,
Fixes her turf-built seat; and wears the garb
Of deep philosophy, and museful sits,
In dreamy twilight of the vacant mind,
Soothed by the whispering shade; for soothing soft
The shades; and vistas lengthening into air,
With moon-beam rainbows tinted—Here each mind
Of finer mould, acute and delicate,
In its high progress to eternal truth
Rests for a space, in fairy bowers entranced;
And loves the softened light and tender gloom;
And, pampered with most unsubstantial food,
Looks down indignant on the grosser world,

And matter's cumbrous shapings. Youth beloved
Of science——of the muse beloved, not here,
Not in the maze of metaphysic lore,
Build thou thy place of resting! lightly tread
The dangerous ground, on noble aims intent;
And be this Circe of the studious cell
Enjoyed, but still subservient. Active scenes
Shall soon with healthful spirit brace thy mind:
And fair exertion, for bright fame sustained,
For friends, for country, chase each spleen-fed fog
That blots the wide creation——
Now heaven conduct thee with a parent's love!

(Wr. 1797, pub. 1799)

21 *from* EIGHTEEN HUNDRED AND ELEVEN

And think'st thou, Britain, still to sit at ease,
An island Queen amidst thy subject seas,
While the vext billows, in their distant roar,
But soothe thy slumbers, and but kiss thy shore?
To sport in wars, while danger keeps aloof,
Thy grassy turf unbruised by hostile hoof?
So sing thy flatterers; but, Britain, know,
Thou who hast shared the guilt must share the woe.
Nor distant is the hour; low murmurs spread,
And whispered fears, creating what they dread;
Ruin, as with an earthquake shock, is here,
There, the heart-witherings of unuttered fear,
And that sad death, whence most affection bleeds,
Which sickness, only of the soul, precedes.
Thy baseless wealth dissolves in air away,
Like mists that melt before the morning ray:
No more on crowded mart or busy street
Friends, meeting friends, with cheerful hurry greet;
Sad, on the ground thy princely merchants bend
Their altered looks, and evil days portend,
And fold their arms, and watch with anxious breast
The tempest blackening in the distant West.

Yes, thou must droop; thy Midas dream is o'er;
The golden tide of Commerce leaves thy shore,
Leaves thee to prove the alternate ills that haunt
Enfeebling Luxury and ghastly Want;
Leaves thee, perhaps, to visit distant lands,
And deal the gifts of Heaven with equal hands.
Yet, O my Country, name beloved, revered,
By every tie that binds the soul endeared,
Whose image to my infant senses came

Mixed with Religion's light and Freedom's holy flame!
If prayers may not avert, if 'tis thy fate
To rank amongst the names that once were great,
Not like the dim, cold Crescent shalt thou fade,
Thy debt to Science and the Muse unpaid;
Thine are the laws surrounding states revere,
Thine the full harvest of the mental year,
Thine the bright stars in Glory's sky that shine,
And arts that make it life to live are thine.
If westward streams the light that leaves thy shores,
Still from thy lamp the streaming radiance pours.
Wide spreads thy race from Ganges to the pole,
O'er half the western world thy accents roll:
Nations beyond the Appalachian hills
Thy hand has planted and thy spirit fills:
Soon as their gradual progress shall impart
The finer sense of morals and of art,
Thy stores of knowledge the new states shall know,
And think thy thoughts, and with thy fancy glow;
Thy Lockes, thy Paleys shall instruct their youth,
Thy leading star direct their search for truth;
Beneath the spreading Platan's tent-like shade,
Or by Missouri's rushing waters laid,
'Old father Thames' shall be the Poet's theme,
Of Hagley's woods the enamoured virgin dream,
And Milton's tones the raptured ear enthral,
Mixt with the roaring of Niagara's fall;
In Thomson's glass the ingenuous youth shall learn
A fairer face of Nature to discern;
Nor of the Bards that swept the British lyre
Shall fade one laurel, or one note expire.
Then, loved Joanna, to admiring eyes
Thy storied groups in scenic pomp shall rise;
Their high-souled strains and Shakespeare's noble rage
Shall with alternate passion shake the stage.
Some youthful Basil from thy moral lay
With stricter hand his fond desires shall sway;
Some Ethwald, as the fleeting shadows pass,
Start at his likeness in the mystic glass;
The tragic Muse resume her just control,
With pity and with terror purge the soul,
While wide o'er transatlantic realms thy name
Shall live in light, and gather *all* its fame.

Where wanders Fancy down the lapse of years
Shedding o'er imaged woes untimely tears?
Fond moody Power! as hopes—as fears prevail,
She longs, or dreads, to lift the awful veil,
On visions of delight now loves to dwell,

Now hears the shriek of woe or Freedom's knell:
Perhaps, she says, long ages past away,
And set in western waves our closing day,
Night, Gothic night, again may shade the plains
Where Power is seated, and where Science reigns;
England, the seat of arts, be only known
By the grey ruin and the mouldering stone;
That Time may tear the garland from her brow,
And Europe sit in dust, as Asia now.

(1812)

22 *from* EIGHTEEN HUNDRED AND ELEVEN

But who their mingled feelings shall pursue
When London's faded glories rise to view?
The mighty city, which by every road,
In floods of people poured itself abroad;
Ungirt by walls, irregularly great,
No jealous drawbridge, and no closing gate;
Whose merchants (such the state which commerce brings)
Sent forth their mandates to dependent kings;
Streets, where the turbaned Moslem, bearded Jew,
And woolly Afric, met the brown Hindu;
Where through each vein spontaneous plenty flowed,
Where Wealth enjoyed, and Charity bestowed.
Pensive and thoughtful shall the wanderers greet
Each splendid square, and still, untrodden street;
Or of some crumbling turret, mined by time,
The broken stairs with perilous step shall climb,
Thence stretch their view the wide horizon round,
By scattered hamlets trace its ancient bound,
And, choked no more with fleets, fair Thames survey
Through reeds and sedge pursue his idle way.

With throbbing bosoms shall the wanderers tread
The hallowed mansions of the silent dead,
Shall enter the long isle and vaulted dome
Where Genius and where Valour find a home;
Awe-struck, midst chill sepulchral marbles breathe,
Where all above is still, as all beneath;
Bend at each antique shrine, and frequent turn
To clasp with fond delight some sculptured urn,
The ponderous mass of Johnson's form to greet,
Or breathe the prayer at Howard's sainted feet.

Perhaps some Briton, in whose musing mind
Those ages live which Time has cast behind,
To every spot shall lead his wondering guests
On whose known site the beam of glory rests:

Here Chatham's eloquence in thunder broke,
Here Fox persuaded, or here Garrick spoke;
Shall boast how Nelson, fame and death in view,
To wonted victory led his ardent crew,
In England's name enforced, with loftiest tone,
Their duty,—and too well fulfilled his own:
How gallant Moore, as ebbing life dissolved,
But hoped his country had his fame absolved.
Or call up sages whose capacious mind
Left in its course a track of light behind;
Point where mute crowds on Davy's lips reposed,
And Nature's coyest secrets were disclosed;
Join with their Franklin, Priestley's injured name,
Whom, then, each continent shall proudly claim.

Oft shall the strangers turn their eager feet
The rich remains of ancient art to greet,
The pictured walls with critic eye explore,
And Reynolds be what Raphael was before.
On spoils from every clime their eyes shall gaze,
Egyptian granites and the Etruscan vase;
And when midst fallen London, they survey
The stone where Alexander's ashes lay,
Shall own with humbled pride the lesson just
By Time's slow finger written in the dust.

(1812)

23 *from* **EIGHTEEN HUNDRED AND ELEVEN**

London exults:—on London Art bestows
Her summer ices and her winter rose;
Gems of the East her mural crown adorn,
And Plenty at her feet pours forth her horn;
While even the exiles her just laws disclaim,
People a continent, and build a name:
August she sits, and with extended hands
Holds forth the book of life to distant lands.

But fairest flowers expand but to decay;
The worm is in thy core, thy glories pass away;
Arts, arms and wealth destroy the fruits they bring;
Commerce, like beauty, knows no second spring.
Crime walks thy streets, Fraud earns her unblessed bread,
O'er want and woe thy gorgeous robe is spread,
And angel charities in vain oppose:
With grandeur's growth the mass of misery grows.
For see,—to other climes the Genius soars,
He turns from Europe's desolated shores;

And lo, even now, midst mountains wrapt in storm,
On Andes' heights he shrouds his awful form;
On Chimborazo's summits treads sublime,
Measuring in lofty thought the march of Time;
Sudden he calls:—''Tis now the hour!' he cries,
Spreads his broad hand, and bids the nations rise.
La Plata hears amidst her torrents' roar;
Potosi hears it, as she digs the ore:
Ardent, the Genius fans the noble strife,
And pours through feeble souls a higher life,
Shouts to the mingled tribes from sea to sea,
And swears—Thy world, Columbus, shall be free.

(1812)

24 LIFE

Animula, vagula, blandula. [Hadrian]

Life! I know not what thou art,
But know that thou and I must part;
And when, or how, or where we meet,
I own to me's a secret yet.
But this I know, when thou art fled,
Where'er they lay these limbs, this head,
No clod so valueless shall be,
As all that then remains of me.
O whither, whither dost thou fly,
Where bend unseen thy trackless course,
And in this strange divorce,
Ah tell where I must seek this compound I?

To the vast ocean of empyreal flame,
From whence thy essence came,
Dost thou thy flight pursue, when freed
From matter's base encumbering weed?
Or dost thou, hid from sight,
Wait, like some spell-bound knight,
Through blank oblivious years the appointed hour,
To break thy trance and reassume thy power?
Yet canst thou without thought or feeling be?
O say what art thou, when no more thou art thee?

Life! we've been long together,
Through pleasant and through cloudy weather;
'Tis hard to part when friends are dear;
Perhaps 'twill cost a sigh, a tear;
Then steal away, give little warning,
Choose thine own time;
Say not Good night, but in some brighter clime
Bid me Good morning.

(Wr. 1805 – 1812? pub. 1825)

HANNAH MORE (1745 – 1833)

She was born in Bristol in 1745 where with her sisters she later ran a school which Mary Robinson attended. In the 1770s she experienced considerable success with her dramas and became acquainted with Mrs Carter, Mrs Montague, Mrs Chapone and other 'Bluestockings'. Her *The Search after Happiness* (Bristol 1773), *Essays on Various Subjects* (1777) and *Sacred Dramas... to which is added, Sensibility, a Poem* (1782) engage the problem of the benefits and costs of 'sensibility' in vigorous and original ways. In the 1780s, however, she turned increasingly to religion and produced a series of conduct manuals and essays although she did oppose slavery. See *Thoughts on the Importance of the Manners of the Great to General Society* (1788), *Strictures on the Modern System of Female Education*, 2 vols (1799), *Coelebs in Search of a Wife*, 2 vols (1808). She vigorously opposed the French Revolution and other forms of radicalism in a long series of Cheap Repository Tracts, specifically aimed at the lower classes. In 1784 she encouraged and assisted the working-class poet Ann Yearsley but, on Yearsley's success, refused to hand over the profits from her work. An acrimonious dispute ensued and Yearsley eventually obtained the money. More's refusal stemmed not from financial gain—More had a comfortable income and later left £30,000 to various charities—but from the conviction that the betterment of the working classes would render them unwilling to accept their traditional place in society. With the advent of the French Revolution, her reputation for piety and opposition to most forms of radicalism distanced her from several other women poets but endeared her to the establishment. Cottle recalled her house as being visited by a constant stream of establishment luminaries (*Reminiscences*..., London 1847, pp. 52–4), and De Quincey remembered her with admiration ('Recollections of Hannah More', De Quincey *CW*, xiv, 94–131). Her poems were collected in 1816 and again in 1829. There are several collected editions of her works, 19 vols (1818–19), 11 vols (1830), 6 vols (1833–34).

25 *from* THE SEARCH AFTER HAPPINESS

Abstruser studies soon my fancy caught,
The poet in the astronomer forgot;
The schoolmen's systems now my mind employed,
Their crystal Spheres, their Atoms, and their Void:
Newton, and Halley all my soul inspired,
And *numbers* less than *calculations* fired;
Descartes, and Euclid shared my varying breast,
And plans and problems all my soul possessed:
Less pleased to sing inspiring Phoebus' ray,
Than mark the flaming comet's devious way:
The pale moon dancing on the silver stream,
And the mild lustre of her trembling beam,
No more could charm my philosophic pride,
Which sought her influence on the flowing tide:
No more ideal beauties fired my thought,
Which only facts and demonstrations sought:
'Let common eyes,' I said, 'with transport view,
The earth's bright verdure, or the Heaven's soft blue,
False is the pleasure, the delight is vain,

Colours exist but in the *vulgar* brain.'
I now with Locke trod *metaphysic* soil,
Now chased coy nature through the tracks of Boyle;
Sighed for their fame, but feared to share their toil
The laurel wreath, in fond idea twined,
To grace my learned temples I designed.

These were my notions, these my constant themes,
My daily longings and my nightly dreams;
The thirst of Fame my bosom robbed of rest,
And envious Spleen became its constant guest....

(1773)

26 *from* **THE SEARCH AFTER HAPPINESS**

To me, no joys could pomp, or fame impart,
Far softer thoughts possessed my virgin heart.
No prudent parent formed my ductile youth,
Nor pointed out the lovely paths of truth.
Left to myself to cultivate my mind,
Pernicious *novels* their soft entrance find:
Their poisonous influence led my mind astray,
I sighed for something; what, I could not say;
I fancied virtues, which were never seen,
And died for heroes, who have never been;
I sickened with disgust at sober sense,
And loathed the pleasures worth and truth dispense;
Contemned the manners of the world I saw,
My guide was fiction, and romance my law.
Strange images my wandering fancy fill,
Each wind a zephyr, and each brook a rill;
I found adventures in each common tale,
And talked and sighed to every passing gale;
Conversed with echoes, woods and shades and bowers,
Cascades and grottoes, fields and streams, and flowers.

Reason perverted, Fancy on her throne,
(My soul to all my sex's softness prone);
I neither spoke, nor looked as mortal ought,
By sense abandoned and by folly taught:
A victim to imagination's sway,
Which stole my health, and rest, and peace away.
Professions, void of meaning, I received,
And still I found them false—and still believed:
Imagined all who courted me, approved,
Who praised, esteemed me, and who flattered, loved.
Fondly I hoped, (now vain those hopes appear),
Each man was faithful and each maid sincere.

Still, disappointment mocked the lingering day:
Still, new-born wishes kept my soul in play

When in the rolling year no joy I find,
I trust the *next*, the *next* will sure be kind;
The next, fallacious as the *last* appears,
And sends me on to still *remoter* years,
They come—they promise, but forget to give;
I *live* not, but I still *intend* to live.

At length, deceived in all my schemes of bliss,
I joined these three in search of Happiness. . . .

(1773)

MARY HAYS (1760 – 1843)

She was born in Southwark to Dissenting parents although little is known of her early life. She was passionately in love with John Eccles from 1778 until his death in 1780, and friendly with leading Dissenters, notably Robert Robinson, William Frend and George Dyer, and later Godwin and Wollstonecraft. She may have edited, or co-edited (with Elizabeth Roberts), *The Lady's Poetical Magazine*, 4 vols (1781–82), and also probably edited the poems of Frances Brooke for the *Monthly Magazine* (1797), i.141–2. For her contributions to the *Monthly Magazine* on other subjects, see Burton R. Pollin, 'Mary Hays on women's rights in the *Monthly Magazine*', *Etudes Anglaises*, xxiv (1971), 271–82. She published *Letters and Essays*... (1793), reprinting some, though not all, her contributions to the *Universal Magazine* 1784–85, *Memoirs of Emma Courtney*, 2 vols (1796), *Appeal to the Men of Great Britain*... (1798). She was ridiculed by Charles Lloyd in *Edmund Oliver*, 2 vols (1798), and by Elizabeth Hamilton in *Memoirs of Modern Philosophers*, 3 vols (1800–01). In 1814 she moved to Clifton, and despite some contact with Hannah More, she drifted into obscurity, and died in 1843.

27 AN INVOCATION TO THE NIGHTINGALE, WRITTEN NEAR THE NEW FOREST IN HAMPSHIRE

Wandering o'er the dewy meadow,
  Oft at evening hour I go;
Fondly courting Philomela's
  Sympathetic plaints of woe.

Sometimes hushed in still attention,
  Leaning pensive o'er a stile;
Fancy bids her sound delusive,
  Lull the yielding sense awhile.

Soft, the visionary music
   Rising floats upon the gale;
Now it sinks in strains more languid,
   Dying o'er the distant vale.

Starting from the dream of fancy,
   Nought my listening ears invade,
Save the hum of falling waters,
   Save the rustling aspen-shade!

Little songstress, sooth my sorrows,
   Lull my soul with softest airs;
Such as erst in 'Lydian measures,'
   Charmed the Grecian hero's cares.

But if forced by cruel rustics,
   To lament thy ruined care;
Breathe thy saddest strains of anguish,
   Strains, that melodize despair!

Deepy versed in sorrow's lessons,
   Best my heart thy griefs can know;
Pity dwells within the bosom,
   Softened by an equal woe.

Would thy melancholy plainings
   All my hapless fate renew;
Heartfelt sighs should load the Zephyr,
   Tears increase the falling dew.

Cease to shun me, lovely mourner,
   Sweetly breathe the melting strain;
Oft, thou deign'st to charm the rustic
   Roving thoughtless o'er the plain:

Yet, to him thy softest trillings
   Can no sympathy impart;
Wouldst thou seek for kindred feelings,
   See them trembling in my heart!

Vain, alas! my invocation,
   Vain the pleadings of the muse!
Deep in silent shades, the charmer
   Doth her tuneful lay refuse.

Homeward as I hopeless wander,
   Faintly sighs the evening breeze;
Shadowy beams the moon's pale lustre,
   Glittering through the waving trees.

(1781, repr. 1793)

While gazing round the wide-extended scene
Of waving corn-fields and embowering green;
Soft murmuring streams, whose mild transparent rills,
Responsive, echo to the woodlark's trills;
While from their banks the humble field-flower laves
Her modest bosom in the crystal waves,
Or views enamoured as the waters glide
Her fair reflected form beneath the tide;
My pensive soul essays the frequent sigh,
And gathering drops stand trembling in each eye,
While keen reflection wakes each latent pain,
And sudden anguish throbs in every vein;
Black Melancholy spreads her awful veil,
And chilling damps o'er every sense prevail;
The fading landscape swims before my sight,
And wraps my soul in shades of mental night.
In vain for me luxuriant Nature blooms!
In vain the flowers exhale their sweet perfumes!
Oh let me then with trembling footsteps haste
To where fair Science gilds the dreary waste!
And seek from philosophic lore to find,
A lenient balm to heal my wounded mind.
Behold majestic Reason first appear;
Her awful presence checks the starting tear;
Around her form a light diffusive spread,
Her radiant eyes a beaming lustre shed:
'Forbear, fond maid, thy fruitless grief,' she cried,
'Attend my voice, and let thy woes subside;
Survey the boundless prospect of mankind,
And mark the lot by heaven to each assigned;
Fleeting their joys, but real in their pain;
See various ills—a complicated train,
Disease, Intemperance, Want, and fell Despair,
The thrill of anguish, and corroding care,
By turns usurp the breast with dire control,
And rend with keenest pangs the feeling soul;
The Great, the Fair, the Hero, and the Sage,
Alike must yield to stern Misfortune's rage;
Till Death, oblivious power, shall intervene,
And close with friendly hand the final scene;
The soul exhausted gladly meets her doom,
And sinks in endless rest beneath the tomb.
No longer then thy woes peculiar deem,
Since life is but an unsubstantial dream;
Swift Time approaches with expanded wing,
And levels in the dust, the slave and king.'
This said, she paused—while wrapt in studious thought.

My mind revolved the awful truths she taught,
When lo! a form severe approached my view,
Whose bosom ne'er the social passions knew.
His iron heart no genuine transports move,
The glow of Friendship, or the thrill of Love;
Nor heaved with kind concern when Misery sighed,
But gloried in a Stoic's hateful pride.
All Nature sickened at his rugged mien,
And baneful damps o'erspread the misty green;
In sounds discordant he would still decry
The softer feelings of Humanity;
Or weakness deem the tender, sacred tear,
Which Friendship pours o'er Virtue's hallowed bier.
His precepts stern a kindling rage inspire,
My soul indignant shook with sudden ire;
'Hence from my sight,' with trembling voice, I cried,
'Offspring accurst of Apathy, and Pride;
Thy frigid counsels can no aid impart
To heal the pangs which rend the impassioned heart;
Unerring Reason points a sure relief
In death, the lenient balm for every grief.
Clasped in his icy arms, his aching breast
No more shall throb with various woes oppressed,
Ah! let me then her awful voice obey,
Yon limpid stream upbraids my coward stay.'
I spoke, intent to plunge beneath the waves,
And whelm my sorrows in a watery grave,
When solemn sounds my trembling footsteps stay,
And sudden glory flashed unusual day;
Clothed in refulgent rays of radiant light,
Three Cherub forms appeared revealed in sight,
Ethereal Piety, divinely fair,
Soft Hope, and heaven-born Peace, celestial pair;
Their sacred influence all my soul possessed;
And each tumultuous passion sunk to rest;
A gentle calmness o'er my senses spread,
Bright rays of comfort beamed around my head;
The tarnished grove assumed their verdant hue,
And renovated Nature bloomed anew.

(1784)

29 SONNET

Ah! let not hope fallacious, airy, wild,
   Illusive rays amid the tempest blend!
   No more my soul with varied feelings rend,
Soft sensibility—refinement's child!

May apathy her wand oblivious spread
  Steeped in lethean waves, with poppies twined,
And gently bending o'er my languid head,
  To long repose beguile a wayward mind.

While keen reflection throbs in every vein,
  Thy aid oblivion, vainly I implore!
This heart shall tremble with the sense of pain,
  Till death's cold hand a lasting peace restore.

Ah! say can reason's feebler power control,
The finer movements of the feeling soul?

(1785, repr. 1793)

CHARLOTTE SMITH (née TURNER) (1749 – 1806)

She first came to prominence with the publication of several sonnets in *The European Magazine* (1782), although she had earlier written verse for *The Lady's Magazine*. She was married off to Benjamin Smith in 1765 and lived in some poverty in London, frequently returning to Bignor Hall, the family home. By 1784, however, she was in the debtors' gaol with her husband when her *Elegaic Sonnets, and Other Essays* were published, (eighth edition, 2 vols, 1797). The sonnets attracted considerable attention. See J[oshua?] T[oumlin?], 'An Essay on the English Sonnet; Illustrated by a Comparison between the Sonnets of Milton and those of Charlotte Smith', *Universal Magazine*, xci (1792), pp. 408–14, Wordsworth's retrospective recognition (Note to 'Stanzas Suggested in a Steamboat...' (1833), *The Poetical Works*, ed. E. de Selincourt and Helen Darbishire, London 1947, iv,403), and Coleridge's assessment, *Poetical Works*, ed. E. H. Coleridge, 2 vols (1912), ii.1139. The sonnets, with pervading themes of melancholy and isolation, possibly intensified by her own confinement within an unhappy marriage and in the debtors' gaol, nevertheless reveal a relish for natural description and attachment to landscape which extended the range of options open to the romantics. Although initially a supporter of the French Revolution, the larger canvas of distress which she witnessed as a result of it, together with fears of invasion (which would have been directly through the landscape she was most attached to), led to two ambitious and complicated works, *The Emigrants* (1793) and *Beachy Head* (pub. 1807), which explore personal isolation against the background of larger themes of the exile of classes and the conflict of nations. Neither work was particularly influential or successful, but they do chart possibilities of engaging private/public themes different from those of the main romantic canon. Financial and marital problems continued and she turned increasingly to writing novels for financial support. Litigation over her father's will and a large family were constant strains throughout her life. She published *The Romance of Real Life*, 3 vols (1797), *Emmeline*, 4 vols (1788), *Celestina*, 4 vols (1791), *Desmond*, 3 vols (1792), *The Wanderings of Warwick* (1794), *Marchmont*, 4 vols (1796), *Montalbert*, 3 vols (1796), *The Young Philosopher*, 4 vols (1798), *Letters of a Solitary Wanderer*, 2 vols (1799). The social and political conflicts of ideas expressed in the novels await but would repay further study.

CHARLOTTE SMITH

She left her husband in 1787, fearing for her safety, and lived in Brighton 1788–93. Wordsworth visited her there in 1791 on his way to France, asking for a letter of introduction to Helen Maria Williams (WW *CL*, i.L20). He had earlier annotated a copy of *Elegaic Sonnets* as an undergraduate in 1789 and re-read them in 1802. His copy of the fifth edition (1789) is at Dove Cottage Library. Just as Hazlitt and De Quincey had remarked on the eclipse of Barbauld, Wordsworth was surprised by the rapid demise of Smith's reputation. However, whereas Hazlitt and De Quincey were energetic promoters of the new canon, in part driven by their road-to-Damascus experiences of reading Wordsworth and Coleridge, Wordsworth himself retained considerable interest in the accuracy of the canon and was one of the first to highlight the disappearance of the women poets and drew attention to Smith's importance on several occasions. Despite continued success with the novels, Smith's financial problems persisted. She died at Tilford in 1806, after years of ill health.

30 SONNET: TO A NIGHTINGALE

Poor melancholy bird—that all night long
Tell'st to the Moon, thy tale of tender woe;
From what sad cause can such sweet sorrow flow,
And whence this mournful melody of song?

Thy poet's musing fancy would translate
What mean the sounds that swell thy little breast,
When still at dewy eve thou leav'st thy nest,
Thus to the listening night to sing thy fate.

Pale Sorrow's victims wert thou once among,
Though now released in woodlands wild to rove,
Say—hast thou felt from friends some cruel wrong,
Or diedst thou—martyr of disastrous love?
Ah! songstress sad!—that such my lot might be,
To sigh and sing at liberty—like thee!

(1782, repr. 1786)

31 SONNET: TO THE SOUTH DOWNS

Ah, hills beloved!—where once, an happy child,
Your beechen shades, 'your turf, your flowers among,'
I wove your blue-bells into garlands wild,
And woke your echoes with my artless song.
Ah, hills beloved!—your turf, your flowers remain;
But can they peace to this sad breast restore,
For one poor moment soothe the sense of pain,
And teach a breaking heart to throb no more?

And you, Aruna!—in the vale below,
As to the sea your limpid waves you bear,
Can you one kind Lethean cup bestow,
To drink a long oblivion to my care?
Ah, no!—when all, e'en hope's last ray is gone,
There's no oblivion—but in death alone!

(1782, repr. 1786)

32 SONNET: ON THE DEPARTURE OF THE NIGHTINGALE

Sweet poet of the woods—a long adieu!
Farewell, soft minstrel of the early year!
Ah! 'twill be long ere thou shalt sing anew,
And pour thy music on the 'night's dull ear'.
Whether on spring thy wandering flights await,
Or whether silent in our groves you dwell,
The pensive muse shall own thee for her mate,
And still protect the song she loves so well.
With cautious step, the love-lorn youth shall glide
Though the lone brake that shades thy mossy nest;
And shepherd girls, from eyes profane shall hide
The gentle bird, who sings of pity best.
For still thy voice shall soft affections move,
And still be dear to sorrow, and to love!

(1782, repr. 1786)

33 SONNET: COMPOSED DURING A WALK ON THE DOWNS, IN NOVEMBER 1787

The dark and pillowy cloud; the sallow trees,
Seem o'er the ruins of the year to mourn;
And cold and hollow, the inconstant breeze
Sobs through the falling leaves and withered fern.
O'er the tall brow of yonder chalky bourn,
The evening shades their gathered darkness fling,
While, by the lingering light, I scarce discern
The shrieking night-jar, sail on heavy wing.
Ah! yet a little—and propitious Spring
Crowned with fresh flowers, shall wake the woodland strain;
But no gay change revolving seasons bring,
To call forth pleasure from the soul of pain,
Bid Siren Hope resume her long lost part,
And chase the vulture Care—that feeds upon the heart.

(Wr. 1787, pub. 1789)

34 SONNET

The fairest flowers are gone!—for tempests fell,
And with wild wing swept some unblown away,
While, on the upland lawn or rocky dell,
More faded in the Day-star's ardent ray;
And scarce the copse or hedge-row's shade beneath,
Or by the runnel's grassy course; appear
Some lingering blossoms of the earlier year,
Mingling bright florets, in the yellow wreath
That Autumn with his poppies and his corn
Binds on his tawny temples.—So the schemes
Raised by fond Hope, in life's unclouded morn,
When sanguine youth enjoys delusive dreams,
Experience withers! till scarce one remains,
Flattering the languid heart, where only reason reigns!

(1798)

35 SONNET

Huge vapours brood above the clifted shore,
Night o'er the ocean settles, dark and mute,
Save where is heard the repercussive roar
Of drowsy billows, on the rugged foot
Of rocks remote; or still more distant tone
Of seamen, in the anchored bark, that tell
The watch relieved; or one deep voice alone,
Singing the hour, and bidding 'strike the bell.'
All is black shadow, but the lucid line
Marked by the light surf on the level sand,
Or where afar, the ship-lights faintly shine
Like wandering fairy fires, that oft on land
Mislead the pilgrim; such the dubious ray
That wavering reason lends, in life's long darkling way.

(1798)

36 *from* THE EMIGRANTS, BOOK I

Scene, on the Cliffs to the Eastward of the Town of Brighthelmstone in Sussex
Time, a Morning in November, 1792

Slow in the Wintery Morn, the struggling light
Throws a faint gleam upon the troubled waves;
Their foaming tops, as they approach the shore
And the broad surf that never ceasing breaks
On the innumerous pebbles, catch the beams

Of the pale Sun, that with reluctance gives
To this cold northern Isle, its shortened day.
Alas! how few the morning wakes to joy!
How many murmur at oblivious night
For leaving them so soon; for bearing thus
Their fancied bliss (the only bliss they taste!),
On her black wings away!—Changing the dreams
That soothed their sorrows, for calamities
(And every day brings its own sad proportion)
For doubts, diseases, abject dread of Death,
And faithless friends, and fame and fortune lost;
Fancied or real wants; and wounded pride,
That views the day star, but to curse his beams.
   Yet He, whose Spirit into being called
This wonderous World of Waters; He who bids
The wild wind lift them till they dash the clouds,
And speaks to them in thunder; or whose breath,
Low murmuring o'er the gently heaving tides,
When the fair Moon, in summer night serene,
Irradiates with long trembling lines of light
Their undulating surface; that great Power,
Who, governing the Planets, also knows
If but a Sea-Mew falls, whose nest is hid
In these incumbent cliffs; He surely means
To us, his reasoning Creatures, whom He bids
Acknowledge and revere his awful hand,
Nothing but good: Yet Man, misguided Man,
Mars the fair work that he was bid enjoy,
And makes himself the evil he deplores.
How often, when my weary soul recoils
From proud oppression, and from legal crimes
(For such are in this Land, where the vain boast
Of equal Law is mockery, while the cost
Of seeking for redress is sure to plunge
The already injured to more certain ruin
And the wretch starves, before his Counsel pleads)
How often do I half abjure Society,
And sigh for some lone Cottage, deep embowered
In the green woods, that these steep chalky Hills
Guard from the strong South West; where round their base
The Beach wide flourishes, and the light Ash
With slender leaf half hides the thymy turf!—
There do I wish to hide me; well content
If on the short grass, strewn with fairy flowers,
I might repose thus sheltered; or when Eve
In Orient crimson lingers in the west,
Gain the high mound, and mark these waves remote
(Lucid though distant), blushing with the rays
Of the far-flaming Orb, that sinks beneath them;

For I have thought, that I should then behold
The beauteous works of God, unspoiled by Man
And less affected then, by human woes
I witnessed not; might better learn to bear
Those that injustice, and duplicity
And faithlessness and folly, fix on me:
For never yet could I derive relief,
When my swollen heart was bursting with its sorrows,
From the sad thought, that others like myself
Live but to swell affliction's countless tribes!
—Tranquil seclusion I have vainly sought;
Peace, who delights in solitary shade,
No more will spread for me her downy wings,
But, like the fabled Danaïds—or the wretch,
Who ceaseless, up the steep acclivity,
Was doomed to heave the still rebounding rock,
Onward I labour; as the baffled wave,
Which yon rough beach repulses, that returns
With the next breath of wind, to fail again.—...

(1793)

37 *from* THE EMIGRANTS, BOOK II

Scene, on an Eminence on one of those Downs, which afford to the South a View of the Sea; to the North of the Weald of Sussex.
Time, an Afternoon in April, 1793

Long wintery months are past; the Moon that now
Lights her pale crescent even at noon, has made
Four times her revolution; since with step,
Mournful and slow, along the wave-worn cliff,
Pensive I took my solitary way,
Lost in despondence, while contemplating
Not my own wayward destiny alone,
(Hard as it is, and difficult to bear!)
But in beholding the unhappy lot
Of the lorn Exiles; who, amid the storms
Of wild disastrous Anarchy, are thrown,
Like shipwrecked sufferers, on England's coast,
To see, perhaps, no more their native land,
Where Desolation riots: They, like me,
From fairer hopes and happier prospects driven,
Shrink from the future, and regret the past.
But on this Upland scene, while April comes,
With fragrant airs, to fan my throbbing breast,
Fain would I snatch an interval from Care,
That weighs my wearied spirit down to earth;

Courting, once more, the influence of Hope
(For 'Hope' still waits upon the flowery prime)
As here I mark Spring's humid hand unfold
The early leaves that fear capricious winds,
While, even on sheltered banks, the timid flowers
Give, half reluctantly, their warmer hues
To mingle with the primroses' pale stars.
No shade the leafless copses yet afford,
Nor hide the mossy labours of the Thrush,
That, startled, darts across the narrow path;
But quickly reassured, resumes his task,
Or adds his louder notes to those that rise
From yonder tufted brake; where the white buds
Of the first thorn are mingled with the leaves
Of that which blossoms on the brow of May.
   Ah! 'twill not be:—So many years have passed,
Since, on my native hills, I learned to gaze
On these delightful landscapes; and those years
Have taught me so much sorrow, that my soul
Feels not the joy reviving Nature brings;
But, in dark retrospect, dejected dwells
On human follies, and on human woes.—
What is the promise of the infant year,
The lively verdure, or the bursting blooms,
To those, who shrink from horrors such as War
Spreads o'er the affrighted world? With swimming eye,
Back on the past they throw their mournful looks,
And see the Temple, which they fondly hoped
Reason would raise to Liberty, destroyed
By ruffian hands; while, on the ruined mass,
Flushed with hot blood, the Fiend of Discord sits
In savage triumph; mocking every plea
Of policy and justice, as she shews
The headless corse of one, whose only crime
Was being born a Monarch—Mercy turns,
From spectacle so dire, her swollen eyes;
And Liberty, with calm, unruffled brow
Magnanimous, as conscious of her strength
In Reason's panoply, scorns to disdain
Her righteous cause with carnage, and resigns
To Fraud and Anarchy the infuriate crowd.—
   What is the promise of the infant year
To those, who (while the poor but peaceful hind
Pens, unmolested, the increasing flock
Of his rich master in this sea-fenced isle)
Survey, in neighbouring countries, scenes that make
The sick heart shudder; and the Man, who thinks,
Blush for his species? *There* the trumpet's voice
Drowns the soft warbling of the woodland choir;

And violets, lurking in their turfy beds
Beneath the flowering thorn, are stained with blood.
There fall, at once, the spoiler and the spoiled;
While War, wide-ravaging, annihilates
The hope of cultivation; gives to Fiends,
The meagre, ghastly Fiends of Want and Woe,
The blasted land—There, taunting in the van
Of vengeance-breathing armies, Insult stalks;
And, in the ranks, 'Famine, and Sword, and Fire,
Crouch for employment.'—...

(1793)

38 STUDIES BY THE SEA

Ah! wherefore do the incurious say,
    That this stupendous ocean wide,
No change presents from day to day,
    Save only the alternate tide;
Or save when gales of summer glide
    Across the lightly crisped wave;
Or, when against the cliff's rough side,
    As equinoxial tempests rave,
It wildly bursts; o'erwhelms the deluged strand,
Tears down its bounds, and desolates the land?

He who with more enquiring eyes
    Doth this extensive scene survey,
Beholds innumerous changes rise,
    As various winds its surface sway;
Now o'er its heaving bosom play
    Small sparkling waves of silver gleam,
And as they lightly glide away
    Illume with fluctuating beam
The deepening surge; green as the dewy corn
That undulates in April's breezy morn.

The far off waters then assume
    A glowing amethystine shade,
That changing like the peacock's plume,
    Seems in celestial blue to fade;
Or paler, colder hues of lead,
    As lurid vapours float on high,
Along the ruffling billows spread,
    While darkly lours the threatening sky;
And the small scattered barks with outspread shrouds,
Catch the long gleams, that fall between the clouds.

Then day's bright star with blunted rays
Seems struggling through the sea-fog pale,
And doubtful in the heavy haze,
Is dimly seen the nearing sail;
Till from the land a fresher gale
Disperses the white mist, and clear,
As melts away the gauzy veil,
The sun-reflecting waves appear;
So, brighter genuine virtue seems to rise
From envy's dark invidious calumnies.

What glories on the sun attend,
When the full tides of evening flow,
Where in still changing beauty, blend
With amber light, the opal's glow;
While in the east the diamond bow
Rises in virgin lustre bright,
And from the horizon seems to throw,
A partial line of trembling light
To the hushed shore; and all the tranquil deep
Beneath the modest moon, is soothed to sleep.

Forgotten then, the thundering break
Of waves, that in the tempest rise,
The falling cliff, the shattered wreck,
The howling blast, the sufferer's cries;
For soft the breeze of evening sighs,
And murmuring seems in Fancy's ear
To whisper fairy lullabies,
That tributary waters bear
From precipices, dark with piny woods,
And inland rocks, and healthy solitudes.

The vast encircling seas within,
What endless swarms of creatures hide,
Of burnished scale, and spiny fin!
These providential instincts guide,
And bid them know the annual tide,
When, from unfathomed waves that swell,
Beyond Fuego's stormy side,
They come, to cheer the tribes that dwell
In Boreal climes; and through his half year's night
Give to the Lapland savage, food and light.

From cliffs, that pierce the northern sky,
Where eagles rear their sanguine brood,
With long awaiting patient eye,
Baffled by many a sailing cloud,
The Highland native marks the flood,

Till bright the quickening billows roll,
And hosts of sea-birds, clamouring loud,
Track with wild wing the welcome shoal,
Swift o'er the animated current sweep,
And bear their silver captives from the deep.

Sons of the North! your streamy vales
With no rich sheaves rejoice and sing;
Her flowery robe no fruit conceals,
Though sweetly smile your tardy spring;
Yet every mountain, clothed with ling,
Doth from its purple brow survey
Your busy sails, that ceaseless bring
To the broad frith, and sheltering bay,
Riches, by Heaven's parental power supplied,—
The harvest of the far embracing tide.

And, where those fractured mountains lift
O'er the blue wave their towering crest,
Each salient ledge and hollow cleft
To sea-fowl give a rugged nest.
But with instinctive love is dressed
The Eider's downy cradle; where
The mother-bird, her glossy breast
Devotes, and with maternal care,
And plumeless bosom, stems the toiling seas,
That foam round the tempestuous Orcades.

From heights, whence shuddering sense recoils,
And cloud-capped headlands, steep and bare,
Sons of the North! your venturous toils
Collect your poor and scanty fare.
Urged by imperious Want, you dare
Scale the loose cliff, where Gannets hide,
Or scarce suspended, in the air
Hang perilous; and thus provide
The soft voluptuous couch, which not secures
To Luxury's pampered minions, sleep like yours.

Revolving still, the waves that now
Just ripple on the level shore,
Have borne perchance the Indian's prow,
Or half congealed, 'mid ice rocks hoar,
Raved to the Walrus' hollow roar;
Or have by currents swift conveyed
To the cold coast of Labrador,
The relics of the tropic shade;
And to the wondering Eskimos have shown
Leaves of strange shape, and fruits unlike their own.

No more then, let the incurious say,
No change this world of water shows,
But as the tides the moon obey,
Or tempests rave, or calms repose.—
Show them, its bounteous breast bestows
On myriads life; and bid them see
In every wave that circling flows,
Beauty and use, and harmony—
Works of the Power Supreme, who poured the flood,
Round the green peopled earth, and called it very good!

(1804)

39 THE SWALLOW

The gorse is yellow on the heath,
The banks with speedwell flowers are gay,
The oaks are budding; and beneath,
The hawthorn soon will bear the wreath,
The silver wreath of May.

The welcome guest of settled Spring,
The Swallow too is come at last;
Just at sun-set, when thrushes sing,
I saw her dash with rapid wing,
And hailed her as she passed.

Come, summer visitant, attach
To my reed roof your nest of clay,
And let my ear your music catch
Low twittering underneath the thatch
At the grey dawn of day.

As fables tell, an Indian Sage,
The Hindustani woods among,
Could in his desert hermitage,
As if 'twere marked in written page,
Translate the wild bird's song.

I wish I did his power possess,
That I might learn, fleet bird, from thee,
What our vain systems only guess,
And know from what wide wilderness
You came across the sea.

I would a little while restrain
   Your rapid wing, that I might hear
Whether on clouds that bring the rain,
You sailed above the western main,
   The wind your charioteer.

In Afric, does the sultry gale
   Through spicy bower, and palmy grove,
Bear the repeated Cuckoo's tale?
Dwells *there* a time, the wandering Rail
   Or the itinerant Dove?

Were you in Asia? O relate,
   If there your fabled sister's woes
She seemed in sorrow to narrate;
Or sings she but to celebrate
   Her nuptials with the rose?

I would enquire how journeying long,
   The vast and pathless ocean o'er,
You ply again those pinions strong,
And come to build anew among
   The scenes you left before;

But if, as colder breezes blow,
   Prophetic of the waning year,
You hide, though none know when or how,
In the cliff's excavated brow,
      And linger torpid here;

Thus lost to life, what favouring dream
   Bids you to happier hours awake;
And tells, that dancing in the beam,
The light gnat hovers o'er the stream,
   The May-fly on the lake?

Or if, by instinct taught to know
   Approaching dearth of insect food;
To isles and willowy aits you go,
And crowding on the pliant bough,
   Sink in the dimpling flood:

How learn ye, while the cold waves boom
   Your deep and oozy couch above,
The time when flowers of promise bloom,
And call you from your transient tomb,
   To light, and life, and love?

Alas! how little can be known,
   Her sacred veil where Nature draws;
Let baffled Science humbly own,
Her mysteries understood alone,
   By *Him* who gives her laws.

(pub. 1807)

40 BEACHY HEAD

On thy stupendous summit, rock sublime!
That o'er the channel reared, half way at sea
The mariner at early morning hails,
I would recline; while Fancy should go forth,
And represent the strange and awful hour
Of vast concussion; when the Omnipotent
Stretched forth his arm, and rent the solid hills,
Bidding the impetuous main flood rush between
The rifted shores, and from the continent
Eternally divided this green isle.
Imperial lord of the high southern coast!
From thy projecting head-land I would mark
Far in the east the shades of night disperse,
Melting and thinned, as from the dark blue wave
Emerging, brilliant rays of arrowy light
Dart from the horizon; when the glorious sun
Just lifts above it his resplendent orb.
Advances now, with feathery silver touched,
The rippling tide of flood; glisten the sands,
Whiie, inmates of the chalky clefts that scar
Thy sides precipitous, with shrill harsh cry,
Their white wings glancing in the level beam,
The terns, and gulls, and tarrocks, seek their food,
And thy rough hollows echo to the voice
Of the gray choughs, and ever restless daws,
With clamour, not unlike the chiding hounds,
While the lone shepherd, and his baying dog,
Drive to thy turfy crest his bleating flock.

The high meridian of the day is past,
And Ocean now, reflecting the calm Heaven,
Is of cerulean hue; and murmurs low
The tide of ebb, upon the level sands.
The sloop, her angular canvas shifting still.
Catches the light and variable airs
That but a little crisp the summer sea,
Dimpling its tranquil surface.

Afar off,
And just emerging from the arch immense
Where seem to part the elements, a fleet
Of fishing vessels stretch their lesser sails;
While more remote, and like a dubious spot
Just hanging in the horizon, laden deep,
The ship of commerce richly freighted, makes
Her slower progress, on her distant voyage,
Bound to the orient climates, where the sun
Matures the spice within its odorous shell,
And, rivalling the grey worm's filmy toil,
Bursts from its pod the vegetable down;
Which in long turbaned wreaths, from torrid heat
Defends the brows of Asia's countless casts.
There the Earth hides within her glowing breast
The beamy adamant, and the round pearl
Enchased in rugged covering; which the slave,
With perilous and breathless toil, tears off
From the rough sea-rock, deep beneath the waves.
These are the toys of Nature; and her sport
Of little estimate in Reason's eye:
And they who reason, with abhorrence see
Man, for such gaudes and baubles, violate
The sacred freedom of his fellow man—
Erroneous estimate! As Heaven's pure air,
Fresh as it blows on this aërial height,
Or sound of seas upon the stony strand,
Or inland, the gay harmony of birds,
And winds that wander in the leafy woods;
Are to the unadulterate taste more worth
Than the elaborate harmony, brought out
From fretted stop, or modulated airs
Of vocal science.—So the brightest gems,
Glancing resplendent on the regal crown,
Or trembling in the high born beauty's ear,
Are poor and paltry, to the lovely light
Of the fair star, that as the day declines,
Attendant on her queen, the crescent moon,
Bathes her bright tresses in the eastern wave.
For now the sun is verging to the sea,
And as he westward sinks, the floating clouds
Suspended, move upon the evening gale,
And gathering round his orb, as if to shade
The insufferable brightness, they resign
Their gauzy whiteness; and more warmed, assume
All hues of purple. There, transparent gold
Mingles with ruby tints, and sapphire gleams,
And colours, such as Nature through her works
Shows only in the ethereal canopy.

Thither aspiring Fancy fondly soars,
Wandering sublime through visionary vales,
Where bright pavilions rise, and trophies, fanned
By airs celestial; and adorned with wreaths
Of flowers that bloom amid elysian bowers.
Now bright, and brighter still the colours glow,
Till half the lustrous orb within the flood
Seems to retire: the flood reflecting still
Its splendour, and in mimic glory dressed;
Till the last ray shot upward, fires the clouds
With blazing crimson; then in paler light,
Long lines of tenderer radiance, lingering yield
To partial darkness; and on the opposing side
The early moon distinctly rising, throws
Her pearly brilliance on the trembling tide.

The fishermen, who at set seasons pass
Many a league off at sea their toiling night,
Now hail their comrades, from their daily task
Returning; and make ready for their own,
With the night tide commencing:—The night tide
Bears a dark vessel on, whose hull and sails
Mark her a coaster from the north. Her keel
Now ploughs the sand; and sidelong now she leans,
While with loud clamours her athletic crew
Unload her; and resounds the busy hum
Along the wave-worn rocks. Yet more remote,
Where the rough cliff hangs beetling o'er its base,
All breathes repose; the water's rippling sound
Scarce heard; but now and then the sea-snipe's cry
Just tells that something living is abroad;
And sometimes crossing on the moonbright line,
Glimmers the skiff, faintly discerned awhile,
Then lost in shadow.

Contemplation here,
High on her throne of rock, aloof may sit,
And bid recording Memory unfold
Her scroll voluminous—bid her retrace
The period, when from Neustria's hostile shore
The Norman launched his galleys, and the bay
O'er which that mass of ruin frowns even now
In vain and sullen menace, then received
The new invaders; a proud martial race,
Of Scandinavia the undaunted sons,
Whom Dogon, Fier-a-bras, and Humfroi led
To conquest: while Trinacria to their power
Yielded her wheaten garland; and when thou,

Parthenope! within thy fertile bay
Received the victors—

In the mailed ranks
Of Normans landing on the British coast
Rode Taillefer; and with astounding voice
Thundered the war song daring Roland sang
First in the fierce contention: vainly brave,
One not inglorious struggle England made—
But failing, saw the Saxon heptarchy
Finish for ever.—Then the holy pile,
Yet seen upon the field of conquest, rose,
Where to appease heaven's wrath for so much blood,
The conqueror bade unceasing prayers ascend,
And requiems for the slayers and the slain.
But let not modern Gallia form from hence
Preumptuous hopes, that ever thou again,
Queen of the isles! shalt crouch to foreign arms.
The enervate sons of Italy may yield;
And the Iberian, all his trophies torn
And wrapped in Superstition's monkish weed,
May shelter his abasement, and put on
Degrading fetters. Never, never thou!
Imperial mistress of the obedient sea;
But thou, in thy integrity secure,
Shalt now undaunted meet a world in arms.

England! 'twas where this promontory rears
Its rugged brow above the channel wave,
Parting the hostile nations, that thy fame,
Thy naval fame was tarnished, at what time
Thou, leagued with the Batavian, gavest to France
One day of triumph—triumph the more loud,
Because even then so rare. Oh! well redeemed,
Since, by a series of illustrious men,
Such as no other country ever reared,
To vindicate her cause. It is a list
Which, as Fame echoes it, blanches the cheek
Of bold Ambition; while the despot feels
The extorted sceptre tremble in his grasp.

From even the proudest roll by glory filled,
How gladly the reflecting mind returns
To simple scenes of peace and industry,
Where, bosomed in some valley of the hills
Stands the lone farm; its gate with tawny ricks
Surrounded, and with granaries and sheds,
Roofed with green mosses, and by elms and ash
Partially shaded; and not far removed
The hat of sea-flints built; the humble home
Of one, who sometimes watches on the heights,

When hid in the cold mist of passing clouds,
The flock, with drippling fleeces, are dispersed
O'er the wide down; then from some ridged point
That overlooks the sea, his eager eye
Watches the bark that for his signal waits
To land its merchandise:—Quitting for this
Clandestine traffic his more honest toil,
The crook abandoning, he braves himself
The heaviest snow-storm of December's night,
Where with conflicting winds the ocean raves,
And on the tossing boat, unfearing mounts
To meet the partners of the perilous trade,
And share their hazard. Well it were for him,
If no such commerce of destruction known,
He were content with what the earth affords
To human labour; even where she seems
Reluctant most. More happy is the hind,
Who, with his own hands rears on some black moor,
Or turbary, his independent hut
Covered with heather, whence the slow white smoke
Of smouldering peat arises——A few sheep,
His best possession, with his children share
The rugged shed when wintery tempests blow;
But, when with Spring's return the green blades rise
Amid the russet heath, the household live
Joint tenants of the waste throughout the day,
And often, from her nest, among the swamps,
Where the gemmed sun-dew grows, or fringed buck-bean,
They scare the plover, that with plaintive cries
Flutters, as sorely wounded, down the wind.
Rude, and but just removed from savage life
Is the rough dweller among scenes like these,
(Scenes all unlike the poet's fabling dreams
Describing Arcady)—But he is free;
The dread that follows on illegal acts
He never feels; and his industrious mate
Shares in his labour. Where the brook is traced
By crowding osiers, and the black coot hides
Among the plashy reeds, her diving brood,
The matron wades; gathering the long green rush
That well prepared hereafter lends its light
To her poor cottage, dark and cheerless else
Through the drear hours of Winter. Otherwhile
She leads her infant group where charlock grows
'Unprofitably gay,' or to the fields,
Where congregate the linnet and the finch,
That on the thistles, so profusely spread,
Feast in the desert; the poor family
Early resort, extirpating with care

These, and the guadier mischief of the ground;
Then flames the high raised heap; seen afar off
Like hostile war-fires flashing to the sky.
Another task is theirs: On fields that shew
As angry Heaven had rained sterility,
Stony and cold, and hostile to the plough,
Where clamouring loud, the evening curlew runs
And drops her spotted eggs among the flints;
The mother and the children pile the stones
In rugged pyramids;—and all this toil
They patiently encounter; well content
On their flock bed to slumber undisturbed
Beneath the smoky roof they call their own.
Oh! little knows the sturdy hind, who stands
Gazing, with looks where envy and contempt
Are often strangely mingled, on the car
Where prosperous Fortune sits; what secret care
Or sick satiety is often hid,
Beneath the splendid outside: *He* knows not
How frequently the child of Luxury
Enjoying nothing, flies from place to place
In chase of pleasure that eludes his grasp;
And that content is e'en less found by him,
Than by the labourer, whose pick-axe smooths
The road before his chariot; and who doffs
What *was* an hat; and as the train pass on,
Thinks how one day's expenditure, like this,
Would cheer him for long months, when to his toil
The frozen earth closes her marble breast.

Ah! who *is* happy? Happiness! a word
That like false fire, from marsh effluvia born,
Misleads the wanderer, destined to contend
In the world's wilderness, with want or woe—
Yet *they* are happy, who have never asked
What good or evil means. The boy
That on the river's margin gaily plays,
Has heard that Death is there—He knows not Death,
And therefore fears it not; and venturing in
He gains a bullrush, or a minnow—then,
At certain peril, for a worthless prize,
A crow's, or raven's nest, he climbs the boll
Of some tall pine; and of his prowess proud,
Is for a moment happy. Are *your* cares,
Ye who despise him, never worse applied?
The village girl is happy, who sets forth
To distant fair, gay in her Sunday suit,
With cherry coloured knots, and flourished shawl,
And bonnet newly purchased. So is he

Her little brother, who his mimic drum
Beats, till he drowns her rural lovers' oaths
Of constant faith, and still increasing love;
Ah! yet a while, and half those oaths believed,
Her happiness is vanished; and the boy
While yet a stripling, finds the sound he loved
Has led him on, till he has given up
His freedom, and his happiness together.
I once was happy, when while yet a child,
I learned to love these upland solitudes,
And, when elastic as the mountain air,
To my light spirit, care was yet unknown
And evil unforeseen:—Early it came,
And childhood scarcely passed, I was condemned,
A guiltless exile, silently to sigh,
While Memory, with faithful pencil, drew
The contrast; and regretting, I compared
With the polluted smoky atmosphere
And dark and stifling streets, the southern hills
That to the setting Sun, their graceful heads
Rearing, o'erlook the frith, where Vecta breaks
With her white rocks, the strong impetuous tide,
When western winds the vast Atlantic urge
To thunder on the coast—Haunts of my youth!
Scenes of fond day-dreams, I behold ye yet!
Where 'twas so pleasant by thy northern slopes
To climb the winding sheep-path, aided oft
By scattered thorns: whose spiny branches bore
Small woolly tufts, spoils of the vagrant lamb
There seeking shelter from the noon-day sun;
And pleasant, seated on the short soft turf,
To look beneath upon the hollow way
While heavily upward moved the labouring wain,
And stalking slowly by, the sturdy hind
To ease his panting team, stopped with a stone
The grating wheel.

Advancing higher still
The prospect widens, and the village church
But little, o'er the lowly roofs around
Rears its grey belfry, and its simple vane;
Those lowly roofs of thatch are half concealed
By the rude arms of trees, lovely in spring,
When on each bough, the rosy-tinctured bloom
Sits thick, and promises autumnal plenty.
For even those orchards round the Norman farms,
Which, as their owners mark the promised fruit,
Console them for the vineyards of the south,
Surpass not these.

Where woods of ash, and beech,
And partial copses, fringe the green hill foot,
The upland shepherd rears his modest home,
There wanders by, a little nameless stream
That from the hill wells forth, bright now and clear,
Or after rain with chalky mixture grey,
But still refreshing in its shallow course,
The cottage garden; most for use designed,
Yet not of beauty destitute. The vine
Mantles the little casement; yet the briar
Drops fragrant dew among the July flowers;
And pansies rayed, and freaked and mottled pinks
Grow among balm, and rosemary and rue:
There honeysuckles flaunt, and roses blow
Almost uncultured: Some with dark green leaves
Contrast their flowers of pure unsullied white;
Others, like velvet robes of regal state
Of richest crimson, while in thorny moss
Enshrined and cradled, the most lovely, wear
The hues of youthful beauty's glowing cheek.—
With fond regret I recollect e'en now
In Spring and Summer, what delight I felt
Among these cottage gardens, and how much
Such artless nosegays, knotted with a rush
By village housewife or her ruddy maid,
Were welcome to me; soon and simply pleased.

An early worshipper at Nature's shrine,
I loved her rudest scenes—warrens, and heaths,
And yellow commons, and birch-shaded hollows,
And hedge rows, bordering unfrequented lanes
Bowered with wild roses, and the clasping woodbine
Where purple tassels of the tangling vetch
With bittersweet, and bryony inweave,
And the dew fills the silver bindweed's cups—
I loved to trace the brooks whose humid banks
Nourish the harebell, and the freckled pagil;
And stroll among o'ershadowing woods of beech,
Lending in Summer, from the heats of noon
A whispering shade; while haply there reclines
Some pensive lover of uncultured flowers,
Who, from the tumps with bright green mosses clad,
Plucks the wood sorrel, with its light thin leaves,
Heart-shaped, and triply folded; and its root
Creeping like beaded coral; or who there
Gathers, the copse's pride, anemones,
With rays like golden studs on ivory laid
Most delicate: but touched with purple clouds,
Fit crown for April's fair but changeful brow.

Ah! hills so early loved! in fancy still
I breathe your pure keen air; and still behold
Those widely spreading views, mocking alike
The Poet and the Painter's utmost art.
And still, observing objects more minute,
Wondering remark the strange and foreign forms
Of sea-shells; with the pale calcareous soil
Mingled, and seeming of resembling substance.
Though surely the blue Ocean (from the heights
Where the downs westward trend, but dimly seen)
Here never rolled its surge. Does Nature then
Mimic, in wanton mood, fantastic shapes
Of bivalves, and inwreathed volutes, that cling
To the dark sea-rock of the watery world?
Or did this range of chalky mountains, once
Form a vast basin, where the Ocean waves
Swelled fathomless? What time these fossil shells,
Buoyed on their native element, were thrown
Among the imbedding calx: when the huge hill
Its giant bulk heaved, and in strange ferment
Grew up a guardian barrier, 'twixt the sea
And the green level of the sylvan weald.

Ah! very vain is Science' proudest boast,
And but a little light its flame yet lends
To its most ardent votaries; since from whence
These fossil forms are seen, is but conjecture,
Food for vague theories, or vain dispute,
While to his daily task the peasant goes,
Unheeding such inquiry; with no care
But that the kindly change of sun and shower,
Fit for his toil the earth he cultivates.
As little recks the herdsman of the hill,
Who on some turfy knoll, idly reclined,
Watches his wether flock; that deep beneath
Rest the remains of men, of whom is left
No traces in the records of mankind,
Save what these half obliterated mounds
And half filled trenches doubtfully impart
To some lone antiquary; who on times remote,
Since which two thousand years have rolled away,
Loves to contemplate. He perhaps may trace,
Or fancy he can trace, the oblong square
Where the mailed legions, under Claudius, reared
The rampire, or excavated fosse delved;
What time the huge unwieldy Elephant
Auxiliary reluctant, hither led,
From Afric's forest glooms and tawny sands,
First felt the Northern blast, and his vast frame

Sunk useless; whence in after ages found,
The wondering hinds, on those enormous bones
Gazed; and in giants dwelling on the hills
Believed and marvelled—

Hither, Ambition, come!
Come and behold the nothingness of all
For which you carry through the oppressed Earth,
War, and its train of horrors—see where tread
The innumerous hoofs of flocks above the works
By which the warrior sought to register
His glory, and immortalize his name—
The pirate Dane, who from his circular camp
Bore in destructive robbery, fire and sword
Down through the vale, sleeps unremembered here;
And here, beneath the green sward, rests alike
The savage native, who his acorn meal
Shared with the herds, that ranged the pathless woods;
And the centurion, who on these wide hills
Encamping, planted the Imperial Eagle.
All, with the lapse of Time, have passed away,
Even as the clouds, with dark and dragon shapes,
Or like vast promontories crowned with towers,
Cast their broad shadows on the downs: then sail
Far to the northward, and their transient gloom
Is soon forgotten.

But from thoughts like these,
By human crimes suggested, let us turn
To where a more attractive study courts
The wanderer of the hills; while shepherd girls
Will from among the fescue bring him flowers,
Of wonderous mockery; some resembling bees
In velvet vest, intent on their sweet toil,
While others mimic flies, that lightly sport
In the green shade, or float along the pool,
But here seem perched upon the slender stalk,
And gathering honey dew. While in the breeze
That wafts the thistle's plumed seed along,
Blue bells wave tremulous. The mountain thyme
Purples the hassock of the heaving mole,
And the short turf is gay with tormentil,
And bird's foot trefoil, and the lesser tribes
Of hawkweed; spangling it with fringed stars.—
Near where a richer tract of cultured land
Slopes to the south; and burnished by the sun,
Bend in the gale of August, floods of corn;
The guardian of the flock, with watchful care,
Repels by voice and dog the encroaching sheep—

While his boy visits every wired trap
That scars the turf; and from the pit-falls takes
The timid migrants, who from distant wilds,
Warrens, and stone quarries, are destined thus
To lose their short existence. But unsought
By Luxury yet, the Shepherd still protects
The social bird, who from his native haunts
Of willowy current, or the rushy pool,
Follows the fleecy crowd, and flirts and skims,
In fellowship among them.

Where the knoll
More elevated takes the changeful winds,
The windmill rears its vanes; and thitherward
With his white load, the master travelling,
Scares the rooks rising slow on whispering wings,
While o'er his head, before the summer sun
Lights up the blue expanse, heard more than seen,
The lark sings matins; and above the clouds
Floating, embathes his spotted breast in dew.
Beneath the shadow of a gnarled thorn,
Bent by the sea blast, from a seat of turf
With fairy nosegays strewn, how wide the view!
Till in the distant north it melts away,
And mingles indiscriminate with clouds:
But if the eye could reach so far, the mart
Of England's capital, its domes and spires
Might be perceived—Yet hence the distant range
Of Kentish hills, appear in purple haze;
And nearer, undulate the wooded heights,
And airy summits, that above the mole
Rise in green beauty; and the beaconed ridge
Of Black-down shagged with heath, and swelling rude
Like a dark island from the vale; its brow
Catching the last rays of the evening sun
That gleam between the nearer park's old oaks,
Then lighten up the river, and make prominent
The portal, and the ruined battlements
Of that dismantled fortress; raised what time
The Conqueror's successors fiercely fought,
Tearing with civil feuds the desolate land.
But now a tiller of the soil dwells there,
And of the turret's looped and raftered halls
Has made an humbler homestead—Where he sees,
Instead of armed foemen, herds that graze
Along his yellow meadows; or his flocks
At evening from the upland driven to fold—

In such a castellated mansion once
A stranger chose his home; and where hard by
In rude disorder fallen, and hid with brushwood
Lay fragments grey of towers and buttresses,
Among the ruins, often he would muse—
His rustic meal soon ended, he was wont
To wander forth, listening the evening sounds
Of rushing milldam, or the distant team,
Or night-jar, chasing fern-flies: the tired hind
Passed him at nightfall, wondering he should sit
On the hill top so late: they from the coast
Who sought bypaths with their clandestine load,
Saw with suspicious doubt, the lonely man
Cross on their way: but village maidens thought
His senses injured; and with pity say
That he, poor youth! must have been crossed in love—
For often, stretched upon the mountain turf
With folded arms, and eyes intently fixed
Where ancient elms and firs obscured a grange,
Some little space within the vale below,
They heard him, as complaining of his fate,
And to the murmuring wind, of cold neglect
And baffled hope he told.—The peasant girls
These plaintive sounds remember, and even now
Among them may be heard the stranger's songs.

Were I a Shepherd on the hill
  And ever as the mists withdrew
Could see the willows of the rill
Shading the footway to the mill
  Where once I walked with you—

And as away Night's shadows sail,
  And sounds of birds and brooks arise,
Believe, that from the woody vale
I hear your voice upon the gale
  In soothing melodies;

And viewing from the Alpine height,
  The prospect dressed in hues of air,
Could say, while transient colours bright
Touched the fair scene with dewy light,
  'Tis, that *her* eyes are there!

I think, I could endure my lot
  And linger on a few short years,
And then, by all but you forgot,
Sleep, where the turf that clothes the spot
  May claim some pitying tears.

For 'tis not easy to forget
   One, who through life has loved you still,
And you, however late, might yet
With sighs to Memory given, regret
   The Shepherd of the Hill.

Yet otherwhile it seemed as if young Hope
Her flattering pencil gave to Fancy's hand,
And in his wanderings, reared to sooth his soul
Ideal bowers of pleasure—Then, of Solitude
And of his hermit life, still more enamoured,
His home was in the forest; and wild fruits
And bread sustained him. There in early spring
The Barkmen found him, e'er the sun arose;
There at their daily toil, the Wedgecutters
Beheld him through the distant thicket move.
The shaggy dog following the truffle hunter,
Barked at the loiterer; and perchance at night
Belated villagers from fair or wake,
While the fresh night-wind let the moonbeams in
Between the swaying boughs, just saw him pass,
And then in silence, gliding like a ghost
He vanished! Lost among the deepening gloom.—
But near one ancient tree, whose wreathed roots
Formed a rude couch, love-songs and scattered rhymes,
Unfinished sentences, or half erased,
And rhapsodies like this, were sometimes found—

Let us to woodland wilds repair
   While yet the glittering night-dews seem
To wait the freshly-breathing air,
   Precursive of the morning beam,
That rising with advancing day,
Scatters the silver drops away.

An elm, uprooted by the storm,
   The trunk with mosses grey and green,
Shall make for us a rustic form,
   Where lighter grows the forest scene;
And far among the bowery shades,
Are ferny lawns and grassy glades.

Retiring May to lovely June
   Her latest garland now resigns;
The banks with cuckoo-flowers are strewn,
   The woodwalks blue with columbines,
And with its reeds, the wandering stream
Reflects the flag-flower's golden gleam.

There, feathering down the turf to meet,
   Their shadowy arms the beeches spread,
While high above our sylvan seat,
   Lifts the light ash its airy head;
And later leaved, the oaks between
Extend their boughs of vernal green.

The slender birch its paper rind
   Seems offering to divided love,
And shuddering even without a wind
   Aspens, their paler foliage move,
As if some spirit of the air
Breathed a low sigh in passing there.

The Squirrel in his frolic mood,
   Will fearless bound among the boughs;
Yaffils laugh loudly through the wood,
   And murmuring ring-doves tell their vows;
While we, as sweetest woodscents rise,
Listen to woodland melodies.

And I'll contrive a sylvan room
   Against the time of summer heat,
Where leaves, inwoven in Nature's loom,
   Shall canopy our green retreat;
And gales that 'close the eye of day'
Shall linger, e'er they die away.

And when a sear and sallow hue
   From early frost the bower receives,
I'll dress the sand rock cave for you,
   And strew the floor with heath and leaves,
That you, against the autumnal air
May find securer shelter there.

The Nightingale will then have ceased
   To sing her moonlight serenade;
But the gay bird with blushing breast,
   And Woodlarks still will haunt the shade,
And by the borders of the spring
Reed-wrens will yet be carolling.

The forest hermit's lonely cave
   None but such soothing sounds shall reach,
Or hardly heard, the distant wave
Slow breaking on the stony beach;
Or winds, that now sigh soft and low,
Now make wild music as they blow.

And then, before the chilling North
   The tawny foliage falling light,
Seems, as it flits along the earth,
   The footfall of the busy Sprite,
Who wrapt in pale autumnal gloom,
Calls up the mist-born Mushroom.

Oh! could I hear your soft voice there,
   And see you in the forest green
All beauteous as you are, more fair
   You'd look, amid the sylvan scene,
And in a wood-girl's simple guise,
Be still more lovely in mine eyes.

Ye phantoms of unreal delight,
   Visions of fond delirium born!
Rise not on my deluded sight,
   Then leave me drooping and forlorn
To know, such bliss can never be,
Unless [   ] loved like me.

The visionary, nursing dreams like these,
Is not indeed unhappy. Summer woods
Wave over him, and whisper as they wave,
Some future blessings he may yet enjoy.
And as above him sail the silver clouds,
He follows them in thought to distant climes,
Where, far from the cold policy of this,
Dividing him from her he fondly loves,
He, in some island of the southern sea,
May haply build his cane-constructed bower
Beneath the bread-fruit, or aspiring palm,
With long green foliage rippling in the gale.
Oh! let him cherish his ideal bliss—
For what is life, when Hope has ceased to strew
Her fragile flowers along its thorny way?
And sad and gloomy are his days, who lives
Of Hope abandoned!

                                        Just beneath the rock
Where Beachy overpeers the channel wave,
Within a cavern mined by wintery tides
Dwelt one, who long disgusted with the world
And all its ways, appeared to suffer life
Rather than live; the soul-reviving gale,
Fanning the bean-field, or the thymy heath,
Had not for many summers breathed on him;
And nothing marked to him the season's change,
Save that more gently rose the placid sea,

And that the birds which winter on the coast
Gave place to other migrants; save that the fog,
Hovering no more above the beetling cliffs
Betrayed not then the little careless sheep
On the brink grazing, while their headlong fall
Near the lone Hermit's flint-surrounded home,
Claimed unavailing pity; for his heart
Was feelingly alive to all that breathed;
And outraged as he was, in sanguine youth,
By human crimes, he still acutely felt
For human misery.

Wandering on the beach,
He learned to augur from the clouds of heaven,
And from the changing colours of the sea,
And sullen murmurs of the hollow cliffs,
Or the dark porpoises, that near the shore
Gambolled and sported on the level brine
When tempests were approaching: then at night
He listened to the wind; and as it drove
The billows with o'erwhelming vehemence
He, starting from his rugged couch, went forth
And hazarding a life, too valueless,
He waded through the waves, with plank or pole
Towards where the mariner in conflict dread
Was buffeting for life the roaring surge;
And now just seen, now lost in foaming gulfs,
The dismal gleaming of the clouded moon
Showed the dire peril. Often he had snatched
From the wild billows, some unhappy man
Who lived to bless the hermit of the rocks.
But if his generous cares were all in vain,
And with slow swell the tide of morning bore
Some blue swollen corse to land; the pale recluse
Dug in the chalk a sepulchre—above
Where the dank sea-wrack marked the utmost tide,
And with his prayers performed the obsequies
For the poor helpless stranger.

One dark night
The equinoxial wind blew south by west,
Fierce on the shore;—the bellowing cliffs were shook
Even to their stony base, and fragments fell
Flashing and thundering on the angry flood.
At day-break, anxious for the lonely man,
His cave the mountain shepherds visited,
Though sand and banks of weeds had choked their way—
He was not in it; but his drowned corse
By the waves wafted, near his former home

Received the rites of burial. Those who read
Chiselled within the rock, these mournful lines,
Memorials of his sufferings, did not grieve,
That dying in the cause of charity
His spirit, from its earthly bondage freed,
Had to some better region fled for ever.

(pub. 1807)

ELIZA KNIPE (later CLARKE, later COBBOLD) (1767 – 1824)

She was born in London but grew up in Liverpool and Manchester. She published *Poems on Various Subjects* (1783), and *Six Narrative Poems* (1787). In 1790 she married William Clarke, who died shortly afterwards. She remained in Ipswich and married John Cobbold, a local brewer, the following year. Her later published verse became increasingly lightweight although a number of loco-descriptive poems remain in manuscript. An incomplete edition of her poems was edited by Laetitia Jermyn (Ipswich 1825).

41 ON THE LAKE OF WINDERMERE

Haste, airy Fancy! and assist my song;
To thee each thought poetic must belong:
Whilst led by thee I tune the softened lay,
Windermere, pleased, shall own thy magic sway.
That beauteous lake! whose charming prospects shew,
In varied lights, as thou dost bid them glow.
And lo! attentive to her suppliant's prayer,
The goddess, swiftly, cleaves the ambient air:
Drawn by six harnessed griffins, see! she rides;
Diamonds and sapphires deck her chariot sides;
The laughing loves around her person play,
And spread their plumage to the sunny ray:
The goddess' self, in painted vest arrayed,
Has, o'er her head, Thaumantia's bow displayed,
Whose changing shades, presented to the sight,
Display rich scenes of variegated light.
Here, the full purple tinct imperial glows;
There, blooming lustre emulates the rose;
The edges glistening with the hue of day,
In golden beams reluctant melt away:
With hair loose floating, and disordered mien,
Swift from her car steps the fantastic queen:
Her right hand holds a book, whose leaves close sealed,
Were ne'er, save to the eye of thought, revealed:
Her left an ebon wand, whose magic power
Varies the face of Nature every hour;

Transports the lively soul to realms unknown,
Or wafts the ideas o'er each distant zone.
Blest with imagination's subtle fire!
I feel the goddess all my soul inspire:
I range, with her, o'er each Arcadian scene,
The waving wood, and primrose-dimpled green:
But all ideal beauties disappear,
When, once, compared with lovely Windermere.
Here, bounteous Nature holds her rural court,
Where the delighted Graces all resort.
Forgive, Oh Muse! if I attempt to paint
Those prospects, where the boldest tincts prove faint.
First, from Lowe Wood, across the watery plain
Cast your pleased eye, and view the wide domain
Where all the fairest of the Naiads reign:
Mark the rich lustre of each golden ray,
When, on the curling waves, the sun beams play.
The cooling zephyrs now their wings expand,
We hoist our sails, and leave the lessening land:
See, o'er the gentle flood the vessel dance,
As swift she cleaves the liquid wide expanse:
Wantonly gay, her milk-white sides she laves,
And gladly kisses the translucent waves:
As now, more distant from Lowe Wood she flies,
What pleasing prospects strike our ravished eyes!
The White House peeping through the tufted grove,
The rising mount, and bowling-green alcove;
While, in perspective, distant hills arise,
Whose airy summits seem to touch the skies.
Now, Bowness comes in sight, turn round and say,
If with indifference, you can well survey
The scene, where Nature's greatest charms unite,
To form such mingled hues of shade and light,
That e'en the pencil of a Claude must fail—
How little, here, would all his art avail!
The dark slope interspersed with broken rocks,
The verdant meadows, and the fleecy flocks;
The isle where winter hardly dares appear,
But spring eternal blossoms through the year:
The bold rotunda, full before us placed,
By situation, more than style, is graced;
And while the scenes a double beauty wear,
We bless the Architect who raised it there.
How pleasant, on the surface of the lake,
With hook and line, the scaly fry to take!
Dear sport! congenial to the pensive mind,
To soft ideas, and a soul refined:
Where, gazing on the wonders of the deep,
We lull each wild, tumultuous, thought to sleep.

Reader, forgive, if fancy tired, omits
Some striking beauties, and the less forgets;
Benevolence will surely intervene,
And overlook the errors of eighteen.

(1783)

42 KESWICK

Lo! how the orient morning sweetly lights
The western side of Keswick's beauteous vale;
And gilds, with yellow beams, the mountain tops;
While on the east, the brown projecting rocks
Cast a dark shade; majestically grand!
Purpling the dale beneath; through which, the lake
Spontaneous rolls along his silver tide.
Where shall the eye find rest, in this wide scene
Of beauteous horror? where the o'erhanging cliff
Threatens with ruin, all who are so bold,
To pass beneath his darkly, lowering brow.
Here, mountains piled on mountains, meet the view,
Upon whose cloud-enveloped heights, the bird,
Sacred to mighty Jove, her eyrie builds.
The roaring water, down the rocky steep,
Rushes impetuous, with resistless force;
Now dashing on the broken crags, it foams
And rages with redoubled violence:
Now, falling in wide sheets from rock to rock,
Till tumbling down some rugged precipice,
It gains the bottom of the dale below;
Then joins the shining flood, and gently flows.
Behold the surface of the crystal lake,
Studded with islands of perpetual green;
Within whose shady woods, the feathered choir
Chant their sweet songs, nor dread the arts of man.
The halcyon here, recluse, sequestered bird,
Spreads her bright plumage to the view of Heaven:
Here, living groves of the Dodonean tree,
Shade above shade, climb the adjacent hills;
Upon whose sides, the yellow waving corn,
A noble contrast forms to the dark oaks,
And charms the sight with golden brilliancy.
All round this lovely scene, the mountains raise
Their spiry heads above the swelling clouds
That rest upon their shoulders, and, sometimes,
Driven by the winds with rudest violence,
Against their fellow clouds with fury dash.

Here, the god Æolus his empire holds,
In hollow caves, and here he reigns supreme:
Oft times his blustering subjects issue forth
With deafening roar, from some wide cavern's mouth,
And make mock thunder echo through the rocks:
Inflated by their breath, the turbid lake
Swells high in heaving waves, and boldly threats
The banks which stop its furious mad career—
Horror magnificent! how shall I paint
The majesty and grandeur of the scene?
My pen's unequal to the task—I stop.

(1783)

ANNE HUNTER (née HOME) (1742 – 1821)

She was born in Berwickshire in 1742 and was a cousin of Joanna and Agnes Baillie. After a long courtship she married John Hunter, the eminent surgeon, in 1771. She was on good terms with many of the leading 'Bluestockings', particularly, Mrs Piozzi and Elizabeth Carter. In the 1790s she became acquainted with Haydn, who dedicated a work to her. Her husband died in 1793, leaving a complicated will, which raised the spectre of poverty, finally dispelled when Parliament bought the Hunterian Museum in 1799. She collected her poems in 1802 but published little of note after 1804.

43 NOVEMBER, 1784

Now yellow autumn's leafy ruins lie
   In faded splendour, on deserted plains,
Far from the madding crowd, alone I fly,
   To wake in solitude the mystic strains.
On themes of high import I dare to sing,
While Fate impels my hand to strike the trembling string.

Bright on my harp the meteors gleam,
   As through the shades they glancing shine;
Now the winds howl, the night birds scream,
   And yelling ghosts the chorus join:
Chimeras dire, from fancy's deepest hell,
Fly o'er yon hallowed tower, and toll the passing bell.

November hears the dismal sound,
   As slow advancing from the pole;
He leads the months their wintery round;
   See blackening clouds attendant roll,
Where frowns a giant band, the sons of care,
Dark thoughts, presages fell, and comfortless despair!

O'er Britain's isle they spread their wings,
And shades of death dismay the land;
November wide his mantle flings,
And lifting high his vengeful hand,
Hurls down the demon Spleen, with powers combined,
To check the springs of life, and crush the enfeebled mind.

His drear dominion he maintains,
Beneath a cold inclement sky;
While noxious fogs, and drizzling rains,
On Nature's sickening bosom lie.
The opening rose of youth untimely fades,
And Hope's fair friendly light beams dimly through the shades.

Now prowls abroad the ghastly fiend,
Fell Suicide, whom Frenzy bore;
His brows with writhing serpents twined,
His mantle steeped in human gore!
The livid flames around his eye-balls play,
Stern Horror stalks before, and Death pursues his way!

Hark! is not that the fatal stroke?
See where the bleeding victim lies;
The bonds of social feeling broke,
Dismayed the frantic spirit flies:
Creation starts, and shrunken Nature views
Appalled the blow, which heaven's first right subdues.

Behold! the weight of woes combined,
A woman has the power to scorn;
Her infant race to shame consigned,
A name disgraced, a fortune torn,
She meets resolved; and combating despair,
Supports alone the ills a coward durst not share.

On languid Luxury and Pride
The subtle fiend employs his spell;
Where selfish, sordid passions bide,
Where weak impatient spirits dwell;
Where thought oppressive from itself would fly,
And seeks relief from time in dark eternity.

Far from the scenes of guilt and death
My wearied spirit seeks to rest;
Why sudden stops my struggling breath,
Why heaves so strong my aching breast?
Hark! sounds of horror sweep the troubled glade!
Far on a whirlwind borne the fatal month is fled!

I watched his flight, and saw him bear
   To Saturn's orb the sullen band;
Where winter chills the lingering year,
   And gloom eternal shades the land.
On a lone rock, far in a stormy main,
In cheerless prison pent, I heard the ghosts complain.

Some power unseen denies my verse
   The hallowed veil of fate to rend;
Now sudden blasts the sounds disperse,
   And Fancy's inspirations end:
While rushing winds in wild discordance jar,
Old Hyem calls the storms around his icy car.

(Wr. 1784, pub. 1790, repr. 1802)

44 TO THE NIGHTINGALE

Why from these shades, sweet bird of eve,
   Art thou to other regions wildly fled?
Thy pensive song would oft my cares relieve,
   Thy melancholy softness oft would shed
Peace on my weary soul: return again,
Return, and, sadly sweet, in melting notes complain.

At the still hour I'll come alone,
   And listen to thy love-lorn plaintive lay;
Or when the moon beams o'er yon mossy stone,
   I'll watch thy restless wing from spray to spray,
And when the swelling cadence slow shall rise,
I'll join the harmony with low and murmuring sighs.

Oh, simple bird! where art thou flown?
   What distant woodland now receives thy nest?
What distant echo answers to thy moan,
   What distant thorn supports thy aching breast?
Whoe'er can feel thy misery like me,
Or pay thee for thy song with such sad sympathy?

(1802)

HELEN MARIA WILLIAMS (later STONE?) (1761 – 1827)

She was born in London in 1761 but was brought up in Berwick-on-Tweed. In 1781, she returned to London and was befriended by Andrew Kippis, an eminent Dissenter, who had been one of Godwin's tutors at Hoxton. He introduced her to London literary society where she met Johnson, Elizabeth Montagu, Anna Seward and many other leading figures. He also brought her into contact with Dissenting radicals, notably Priestley, Price and Godwin. On an invitation from a friend, she visited Paris in 1790, and became an enthusiastic apologist for the Revolution, of which she published an account, *Letters Written from France* (1790). She returned to Paris in 1791 and became a strong supporter of the Girondins. Around this time she entered into a long-term relationship with another radical, John Hurford Stone, until his death in 1818. She probably married him in 1794, and was later buried beside him (see *Thraliana*, ed. K.C. Balderston, 2 vols, Oxford, 1951, ii.894n.). In October 1793 she was under house arrest and her papers, including some poems, were confiscated. Early publications included *Peru* (1784), an important revisionist reading of European activity in South America, and *A poem...on the Slave Trade* (1788), which galvanised More and Yearsley on the subject. Her novel *Julia*, 2 vols (1790), containing much poetry before Ann Radcliffe made it fashionable in that form, is unjustly neglected and an important response to Rousseau (see note to **8–9**). Her *Poems*, 2 vols (1786), 2 vols (1791), revised 1823, brought her to the attention of younger poets, notably Wordsworth who admired several sonnets. She also published *A Farewell for two Years to England* (1791), *A Tour in Switzerland*, 2 vols (1798), and several updates of her reports of the French Revolution. After news of the excesses of the French Revolution reached England, she was constantly vilified for her politics and sexual morality. She remained steadfast in her support of the Revolution, although critical of its excesses. Of all the women poets, with the possible exception of Mary Robinson, she was the most vigorously excluded in subsequent literary histories.

45 SONNET: TO TWILIGHT

Meek Twilight! soften the declining day,
   And bring the hour my pensive spirit loves;
When, o'er the mountain slow descends the ray
   That gives to silence the deserted groves.
Ah, let the happy court the morning still,
   When, in her blooming loveliness arrayed,
She bids fresh beauty light the vale, or hill,
   And rapture warble in the vocal shade.
Sweet is the odour of the morning's flower,
   And rich in melody her accents rise;
Yet dearer to my soul the shadowy hour,
   At which her blossoms close, her music dies—
For then, while languid nature droops her head,
She wakes the tear 'tis luxury to shed.

(1784, repr. 1786)

46 SONNET: TO EXPRESSION

Expression, child of soul! I fondly trace
Thy strong enchantments, when the poet's lyre,
The painter's pencil catch thy sacred fire,
And beauty wakes for thee her touching grace—
But from this frighted glance thy form avert
When horrors check thy tear, thy struggling sigh,
When frenzy rolls in thy impassioned eye,
Or guilt sits heavy on thy labouring heart—
Nor ever let my shuddering fancy bear
The wasting groan, or view the pallid look
Of him the Muses loved—when hope forsook
His spirit, vainly to the Muses dear!
For charmed with heavenly song, this bleeding breast,
Mourns the blest power of verse could give despair no rest.

(1784, repr. 1786)

47 AN ADDRESS TO POETRY

While envious crowds the summit view,
Where danger with ambition strays;
Or far, with anxious step, pursue
Pale avarice, through his winding ways;
The selfish passions in their train,
Whose force the social ties unbind,
And chill the love of human kind,
And make fond Nature's best emotions vain;

Oh Poesy! Oh nymph most dear,
To whom I early gave my heart,
Whose voice is sweetest to my ear
Of aught in nature or in art;
Thou, who canst all my breast control,
Come, and thy harp of various cadence bring,
And long with melting music swell the string
That suits the present temper of my soul.

Oh! ever gild my path of woe,
And I the ills of life can bear;
Let but thy lovely visions glow,
And chase the forms of real care;
Oh still, when tempted to repine
At partial fortune's frown severe,
Wipe from my eyes the anxious tear,
And whisper, that thy soothing joys are mine!

When did my fancy ever frame
A dream of joy by thee unblest?
When first my lips pronounced thy name,
New pleasure warmed my infant breast.
I loved to form the jingling rhyme,
The measured sounds, though rude, my ear could please,
Could give the little pains of childhood ease,
And long have soothed the keener pains of time.

The idle crowd in fashion's train,
Their trifling comment, pert reply,
Who talk so much, yet talk in vain,
How pleased for thee, Oh nymph, I fly!
For thine is all the wealth of mind,
Thine the unborrowed gems of thought,
The flash of light, by souls refined,
From heaven's empyreal source exulting caught.

And ah! when destined to forgo
The social hour with those I love,
That charm which brightens all below,
That joy all other joys above,
And dearer to this breast of mine,
Oh Muse! than aught thy magic power can give;
Then on the gloom of lonely sadness shine,
And bid thy airy forms around me live.

Thy page, Oh Shakespeare! let me view,
Thine! at whose name my bosom glows;
Proud that my earliest breath I drew
In that blest isle where Shakespeare rose!—
Where shall my dazzled glances roll?
Shall I pursue gay Ariel's flight,
Or wander where those hags of night
With deeds unnamed shall freeze my trembling soul?

Plunge me, foul sisters! in the gloom
Ye wrap around yon blasted heath,
To hear the harrowing rite I come,
That calls the angry shades from death!—
Away—my frighted bosom spare!
Let true Cordelia pour her filial sigh,
Let Desdemona lift her pleading eye,
And poor Ophelia sing in wild despair!

When the bright noon of summer streams
In one wide flash of lavish day,
As soon shall mortal count the beams,
As tell the powers of Shakespeare's lay;

Oh Nature's Poet! the untaught
The simple mind thy tale pursues,
And wonders by what art it views
The perfect image of each native thought.

In those still moments when the breast,
Expanded, leaves its cares behind,
Glows by some higher thought possest,
And feels the energies of mind;
Then, awful Milton, raise the veil
That hides from human eye the heavenly throng!
Immortal sons of light! I hear your song,
I hear your high-tuned harps creation hail!

Well might creation claim your care,
And well the string of rapture move,
When all was perfect, good, and fair,
When all was music, joy, and love!
Ere evil's inauspicious birth
Changed nature's harmony to strife;
And wild remorse, abhorring life,
And deep affliction, spread their shade on earth.

Blest Poesy! Oh sent to calm
The human pains which all must feel;
Still shed on life thy precious balm,
And every wound of nature heal!
Is there a heart of human frame
Along the burning track of torrid light,
Or 'mid the fearful waste of polar night,
That never glowed at thy inspiring name?

Ye southern isles, emerged so late
Where the pacific billow rolls,
Witness, though rude your simple state,
How heaven-taught verse can melt your souls:
Say, when you hear the wandering bard,
How thrilled ye listen to his lay,
By what kind arts ye court his stay,
All savage life affords, his sure reward.

So, when great Homer's chiefs prepare,
A while from war's rude toils released,
The pious hecatomb, and share
The flowing bowl, and genial feast;
Some heavenly minstrel sweeps the lyre,
While all applaud the poet's native art,
For him they heap the viands choicest part,
And copious goblets crown the muse's fire.

Even *here*, in scenes of pride and gain,
Where faint each genuine feeling glows;
Here, Nature asks, in want and pain,
The dear illusions verse bestows;
The poor, from hunger, and from cold,
Spare one small coin, the ballad's price;
Admire their poet's quaint device,
And marvel much at all his rhymes unfold.

Ye children, lost in forests drear,
Still o'er your wrongs each bosom grieves,
And long the red-breast shall be dear
Who strewed each little corpse with leaves;
For you, my earliest tears were shed,
For you, the gaudy doll I pleased forsook,
And heard with hands up-raised, and eager look,
The cruel tale, and wished ye were not dead!

And still on Scotia's northern shore,
'At times, between the rushing blast,'
Recording memory loves to pour
The mournful song of ages past;
Come, lonely bard 'of other years!'
While dim the half-seen moon of varying skies,
While sad the wind along the grey-moss sighs,
And give my pensive heart 'the joy of tears!'

The various tropes that splendour dart
Around the modern poet's line,
Where, borrowed from the sphere of art,
Unnumbered gay allusions shine,
Have not a charm my breast to please
Like the blue mist, the meteor's beam,
The dark-browed rock, the mountain stream,
And the light thistle waving in the breeze.

Wild Poesy, in haunts sublime,
Delights her lofty note to pour;
She loves the hanging rock to climb,
And hear the sweeping torrent roar:
The little scene of cultured grace
But faintly her expanded bosom warms;
She seeks the daring stroke, the aweful charms,
Which Nature's pencil throws on Nature's face.

Oh Nature! thou whose works divine
Such rapture in this breast inspire,
As makes me dream one spark is mine
Of Poesy's celestial fire;

HELEN MARIA WILLIAMS

When doomed for London smoke to leave
The kindling morn's unfolding view,
Which ever wears some aspect new,
And all the shadowy forms of soothing eve;

Then, Thomson, then be ever near,
And paint whatever season reigns;
Still let me see the varying year,
And worship Nature in thy strains;
Now, when the wintery tempests roll,
Unfold their dark and desolating form,
Rush in the savage madness of the storm,
And spread those horrors that exalt my soul.

And Pope, the music of thy verse
Shall winter's dreary gloom dispel,
And fond remembrance oft rehearse
The moral song she knows so well;
The sportive sylphs shall flutter here,
There Eloise, in anguish pale,
'Kiss with cold lips the sacred veil,
And drop with every bead too soft a tear!'

When disappointment's sickening pain,
With chilling sadness numbs my breast;
That feels its dearest hope was vain,
And bids its fruitless struggles rest;
When those for whom I wish to live,
With cold suspicion wrong my aching heart;
Or, doomed from those for ever loved to part,
And feel a sharper pang than death can give;

Then with the mournful bard I go,
Whom 'melancholy marked her own,'
While tolls the curfew, solemn, slow,
And wander amid graves unknown;
With yon pale orb, loved poet, come!
While from those elms long shadows spread,
And where the lines of light are shed,
Read the fond record of the rustic tomb!

Or let me o'er old Conway's flood
Hang on the frowning rock, and trace
The characters, that wove in blood,
Stamped the dire fate of Edward's race;
Proud tyrant, tear thy laurelled plume;
How poor thy vain pretence to deathless fame!
The injured muse records thy lasting shame,
And she has power to 'ratify thy doom.'

Nature, when first she smiling came,
To wake within the human breast
The sacred muses' hallowed flame,
And earth, with heaven's rich spirit blest!
Nature in that auspicious hour,
With aweful mandate, bade the bard
The register of glory guard,
And gave him o'er all mortal honours power.

Can fame on painting's aid rely,
Or lean on sculpture's trophyed bust?
The faithless colours bloom to die,
The crumbling pillar mocks its trust;
But thou, oh muse, immortal maid!
Canst paint the godlike deeds that praise inspire,
Or worth that lives but in the mind's desire,
In tints that only shall with Nature fade!

Oh tell me, partial nymph! what rite,
What incense sweet, what homage true,
Draws from thy fount of purest light
The flame it lends a chosen few?
Alas! these lips can never frame
The mystic vow that moves thy breast;
Yet by thy joys my life is blest,
And my fond soul shall consecrate thy name.

(1790)

48 SONNET: TO HOPE

Oh, ever skilled to wear the form we love!
To bid the shapes of fear and grief depart,
Come, gentle Hope! with one gay smile remove
The lasting sadness of an aching heart.
Thy voice, benign enchantress! let me hear;
Say that for me some pleasures yet shall bloom!
That fancy's radiance, friendship's precious tear,
Shall soften, or shall chase, misfortune's gloom.—
But come not glowing in the dazzling ray
Which once with dear illusions charmed my eye!
Oh strew no more, sweet flatterer! on my way
The flowers I fondly thought too bright to die.
Visions less fair will sooth my pensive breast,
That asks not happiness, but longs for rest!

(1790)

HELEN MARIA WILLIAMS

49 TO DR MOORE, IN ANSWER TO A POETICAL EPISTLE WRITTEN BY HIM, IN WALES, TO HELEN MARIA WILLIAMS

While in long exile far from you I roam,
To soothe my heart with images of home,
For me, my friend, with rich poetic grace,
The landscapes of my native isle you trace;
Her cultured meadows, and her lavish shades,
Her winding rivers, and her verdant glades;
Far, as where frowning on the flood below,
The rough Welsh mountain lifts its craggy brow;
Where nature throws aside her softer charms,
And with sublimer views the bosom warms.

Meanwhile, my steps have strayed where Autumn yields
A purple harvest on the sunny fields;
Where, bending with their luscious weight, recline
The loaded branches of the clustering vine;
There, on the Loire's sweet banks, a joyful band
Culled the rich produce of the fruitful land;
The youthful peasant, and the village maid,
And feeble age and childhood lent their aid.
The labours of the morning done, they haste
Where the light dinner in the field is placed;
Around the soup of herbs a circle make,
And all from one vast dish at once partake:
The vintage-baskets serve, reversed, for chairs,
And the gay meal is crowned with tuneless airs;
For each in turn must sing with all his might;
And some their carols pour in nature's spite.

Delightful land! Ah, now with general voice
Thy village sons and daughters may rejoice.
Thy happy peasant, now no more a slave,
Forbad to taste one good that nature gave,
Views with the anguish of indignant pain
The bounteous harvest spread for him in vain.
Oppression's cruel hand shall dare no more
To seize with iron gripe his scanty store;
And from his famished infants wring those spoils,
The hard-earned produce of his useful toils:
For now on Gallia's plain the peasant knows
Those equal rights impartial Heaven bestows.
He now, by freedom's ray illumined, taught
Some self-respect, some energy of thought,
Discerns the blessings that to all belong,
And lives to guard his humble shed from wrong.

Auspicious Liberty! in vain thy foes
Deride thy ardour, and thy force oppose;

In vain refuse to mark thy spreading light,
While, like the mole, they hide their heads in night;
Or hope their eloquence with taper-ray
Can dim the blaze of philosophic day;
Those reasoners who pretend that each abuse,
Sanctioned by precedent, has some blest use.
Does then some chemic power to time belong,
Extracting, by some process, right from wrong?
Must feudal governments for ever last?
Those Gothic piles, the work of ages past;
Nor may obtrusive reason boldly scan,
Far less reform the rude mishapen plan;
The winding labyrinths, the hostile towers,
Whence danger threatens, and where horror lours;
The jealous draw-bridge, and the moat profound,
The lonely dungeon in the caverned ground;
The sullen dome above those central caves,
Where lives one tyrant, and a host of slaves?
Ah, Freedom, on this renovated shore,
That fabric frights the moral world no more!
Shook to its basis, by thy powerful spell,
Its triple walls in massy fragments fell;
While, rising from the hideous wreck, appears
The temple thy firm arm sublimely rears;
Of fair proportions, and of simple grace,
A mansion worthy of the human race.
For me, the witness of those scenes, whose birth
Forms a new era in the storied earth;
Oft while with glowing breast those scenes I view,
They lead, ah friend beloved, my thoughts to you!
Ah, still each fine emotion they impart,
With your idea mingles in my heart;
You, whose warm bosom, whose expanded mind,
Have shared this glorious triumph of mankind;
You, whom I oft have heard, with generous zeal,
With all that truth can urge, or pity feel,
Refute the pompous argument that tried
The common cause of millions to deride;
With reason's force the plausive sophist hit,
Or dart on folly the quick flash of wit.
Too swift, my friend, the moments winged their flight,
That gave at once instruction and delight;
That ever from your ample stores of thought
To my small stock some new accession brought.
How oft remembrance, while this bosom bleeds,
My pensive fancy to your dwelling leads;
Where, round your cheerful hearth, I weeping trace
The social circle, and my vacant place!—
When to that dwelling friendship's tie endears,

When shall I hasten with the 'joy of tears?'
That joy whose keen sensation swells to pain,
And strives to utter what it feels, in vain.

(1792)

50 SONNET: TO LOVE

Ah Love! 'ere yet I knew thy fatal power,
Bright glowed the colour of my youthful days,
As, on the sultry zone, the torrid rays
That paint the broad leaved plantain's glossy bower:
Calm was my bosom as this silent hour,
When o'er the deep, scarce heard, the zephyr strays,
'Midst the cool tamarinds indolently plays,
Nor from the orange shakes its odorous flower:
But ah! since Love has all my heart possest,
That desolated heart what sorrows tear?
Disturbed, and wild as ocean's troubled breast,
When the hoarse tempest of the night is there!
Yet my complaining spirit asks no rest—
This bleeding bosom cherishes despair.

(1795)

51 SONNET: TO DISAPPOINTMENT

Pale Disappointment! at thy freezing name
Chill fears in every shivering vein I prove,
My sinking pulse almost forgets to move,
And life almost forsakes my languid frame—
Yet thee, relentless nymph! no more I blame—
Why do my thoughts midst vain illusions rove?
Why gild the charms of friendship and of love
With the warm glow of fancy's purple flame?
When ruffling winds have some bright fane o'erthrown,
Which shone on painted clouds, or seemed to shine,
Shall the fond gazer dream for him alone
Those clouds were stable, and at fate repine?—
I feel, alas! the fault is all my own,
And ah, the cruel punishment is mine!—

(1795)

52 SONNET: TO SIMPLICITY

Nymph of the desert! on this lonely shore
Simplicity, thy blessings still are mine,
And all thou canst not give I pleased resign,
For all beside can sooth my soul no more.
I ask no lavish heaps to swell my store,
And purchase pleasures far remote from thine.
Ye joys, for which the race of Europe pine,
Ah, not for me your studied grandeur pour—
Let me where yon tall cliffs are rudely piled,
Where towers the palm amidst the mountain trees,
Where pendent from the steep, with graces wild,
The blue liana floats upon the breeze,
Still haunt those bold recesses, nature's child,
Where thy majestic charms my spirit seize!

(1795)

53 SONNET: TO THE STRAWBERRY

The Strawberry blooms upon its lowly bed,
Plant of my native soil!—the lime may fling
More potent fragrance on the zephyr's wing;
The milky cocoa richer juices shed;
The white Guava lovelier blossoms spread—
But not like thee to fond remembrance bring
The vanished hours of life's enchanting spring,
Short calendar of joys for ever fled!—
Thou bidst the scenes of childhood rise to view,
The wild-wood path which fancy loves to trace;
Where veiled in leaves, thy fruit of rosy hue
Lurked on its pliant stem with modest grace—
But ah! when thought would later years renew,
Alas, successive sorrows crowd the space!

(1795)

54 SONNET: TO THE CURLEW

Soothed by the murmurs on the sea-beat shore,
His dun-grey plumage floating to the gale,
The Curlew blends his melancholy wail,
With those hoarse sounds the rushing waters pour—
Like thee, congenial bird! my steps explore
The bleak lone sea-beach, or the rocky dale,
And shun the orange bower, the myrtle vale,

Whose gay luxuriance suits my soul no more.
I love the ocean's broad expanse, when drest
In limpid clearness, or when tempests blow;
When the smooth currents on its placid breast
Flow calm as my past moments used to flow;
Or, when its troubled waves refuse to rest,
And seem the symbol of my present woe.

(1795)

55 SONNET: TO THE TORRID ZONE

Pathway of light! o'er thy empurpled zone
With lavish charms perennial summer strays;
Soft 'midst thy spicy groves the zephyr plays,
While far around the rich perfumes are thrown;
The amadavid-bird for thee alone
Spreads his gay plumes that catch thy vivid rays;
For thee the gems with liquid lustre blaze,
And nature's various wealth is all thy own.
But ah! not thine is twilight's doubtful gloom,
Those mild gradations, mingling day with night;
Here, instant darkness shrouds thy genial bloom,
Nor leaves my pensive soul that lingering light,
When musing memory would each trace resume
Of fading pleasures in successive flight.

(1795)

56 SONNET: TO THE CALBASSIA TREE

Sublime Calbassia! luxuriant tree,
How soft the gloom thy bright-hued foliage throws,
While from thy pulp a healing balsam flows,
Whose power the suffering wretch from pain can free:
My pensive footsteps ever turn to thee!
Since oft while musing on my lasting woes,
Beneath thy flowery white-bells I repose,
Symbol of friendship, dost thou seem to me;—
For thus has friendship cast her soothing shade
O'er my unsheltered bosom's keen distress;
Thus fought to heal the wounds which love has made,
And temper bleeding sorrow's sharp excess!
Ah! not in vain she lends her balmy aid—
The agonies she cannot cure, are less!

(1795)

57 SONNET: TO THE WHITE BIRD OF THE TROPIC

HELEN MARIA WILLIAMS

Bird of the Tropic! thou, who lov'st to stray,
Where thy long pinions sweep the sultry line,
Or mark'st the bounds which torrid beams confine
By thy averted course, that shuns the ray
Oblique, enamoured of sublimer day—
Oft on yon cliff thy folded plumes recline,
And drop those snowy feathers Indians twine,
To crown the warrior's brow with honours gay—
O'er trackless oceans what impels thy wing?
Does no soft instinct in thy soul prevail?
No sweet affection to thy bosom cling,
And bid thee oft thy absent nest bewail?—
Yet thou again to that dear spot canst spring—
But I my long-lost home no more shall hail!

(1795)

58 A HYMN WRITTEN AMONG THE ALPS

Creation's God! with thought elate,
 Thy hand divine I see;
Impressed on scenes where all is great,
 Where all is full of thee!;

Where stern the Alpine mountains raise
 Their heads of massive snow;
Whence, on the rolling storm I gaze,
 That hangs—how far below!;

Where, on some bold stupendous height,
 The eagle sits alone;
Or soaring wings his sullen flight
 To haunts yet more his own;

Where the sharp rock the chamois treads,
 Or slippery summit scales;
Or where the whitening snow-bird spreads
 Her plumes to icy gales;

Where the rude cliff's steep column glows
 With morning's tint of blue;
Or evening on the Glacier throws
 The rose's blushing hue;

Or where by twilight's softer light,
 The mountain shadow bends;
And sudden casts a partial night,
 As black its form descends;

Where the full ray of noon, alone
   Down the deep valley falls;
Or, where the sun-beam never shone
   Between its rifted walls;

Where cloudless regions calm the soul,
   Bid mortal cares be still;
Can passion's wayward wish control,
   And rectify the will;

Where midst some vast expanse, the mind
   Which swelling virtue fires,
Forgets that earth it leaves behind,
   And to its heaven aspires;

Where far along the desart-sphere
   Resounds no creature's call;
And undisturbing mortal ear,
   The Avalanches fall;

Where, rushing from their snowy source,
   The daring torrents urge
Their loud-toned waters headlong course,
   And lift their feathered surge;

Where swift the lines of light, and shade,
   Flit o'er the lucid lake,
Or the shrill winds its breast invade,
   And its green billows wake;

Where on the slope, with speckled dye,
   The pigmy herds I scan,
Or soothed the scattered *chalets* spy,
   The last abodes of man;

Or, where the flocks refuse to pass,
   And the lone peasant mows,
Fixed on his knees, the pendant grass,
   Which down the steep he throws;

Or where the dangerous pathway leads
   High o'er the gulf profound;
From whence the shrinking eye recedes,
   Nor finds repose around;

Where red the mountain-ash reclines
   Along the clefted rock;
Where firm, the dark unbending pines
   The howling tempests mock;

Where, level with ice-ribbed bound,
  The yellow harvests glow;
Or vales with purple vines are crowned
  Beneath impending snow;

Where the rich minerals catch the ray
  With varying lustre bright,
And glittering fragments strew the way,
  With sparks of liquid light;

Or, where the moss forbears to creep,
  Where loftier summits rear
Their untrod snows, and frozen sleep
  Locks all the uncoloured year;

In every scene, where every hour
  Sheds some terrific grace,
In nature's vast, overwhelming power,
  THEE, THEE, my GOD, I trace!

(1798)

MARY HUNT (1764 – 1834)

She was born on 12th November 1764 at Stoke Doyle, where her father Rowland Hunt (1707–85) was Rector from 1756. Her mother, Mary, was the daughter of the Rev. Francis Wells, Vicar of Oundle. Mary Hunt was an intimate friend of Henrietta Maria and Jane Bowdler and was later preceptress to Princess Charlotte. She lived in Exeter but frequently visited Bath. She died on 5 December 1834, and was buried in the Cathedral yard. See George Streynsham Master, *Notices of the Family of Hunt*..., London 1880.

59 WRITTEN ON VISITING THE RUINS OF DUNKESWELL ABBEY, IN DEVONSHIRE, SEPTEMBER 1786

Blest by the power, by heaven's own flame inspired,
That first through shades monastic poured the light;
Where, with unsocial indolence retired,
Fell Superstition reigned in tenfold night;
Where, long sequestered from the vulgar sight,
Religion fettered lay, her form unknown
'Mid direful gloom, and many a secret rite;
Till now released she claims her native throne,
And gilds the awakening world with radiance all her own.

O sacred source of sweet celestial peace,
From age to age in darksome cells confined!
Blest be the voice that bade thy bondage cease,
And sent thee forth, to illuminate the blind,
Support the weak, and raise the sinking mind:
By thee the soul her native strength explores,
Pursues the plan by favouring heaven assigned,
Through Truth's fair path the enlightened spirit soars,
And the Great Cause of All with purer rites adores.

How oft confined within this narrow grate,
With souls aspiring to a world's applause,
Have free-born spirits mourned their hapless fate!
Some hero ardent in his country's cause,
Some patriot formed to give a nation laws,
Or in life's milder scenes with honour shine;
When each bright hope a father's hand withdraws,
And dooms his child, from every prospect fair,
To long unvarying years of lonely deep despair.

When darkness now with silence reigns around,
As the faint sun withdraws his glimmering beams;
(Save when to render horror more profound,
On the rough grate the pale moon quivering gleams,
And through the lengthening aisle the owlet screams)
Then, lulled by Fancy's visionary train,
His long-lost friends frequent his blissful dreams;
He spends his days of childhood o'er again,
Till sounds the midnight bell, and proves the vision vain.

Yet let the hand of desolating time
These sinking towers and mouldering walls revere;
For not with useless pride they rose sublime:
Fair Science stored her choicest treasures here,
When Rapine whirled aloft her threatening spear,
When Murder reigned, by Gothic ignorance crowned:
On every plain the barbarous bands appear;
Fierce Discord bids her hostile trumpet sound,
And War, in crimsoned robe, tremendous stalks around.

Though now in ruined majesty they lie,
The fading relics of departed days;
Yet shall their change no useless theme supply,
No trivial subject for the poet's lays:
For as the thoughtful mind these scenes surveys,
Whose solemn shades reflection's powers invite,
Their falling pomp that awful hand displays,
Which can from transient ill, and mental night,
Educe eternal good, and intellectual light.

(1786, repr. 1792)

ANN YEARSLEY (née CROMARTIE) (1752 – 1806)

She was born at Clifton Hall near Bristol. Her father was a labourer and her mother a milkwoman, which she too became. She married John Yearsley in 1774. Hannah More read her verse in 1784 and arranged for the publication of *Poems on Several Occasions* (1785), to which there were more than a thousand subscribers. More placed the profits in trust and they quarrelled. Yearsley eventually regained the profits and set up a circulating library in 1793, which was successful. Although she shared many radical positions and supported the anti-slavery campaign, her perspective on events in France was dictated by the sympathies she felt for Louis XVI and Marie Antoinette. She published *Poems on Several Occasions* (1785), *A Second Book of Poems on Various Subjects* (1787), *A Poem on the Inhumanity of the Slave-trade* (1788), *Stanzas of Woe* (1790), *The Rural Lyre* (1796) and a novel, *The Royal Captives*, 4 vols (1796). In 1803, she retired to Melksham in Wiltshire in ill health and died in 1806.

60 TO MR * * * *, AN UNLETTERED POET, ON GENIUS UNIMPROVED

Florus, canst thou define that innate spark
Which blazes but for glory? Canst thou paint
The trembling rapture in its infant dawn,
Ere young Ideas spring; to local Thought
Arrange the busy phantoms of the mind,
And drag the distant timid shadows forth,
Which, still retiring, glide unformed away,
Nor rush into expression? No; the pen,
Though dipped in awful Wisdom's deepest tint,
Can *never* paint the wild ecstatic mood.

Yet, when the bolder Image strikes thine eye,
And uninvited grasps thy strongest thought,
Resolved to shoot into this World of Things,
Wide fly the gates of Fancy; all alarmed,
The thin ideal troop in haste advance,
To usher in the substance-seeking Shade.

And what's the Shade which rushes on the world
With powerful glare, but emblem of the soul?

Ne'er hail the fabled Nine, or snatch rapt Thought
From the Castalian spring; 'tis not for *thee*,
From embers, where the Pagan's light expires,
To catch a flame divine. From one bright spark
Of never-erring Faith, more rapture beams
Than wild Mythology could ever boast.

Pursue the Eastern Magi through their groves,
Where Zoroaster holds the mystic clue,
Which leads to great Ormazes; there thou'lt find

His God thy own; or bid thy Fancy chase
Restless Pythagoras through his varied forms,
And she shall see him sitting on a heap
Of poor Absurdity; where chearful Faith
Shall never rest, nor great Omniscience claim.

What are the Muses, or Apollo's strains,
But harmony of soul? Like thee, estranged
From Science, and old Wisdom's classic lore,
I've patient trod the wild entangled path
Of unimproved Idea. Dauntless Thought
I eager seized, no formal Rule e'er awed;
No Precedent controlled; no Custom fixed
My independent spirit: on the wing
She still shall guideless soar, nor shall the Fool,
Wounding her powers, e'er bring her to the ground.

Yet Florus, lift! to thee I loudly call;
Dare thee, by all the transport Mind can reach,
Yea, by the boasted privilege of *Man*,
To stretch with me the spirit-raising wing
Of artless Rapture! Seek Earth's farthest bound,
Till Fancy panting, drops from endless space.

Deep in the soul live ever tuneful springs,
Waiting the touch of Ecstasy, which strikes
Most powerful on defenceless, untaught Minds;
Then, in soft unison, the trembling strings
All move in one direction. Then the soul
Sails on Idea, and would eager dart
Through yon ethereal way; restless awhile,
Again she sinks to sublunary joy.

Florus, rove on! pluck from the pathless vale
Of Fancy, all her loveliest, wildest sweets;
These best can please; but ah! beware, my Friend:
Timid Idea shrinks, when coldly thou
Would'st hail the tender shade; then strongly clasp
The coy, reluctant fugitive, or seize
The rover, as she flies; that breast alone
Is hers, all glowing with immortal flame;
And that be thine.

(1787)

61 ANARCHY

Furies! Why sleep amid the carnage?—rise!
 Bring up my wolves of war, my pointed spears.
Daggers, yet reeking, banners filled with sighs,
 And paint your cheeks with gore, and lave your locks in tears.

On yon white bosom see that happy child!
 Seize it, deface its infant charms! And say,
Anarchy viewed its mangled limbs and smiled.
 Strike the young mother to the earth!—Away!

This is my era! O'er the dead I go!
 From my hot nostrils minute murders fall!
Behind my burning car lurks feeble Woe!
 Filled with my dragon's ire, my slaves for kingdoms call!

Hear them not, Father of the ensanguined race!—
World! Give my monsters way!—Death! keep thy steady chase!

(1796)

62 PEACE

What howlings wake me!—my fair olives die!
 Storms shake my bower, and drive me to the plain.—
Ah! direful Anarchy, thy chariots fly
 O'er worlds of weeping babes, o'er worlds of heroes slain!

Order! Bright angel down yon rainbow glide!
 From the mild bosom of my God appear!
O'er Gallia spread thy snowy pinions wide—
 O! cool the fevered mind! and whisper to Despair.

Envenomned and unwelcome war! will man,
 Long nurse thy furies or prolong thy stay?
Will not his fine, reflective spirit scan
 Those desolations that have marked thy way?

Yes!—He shall wearied leave thy crimes, and prove,
All that is worth Man, is found with Me and Love.

(1796)

63 DEDICATED TO LOUIS XIV

Cold was the star
That ruled my natal hour! and pale the beams
That trembled o'er my head, as they distilled
The damps of woe—yet soon! bear witness Heaven!
I loved thee, Contemplation! And, by thee
I was beloved—O mutual bliss! The Night
Threw off her sadness, when with thee I lay
Dissolved in grateful wonder! Worlds on worlds,
Ponderous with their inhabitants came on—
And still another, and another rolled,
Forced by the arm of Time from the dark breast
Of great Eternity: the Infinite
At length shut up my wearied sense, and gave
A guiltless slumber.—Dawn no sooner shed
Her tints in wild profusion from the East,
Than cheered I rose to follow thee. How oft
We paused on ruined towers, watched down the moon,
And listened to the mariner afar,
Who sang across the main? To my young eye
Thou heldst aërial vision. There I saw
Unshapely Matter moving into life;
Myriads of atoms glistening in the wind—
Insects conglobed, and yet so finely formed,
That Zephyr breathed them into being—Tones
Of harmony they gave too thin to touch
The nerve of mortal hearing. Taught by thee,
My soul expanded, soared, and stooped again
To view the animalcula that join
Eternally through minutes, days and years;
Tilling the mighty universe. Thus charmed
By Contemplation, my rough passions sleep;
Whilst heavenly Sympathy, to Nature true,
Droops her white pinions, mourns the ills of War,
And through her tears e'en foes forget to frown.

I would complain! but never for myself!
For whilst I mourn I stand aloof!—So stood
The Persian King, weeping that life's poor farce
Should end by Fate within an hundred years;
Whilst, as he wept, his actors died away.

For ye who revel on fair Gallia's lap,
Content to wear her honours fiercely won
By your proud ancestors, the tuneful bard
Should ne'er atune his lyre—the streaming blaze,
In which you bask encircled, long hath played
Around the elder brothers of mankind—

Shine in your tinsel, but be humble!—Own
There are in Gallia's family some men
Who are poor younger sons! For these the sage
Should waste his midnight taper, wander o'er
The wilds of thought, cull from the mouldering page
Strong precept, patient-virtue, all that tend
To meliorate the mind—for these the Bard
Should breath his tones of harmony, and soothe
Their souls to social love. Here sits a youth,
By Science favoured, though by Fortune scorned;
His passions and his virtues highly burn
As that same Lord's, who with unwieldy pride
Lolls laughing at the world!—May Wisdom bind
Around the stripling's soul her starry zone,
And bid his wishes travel with his fate.

Passions we have! Nor can the rod of Power
Whip out these elements of life; the art
Of beauteous order is to bid them play;
And trust me, when once touched with skill, they make
True melody: hence rise unerring tones
Of noble friendship, and of dearer love,
Whose union alone can bless mankind,
And save a sinking Realm. O! then beware!
Ye who have power how wantonly ye sport
With the fine fibres of the heart—not all
Is harmony within. The soul of man
Is wrought with energy. What though it yield
To Nature's plastic touch, when Misery wounds,
Or Love dissolves—Within its cells remote
Sleep phantoms of most ugly hue, designed
To execute, by Nature, plans more wild
Than Policy can meditate. From these
Are born the horrid, wonderful, and great;
Possessing these, man rears himself above
The present wrong; and, big with fell revenge,
Looks on through ages for a Name; such fill
The plain with murder; every vale with tears,
When Monarchs buy their glories with a crime.
These forced the soul of Caesar from the world,
Shook down the Grecian towers, strongly drew up
Rome's deep foundations; in their grasp have died,
Promiscuously, the Sovereign and the Slave.

Much soothing do they need who bite their bread
With insult! Wildly grand are they whose souls
Rise stubborn from despair! Superior he
Who lulls them to repose!—You'll say, great Sire!
That blessings are divided; and that all

Are not to crowns hereditary heirs.
But since such passions in the heart of man
For ever lurk, be it your tenderest care
Not to provoke them with the barbed dart
Of hot Oppression. For the haughty train,
The elder sons of Gallia, bid them grace
The bosom with a star, within their halls
Hang high their family achievements; lay
Luxurious purple on their pillows, sink
To Sapphic measures, but whilst melting thus,
O! bid them spare a brother's heart! 'Tis vile!
So wantonly to loose the wolves of law
On that defenceless frame whose fortune pleads
Against its wretched owner. Plunge not man
So deeply down within your prison walls,
To linger out the bloom of life! Draw near
This iron grate, and you shall hear the groan
Of a dejected Father! Cold Despair
Shall on your forehead breathe its piteous blast,
And foul contagion spot you! Is it well
To charge this dungeon with the human heart!
Where it must long be perishing? Behold
How dismal spectres sweep along the walls,
Frightening the angel Pity from her stand.
Go; tell your Legislators! were your laws
More lenient, Gallia's crown would closer sit
On him who wears it. Know—though horrid gloom
Wrap the lost captive from a social world;
Not unobserving is that world: the bands
Of Friendship bind the wretched link unseen;
Millions of spirits, who to woe inured,
Shall burst upon the light, when sanguine power
Shall sink abashed, and see her fetters rust.

For me, who am so used to rove, the field
Of Nature yields delight; the flowery vale
Resigns her fragrance to my grateful sense;
And on the mountain I inhale the breath
Of Love, as the soft cherub warms the air.
Haste, then ye gentler spirits, who have long
Subdued the fiercer passions: ye who deaf
To court cabal and revelry can dare
To woo bright Contemplation, hither haste!

O, Nature! Thou dear Goddess of the hills,
Give me thy sweet variety! When scenes
Where shepherds languish open to my view,
Teach me to charm with numbers chastely soft,
And make the flame divine! To paint the lawn,

Lend me thy mellow tints; when through the air
I chase the infant atom born of Light,
Reduce my heart to ether; but when Man,
Enchained in the deep chambers of the earth,
Calls loud for justice, give Cassandra's fire.

(1796)

MARY O'BRIEN (fl. 1779 – 90)

An Irish woman, possibly the wife of Patrick O'Brien. She published drama, verse and possibly a novel. Little else is known of her life. A manuscript opera was collected by the Rev. F.J. Stainforth and is in the BL. The 'Ode to Milton' is discussed by Joseph Wittreich, *Feminist Milton*, Ithaca 1987.

64 ODE TO MILTON

Hail, happy bard! with glorious thoughts inspired!
Immortal themes thy lofty judgment fired,
Thy soul with sweet celestial strains was won,
While secret powers led thy fancy on;
In tuneful bands cherubs around thee hung,
And lent new graces as the poet sung.

Oh thou, poetic prince of graceful ease,
Whose seraph notes even savage minds can please;
In the smooth numbers of thy verse we stray,
Through sable mazes to eternal day;
Where on the rosy beams of bliss we soar,
And the sweet plains of paradise explore.

Still as we read, our sense is more refined,
A glow of rapture animates the mind,
Impressed with beauties rising to our view,
With eager haste the pleasing tracks pursue.
First of thy race that trod the hallowed ground,
And gained the top of Sion's sacred mound,
Or dared with soul sublime attempt the lyre,
Light by the mystic torch of gospel fire.

Had the Almighty king, enthroned in state,
Revealed the hidden mysteries of fate;
Unfurled the clouds, unveiled the expanded sky,
And stood confessed a god to mortals' eye:

Descending deigned, in voice celestial rare,
The wondrous story of the fallen pair,
A secret long to angels knowledge given,
Locked in the bosoms of the blest in heaven;
In Milton's phrase, the sovereign Lord of Grace,
Had taught the sacred facts to human race.

No more shall Pagan poetry decoy,
Our riper judgment to the feats of Troy.
To Greece and Rome such mortal themes belong;
More perfect truths beam forth in Milton's song.
How poor that painter's skill, how unrefined,
Who drew the meditating poet blind!
His thoughts beyond weak nature ne'er aspired;
He knew not Milton's light to Heaven retired!

As round the world the lamp of Phoebus plays,
In different quarters darts refulgent rays,
To eastern climes he moves in awful plight,
And bursts in floods of glory on their sight;
So Milton's orbs, eclipsed to human eye,
Blazed in meridian flame beyond the sky;
His lamps of light in higher regions burned,
From earthly sparks to heavenly glory turned!

(1790)

JOANNA BAILLIE (1762 – 1851)

She was born in Bothwell, Lanarkshire and went to school in Glasgow where her father was Professor of Divinity at the University. Her maternal uncle was John Hunter, husband of Anne Hunter (see **43–4**). In 1784 she moved to London. In 1790, she published anonymously, *Poems: Wherein it is Attempted to Describe Certain Views of Nature and of Rustic Manners*..., reprinting it, with revisions, in *Fugitive Verses* (1840). *A Series of Plays: in which it is Attempted to Delineate the Stronger Passions of the Mind*..., 3 vols (1798–1812), contained an important introductory discourse (i.1–72) and made her reputation as the leading female dramatist of the day. She moved to Hampstead with her mother and her sister, Agnes, in 1801, where she became friendly with Anna Barbauld, and was visited by Wordsworth, Scott, Rogers, Henry Crabb Robinson, Holland and many others. She died in Hampstead in 1851.

65 *from* A WINTER DAY

The night comes on apace—
Chill blows the blast, and drives the snow in wreaths.
Now every creature looks around for shelter,
And, whether man or beast, all move alike
Towards their several homes; and happy they

Who have a house to screen them from the cold!
Lo, o'er the frost a reverend form advances!
His hair white as the snow on which he treads,
His forehead marked with many a care-worn furrow,
Whose feeble body, bending o'er a staff,
Still show that once it was the seat of strength,
Though now it shakes like some old ruined tower.
Clothed indeed, but not disgraced with rags,
He still maintains that decent dignity
Which well becomes those who have served their country.
With tottering steps he to the cottage moves:
The wife within, who hears his hollow cough,
And pattering of his stick upon the threshold,
Sends out her little boy to see who's there.
The child looks up to view the stranger's face,
And seeing it enlightened with a smile,
Holds out his little hand to lead him in.
Roused from her work, the mother turns her head,
And sees them, not ill-pleased.—
The stranger whines not with a piteous tale,
But only asks a little, to relieve
A poor old soldier's wants.—
The gentle matron brings the ready chair,
And bids him sit, to rest his wearied limbs,
And warm himself before her blazing fire.
The children, full of curiosity,
Flock round, and with their fingers in their mouths,
Stand staring at him; whilst the stranger, pleased,
Takes up the youngest boy upon his knee.
Proud of its seat, it wags its little feet,
And prates, and laughs, and plays with his white locks.
But soon the soldier's face lays off its smiles;
His thoughtful mind is turned on other days,
When his own boys were wont to play around him,
Who now lie distant from their native land
In honourable, but untimely graves.
He feels how helpless and forlorn he is,
And bitter tears gush from his dim-worn eyes.
His toilsome daily labour at an end,
In comes the wearied master of the house,
And marks with satisfaction his old guest,
With all his children round.—
His honest heart is filled with manly kindness;
He bids him stay, and share their homely meal,
And take with them his quarters for the night.
The weary wanderer thankfully accepts,
And, seated with the cheerful family,
Around the plain but hospitable board,
Forgets the many hardships he has passed.

When all are satisfied, about the fire
They draw their seats, and form a cheerful ring.
The thrifty housewife turns her spinning wheel;
The husband, useful even in his rest,
A little basket weaves of willow twigs,
To bear her eggs to town on market days;
And work but serves to enliven conversation.
Some idle neighbours now come straggling in,
Draw round their chairs, and widen out the circle.
Without a glass the tale and jest go round;
And every one, in his own native way,
Does what he can to cheer the merry group.
Each tells some little story of himself,
That constant subject upon which mankind,
Whether in court or country, love to dwell.
How at a fair he saved a simple clown
From being tricked in buying of a cow;
Or laid a bet upon his horse's head
Against his neighbour's, bought for twice his price,
Which failed not to repay his better skill:
Or on a harvest day, bound in an hour
More sheaves of corn than any of his fellows,
Though ne'er so keen, could do in twice the time.
But chief the landlord, at his own fire-side,
Doth claim the right of being listened to;
Nor dares a little bawling tongue be heard,
Though but in play, to break upon his story.
The children sit and listen with the rest;
And should the youngest raise its little voice,
The careful mother, ever on the watch,
And always pleased with what her husband says,
Gives it a gentle rap upon the fingers,
Or stops its ill timed prattle with a kiss.
The soldier next, but not unasked, begins,
And tells in better speech what he has seen;
Making his simple audience to shrink
With tales of war and blood. They gaze upon him,
And almost weep to see the man so poor,
So bent and feeble, helpless and forlorn,
That oft has stood undaunted in the battle
Whilst thundering cannons shook the quaking earth,
And showering bullets hissed around his head.
With little care they pass away the night,
Till time draws on when they should go to bed;
Then all break up, and each retires to rest
With peaceful mind, nor torn with vexing cares,
Nor dancing with the unequal beat of pleasure.

But long accustomed to observe the weather,
The labourer cannot lay him down in peace
Till he has looked to mark what bodes the night.
He turns the heavy door, thrusts out his head,
Sees wreathes of snow heaped up on every side,
And black and grumly all above his head,
Save when a red gleam shoots along the waste
To make the gloomy night more terrible.
Loud blows the northern blast—
He hears it hollow grumbling from afar,
Then, gathering strength, roll on with doubled might,
And break in dreadful bellowings o'er his head;
Like pithless saplings bend the vexed trees,
And their wide branches crack. He shuts the door,
And, thankful for the roof that covers him,
Hies him to bed....

(1790)

66 *from* **A SUMMER DAY**

Now weary labourers perceive, well-pleased,
The shadows lengthen, and the oppressive day
With all its toil fast wearing to an end.
The sun, far in the west, with side-long beam
Plays on the yellow head of the round hay-cock,
And fields are checkered with fantastic shapes
Or tree, or shrub, or gate, or rugged stone,
All lengthened out, in antic disproportion,
Upon the darkened grass.——
They finish out their long and toilsome task,
Then, gathering up their rakes and scattered coats,
With the less cumberous fragments of their feast,
Return right gladly to their peaceful homes.

The village, lone and silent through the day,
Receiving from the fields its merry bands,
Sends forth its evening sound, confused but cheerful;
Whilst dogs and children, eager housewives' tongues,
And true love ditties, in no plaintive strain,
By shrill voiced maid, at open window sung;
The lowing of the home-returning kine,
The herd's low droning trump, and tinkling bell
Tied to the collar of his favourite sheep,
Make no contemptible variety
To ears not over nice.—
With careless lounging gait, the sauntering youth

Upon his sweetheart's open window leans,
And as she turns about her buzzing wheel
Diverts her with his jokes and harmless taunts.
Close by the cottage door, with placid mien,
The old man sits upon his seat of turf,
His staff with crooked head laid by his side,
Which oft the younger race in wanton sport,
Gambolling round him, slyly steal away,
And straddling o'er it, show their horsemanship
By raising round the clouds of summer sand,
While still he smiles, yet chides them for the trick.
His silver locks upon his shoulders spread,
And not ungraceful is his stoop of age.
No stranger passes him without regard;
And every neighbour stops to wish him well,
And ask him his opinion of the weather.
They fret not at the length of his discourse,
But listen with respect to his remarks
Upon the various seasons he remembers;
For well he knows the many divers signs
Which do foretell high winds, or rain, or drought,
Or aught that may affect the rising crop.
The silken clad, who courtly breeding boast,
Their own discourse still sweetest to their ears,
May grumble at the old man's lengthened story,
But here it is not so.——

From every chimney mounts the curling smoke,
Muddy and grey, of the new evening fire;
On every window smokes the family supper,
Set out to cool by the attentive housewife,
While cheerful groups at every door convened
Bawl cross the narrow lane the parish news,
And oft the bursting laugh disturbs the air.
But see who comes to set them all agag!
The weary-footed pedlar with his pack.
How stiff he bends beneath his bulky load!
Covered with dust, slip-shod, and out at elbows;
His greasy hat sits backward on his head;
His thin straight hair divided on his brow
Hangs lank on either side his glistening cheeks,
And woe-begone, yet vacant is his face.
His box he opens and displays his ware.
Full many a varied row of precious stones
Cast forth their dazzling lustre to the light.
To the desiring maiden's wishful eye
The ruby necklace shows its tempting blaze:
The china buttons, stamped with love device,
Attract the notice of the gaping youth;

Whilst streaming garters, fastened to a pole,
Aloft in air their gaudy stripes display,
And from afar the distant stragglers lure.
The children leave their play and round him flock;
E'en sober aged grand-dame quits her seat,
Where by the door she twines her lengthened threads,
Her spindle stops, and lays her distaff by,
Then joins with step sedate the curious throng.
She praises much the fashions of her youth,
And scorns each gaudy nonsense of the day;
Yet not ill-pleased the glossy ribband views,
Uprolled, and changing hues with every fold,
New measured out to deck her daughter's head.

Now red, but languid, the last weakly beams
Of the departing sun, across the lawn
Deep gild the top of the long sweepy ridge,
And shed a scattered brightness, bright but cheerless,
Between the openings of the rifted hills;
Which like the farewell looks of some dear friend,
That speaks him kind, yet sadden as they smile,
But only serve to deepen the low vale,
And make the shadows of the night more gloomy.
The varied noises of the cheerful village
By slow degrees now faintly die away,
And more distinct each feeble sound is heard
That gently steals adown the river's bed,
Or through the wood comes with the ruffling breeze.
The white mist rises from the swampy glens,
And from the dappled skirting of the heavens
Looks out the evening star.——
The lover skulking in the neighbouring copse,
(Whose half-seen form shown through the thickened air,
Large and majestic, makes the traveller start,
And spreads the story of the haunted grove,)
Curses the owl, whose loud ill-omened scream,
With ceaseless spite, robes from his watchful ear
The well known footsteps of his darling maid;
And fretful, chases from his face the night-fly,
Who buzzing round his head doth often skim,
With fluttering wing, across his glowing cheek:
For all but him in deep and balmy sleep
Forget the toils of the oppressive day;
Shut is the door of every scattered cot,
And silence dwells within. . . .

(1790)

67 *from* THUNDER

Spirit of strength, to whom in wrath 'tis given
To mar the earth, and shake the vasty heaven:
Behold the gloomy robes, that spreading hide
Thy secret majesty, lo! slow and wide,
Thy heavy skirts fail in the middle air,
Thy sultry shroud is o'er the noonday glare:
The advancing clouds sublimely rolled on high,
Deep in their pitchy volumes clothe the sky:
Like hosts of gathering foes arrayed in death,
Dread hangs their gloom upon the earth beneath.
It is thy hour: the awful deep is still,
And laid to rest the wind of every hill.
Wild creatures of the forest homeward scour,
And in their dens with fear unwonted cower.

Pride in the lordly palace is forgot;
And in the lowly shelter of the cot
The poor man sits, with all his family round,
In awful expectation of thy sound.
Lone on his way the traveller stands aghast;
The fearful looks of man to heaven are cast,
When, lo! thy lightning gleams on high,
As swiftly turns his startled eye;
And swiftly as thy shooting blaze
Each half performed motion stays,
Deep awe, all human strife and labour stills,
And thy dread voice alone, the earth and heaven fills.

Bright bursts the lightning from the cloud's dark womb,
As quickly swallowed in the closing gloom.
The distant streamy flashes, spread askance
In paler sheetings, skirt the wide expanse.
Dread flaming from aloft, the cataract dire
Oft meets in middle space the nether fire.
Fierce, red, and ragged, shivering in the air,
Athwart mid-darkness shoots the lengthened glare.
Wild glancing round, the feebler lightning plays;
The rifted centre pours the general blaze;
And from the warring clouds in fury driven,
Red writhing falls the keen embodied bolt of heaven.

From the dark bowels of the burthened cloud
Dread swells the rolling peal, full, deepening, loud.
Wide rattling claps the heavens scattered o'er,
In gathered strength lift the tremendous roar;
With weaning force it rumbles over head,
Then, growling, wears away to silence dread.
Now waking from afar in doubled might,

Slow rolling onward to the middle height;
Like crash of mighty mountains downward hurled,
Like the upbreaking of a wrecking world,
In dreadful majesty, the explosion grand
Bursts wide, and awful, o'er the trembling land.
The lofty mountains echo back the roar,
Deep from afar rebounds earth's rocky shore;
All else existing in the senses bound
Is lost in the immensity of sound.
Wide jarring sounds by turns in strength convene,
And deep, and terrible, the solemn pause between....

(1790)

68 *from* **WIND**

Power uncontrollable, who hold'st thy sway
In the unbounded air, whose trackless way
Is in the firmament, unknown of sight,
Who bend'st the sheeted heavens in thy might,
And lift'st the ocean from its lowest bed
To join in middle space the conflict dread;
Who o'er the peopled earth in ruin scours,
And buffets the firm rock that proudly lours,
Thy signs are in the heavens. The upper clouds
Draw shapeless o'er the sky their misty shrouds;
Whilst darker fragments rove in lower bands,
And mournful purple clothes the distant lands.
In gathered tribes, upon the hanging peak
The sea-fowl scream, ill-omened creatures shriek:
Unwonted sounds groan on the distant wave,
And murmurs deep break from the downward cave.
Unlooked-for gusts the quiet forests shake,
And speak thy coming—awful Power, awake!

Like burst of mighty waters wakes the blast,
In wide and boundless sweep: through regions vast
The floods of air in loosened fury drive,
And meeting currents strong, and fiercely strive.
First wildly raving on the mountain's brow
'Tis heard afar, till o'er the plains below
With even rushing force it bears along,
And gradual swelling, louder, full, and strong,
Breaks wide in scattered bellowing through the air.
Now is it hushed to calm, now roused to war,
Whilst in the pauses of the nearer blast,
The farther gusts howl from the distant waste.

JOANNA
BAILLIE

Now rushing furious by with loosened sweep,
Now rolling grandly on, solemn and deep,
Its bursting strength the full embodied sound
In wide and shallow brawlings scatters round;
Then wild in eddies shrill, with rage distraught,
And force exhausted, whistles into naught.
With growing might, arising in its room,
From far, like waves of ocean onward come
Succeeding gusts, and spend their wasteful ire,
Then slow, in grumbled mutterings retire:
And solemn stillness overawes the land,
Save where the tempest growls along the distant strand.
But great in doubled strength, afar and wide,
Returning battle wakes on every side;
And rolling on with full and threatening sound,
In wildly mingled fury closes round.
With bellowings loud, and hollow deepening swell,
Reiterated hiss, and whistlings shrill,
Fierce wars the varied storm, with fury tore,
Till all is overwhelmed in one tremendous roar.

The vexed forest, tossing wide,
Uprooted strews its fairest pride;
The lofty pine in twain is broke,
And crushing falls the knotted oak.
The huge rock trembles in its might;
The proud tower tumbles from its height;
Uncovered stands the social home;
High rocks aloft the city dome;
Whilst bursting bar, and flapping gate,
And crashing roof, and clattering grate,
And hurling wall, and falling spire,
Mingle in jarring din and ruin dire.
Wild ruin scours the works of men;
Their motley fragments strew the plain.
E'en in the desert's pathless waste,
Uncouth destruction marks the blast:
And hollow caves whose secret pride,
Grotesque and grand, was never eyed
By mortal man, abide its drift,
Of many a goodly pillar reft.
Fierce whirling mounts the desert sand,
And threats aloft the peopled land.
The great expanded ocean, heaving wide,
Rolls to the farthest bound its lashing tide;
Whilst in the middle deep afar are seen,
All stately from the sunken gulfs between,
The towering waves, which bend with hoary brow,
Then dash impetuous to the deep below.

With broader sweepy base, in gathered might
Majestic, swelling to stupendous height,
The mountain billow lifts its awful head,
And, curving, breaks aloft with roarings dread.
Sublimer still the mighty waters rise,
And mingle in the strife of nether skies.
All wildness and uproar, above, beneath,
A world immense of danger, dread, and death....

(1790)

69 AN ADDRESS TO THE NIGHT: A FEARFUL MIND

Uncertain, awful as the gloom of death,
The Night's grim shadows cover all beneath.
Shapeless and black is every object round,
And lost in thicker gloom the distant bound.
Each swelling height is clad with dimmer shades,
And deeper darkness marks the hollow glades.
The moon in heavy clouds her glory veils,
And slow along their passing darkness fails;
While lesser clouds in parted fragments roam,
And red stars glimmer through the river's gloom.

Nor cheerful voice is heard from man's abode,
Nor sounding footsteps on the neighbouring road;
Nor glimmering fire the distant cottage tells;
On all around a fearful stillness dwells:
The mingled noise of industry is laid,
And silence deepens with the nightly shade.
Though still the haunts of men, and shut their light,
Thou art not silent, dark mysterious Night.
The cries of savage creatures wildly break
Upon thy quiet; birds ill-omened shriek;
Commotions strange disturb the rustling trees;
And heavy plaints come on the passing breeze.
Far on the lonely waste, and distant way,
Unwonted sounds are heard, unknown of day.
With shrilly screams the haunted cavern rings;
And heavy treading of unearthly things
Sounds loud and hollow through the ruined dome;
Yea, voices issue from the secret tomb.

But lo! a sudden flow of bursting light!
What wild surrounding scenes break on the sight!
Huge rugged rocks uncouthly lour on high,
Whilst on the plain their lengthened shadows lie.

The wooded banks in streamy brightness glow;
And waving darkness skirts the flood below.
The roving shadow hastens o'er the stream;
And like a ghost's pale shroud the waters gleam.
Black fleeting shapes across the valley stray:
Gigantic forms tower on the distant way:
The sudden winds in wheeling eddies change:
'Tis all confused, unnatural, and strange.
Now all again in horrid gloom is lost:
Wild wakes the breeze like sound of distant host:
Bright shoots along the swift returning light:
Succeeding shadows close the startled sight.
Some restless spirit holds the nightly sway:
Long is the wild, and doubtful is my way.
Inconstant Night, whate'er thy changes be,
It suits not man to be alone with thee.
O! for the sheltering roof of lowest kind,
Secure to rest with others of my hind!

(1790)

70 LONDON

It is a goodly sight through the clear air,
From Hampstead's heathy height to see at once
England's vast capital in fair expanse,
Towers, belfries, lengthened streets, and structures fair,
St Paul's high dome amidst the vassal bands
Of neighbouring spires, a regal chieftain stands,
And over fields of ridgy roofs appear,
With distance softly tinted, side by side,
In kindred grace, like twain of sisters dear,
The Towers of Westminster, her Abbey's pride;
While, far beyond, the hills of Surrey shine
Through thin soft haze, and show their wavy line.
Viewed thus, a goodly sight! but when surveyed
Through denser air when moistened winds prevail,
In her grand panoply of smoke arrayed,
While clouds aloft in heavy volumes sail,
She is sublime.—She seems a curtained gloom
Connecting heaven and earth,—a threatening sign of doom.
With more than natural height, reared in the sky
'Tis then St Paul's arrests the wondering eye;
The lower parts in swathing mist concealed,
The higher through some half spent shower revealed,
So far from earth removed, that well, I trow,
Did not its form man's artful structure show,

It might some lofty alpine peak be deemed,
The eagle's haunt, with cave and crevice seamed.
Stretched wide on either hand, a rugged screen,
In lurid dimness, nearer streets are seen
Like shoreward billows of a troubled main,
Arrested in their rage. Through drizzly rain,
Cataracts of tawny sheen pour from the skies,
Of furnace smoke black curling columns rise,
And many tinted vapours, slowly pass
O'er the wide draping of that pictured mass.

So shows by day this grand imperial town,
And, when o'er all the night's black stole is thrown,
The distant traveller doth with wonder mark
Her luminous canopy athwart the dark,
Cast up, from myriads of lamps that shine
Along her streets in many a starry line:—
He wondering looks from his yet distant road,
And thinks the northern streamers are abroad.
'What hollow sound is that?' approaching near,
The roar of many wheels break on his ear.
It is the flood of human life in motion!
It is the voice of a tempestuous ocean!
With sad but pleasing awe his soul is filled,
Scarce heaves his breast, and all within is stilled,
As many thoughts and feelings cross his mind,—
Thoughts, mingled, melancholy, undefined,
Of restless, reckless man, and years gone by,
And Time fast wending to Eternity.

(Wr. *c.* 1800, pub. 1840)

71 *from* THE TRAVELLER BY NIGHT IN NOVEMBER

Through village, lane or hamlet going,
The light from cottage window, shewing
Its inmates at their evening fare,
By rousing fire, where earthenware
With pewter trenchers, on the shelf,
Give some display of worldly pelf,
Is transient vision to the eye
Of him our hasty passer-by;
Yet much of pleasing import tells,
And cherished in his fancy dwells,
Where simple innocence and mirth
Encircle still the cottage hearth.
Across the road a fiery glare

Doth now the blacksmith's forge declare,
Where furnace-blast, and measured din
Of heavy hammers, and within
The brawny mates their labour plying,
From heated bar the red sparks flying,
Some idle neighbours standing by
With open mouth and dazzled eye;
The rough and sooty walls with store
Of chains and horse-shoes studded o'er,
And rusty blades and bars between,
All momently are heard and seen.

Nor does he often fail to meet,
In market town's dark, narrow street,
(Even when the night with onward wings
The sober hour of bed-time brings,)
Amusement. From the alehouse door,
Having full bravely paid his score,
Issues the tipsy artisan,
With some sworn brother of the can,
While each to keep his footing tries,
And utters words solemn and wise.

The dame demure, from visit late,
Her lantern borne before in state
By sloven footboy, paces slow
With pattened feet and hooded brow.

Where the seamed window-board betrays
Interior light, right closely lays
The eaves-dropper his curious ear,
Some neighbour's fire-side talk to hear;
While, from an upper casement bending,
A household maid, perhaps, is sending
From jug or pot, a sloppy shower
That makes him homeward fleetly scour.
From lower rooms few gleams are sent
Through shortened shutter-hole or rent;
But from the loftier chambers peer
(Where damsels doff their gentle gear
For rest preparing) tapers bright,
That give a momentary sight
Of some fair form with visage glowing,
With loosened braids and tresses flowing,
Who busied by the mirror stands
With bending head and upraised hands
Whose moving shadow strangely falls
With size enlarged on roof and walls.
Ah! lovely are the things, I ween,

By speed's light, passing glamoury seen!
Fancy so touched will oft restore
Things once beheld and seen no more.

But now he spies the flaring door
Of bridled Swan or gilded Boar,
At which the bowing waiter stands
To know the alighting guest's commands.
A place of bustle, dirt and din,
Swearing without, scolding within;
Of narrow means and ample boast,
The traveller's stated halting post,
Where trunks are missing or deranged,
And parcels lost and horses changed.

Yet this short scene of noisy coil
But serves our traveller as a foil,
Enhancing what succeeds, and lending
A charm to pensive quiet, sending
To home and friends, left far behind,
The kindliest musings of his mind;
Or, should they stray to thoughts of pain,
A dimness o'er the haggard train
A mood and hour like this will throw,
As vexed and burthened spirits know.
Night, loneliness and motion are
Agents of power to distance care;
To distance, not discard; for then,
Withdrawn from busy haunts of men,
Necessity to act suspended,
The present, past and future blended,
Like figures of a mazy dance,
Weave round the soul a dreamy trance,
Till jolting stone or turnpike gate
Arouse him from the soothing state.

And when the midnight hour is past,
If through the night his journey last,
When still and lonely is the road,
Nor living creature moves abroad,
Then most of all, like fabled wizard,
Night slily dons her cloak and vizard,
His eyes at every corner meeting
With some new slight of dexterous cheating,
And cunningly his sight betrays
Even with his own lamp's partial rays.

The road that in fair, honest day
Through pasture-land or corn-fields lay,

A broken hedge-row's ragged screen
Skirting its margin rank and green,
With boughs projecting, interlaced
With thorn and briar, distinctly traced
On the deep shadows at their back
That deeper sink to pitchy black,
Appearing soothly to the eye
Like woven boughs of tapestry,—
Seems now to wind through tangled wood
On forest wild, where Robin Hood
With all his out-laws stout and bold
In olden days his reign might hold.
Yea, roofless barn and ruined walls,
As passing light upon them falls,
When favoured by surrounding gloom,
The castle's stately form assume.

The steaming vapour that proceeds
From moistened hide of weary steeds,
And high on either side will rise,
Like clouds storm-drifted, past him flies;
While mire cast up by their hoofed feet
Adds curious magic to deceit,
Glancing presumptuously before him,
Like yellow diamonds of Cairngorm....

(Wr. *c.* 1800–10?, pub. 1840)

72 ADDRESS TO A STEAMVESSEL

Freighted with passengers of every sort,
A motley throng, thou leavest the busy port:
Thy long and ample deck,—where scattered lie
Baskets and cloaks and shawls of crimson dye;
Where dogs and children through the crowd are straying,
And on his bench apart the fiddler playing,
While matron dames to tresselled seats repair,—
Seems, on the glassy waves, a floating fair.

Its dark form on the sky's pale azure cast,
Towers from this clustering group thy pillared mast;
The dense smoke, issuing from its narrow vent,
Is to the air in curly volumes sent,
Which coiling and uncoiling on the wind,
Trail, like a writhing serpent, far behind.
Beneath, as each merged wheel its motion plies,
On either side the white-churned waters rise,

And newly parted from the noisy fray,
Track with light ridgy foam thy recent way,
Then far diverged, in many a lustrous line
On the still-moving distant surface shine.

Thou holdst thy course in independent pride;
No leave ask'st thou of either wind or tide.
To whate'er point the breeze inconstant veer,
Still doth thy careless helmsman onward steer;
As if the stroke of some magician's wand
Had lent thee power the ocean to command.
What is this power which thus within thee lurk
And all unseen, like a masked giant works?
E'en that which gentle dames at morning tea,
From silver urn ascending, daily see
With tressy wreathings borne upon the air
Like loosened ringlets of a lady's hair;
Or rising from the enamelled cup beneath,
With the soft fragrance of an infant's breath:
That which within the peasant's humble cot
Comes from the uncovered mouth of savoury pot,
As his kind mate prepares his noonday fare.
Which cur and cat and rosy urchins share;
That which, all silvered by the moon's pale beam
Precedes the mighty Geyser's up-cast stream,
What time, with bellowing din, exploded forth,
It decks the midnight of the frozen north,
While travellers from their skin-spread couches rise
To gaze upon the sight with wondering eyes.

Thou hast to those 'in populous city pent'
Glimpses of wild and beauteous nature lent,
A bright remembrance ne'er to be destroyed,
That proves to them a treasure long enjoyed,
And for this scope to beings erst confined,
I fain would hail thee with a grateful mind.
They who had nought of verdant freshness seen,
But suburb orchards choked with coleworts green,
Now, seated at their ease, may glide along,
Loch Lomond's fair and fairy Isles among;
Where bushy promontories fondly peep
At their own beauty in the nether deep,
O'er drooping birch and rowan red that lave
Their fragrant branches in the glassy wave:
They who on higher objects scarce have counted
Than church-spire with its gilded vane surmounted,
May view within their near, distinctive ken
The rocky summits of the lofty Ben;
Or see his purple shoulders darkly lower

Through the dim drapery of a summer shower.
Where, spread in broad and fair expanse, the Clyde
Mingles his waters with the briny tide,
Along the lesser Cumbray's rocky shore,
With moss and crusted lichens fleckered o'er,
He who but warfare held with thievish cat,
Or from his cupboard chased a hungry rat,
The city cobbler,—scares the wild sea-mew
In its mid-flight with loud and shrill halloo;
Or valiantly with fearful threatening shakes
His lank and greasy head at Kittywakes.
The eyes that have no fairer outline seen,
Than chimneyed walls with slated roofs between,
Which hard and harshly edge the smoky sky,
May Arran's softly-visioned peaks descry,
Coping with graceful state her steepy sides
O'er which the cloud's broad shadow swiftly glides,
And interlacing slopes that gently merge
Into the pearly mist of ocean's verge.
Eyes which admired that work of sordid skill,
The storeyed structure of a cotton mill,
May wondering now behold the unnumbered host
Of marshalled pillars on fair Ireland's coast,
Phalanx on phalanx ranged with sidelong bend,
Or broken ranks that to the main descend,
Like Pharaoh's army on the Red Sea shore,
Which deep and deeper sank, to rise no more.

Yet ne'ertheless, whate'er we owe to thee,
Rover at will on river, lake, and sea,
As profit's bait or pleasure's lure engage,
Offspring of Watt, that philosophic sage,
Who in the heraldry of science ranks
With those to whom men owe high meed of thanks
For genius usefully employed, whose fame
Shall still be linked with Davy's splendid name;
Dearer to fancy, to the eye more fair
Are the light skiffs, that to the breezy air
Unfurl their swelling sails of snowy hue
Upon the moving lap of ocean blue:
As the proud swan on summer lake displays,
With plumage brightening in the morning rays,
Her fair pavilion of erected wings,
They change, and veer, and turn like living things.

With ample store of shrouding, sails, and mast,
To brave with manly skill the winter blast
Of every clime,—in vessels rigged like these
Did great Columbus cross the western seas,

And to the stinted thoughts of man revealed
What yet the course of ages had concealed:
In such as these, on high adventure bent,
Round the vast world Magellan's comrades went.
To such as these are hardy seamen found
As with the ties of kindred feeling bound,
Boasting, while cans of cheering grog they sip,
The varied fortunes of 'our gallant ship:'
The offspring these of bold sagacious man,
Ere yet the reign of lettered lore began.

In very truth, compared to these, thou art
A daily labourer, a mechanic swart,
In working weeds arrayed of homely grey,
Opposed to gentle nymph or lady gay,
To whose free robes the graceful right is given
To play and dally with the winds of heaven.
Beholding thee, the great of other days
And modern men with all their altered ways,
Across my mind with hasty transit gleam,
Like fleeting shadows of a feverish dream:
Fitful I gaze, with adverse humours teased,
Half sad, half proud, half angry, and half pleased.

(1823)

ANNA MARIA JONES (née SHIPLEY) (1748 – 1829)

She was born on 5 December 1748, the eldest daughter of Jonathan Shipley (1714–88), Bishop of St Asaph, who married Anna Maria Mordaunt *c.* 1743, a niece of the Earl of Peterborough. Her father was a significant figure in the opposition to the American War and viewed America as 'the last great nursery of free men left on the face of the earth'. Her uncle, William Shipley, was the founder of the Royal Society of Arts in 1754. Jonathan Shipley educated his daughters in modern and classical languages, and on meeting Anna Maria in 1766 at the home of Lady Spencer at Althorpe, Sir William Jones, later the greatest authority on oriental languages, entered into a long courtship, marrying her on 8 April 1783. Following his appointment as judge to the High Court of Calcutta, they sailed for India. Both her father and her husband were friends of Benjamin Franklin (who wrote part of his autobiography at St Asaph) and were moderate reformers along the lines of Price and Priestley. In India, she shared many of her husband's interests and edited his works after his death. Contemporaries recall her dancing minuets and wearing saris. In 1793, shortly before her husband's death she returned to England, where she became increasingly involved in complicated family affairs. (Her letters from India and her journals were destroyed in 1857 by Esther Maurice, the sister of F.D. Maurice, who had married Julius Hare.) In 1806, she adopted the children of her spirited sister, Georgiana, and lived at Worting House, near Basingstoke, though she still spent long periods in London. In contrast to Georgiana, she was thought to be rather stern and became increasingly evangelical in later life. She died on 7 July 1829.

73 SONNET: TO ECHO

I saw her in the fleeting Wind,
   I heard Her on the sounding Shore;
The fairy Nymph of shadowy Kind,
   That oft derides the Winter's Roar:
I heard her lash from Rock to Rock,
With shrill repeating solemn Shock;
I met her in the twilight's Shade
As flitting o'er my pensive Glade;
O'er yonder tepid Lake she flew,
Her Mantle gemmed with silver Dew;
The bursting Note swept through the Sky
As the young Valleys passed the Sigh:
In Accents varied as the Passions change,
The Nymph, wild Echo, sweeps the hallow Range.

(1793)

74 STANZAS: MARIE ANTOINETTE'S COMPLAINT IN PRISON

Slow creeps the Hour to sad Reflection due,
   Coy's the bleak Whisper of the dreary Night;
Where no faint *Hope* arrests the timid View,
   Or softened *Pity* beams her gentle Light.

Why sacred *Heaven* permit my throbbing Heart,
   Still in its feeble Cell so rude to beat;
Why *Death* recede the kind consoling Dart,
   That soothes the Pulse of Life's departing Heat?—

Say, am I doomed by desolating Fate,
   The wretched Victim of acute Despair;
Has bright-eyed Mercy shut her crystal Gate,
   With stern Denial of Admission there?—

Ah no!—my soul yet looks for Joys supreme,
   For rosy Bliss that Angels taste on high;
E'en *new*, the Transports of the golden Dream,
   Bear my frail Being through the purple Sky.

Yes—dear Illusion, thou dost kindly throw
   A twilight Glory o'er my shattered Sense;
I feel the transient momentary Glow,
   The tender Solaces of Heaven dispense.

Hush!—'twas the Murmur of the hurtling Wind,
   That nightly rushes on my wounded Ear;
Twas the deep Sigh, by Echo's Voice refined,
   Sped from the pallid Lips of frenzied Fear.

Cold through the languid Pulse does *Terror* creep,
   The foulest Fiend of Midnight's torpid Hour;
At thy Approach the drowsy Prince of Sleep,
   Starts from his Couch and owns thy freezing Power.

O! could I pass these solitary Walls,
   I'd seek wild Deserts and enchanted Caves;
Where pale *Disorder* on her Votaries calls,
   Where gasping Madness at her Shadow raves.

And, I would tell unto the *weeping* Moon,
   That showered her Tears upon my frantic Head;
Yes—I would tell her all my Woes, and soon
   This widowed Form should join its kindred Dead.

Soon should my wearied Spirit take her Flight,
   From the keen Agony of mental Pain;
Soon with her Lord enjoy celestial Light,
   'Mid the pure Regions of the starry Plain.

Ah!—holy Saint, if from thy lustrous Goal,
   Thou view'st me sink beneath Affliction's Rod;
In Pity waft my trembling, fainting Soul,
   To the chaste Presence of her Maker—God!—

O'er our sweet Infants may thy partial Care,
   Guard them from rude Oppression's savage Ire;
For this, a Mother's melancholy Prayer,
   Ascends with Fervour to their murdered Sire!

(1793)

O! lead me at the Close of Day,
To view the ruby Orb of Fire,
Beneath Night's Canopy retire,
As down the West he speeds away:—
To gaze upon the Clouds of Gold,
O'er amber Evening's Beauties rolled,
In visionary Forms sublime;
Where mingled with the dappled Skies,
The crimson Blushes proudly rise,
To meliorate Departing Time!

Now Cynthia throws her spangled Dew,
O'er Night's enchanting sabling Hue,
And bids the Stars their Glories hide;
While in her Beams are seen to sport,
The tiny Fairies of her Court,
In all their variegated Pride:—
There Fancy thou art known to reign,
Light robed among the mystic Train:
Transparent Gossamer doth veil
Thy Graces from the tepid Gale;
And round thy Brows the *Ariels* twine,
A filmy Wreath of Power divine:—
Then, as the little *Moon* glides down,
And deeper Shadows dim the Light;
The bashful Stars, a radiant Crown,
Weave for the sable *Queen of Night*:
While Fancy, thou art seen to stray,
Through the bright constellated Way.

Alike, when rosy-fingered Morn
Her Glories on the Twilight flings;
The lovely Cherubs of the Dawn,
Wanton on their purple Wings:
And see, the flaky Mists arise,
In spiral Columns to the Skies;
While vestal *Health* with Joy elate,
Stands tip-toe on the golden Gate,
Where fair *Aurora* leads the *Hours*
To carol through their sunny Bowers;
There Fancy, with imperial Gaze,
Adores *Apollo's* radiant Blaze;
And, with a conscious Bliss, impearls
Her sparkling Diamonds in his golden Curls.

Yes, central Nymph, thou too art seen
To hie across the russet Green;

O'er bending Grass and ripened Corn,
Gay with the Freshness of the Morn.
I've marked *Thee* loiter down the Glade,
In search of *Love's* romantic Maid;
Whom disappointed Passion drove,
To seek the Woodbine's sheltered Grove:
Fancy, 'tis thine, with brilliant Fire,
To sweep the Muse's trilling Lyre;
From *Thee*, the sweet Ideas spring,
Which Ida's Nymphs are heard to sing;
'Tis thine, to bid their Fervours roll,
With melting Transport to the Soul:—
O Fancy, could thy Strains divine
Impress the *Minstrel's* chary Line;
I'd crown *Thee* with such lustrous Rays,
Should rival e'en the God of Day's proud Blaze!

(1793)

76 ADIEU TO INDIA

Et vix sustinuit dicere Lingua – vale! [Ovid]

Ocean, I call thee from the sapphire Deep,
Where the young Billows on their pearl-beds sleep;
And the fair Beauties of the boisterous Main,
Far from the jarring Elements complain:
Where in the coral Grove's transparent Court,
The green-haired Tritons and their Nymphs resort:
Haste and subdue the Turbulence that laves
The long-drawn Shadows of the mountain Waves;
Still the proud Tempest, whose impetuous Sway,
Heaves into monstrous Forms the watery Way.
Maria asks—nor thou the Boon refuse,
Urged by the pensive melancholy Muse!
Who oft to *Thee*, when keen Despair hath spread
Her awful Terrors o'er her timid Head,
Has poured with fervid Lay the suppliant Prayer,
And twined her Sorrows in thy sedgy Hair:
While *Thou* attentive to the weeping Tale,
Dispersed her Fears, and quelled the ruthless Gale.

Adieu to India's fertile Plains,
Where *Brahma's* holy Doctrine reigns;
Whose virtuous Principles still bind
The *Hindu's* meek untainted Mind;
Far other Scenes my Thoughts employ,
Source of Anguish, Hope and Joy;
I hasten to my Native Shore,

Where *Art* and *Science* blend their Lore:
There *Learning* keeps her chosen Seat—
A million Votaries at her Feet,
Ambitious of the Laurel Bough,
To wind about their honoured Brow.
Yet ere I go—a grateful Pain
Involves the Muse's parting Strain;
The sad Regret my Mind imbues,
And fills with Grief—*my last Adieus!*
For I have felt the subtle Praise,
That cheered the *Minstrel's* doubtful Lays;
That fed the infant lambent Flame,
And bade me hope for Future Fame.

Farewell, ye sacred Haunts, where oft I've strayed
With mild Reflection—solitary Maid!—
Ye Streams that swell the winding *Hougly's* Tide,
The Seat of Commerce and the Muse's Pride,
Farewell!—the Mariners unfurl the Sails,
Eager to meet the Pressure of the Gales;
And now the lofty Vessel cleaves the Way,
Dashing the impelling Waves with silver Spray.—
Why springs my Heart with many an aching Sigh,
Why stands impearled the *Trembler* on mine eye?—
Alas!—fond Memory weeps the Vision past,
'For ever fled, like yonder sweeping Blast:'
Those Hours of Bliss, those Scenes of soft Delight,
Vanish like Mists before the Rays of Light;
But still Remembrance holds the Objects dear,
And bathes their *Shadows* with Regret's pure Tear;
Nor shall the oblivious Power of Time subdue,
The painful Feelings of the last—Adieu!

(1793)

MARY ROBINSON (née DARBY) (1758 – 1800)

She was born in Bristol where she went to the school run by Hannah More and her sisters. She later attended schools in Chelsea, Battersea and Marylebone. She was married off in 1774 to Thomas Robinson. He turned out to have no fortune and no prospects, gambled heavily, and was later gaoled for debt. She accompanied him to prison where she wrote some poetry. She had earlier met Garrick and in December 1776 she appeared as Juliet in Drury Lane with great success and continued acting. She came to the attention of the Prince of Wales and became his mistress in 1778. He later abandoned her. In 1781 after difficult negotiations, she was granted an annuity of £500 a year. Around 1782 she formed a liaison with Banastre Tarleton which lasted for sixteen years until he, too, abandoned her. She published early but unremarkable verse, *Poems* (1775) and *Captivity* (1777). In the late 1780s she published 'Della Cruscan' verse in *The World* and *The Oracle*. Her *Poems* (1791), followed by a second volume in 1793, were widely admired, and a selection, *The Beauties of Mrs Robinson* (1791), might seem to indicate imminent entry into the canon. However, it was probably her notoriety that prompted the volume. She also published an important collection of longer poems, *Sight, the Cavern of Woe, and Solitude* (1793). Financial problems persisted and she turned to novel writing, *Vacenza*, 2 vols (1792), *Angelina*, 3 vols (1796), and *Walsingham*, 4 vols (1797), as well as poetry, *Sappho and Phaon* (1796), and *Lyrical Tales* (1800). She also published an important and unjustly neglected feminist tract, *A Letter to the Women of England, on the Injustice of Mental Subordination* (1799). Between 1798 and 1800, she contributed a number of important poems to *The Morning Post*. She is probably unique among the women poets in terms of development, from the polite verse of the 1770s, through polished Della Cruscan poetry, to *Lyrical Tales* (1800), sharp social satire and romantic subject matter. Her novels are unjustly neglected and display both radical concerns and conflicts between reason and passion (a central problem for Dissenting radicals), which were to a large extent bypassed by Wordsworth, Coleridge and Southey. She died crippled and impoverished in 1800. Her daughter, Maria Elizabeth, edited *Memoirs... With some Posthumous Pieces*, 4 vols, (1801) and her *Poetical Works*, 3 vols (1806).

77 ODE: TO THE NIGHTINGALE

Sweet Bird of Sorrow!—why complain
   In such soft melody of Song,
That Echo, amorous of thy Strain,
   The lingering cadence doth prolong?
Ah! tell me, tell me, why,
Thy dulcet Notes ascend the sky.
Or on the filmy vapours glide
Along the misty mountain's side?
And wherefore dost Thou love to dwell,
In the dark wood and moss-grown cell,
Beside the willow-margined stream—
Why dost Thou court wan Cynthia's beam?
Sweet Songstress—if thy wayward fate
Hath robbed Thee of thy bosom's mate,

Oh, think not thy heart-piercing moan
Evaporates on the breezy air,

Or that the plaintive Song of Care
Steals from Thy Widowed Breast alone.
Oft have I heard thy mournful Tale,
On the high Cliff, that o'er the Vale
Hangs its dark brow, whose awful shade
Spreads a deep gloom along the glade:
Led by its sound, I've wandered far,
Till crimson evening's flaming Star
On Heaven's vast dome refulgent hung,
And round ethereal vapours flung;
And oft I've sought the Hygeian Maid,
In rosy dimpling smiles arrayed,
Till forced with every Hope to part,
Resistless Pain subdued my Heart.

Oh then, far o'er the restless deep
Forlorn my poignant pangs I bore,
Alone in foreign realms to weep,
Where Envy's voice could taunt no more.
I hoped, by mingling with the gay,
To snatch the veil of Grief away;
I hoped, amid the joyous train,
To break Affliction's ponderous chain;
Vain was the Hope—in vain I sought
The placid hour of careless thought,
Where Fashion winged her light career,
And sportive Pleasure danced along,
Oft have I shunned the blithsome throng,
To hide the involuntary tear,
For e'en where rapturous transports glow,
From the full Heart the conscious tear will flow,
When to my downy couch removed,
Fancy recalled my wearied mind
To scenes of Friendship left behind,
Scenes still regretted, still beloved!
Ah, then I felt the pangs of Grief,
Grasp my warm Heart, and mock relief;
My burning lids Sleep's balm defied,
And on my feverish lip imperfect murmurs died.

Restless and sad—I sought once more
A calm retreat on Britain's shore;
Deceitful Hope, e'en there I found
That soothing Friendship's specious name
Was but a short-lived empty sound,
And Love a false delusive flame.

Then come, Sweet Bird, and with thy strain,
Steal from my breast the thorn of pain;
Blest solace of my lonely hours,
In craggy caves and silent bowers,
When Happy Mortals seek repose,
By Night's pale lamp we'll chaunt our woes,
And, as her chilling tears diffuse
O'er the white thorn their silvery dews,
I'll with the lucid boughs entwine
A weeping Wreath, which round my Head
Shall by the waning Crescent shine,
And light us to our leafy bed.—
But ah! nor leafy beds nor bowers
Fringed with soft May's enamelled flowers,
Nor pearly leaves, nor Cynthia's beams,
Nor smiling Pleasure's shadowy dreams,
Sweet Bird, not e'en Thy melting Strains
Can calm the Heart, where Tyrant Sorrow reigns.

(1791)

78 STANZAS WRITTEN BETWEEN DOVER AND CALAIS, IN JULY 1792

Bounding Billow, cease thy motion;
Bear me not so swiftly o'er!
Cease thy roaring, foamy Ocean!
I will tempt thy rage no more.

Ah! within my bosom beating,
Varying passions wildly reign!
Love, with proud Resentment meeting;
Throbs by turns, of joy and pain!

Joy, that far from foes I wander,
Where their Arts can reach no more;
Pain, that woman's heart grows fonder,
When the dream of bliss is o'er!

Love, by fickle fancy banished,
Spurned by Hope, indignant flies!
Yet, when love and hope are vanished,
Restless Memory never dies!

Far I go! where Fate shall lead me,
Far across the troubled deep!
Where no stranger's ear shall heed me;
Where no eye for Me shall weep.

Proud has been my fatal passion!
  Proud my injured heart shall be!
While each thought and inclination
  Proves that heart was formed for Thee!

Not one Sigh shall tell my story;
  Not one Tear my cheek shall stain!
Silent grief shall be my glory;
  Grief that stoops not to Complain!

Let the bosom, prone to ranging,
  Still, by ranging, seek a cure!
Mine disdains the thought of changing,
  Proudly destined to Endure!

Yet ere far from all I treasured,
  * * * * * * * * ! ere I bid adieu,
Ere my days of pain are measured
  Take the song that's Still thy due!

Yet believe, no servile passions
  Seek to charm thy wandering mind;
Well I know thy inclinations,
  Wavering as the passing wind!

I have loved thee! Dearly loved thee!
  Through an age of worldly woe!
How ungrateful I have proved thee,
  Let my mournful exile show!

Ten long years of anxious sorrow,
  Hour by hour, I counted o'er;
Looking forward till to morrow,
  Every day I loved thee more!

Power and Splendour could not charm me;
  I no joy in Wealth could see;
Nor could threats or fears alarm me—
  Save the Fear of losing Thee!

When the storms of fortune pressed thee,
  I have sighed to hear *thee* sigh!
Or when sorrows dire distressed thee,
  I have bid those sorrows fly!

Often hast thou smiling told me,
  Wealth and Power were trifling things,
While Love, smiling to behold me,
  Mocked cold Time's destructive wings.

When with thee, what ills could harm me?
  Thou couldst every pang assuage!
Now, Alas! what Hope shall charm me?
  Every moment seems an age!

Fare thee well, ungrateful Rover!
  Welcome Gallia's hostile shore;
Now, the breezes waft me over;
  Now we part—to meet no more!

(1793)

79 STANZAS WRITTEN AFTER SUCCESSIVE NIGHTS OF MELANCHOLY DREAMS

Ye airy Phantoms, by whose power
  Night's curtains spread a deeper shade;
Who, prowling in the murky hour,
  The weary sense with spells invade;
Why round the fibres of my brain,
  Such desolating miseries fling,
And, with new scenes of mental pain,
Chase from my languid eye, sleep's balm-dispensing wing?

Ah! why, when o'er the darkened globe
  All Nature's children sink to rest—
Why, wrapped in horrors ghastly robe,
  With shadowy hand assail my breast?
Why conjure up a tribe forlorn,
  To menace, where I bend my way?
Why round my pillow plant the thorn,
  Or fix the Demons dire, in terrible array?

Why, when the busy day is o'er—
  A day, perhaps, of *tender thought*—
Why bid my eager gaze explore
  New prospects, with new anguish fraught?
Why bid my maddening sense descry
  The Form, in silence I adore!
His magic smile! his murderous eye!
Then bid me wake to prove, the fond illusion o'er!

When, feverish with the throbs of pain,
  And bathed with many a trickling tear,
I close my cheated eyes again,
  Despair's wild bands are hovering near;

Now borne upon the yelling blast,
O'er craggy Peaks I bend my flight;
Now, on the yawning Ocean cast,
I plunge unfathomed depths, amid the shades of night!

Or, borne upon the billow's Ire,
O'er the vast waste of water's drear,
Where shipwrecked Mariners expire,
No friend their dying plaints to hear,
I view far off the craggy cliff,
Whose white top mingles with the skies;
While, at its base, the shattered Skiff,
Washed by the foaming wave, in many a fragment lies.

Oft, when the Morning's gaudy beams
My lattice gild with sparkling light,
O'erwhelmed with agonizing dreams,
And bound in spells of Fancied Night,
I start, convulsive, wild, distraught!
By some pale Murderer's poignard pressed,
Or by the grinning Phantom caught,
Wake from the maddening grasp with horror-freezing breast!

Then, down my cold and pallid cheek,
The mingling tears of joy and grief,
The soul's tumultuous feelings speak,
And yield the struggling heart relief;
I smile to know the danger past!
But soon the radiant moment flies;
Soon is the transient Day o'ercast,
And hope steels trembling from my languid eyes!

If Thus, for Moments of repose,
Whole Hours of misery I must know;
If, when each sunny day shall close,
I must each gleam of Peace forgo!
If, for one Little Morn of Mirth,
This breast must feel long nights of pain;
Oh! Life, thy joys are nothing worth;
Then let me sing to rest—and never wake again!

(1793)

80 ODE TO MY BELOVED DAUGHTER, ON HER BIRTH-DAY, OCTOBER 18, 1794

'Tis not an April-day,
Nor rosy Summer's burning hour,
Nor Evening's sinking ray,
That gilds rich Autumn's yellow bower,
Alone, that fades away!
Life is a variegated, tedious span,
A sad and toilsome road, the weary traveller, Man!

'Tis not the base alone
That wander through a desert drear,
Where Sorrow's plaintive tone
Calls Echo from her cell to hear
The soul-subduing moan;
In haunts where Virtue lives retired we see
The agonizing wounds of hopeless Misery!

'Tis not in titles vain,
Or yet in costly trappings rare,
Or Courts where Monarchs reign,
Or Sceptre, Crown, or regal Chair,
To quell the throb of pain;
The balmy hour of rest alone, we find,
Springs from that sacred source, Integrity of Mind!

Power cannot give us health,
Or lengthen out our breathing day!
Nor all the stores of wealth
The sting of conscience chase away!
Time seals each charm by stealth,
And, spite of all that Wisdom can devise,
Still to the vale of Death our dreary pathway lies!

Mark how the Seasons go!
Spring passes by in liveliest green,
Then Summer's trappings glow,
Then Autumn's tawny vest is seen,
Then Winter's locks of snow!
With true Philosophy each change explore,
Read Nature's page divine! and mock the Pedant's lore.

Life's race prepared to run,
We wake to Youth's exulting glee;
Alas! how soon 'tis done!
We fall, like blossoms from the tree,
Yet ripe, by Reason's sun;
The cherished fruit in Winter's gloom shall be
An earnest bright and fair—of Immortality!

Sweet comfort of my days!
While yet in Youth's ecstatic prime,
Illumed by Virtue's rays,
Thy hand shall snatch from passing Time
A wreath that ne'er decays!
That when cold age shall shrink from worldly cares,
A Crown of conscious Peace may deck thy silver hairs!

We are but busy Ants,
We toil through Summer's vivid glow
To hoard for Winter's wants;
Our brightest prospects fraught with woe,
And thorny all our haunts!
Then let it be the Child of Wisdom's plan,
To make his little hour as cheerful as he can!

The Being we adore
Bids all the face of Nature smile!
The wisest can no more
Than view it, and revere the while!
Then let us not explore
Things hidden in the mysteries of Fate;
Man should rely on Heaven, nor murmur at his state!

Thou art more dear to me
Than sight, or sense, or vital air!
For every day I see
Presents thee with a mind more fair!
Rich pearl, in life's rude Sea!
Oh! may thy mental graces still impart
The balm that soothes to rest a Mother's trembling heart!

Still may revolving years
Expand the virtues of thy mind!
And may Affliction's tears
Thy peaceful pillow never find;
Nor fruitless hopes—nor fears:
May no keen pangs thy halcyon bower invade,
But every thought be bliss, till thy *last hour shall fade!*

(1794, repr. 1806)

81 JANUARY, 1795

Pavement slippery, people sneezing,
Lords in ermine, beggars freezing;
Titled gluttons dainties carving,
Genius in a garret starving.

Lofty mansions, warm and spacious;
Courtiers cringing and voracious;
Misers scarce the wretched heeding;
Gallant soldiers fighting, bleeding.

Wives who laugh at passive spouses;
Theatres, and meeting-houses;
Balls, where simpering misses languish;
Hospitals, and groans of anguish.

Arts and sciences bewailing;
Commerce drooping, credit failing;
Placemen mocking subjects loyal;
Separations, weddings royal.

Authors who can't earn a dinner;
Many a subtle rogue a winner;
Fugitives for shelter seeking;
Misers hoarding, tradesmen breaking.

Taste and talents quite deserted;
All the laws of truth perverted;
Arrogance o'er merit soaring;
Merit silently deploring.

Ladies gambling night and morning;
Fools the works of genius scorning;
Ancient dames for girls mistaken,
Youthful damsels quite forsaken.

Some in luxury delighting;
More in talking than in fighting;
Lovers old, and beaux decrepid;
Lordlings empty and insipid.

Poets, painters, and musicians;
Lawyers, doctors, politicians:
Pamphlets, newspapers, and odes,
Seeking fame by different roads.

Gallant souls with empty purses,
Generals only fit for nurses;
School-boys, smit with martial spirit,
Taking place of veteran merit.

Honest men who can't get places,
Knaves who show unblushing faces;
Ruin hastened, peace retarded;
Candour spurned, and art rewarded.

(1795, repr. 1806)

82 THE PROGRESS OF MELANCHOLY

By slow progressive steps the poison fell,
Creeps through the sickening brain; the pallid cheek,
The languid down-cast eye, the listless frame,
The desolating toil of ceaseless thought,
Proclaim the mental malady at hand!
Absorbed amidst surrounding revelry,
The child of ruthless Melancholy steals;
Unheeding the loud laugh, the wanton jest,
The sign mysterious, or the whisper low
Of shrewd, sharp-sighted, prying observation.
Nor magic charm, nor herb medicinal,
Nor all the treasured lore of studious skill,
Can draw the victim from the numbing spell
That fascinates and chains her yielding soul!

Seldom she speaks: if questioned, she returns
The answer incoherent and unapt,
Marked by the frequent pause and vacant eye.
Sometimes she weeps; but nature's niggard hand
Denies the copious shower; sweet balmy fount,
That cools and vivifies the burning brain!
And now she starts! and now-and-then, by fits,
She looks aghast, trembles, and deeply sighs;
Then sinks into the torpid dream again.

She loaths the blooms of spring! the glowing hour
Of feast and minstrelsy, and playful mirth!
Her mind, each active faculty possessed,
Resigns itself to ever-musing woe:
For her no orient beam adorns the sky;
No balmy wing ethereal, through the shade
Flings the refreshing breeze; no limpid brook
Sparkles with noon-tide rays, reflected back
With ten-fold lustre from its glassy breast!
The change of season, and the varying hour,
Serve to make up the dull account of time,
But bring no interval of gleaming joy!

Or, if her sense can ought discriminate,
She lingers on the miseries of life;
The barren mountain, where the tottering hut
Rocks as the whirlwind sweeps its rushy roof,
And hurls it fathoms down the shaggy steep!
The chamber, where the paly quivering lamp
Shows the worn sufferer on the bed of death.
For her the woodland nightingale attunes
His song nocturnal, unregarded—lost!
The sad, the sympathetic, plaintive strain,
O'er the dull ear of sorrow passes faint,
If not unheeded; or, if feeling wakes,
Recalled by memory to long past woe,
Reflection glances o'er the page of time,
And marks its progress, with a silent tear!

Pale Melancholy shuns the rural haunt
Where peace, and joy, and revelry preside!
Bliss-breathing Health, that welcomes young desire,
Led on by smiling hope and blooming love,
Starts from her withering form, and steals away;
While apathy, with petrifying hand,
Throws a dim shadow o'er each faded charm.

The twilight gloom amidst embowering woods
She courts, and bending o'er some wizard stream
That winds among the ever-mouldering heaps,
Strewed by the touch of time from antique towers
And arches fretted with fantastic forms,
She sits, the pensive genius of the scene!
Around her cell attentive Stillness reigns;
The breezes sleep; and o'er its pebbly bed
The shallow river bends its silent way;
Death seems to triumph o'er the breathing world,
Save where the bat from the dark ruin flits,
Cleaving the night-mist with his dusky wing.

Nor there alone presides the mournful maid;
She loves to stray, and ponder as she strays,
Along the dreary monumental pile;
Where, from the Gothic roof, with ivy bound,
The whistling wind descends, and through the aisle
Sweeps the long hoarded dust for ages heaped
On the vain records of the sainted dead!
Where the loathed insect weaves it wily web,
And spits foul venom on the sceptred hand,
Mocking the pride and pageantry of kings.

Oft, when the wintery moon o'ertops the hills,
In circling vapour wrapped, she wanders forth

O'er the bleak heath; listening the rising gale,
Or distant village bell, whose sound, once told,
Proclaims the witching hour. Then Fancy comes;
But in her train no lovely forms appear,
No blithesome groups, thridding the roseate wreath,
Or tripping in fantastic measures by;
No Sylvan pipe, no rude, yet dulcet note
Of mountain minstrelsy delights her ear;
But the shrill menace of the freezing blast,
(Throned on whose black and desolating wing
Disease and death hurl the destructive shaft)
Howls o'er her breast. Still, dauntless, she proceeds;
The drizzly dew, the sharp and nipping gale,
Pass o'er her cheek unheeded. All alone
She contemplates the solitary scene,
While horror, maddening, conjures up a host
Of spectres gaunt; of chiefs, whose mouldering bones
Have slept beneath the green-sod where they fell,
Till village legends scarcely say—they died!

Now from their prison graves again they start,
Hurling the airy javelin on the foe;
And now they rush, in mighty legions, on;
Now form the lengthening colums fiercely brave;
And now the broken ranks disordered fly,
Pale as the silvery beam that marks their course;
And now the breathless heaps bestrew the plain,
While on their mangled limbs the battered shield
Gleams horrible; as through the indented steel
The life-stream gushes from the recent wound!
The groan of death fills up the dreadful pause;
Sad, and more sad, it echoes o'er the scene,
Till, oft repeated, the deep murmur dies!
The cherished poison, now more potent grown,
Riots o'er all the faculties at will;
Strong in conceit, with fascination fraught,
Painfully pleasing. As the fever burns
The consciousness of misery recedes;
Till filled with horror, reason's barrier falls,
And frenzy triumphs o'er the infected brain!

Now the wan maniac hurries to the bourn
Whose sandy base the frequent surges lave;
Dishevelled! wild! and fearless of the storm!
There, o'er the dreadful summit she inclines,
While darkness wraps the liquid world below:
She listens, with attention mute, to catch
The mournful murmurs of the distant main;
The tempest wakes; the roused and angry waves

Rise in the mighty elemental strife,
To lash the howling blast, whose forceful breath
Repels them, foaming, to their native deep.
Amidst the din terrific, the doomed bark
Strikes on the rocky shore. The wretched crew
Fill the dread chorus with the groans of death,
Till the tired winds moan o'er the shattered wreck,
That sinks amidst the fathomless abyss!

Roused from her dream, pale Melancholy starts;
Shrieks louder than the blast! but shrieks unheard;
Then plunges headlong from the dizzy steep,
And, in the bosom of Despair, expires!

Now the faint dawn gleams o'er the eastern cliff;
The smooth sea brightens with the coming ray,
And not a vestige of the storm is seen!

(1796)

83 SONNET: TO LIBERTY

Oh! Liberty! transcendent and sublime!
   Born on the mountain's solitary crest;
Nature thy nurse, thy fire unconquered Time,
   Truth, the pure inmate of thy glowing breast!
Oft dost thou wander by the billowy deep,
   Scattering the sands that bind the level shore,
Or, towering, brave the desolating roar
   That bids the tyrant tempest lash the steep!
'Tis thine, when sanguinary daemons lour,
   Amidst the thickening hosts to force thy way;
To quell the minions of oppressive power,
   And shame the vaunting nothings of a day!
Still shall the human mind thy name adore,
   Till chaos reigns—and worlds shall be no more!

(1796)

84 ODE: TO THE SNOW-DROP

The Snow-drop, Winter's timid child,
   Awakes to life, bedewed with tears,
And flings around its fragrance mild;
And where no rival flowerets bloom,
Amidst the bare and chilling gloom,
   A beauteous gem appears!

All weak and wan, with head inclined,
Its parent-breast the drifted snow,
It trembles, while the ruthless wind
Bends its slim form; the tempest lours,
Its emerald eye drops crystal showers
On its cold bed below.

Poor flower! on thee the sunny beam
No touch of genial warmth bestows!
Except to thaw the icy stream
Whose little current purls along,
And whelms thee as it flows.

The night-breeze tears thy silky dress,
Which decked with silvery lustre shone;
The morn returns, not thee to bless.—
The gaudy *Crocus* flaunts its pride,
And triumphs where *its rival*—died
Unsheltered and unknown!

No sunny beam shall gild thy grave,
No bird of pity thee deplore:
There shall no verdant branches wave,
For spring shall all her gems unfold,
And revel 'midst her beds of gold,
When thou art seen no more!

Where'er I find thee, gentle flower,
Thou still art sweet, and dear to me!
For I have known the cheerless hour,
Have seen the sun-beams cold and pale,
Have felt the chilling, wintery gale,
And wept, and shrunk like thee!

(1797, repr. 1806)

85 STANZAS

In this vain busy world, where the Good and the Gay,
By affliction or folly wing moments away;
Where the False are respected, the Virtuous betrayed;
Where Vice lives in sunshine, and Genius in shade;
With a soul-sickened sadness all changes I see;
For the world, the base world, has no pleasure for me!

In cities, where wealth loads the coffers of Pride;
Where Talents and Sorrow are ever allied;
Where Dullness is worshipped, and Wisdom despised
Where none but the Empty and Vicious are prized;

All scenes with disgust and abhorrence I see;
For the world has no corner of comfort for me!

While pale Asiatics, encircled with gold,
The sons of meek Virtue indignant behold;
While the tithe pampered Churchman reviles at the poor,
As the lorn sinking traveller faints at his door;
While Custom dares sanction Oppression's decree—
Oh, keep such hard bosoms, such monsters, from me!

While the flame of a Patriot expires in the breast,
With ribbands, and tinsel, and frippery dressed;
While Pride mocks the children of Want and Despair,
Gives a sneer for each sigh, and a smile for each prayer;
Though he triumphs his day, a short day it must be—
Heaven keep such cold tyrants, oh, keep them from me!

While the Lawyer still lives by the anguish of hearts,
While he wrings the wronged bosom, and thrives as it smarts;
While he grasps the last guinea from Poverty's heir;
While he revels in splendour which rose from Despair;
While the tricks of his office our scourges must be;
Oh, keep the shrewd knave and his quibbles from me!

While the court breeds the Sycophant, trained to ensnare;
While the prisons re-echo the groans of Despair;
While the State deals out taxes, the Army dismay;
While the Rich are upheld, and the Poor doomed to pay;
Humanity saddens with pity, to see
The scale of injustice, and trembles like me!

While Patriots are slandered, and venal Slaves rise;
While Power grows a giant, and Liberty dies;
While a phantom of Virtue o'er Energy reigns;
And the broad wing of Freedom is loaded with chains;
While War spreads its thunders o'er land and o'er sea;
Ah, who but can listen and murmur like me!

While the bosom which loves, and confesses its flame,
By the high-titled Female is branded with shame;
While a Coronet hides what the Humble despise;
And the lowly must fall that the Haughty may rise;
Oh, who can the triumphs of infamy see,
Nor shrink from the reptiles, and shudder like me!

Ah, World, thou vile World, how I sicken to trace
The anguish that hourly augments for thy race!
How I turn from the Worst, while I honour the Best;
The Enlightened adore, and the Venal detest!
And, oh! with what joy to the grave would I flee—
Since the World, the base World has no pleasure for me!

(1797)

86 *from* THE PROGRESS OF LIBERTY

Hail, Liberty sublime! Hail, godlike Power,
Coeval with the skies, to earth new born;
Thou parent of delight, thou source refined
Of human energy! Thou fountain vast
From whose immortal stream the soul of man
Imbibles celestial fervour! But for Thee,
O! best and noblest attribute of God!
Who would the coil endure of mortal woe,
The frowns of Fortune, or the taunts of Pride;
Float with the gale, or buffet with the storm;
Who labour through the busy dream of Time,
War with oppression, or resist the base;
Opposing ever, and by each opposed,
To count succeeding conflicts; and to die?
Hail, Liberty! Legitimate of Heaven!
Who, on a mountain's solitary brow
First started into life; thy Sire, old Time;
Thy mother, blooming, innocent, and gay,
The Genius of the scene! Thy lusty form
She gave to Nature; on whose fragrant lap,
Nursed by the breath of morn, each glowing vein
Soon throbbed with healthful streams. Thy sparkling eyes
Snatched radiance from the Sun! while every limb,
By custom unrestrained, grew firm and strong.
Thy midnight cradle, rocked by howling winds,
Lulled thee to wholesome rest. Thy beverage pure,
The wild brook gushing from the rocky steep,
And foaming, unimpeded, down the vale.
For thee no victim bled: no groan of death
Stole on the sighing gale to pitying Heaven!
Thy food the herbage sweet, or wandering vine
Bursting its luscious bounds, and scattering wide
The purple stream nectareous. O'er the hills,
Veiled with an orient canopy sublime,
'Twas thine to rove unshackled; or to weave
Young mountain flowers, to deck thy flowing hair,
But not confine it. Where thy footsteps fell,
No vagrant bud was crushed; for swift, and light
As summer breezes, flew thy active limbs,
Scarce brushing the soft dews. Thy song divine,
Warbled with all the witchery of sound,
Welcomed the varied year; nor marked the change
Of passing seasons: For to thee the morn
(Whether Favonius oped the sunny East,
Flaunting its lustrous harbinger of light,
Or slow the paly glimpse of Winter's eye
Peered on the frozen brow of sickly day),

Still wore an aspect lovely! Evening's star,
Spangling the purple splendours of the West,
And glowing, 'midst infinity of space,
Tempered by twilight's tears, still smiled on thee,
And bade thee dream of rapture! Nor could night,
With all its glooms opaque, its howling blasts—
Thunders, appalling to the guilty soul—
Or livid fires, winging the shafts of death,
Shake the soft slumbers of thy halcyon home.
The wild was thy domain! at morn's approach
Thy bounding form uprose to meet the Sun,
Thyself its proud Epitome! For thou,
Like the vast Orb, wert destined to illume
The mist-encircled world; to warm the soul,
To call the powers of teeming Reason forth,
And ratify the laws by Nature made!...

(Wr. 1798, pub. 1801)

87 *from* **THE PROGRESS OF LIBERTY**

Albion! still
May thy brave peasantry indignant turn
From priestcraft, ignorance, and bigot fraud,
To view in Nature's wonders, Nature's God!
For where can man so proudly contemplate
The Omniscient's power, as in the tablet vast
Of infinite creation? Every breeze
Seems the soft whispering of Nature's voice
Fraught with the lore of Reason. Every leaf
That flaunts its vernal hue, or eddying falls,
Its fibres withered by autumnal skies,
A moral lesson shows. The rippling rill
Prattles with Nature's tongue. The evening gale,
Moans the decline of day: while Twilight's tears
Fall on the dusky wings of chilling Night,
Spreading to hide its triumphs. The vast dome
Gleams with unnumbered stars; the prying eyes
Of those bright sentinels, etherial borne,
That watch the sleep of Nature. O'er the main,
In ebon car aerial, lightning winged,
The pealing thunder whirling his vast flight,
A short-lived fiend, gigantic born, the son
Of Equinox, rides furious. The freed winds
Howl as he passes by. The foamy waste
Bounds with compulsive horrors; while the waves
Lash the loud-sounding shore. O! Nature's God!
These are the varied pages of that lore

Which Reason searches: These the awful spells
That seize on all the faculties of man,
And bind them to allegiance. For that Power
Which speaks in mighty thunder wakes the soul,
Breathing in balmy gales; is seen alike
In the swift lightning and the lingering hue
Of Evening's purple veil; looks through the stars
And whispers 'mid the solitude sublime
Of thickening glooms nocturnal: from the east
Flames forth his burning eye: the grateful earth
Welcomes his glances with her boundless stores,
And robes herself in splendours: odours rich
And colours varying decorate her breast,
To greet the Lord of Nature: forests wild
And oceans multitudinous unfold
Their wonders to his gaze! Then why should Man
Creep like a reptile, fearful to explore
The page of human knowledge? Why mistrust
The sensate soul, the faculty supreme
Which instinct wakens?...

(Wr. 1800?, pub. 1801)

88 LONDON'S SUMMER MORNING

Who has not waked to list the busy sounds
Of summer's morning, in the sultry smoke
Of noisy London? On the pavement hot
The sooty chimney-boy, with dingy face
And tattered covering, shrilly bawls his trade,
Rousing the sleepy housemaid. At the door
The milk-pail rattles, and the tinkling bell
Proclaims the dustman's office; while the street
Is lost in clouds impervious. Now begins
The din of hackney-coaches, waggons, carts;
While tinmen's shops, and noisy trunk-makers,
Knife-grinders, coopers, squeaking cork-cutters,
Fruit-barrows, and the hunger-giving cries
Of vegetable venders, fill the air.
Now every shop displays its varied trade,
And the fresh-sprinkled pavement cools the feet
Of early walkers. At the private door
The ruddy housemaid twirls the busy mop,
Annoying the smart 'prentice, or neat girl,
Tripping with band-box lightly. Now the sun
Darts burning splendour on the glittering pane,
Save where the canvas awning throws a shade
On the gay merchandise. Now, spruce and trim,
In shops (where beauty smiles with industry,)
Sits the smart damsel; while the passenger

Peeps through the window, watching every charm.
Now pastry dainties catch the eye minute
Of humming insects, while the limy snare
Waits to enthral them. Now the lamp-lighter
Mounts the tall ladder, nimbly venturous,
To trim the half-filled lamp; while at his feet
The pot-boy yells discordant! All along
The sultry pavement, the old-clothes-man cries
In tone monotonous, and side-long views
The area for his traffic: now the bag
Is slyly opened, and the half-worn suit
(Sometimes the pilfered treasure of the base
Domestic spoiler), for one half its worth,
Sinks in the green abyss. The porter now
Bears his huge load along the burning way;
And the poor poet wakes from busy dreams,
To paint the summer morning.

(1800, repr. 1806)

89 TO THE POET COL[E]RIDGE

Rapt in the visionary theme!
   Spirit Divine! with thee I'll wander!
Where the blue, wavy, lucid stream,
   'Mid forest glooms shall slow meander!
With thee I'll trace the circling bounds
   Of thy New Paradise, extended;
And listen to the varying sounds
   Of winds, and foamy torrents blended!

Now by the source, which labouring heaves
   The mystic fountain, bubbling, panting,
While gossamer its net-work weaves,
   Adown the blue lawn, slanting!
I'll mark thy 'sunny dome,' and view
Thy 'caves of ice,' thy fields of dew!
Thy ever-blooming mead, whose flower
Waves to the cold breath of the moon-light hour!
Or when the day-star, peering bright
On the grey wing of parting night;
While more than vegetating power,
Throbs, grateful to the burning hour,
As Summer's whispered sighs unfold
Her million—million buds of gold!
Then will I climb the breezy bounds
   Of thy New Paradise, extended,
And listen to the distant sounds
   Of winds, and foamy torrents blended!

Spirit Divine! with thee I'll trace,
Imagination's boundless space!
With thee, beneath thy 'sunny dome,'
I'll listen to the minstrel's lay,
Hymning the gradual close of day,
In 'caves of ice' enchanted roam,
Where on the glittering entrance plays
The moon's-beam with its silvery rays;
Or, when the glassy stream,
That through the deep dell flows,
Flashes the noon's hot beam,
The noon's hot beam, that midway shows
Thy flaming temple, studded o'er
With all Peruvia's lustrous store!
There will I trace the circling bounds
Of thy New Paradise, extended,
And listen to the awful sounds
Of winds, and foamy torrents blended!

And now I'll pause to catch the moan
Of distant breezes, cavern-pent;
Now, ere the twilight tints are flown,
Purpling the landscape far and wide,
On the dark promontory's side
I'll gather wild-flowers, dew besprent,
And weave a crown for thee,
Genius of Heaven-taught poesy!
While, opening to my wondering eyes,
Thou bidst a new creation rise,
I'll raptured trace the circling bounds
Of thy Rich Paradise, extended,
And listen to the varying sounds
Of winds, and foamy torrents blended.

And now, with lofty tones inviting,
Thy Nymph, her dulcimer swift-smiting,
Shall wake me in ecstatic measures,
Far, far removed from mortal pleasures!
In cadence rich, in cadence strong,
Proving the wondrous witcheries of song!
I hear her voice! thy 'sunny dome,'
Thy 'caves of ice,' aloud repeat,
Vibrations, maddening sweet!
Calling the visionary wanderer home.
She sings of thee, O! favoured child
Of minstrelsy, *sublimely wild!*
Of thee, whose soul can feel the tone
Which gives to airy dreams *a magic all thy own!*

(Wr. 1800, pub. 1801)

90 ODE INSCRIBED TO THE INFANT SON OF S.T. COLERIDGE, ESQ.

Born Sept. 14, 1800, at Keswick, in Cumberland

Spirit of Light! whose eye unfolds
The vast expanse of Nature's plan!
And from thy eastern throne beholds
The mazy paths of the lorn traveller—Man!
To thee I sing! *Spirit of Light*, to thee
Attune the varying strain of wood-wild minstrelsy!

O Power Creative!—but for Thee
Eternal Chaos all things would enfold;
And black as Erebus this system be,
In its ethereal space—benighted—rolled.
But for thy influence, e'en *this day*
Would slowly, sadly, pass away;
Nor proudly mark the Mother's tear of joy,
The smile seraphic of the baby boy,
The Father's eyes, in fondest transport taught
To beam with tender hope—to speak the enraptured thought.

To thee I sing, Spirit of Light! to thee
Attune the strain of wood-wild minstrelsy.
Thou sail'st o'er Skiddaw's heights sublime,
Swift borne upon the wings of joyous time!
The sunny train, with widening sweep,
Rolls blazing down the misty-mantled steep;
And far and wide its rosy ray
Flushes the dewy-silvered breast of day!
Hope-fostering day! which Nature bade impart
Heaven's proudest rapture to the parent's heart.
Day! first ordained to see the baby prest
Close to its beauteous mother's throbbing breast;
While instinct, in its laughing eyes, foretold
The mind susceptible—the spirit bold—
The lofty soul—the virtues prompt to trace
The wrongs that haunt mankind o'er life's tempestuous space.

Romantic Mountains! from whose brows sublime
Imagination might to frenzy turn!
Or to the starry worlds in fancy climb,
Scorning this low earth's solitary bourn—
Bold Cataracts! on whose headlong tide
The midnight whirlwinds howling ride—
Calm-bosomed Lakes! that trembling hail
The cold breath of the morning gale;
And on your lucid mirrors wide display,
In colours rich, in dewy lustre gay,
Mountains and woodlands, as the dappled dawn
Flings its soft pearl-drops on the summer lawn;

Or paly moonlight, rising slow,
While o'er the hills the evening zephyrs blow:—
Ye all shall lend your wonders—all combine
To bless the baby boy with harmonies divine.

O Baby! when thy unchained tongue
   Shall, lisping, speak thy fond surprise;
When the rich strain thy father sung,
   Shall from thy imitative accents rise;
When through thy soul rapt Fancy shall diffuse
The mightier magic of his loftier Muse;
Thy wakened spirit, wondering, shall behold
Thy native mountains, capped with streamy gold!
Thy native Lakes, their cloud-topped hills among,
O! hills! made sacred by thy parent's song!
Then shall thy soul, legitimate, expand,
And the proud Lyre quick throb at thy command!
And Wisdom, ever watchful o'er thee smile,
His white locks waving to the blast the while;
And pensive Reason, pointing to the sky,
Bright as the morning star her clear broad eye,
Unfold the page of Nature's book sublime,
The lore of every age—the boast of every clime!

Sweet Baby Boy! accept a Stranger's song;
   An untaught Minstrel joys to sing of thee!
And, all alone, her forest haunts among,
   Courts the wild tone of mazy harmony!
A Stranger's song! Babe of the mountain wild,
Greets thee as Inspiration's darling child!
O! may the fine-wrought spirit of thy sire
Awake thy soul and breathe upon thy lyre!
And blest, amid thy mountain haunts sublime,
   Be all thy days, thy rosy infant days,
And may the never-tiring steps of time
   Press lightly on with thee o'er life's disastrous maze.

Ye hills, coeval with the birth of time!
   Bleak summits, linked in chains of rosy light!
   O may your wonders many a year invite
Your native son the breezy path to climb;
Where, in majestic pride of solitude,
   Silent and grand, the hermit Thought shall trace,
   Far o'er the wild infinity of space,
The sombre horrors of the waving wood;
The misty glen; the river's winding way;
The last deep blush of summer's lingering day;
The winter storm, that, roaming unconfined,
Sails on the broad wings of the impetuous wind.

O! whether on the breezy height
Where Skiddaw greets the dawn of light,
Ere the rude sons of labour homage pay
To Summer's flaming eye or Winter's banner grey;
Whether Lodore its silver torrent flings—
The mingling wonders of a thousand springs!
Whether smooth Bassenthwaite, at Eve's still hour,
   Reflects the young moon's crescent pale;
Or meditation seeks her silent bower,
   Amid the rocks of lonely Borrowdale,
Still may thy name survive, sweet Boy! till Time
Shall bend to Keswick's vale—thy Skiddaw's brow sublime!

(1800, repr. 1806)

91 THE HAUNTED BEACH

Upon a lonely desart Beach
   Where the white foam was scattered,
A little shed upreared its head
   Though lofty Barks were shattered.
The Sea-weeds gathering near the door,
   A sombre path displayed;
And, all around, the deafening roar,
Re-echoed on the chalky shore,
   By the green billows made.

Above, a jutting cliff was seen
   Where Sea Birds hovered, craving;
And all around, the crags were bound
   With weeds—for ever waving.
And here and there, a cavern wide
   Its shadowy jaws displayed;
And near the sands, at ebb of tide,
A shivered mast was seen to ride
   Where the green billows strayed.

And often, while the moaning wind
   Stole o'er the Summer Ocean;
The moonlight scene, was all serene,
   The waters scarce in motion:
Then, while the smoothly slanting sand
   The tall cliff wrapped in shade,
The Fisherman beheld a band
Of Spectres, gliding hand in hand—
   Where the green billows played.

And pale their faces were, as snow,
   And sullenly they wandered:

And to the skies with hollow eyes
They looked as though they pondered.
And sometimes, from their hammock shroud,
They dismal howlings made,
And while the blast blew strong and loud
The clear moon marked the ghastly crowd,
Where the green billows played!

And then, above the haunted hut
The Curlews screaming hovered;
And the low door with furious roar
The frothy breakers covered.
For, in the Fisherman's lone shed
A murdered Man was laid,
With ten wide gashes in his head
And deep was made his sandy bed
Where the green billows played.

A Shipwrecked Mariner was he,
Doomed from his home to sever;
Who swore to be through wind and sea
Firm and undaunted ever!
And when the wave resistless rolled,
About his arm he made
A packet rich of Spanish gold,
And, like a British sailor, bold,
Plunged, where the billows played!

The Spectre band, his messmates brave
Sunk in the yawning ocean,
While to the mast he lashed him fast
And braved the storm's commotion.
The winter moon, upon the sand
A silvery carpet made,
And marked the Sailor reach the land,
And marked his murderer wash his hand
Where the green billows played.

And since that hour the Fisherman
Has toiled and toiled in vain!
For all the night, the moony light
Gleams on the spectred main!
And when the skies are veiled in gloom,
The Murderer's liquid way
Bounds o'er the deeply yawning tomb,
And flashing fires the sands illume,
Where the green billows play!

Full thirty years his task has been,
Day after day more weary;

For Heaven designed, his guilty mind
   Should dwell on prospects dreary.
Bound by a strong and mystic chain,
   He has not power to stray;
But, destined misery to sustain,
He wastes, in Solitude and Pain—
   A loathsome life away.

(1800)

92 WINKFIELD PLAIN; OR, A DESCRIPTION OF A CAMP IN THE YEAR 1800

Tents, *marquees*, and baggage-wagons;
Suttling houses; beer in flagons;
Drums and trumpets; singing, firing;
Girls seducing; *beaux* admiring;
Country lasses, gay and smiling;
City-lads their hearts beguiling;
Dusty roads, and horses frisky;
Many an Eton boy, in whisky;
Taxed-carts, full of farmers' daughters;
Brutes to kill, and man, who slaughters;
Public-houses, booths, and castles;
Belles of fashion, serving vassals;
Dowagers of sixty, simpering;
Misses for *'their soldiers'* wimpering;
Princesses with heavenly faces;
Beauteous children of the Graces:
Britain's pride, and Virtue's treasure;
Fair and gracious beyond measure;
Aid-de-camps; and *royal* pages;
Prudes and vestals of all ages;
Old coquettes, and matrons surly;
Sounds of distant *hurly burly*;
Mingled sounds of uncouth singing;
Carts, *all sorts* of forage bringing;
Sociables, and horses weary;
Houses warm and dresses airy;
Loads of fattened poultry; pleasure
Served *(for money)* without measure;
Tradesmen leaving shops, and seeming
More of *war* than *business* dreaming.
Martial sounds, and braying asses:
Noise *that every noise surpasses*;
All confusion, din, and riot;
Nothing clean, and nothing quiet.

(1800, repr. 1804)

ANN RADCLIFFE (née WARD) (1764 – 1823)

She was born in London. Her father, William, was a haberdasher in Holborn. The family moved to Bath in 1772 where her father managed a shop selling Wedgwood china. In 1787 she married William Radcliffe. She published *The Castles of Athlin and Dunbayne* (1789) and *A Sicilian Romance*, 2 vols (1790). Her next three novels established her reputation, were highly profitable, and are still regarded as important milestones in the development of 'Gothic horror' fiction: *The Romance of the Forest*, 3 vols (1791), *The Mysteries of Udolpho*, 4 vols (1794), *The Italian*, 3 vols (1797). *The Romance of the Forest* and *The Mysteries of Udolpho* are also important for the incorporation of verse in novels and provided many stock ingredients for poems in the 1790s. (Coleridge's 'The Mad Monk' originally appeared in *The Morning Post*, 13 October 1800, as 'The Voice from the Side of Etna; or The Mad Monk: An Ode in Mrs Radcliff's Manner', and Wordsworth's 'The Borderers' may have been influenced by *The Romance of the Forest.*) Success, shyness, or possible pressure from her husband, led to her virtual retirement from literary society (of which she was never an active member). She also wrote important travel accounts of her journeys to Germany, the Lake District and the south coast. A final novel, *Gaston de Blondeville*, written in 1802, was published posthumously in 4 vols (1826), together with unpublished travel accounts, poetry and a memoir. *The Poems*..., London 1816, is probably an unauthorised reprinting of poems from the novels.

93 TO THE VISIONS OF FANCY

Dear, wild illusions of creative mind!
   Whose varying hues arise to Fancy's art,
And by her magic force are swift combined
   In forms that please, and scenes that touch the heart:
Oh! whether at her voice ye soft assume
   The pensive grace of sorrow drooping low;
Or rise sublime on terror's lofty plume,
   And shake the soul with wildly thrilling woe;
Or, sweetly bright, your gayer tints ye spread,
   Bid scenes of pleasure steal upon my view,
Love wave his purple pinions o'er my head,
   And wake the tender thought to passion true;
O! still—ye shadowy forms! attend my lonely hours,
Still chase my real cares with your illusive powers!

(1791)

94 SONG OF A SPIRIT

In the sightless air I dwell,
   On the sloping sun-beams play;
Delve the cavern's inmost cell,
   Where never yet did day-light stray:

Dive beneath the green sea waves,
And gambol in briny deeps;
Skim every shore that Neptune laves,
From Lapland's plains to India's steeps.

Oft I mount with rapid force
Above the wide earth's shadowy zone;
Follow the day-star's flaming course
Through realms of space to thought unknown:

And listen oft celestial sounds
That swell the air unheard of men,
As I watch my nightly rounds
O'er woody steep, and silent glen.

Under the shade of waving trees,
On the green bank of fountain clear,
At pensive eve I sit at ease,
While dying music murmurs near.

And oft, on point of airy clift,
That hangs upon the western main,
I watch the gay tints passing swift,
And twilight veil the liquid plain.

Then, when the breeze has sunk away,
And ocean scarce is heard to lave,
For me the sea-nymphs softly play
Their dulcet shells beneath the wave.

Their dulcet shells! I hear them now,
Slow swells the strain upon mine ear;
Now faintly falls—now warbles low,
Till rapture melts into a tear.

The ray that silvers o'er the dew,
And trembles through the leafy shade,
And tints the scene with softer hue,
Calls me to rove the lonely glade;

Or hie me to some ruined tower,
Faintly shown by moon-light gleam,
Where the lone wanderer owns my power
In shadows dire that substance seem;

In thrilling sounds that murmur woe,
And pausing silence make more dread;
In music breathing from below
Sad solemn strains, that wake the dead.

Unseen I move—unknown am feared!
  Fancy's wildest dreams I weave;
And oft by bards my voice is heard
  To die along the gales of eve.

(1791)

95 MORNING, ON THE SEA SHORE

What print of fairy feet is here
On Neptune's smooth and yellow sands?
  What midnight revel's airy dance,
  Beneath the moon-beams' trembling glance,
Has blest these shores?—What sprightly bands
    Have chased the waves unchecked by fear?
Whoe'er they were they fled from morn,
  For now all silent and forlorn
These tide-forsaken sands appear—
  Return, sweet sprites! the scene to cheer!

In vain the call!—Till moonlight's hour
Again diffuse its softer power,
Titania, nor her fairy loves,
Emerge from India's spicy groves.
  Then, when the shadowy hour returns,
When silence reigns o'er air and earth,
  And every star in aether burns,
They come to celebrate their mirth;
  In frolic ringlet trip the gróund,
Bid Music's voice on Silence win,
  Till magic echoes answer round—
Thus do their festive rites begin.

O fairy forms! so coy to mortal ken,
  Your mystic steps to poets only shown,
O! lead me to the brook, or hallowed glen,
  Retiring far, with winding woods o'ergrown!
    Where'er ye best delight to rule;
  If in some forest's lone retreat,
  Thither conduct my willing feet
    To the light brink of fountain cool,
  Where, sleeping in the midnight dew,
  Lie Spring's young buds of every hue,
    Yielding their sweet breath to the air;
  To fold their silken leaves from harm,
  And their chill heads in moonshine warm,
    To bright Titania's tender care.

There, to the night-bird's plaintive chaunt
   Your carols sweet ye love to raise,
   With oaten reed and pastoral lays;
And guard with forceful spell her haunt,
   Who, when your antic sports are done,
Oft lulls ye in the lily's cell,
Sweet flower! that suits your slumbers well,
   And shields ye from the rising sun.
When not to India's steeps ye fly
   After twilight and the moon,
In honeyed buds ye love to lie,
   While reigns supreme Light's fervid noon;
Nor quit the cell where peace pervades
Till night leads on the dews and shades.

E'en now your scenes enchanted meet my sight!
      I see the earth unclose, the palace rise,
The high dome swell, and long arcades of light
   Glitter among the deep embowering woods,
   And glance reflected from the trembling floods!
While to soft lutes the portals wide unfold,
      And fairy forms, of fine aetherial dyes,
      Advance with frolic step and laughing eyes,
Their hair with pearl, their garments decked with gold;
Pearls that in Neptune's briny waves they sought,
And gold from India's deepest caverns brought.
Thus your light visions to my eyes unveil,
Ye sportive pleasures, sweet illusions, hail!
   But ah! at morn's first blush again ye fade!
So from youth's ardent gaze life's landscape gay,
   And forms in Fancy's summer hues arrayed,
Dissolve at once in air at Truth's resplendent day!

(1791)

96 RONDEAU

Soft as yon silver ray, that sleeps
Upon the ocean's trembling tide;
Soft as the air, that lightly sweeps
Yon sail, that swells in stately pride:

Soft as the surge's stealing note,
That dies along the distant shores,
Or warbled strain, that sinks remote—
So soft the sigh my bosom pours!

True as the wave to Cynthia's ray,
True as the vessel to the breeze,
True as the soul to music's sway,
Or music to Venetian seas:

Soft as yon silver beams, that sleep
Upon the ocean's trembling breast;
So soft, so true, fond Love shall weep,
So soft, so true, with *thee* shall rest.

(1794)

97 THE SEA-MEW

Forth from her cliffs sublime the sea-mew goes
To meet the storm, rejoicing! To the woods
She gives herself; and, borne above the peaks
Of highest head-lands, wheels among the clouds,
And hears Death's voice in thunder roll around,
While the waves far below, driven on the shore,
Foaming with pride and rage, make hollow moan.
Now, tossed along the gale from cloud to cloud,
She turns her silver wings touched by the beam,
That through a night of vapours darts its long,
Level line; and, vanishing 'mid the gloom,
Enters the secret region of the storm;
But soon again appearing, forth she moves
Out from the mountainous shapes of other clouds,
And, sweeping down them, hastens to new joys.
It was the wailing of the deep she heard!
No fears repel her: when the tumult swells,
Even as the spirit-stirring trumpet glads
The neighing war-horse, is the sound to her.
O'er the waves hovering, while they lash the rocks,
And lift, as though to reach her, their chafed tops,
Dashing the salt foam o'er her downy wings,
Higher she mounts, and from her feathers shakes
The shower, triumphant. As they sink, she sinks,
And with her long plumes sweeps them in their fall,
As if in mockery; then, as they retreat,
She dances o'er them, and with her shrill note
Dares them, as in scorn.

It is not thus she meets their summer smiles;
Then, skimming low along the level tide,
She dips the last point of her crescent wings,
At measured intervals, with playful grace,
And rises, as retreating to her home

High on yon 'pending rock, but poised awhile
In air, as though enamoured of the scene,
She drops, at once, and settles on the sea,
On the green waves, transparent then she rides,
And breathes their freshness, trims her plumage white,
And, listening to the murmur of the surge,
Doth let them bear her wheresoe'er they will.

Oh! bird beloved of him, who, absent long
From his dear native land, espies thee ere
The mountain tops o'er the far waters rise,
And hails thee as the harbinger of home!
Thou bear'st to him a welcome on thy wings.
His white sail o'er the horizon thou hast seen
And hailed it, with thy oft-repeated cry,
Announcing England. 'England is near!' he cries,
And every seaman's heart an echo beats,
And 'England—England!' sounds along the deck,
Mounts to the shrouds, and finds an answering voice,
Even at the top-mast head, where, posted long,
The 'look out' sailor clings, and with keen eye,
By long experience finely judging made,
Reads the dim characters of air-veiled shores.
O happy bird! whom Nature's changing scenes
Can ever please; who mount'st upon the wind
Of Winter and amid the grandeur soar'st
Of tempests, or sinkest to the peaceful deep,
And float'st with sunshine on the summer calm!
O happy bird! lend my thy pinions now.
Thy joys are mine, and I, like thee, would skim
Along the pleasant curve of the salt bays,
Where the blue seas do now serenely sleep;
Or, when they waken to the Evening breeze,
And every crisping wave reflects her tints
Of rose and amber,—like thee, too, would I
Over the mouths of the sea-rivers float,
Or watch, majestic, on the tranquil tide,
The proud ships follow one another down,
And spread themselves upon the mighty main,
Freighted for shores that shall not dawn on sight,
Till a new sky uplift its burning arch,
And half the globe be transversed. Then to him,
The home-bound seaman, should my joyous flight
Once more the rounding river point,—to him
Who comes, perchance, from coasts of darkness, where
Grim Ruin, from his throne of hideous rocks,
O'ercanopied with pine, or giant larch,
Scowls on the mariner, and Terror wild
Looks through the parting gloom with ghastly eye,

Listens to woods, that groan beneath the storm,
And starts to see the river-cedar fall.

How sweet to him, who from such strands returns,
How sweet to glide along his homeward stream
By well-known meads and woods and village cots,
That lie in peace around the ivied spire
And ancient parsonage, where the small, fresh stream
Gives a safe haven to the humbler barks
At anchor, just as last he viewed the scene.
And soft as then upon the surface lies
The sunshine, and as sweet the landscape
Smiles, as on that day he sadly bade farewell
To those he loved. Just so it smiles, and yet
How many other days and months have fled,
What shores remote his steps have wandered o'er,
What scenes of various life unfolded strange,
Since that dim yesterday! The present scene
Unchanged, though fresh, appears the only truth,
And all the interval a dream! May those
He loves still live, as lives the landscape now;
And may to-morrow's sun light the thin clouds
Of doubt with rainbow-hues of hope and joy!

Bird! I would hover with thee o'er the deck,
Till a new tide with thronging ships should tremble;
Then, frightened at their strife, with thee I'd fly
To the free waters and the boundless skies,
And drink the light of heaven and living airs;
Then with thee haunt the seas and sounding shores,
And dwell upon the mountain's beaked top,
Where nought should come but thou and the wild winds.
There would I listen, sheltered in our cell,
The tempest's voice, while midnight wraps the world
But, if a moon-beam pierced the clouds, and shed
Its sudden gleam upon the foaming waves,
Touching with pale light each sharp line of cliff,
Whose head towered darkly, which no eye could trace,—
Then downward I would wheel amid the storm,
And watch, with untired gaze, the embattled surges
Pouring in deep array, line after line,
And hear their measured war-note sound along
The groaning coast, whereat the winds above
Answer the summons, and each secret cave,
Untrod by footsteps, and each precipice,
That oft had on the unconscious fisher frowned,
And every hollow bay and utmost cape
Sighs forth a fear for the poor mariner.
He, meanwhile, hears the sound o'er waters wide;
Lashed to the mast, he hears, and thinks of home.

O bird! lend me thy wings,
That swifter than the blast I may out-fly
Danger, and from yon port the life-boat call.
And see! e'en now the guardian bark rides o'er
The mountain-billows, and descends through chasms
Where lurks Destruction eager for his prey,
With eyes of flashing fire and foamy jaws.
He, by strange storm-lights shown, uplifts his head,
And, from the summit of each rising wave,
Darts a grim glance upon the daring crew,
And sinks the way their little boat must go!
But she, with blessings armed, best shield! as if
Immortal, surmounts the abyss, and rides
The watery ridge upon her pliant oars,
Which conquer the wild, raging element
And that dark demon, with angelic power.
Wave after wave, he sullenly retreats,
With oft repeated menace, and beholds
The poor fisherman, with all his fellows,
Borne from his grasp in triumph to the shore—
There Hope stands watchful, and her call is heard
Wafted on wishes of the crowd. Hark! hark!
Is that her voice rejoicing? 'Tis her song
Swells high upon the gale, and 'tis her smile,
That gladdens the thick darkness. THEY ARE SAVED.

Bird of the winds and waves and lonely shores,
Of loftiest promontories—and clouds,
And tempests—Bird of the sun-beam, that seeks
Thee through the storm, and glitters on thy wings!
Bird of the sun-beam and the azure calm,
Of the green cliff, hung with gay summer plants,
Who lov'st to sit in stillness on the bough,
That leans far o'er the sea, and hearest there
The chasing surges and the hushing sounds,
That float around thee, when tall shadows tremble,
And the rock-weeds stream lightly on the breeze.
O bird of joy! what wanderer of air
Can vie with thee in grandeur of delights,
Whose home is on the precipice, whose sport
Is on the waves? O happy, happy bird!
Lend me thy wings, and let thy joys be mine!

(Wr. 1794–1800?, pub. 1826)

AMELIA ALDERSON

AMELIA ALDERSON (later OPIE) (1769 – 1853)

She was born in Norwich and early came into contact with Dissenting and non-Dissenting radicals. She was admired by Godwin whom she had met in 1794. He wrote a now lost love poem to her, probably in February 1796, which complicates the now discounted story of his possible proposal to her. She wrote verse from as early as 1790, some of which is lost, and contributed to the Norwich-based Dissenting periodical, *The Cabinet*, 3 vols (1795) and to Southey's *Annual Anthology*, 2 vols (1799–1800). She married the painter John Opie in 1798 (a manuscript novel, *The Painter and his Wife*, is lost). She distanced herself from the radicals (though, like other women who did the same, she continued to be active in the anti-slavery campaigns). After 1800 she published most of her verse in the *European Magazine* and several annuals. She published *The Father and Daughter* (1801), *Adeline Mowbray* (1804), *Poems*, London 1802, and *The Warrior's Return*..., London 1808. Her husband died in 1807 and she edited his *Lectures on Painting*, London 1809. She became a Quaker in 1825 and continued to be active in reform rather than radicalism.

98 TO TWILIGHT

Friend of the pensive wanderer, Twilight, hail!
I joy to see thee roll thy sea of clouds
  Athwart the crimson throne
  Of the departing sun.

For then what various objects, dimly seen,
By wonder-working Fancy touched, acquire
  An awe-inspiring air,
  And urge Fear's hurried step.

Lo! thine attendant, the low-sailing bat,
Flaps his brown wing, begins his circling flight;
  E'en Midnight's tuneful bird,
  To hail thee, pours her strain.

I love thy simple garb; no brilliant stars
Adorn thy dusky vest, unlike to that
  Worn by thy sister Night,
  Save when she reigns in storms.

Nor canst thou boast the many-tinted robe
Worn by thy beauteous herald, dewy Eve,
  Thine is a veil of grey,
  Meet for the cloistered maid.

Thou nurse of saddening thoughts, prolong thy stay,
Let me adore thee still! Eve's glowing grace,
  Night's fire-embroidered vest,
  Alike displease my eye;

For I am Sorrow's child, and thy cold showers,
Thy mist-encircled forms, thy doubtful shapes,
Wake a responsive chord
Within my troubled soul.

For oh! to me futurity appears
Wrapt in a chilling veil of glooms and mists,
Nor seems one tint or star
To deck her furrowed brow,

But slowly cross her path, imperfect shapes
Of danger, sorrow, frenzy, and despair,
Force their uneasy way,
And pale my cold, sunk cheek.

But see—the unwelcome moon unveils her head,
(Those hours are gone in which I hailed her beams)
Distinctness spreads around,
And mimic day appears.

I loathe the cheerful sight, as still my fate,
O Twilight! bears a hue resembling thine;
And envy-struck, I shun
The scene I cannot share.

I'll to my couch, yet not alas to rest;
By artificial gloom I'll suit my soul,
And e'en from pity hide
My dim and sleepless eyes.

(Wr. 1792, pub. 1799)

99 ODE TO BORROWDALE IN CUMBERLAND

Hail, Derwent's beauteous pride!
Whose charms rough rocks in threatening grandeur guard,
Whose entrace seems to mortals barred,
But to the Genius of the storm thrown wide.

He on thy rock's dread height,
Reclined beneath his canopy of clouds,
His form in darkness shrouds,
And frowns as fixt to keep thy beauties from the sight.

But rocks and storms are vain:
Midst mountains rough and rude
Man's daring feet intrude,
Till, lo! upon the ravished eye
Burst thy clear stream, thy smiling sky,
Thy wooded valley, and thy matchless plain.

Bright vale! the Muse's choicest theme,
My morning thought, my midnight dream;
Still memory paints thee, smiling scene,
Still views the robe of purest green,
Refreshed by beauty-shedding rains,
Which wraps thy flower-enamelled plains;
Still marks thy mountains' fronts sublime,
Force graces from the hand of time;
Still I thy rugged rocks recall,
Which seem as nodding to their fall,
Whose wonders fixed my aching sight,
Till terror yielded to delight,
And my surprises, pleasures, fears,
Were told by slow delicious tears.

But suddenly the smiling day
That cheered the valley, flies away;
The wooded rocks, the rapid stream,
No longer boast the noon-tide beam;
But storms athwart the mountains sail,
And darkly brood o'er Borrowdale.
The frightened swain his cottage seeks,
Ere the thick cloud in terror speaks:—
And see, pale lightning flashes round!
While as the thunder's awful sound
On Echo's pinion widely flies,
Yon cataract's roar unheeded dies;...
And thee, Sublimity! I hail,
Throned on the gloom of Borrowdale.

But soon the thunder dies away,
The flash withdraws its fearful ray;
Again upon the silver stream
Waves in bright wreaths the noon-tide beam.

O scene sequestered, varied, wild,
Scene formed to soothe Affliction's child,
How blest were I to watch each charm
That decks thy vale in storm or calm!

To see Aurora's hand unbind
The mists by night's chill power confined;
Upon the mountain's dusky brow
Then mark their colours as they flow,
Gliding the colder West to seek,
As from the East day's splendours break.

Now the green plain enchants the sight,
Adorned with spots of yellow light;
While, by its magic influence, shade

With contrast seems each charm to aid,
And clothes the woods in deeper dyes,
To suit the azure-vested skies.
While, lo! the lofty rocks above,
Where proudly towers the bird of Jove;
See from the view yon radiant cloud
His broad and sable pinions shroud,
Till, as he onward wings his flight,
He vanishes in floods of light;
Where feathered clouds on aether sail,
And glittering hang o'er Borrowdale....

Or, at still midnight's solemn hour,
When the dull bat revolves no more,
In search of nature's awful grace,
I'd go, with slow and cautious pace,
Where the loud torrent's foaming tide
Lashes the rock's uneven side,...
That rock which, o'er the stream below
Bending its moss-clad crumbling brow,
Makes pale with fear the wanderer's cheek,
Nor midnight's silence fails to break
By fragments from its aged head,
Which, rushing to the river's bed,
Cause, as they dash the waters round,
A dread variety of sound;
While I the gloomy grandeur hail,
And awe-struck rove through Borrowdale.

Yes, scene sequestered, varied, wild,
So formed to soothe Affliction's child,
Sweet Borrowdale! to thee I'll fly,
To hush my bosom's ceaseless sigh.
If yet in Nature's store there be
One kind heart-healing balm for me,
Now the long hours are told by sighs,
And sorrow steals health's crimson dyes,—
If aught can smiles and bloom restore,
Ah! surely thine's the precious power!

Then take me to thy world of charms,
And hush my tortured breast's alarms;
Thy scenes with unobtrusive art
Shall steal the mourner from her heart,...
The hands in sorrow claspt unclose,
Bid her sick soul on Heaven repose,
And, soothed by time and nature, hail
Health, peace, and hope in Borrowdale.

(Wr. 1794, pub. 1808)

Lo! Winter drives his horrors round;
Wide o'er the rugged soil they fly;
In their cold spells each stream is bound,
While at the magic of their eye
Each sign of Spring's gay beauty fades,
And one white wild the aching sight invades.
It is the time for Woe to reign,
And hark! she bids her haggard train,
Pale poverty and want, appear,
Disease, their darling child, draw near,
And, grateful for the favouring hour,
They feel, they seize, they riot, in their power.
But Winter! not to thee alone
Their heart-appalling sway they owe,
For they to war's despotic throne
As tributary subjects bow;
War, who bids trembling Europe gasp,
With wild convulsions in his bloody grasp.
Whence yonder groans? O wretched land!
Poland, from thee, alas! they came,
A despot speaks, and lo! a band,
Blaspheming pure Religion's name,
Bid cold, deliberate murder live,
And death's dread stroke to helpless thousands give.
And see, on Belgia's reeking plain,
Alternate horrors rise and reign!
What mingled sounds affright the ear!
Now, we the song of victory hear,
And now, despair's appalling tone,
And now, of *death* the deep sepulchral groan.
Freedom! for whose dear sake I'd dare
Each various ill that tortures life,
Though I thy matchless victories share,
While, towering 'midst the bloody strife,
I see thy form sublime, acquire
New power to charm, new beauty to inspire;
I cannot smile; I cannot join
The song of triumph! though thy foes,
Celestial power! are also mine;
And though I weep for all thy woes,
Yet I thy *triumphs* too must weep,
And in my tears thy bloody laurels steep.
For who are they that madly bear
Against thy sons the venal spear?
Are they not men?—then say, what power
Can bid my bosom mourn no more;
O where's the fiend-delighting ban

Forbidding Man to weep for Slaughtered Man!
E'en Victory, when reflection's voice
Breathes in her ear 'thy brothers die,'
Shall bid her sons no more rejoice,
But change her shouts for pity's sigh:
She will her breast in anguish beat,
And wear the sombrous aspect of *defeat*.
O Britain! ill-starred land! no more
Must Peace to thee her olive bear,
But on thy once-triumphant shore,
Must we behold the form of fear
Expecting, on the swelling tide,
To see the Foe in proud defiance ride!
Avert the threatening, awful ill;
For fraught with power, and fraught with will
To make thy hardiest veterans die,
A lurking fiend, alas! is nigh,
Who threatens on thy sons to pour
The fatal cloud thou bad'st on Gallia lower.
Lo! Famine spreads her banners wide;
She comes arrayed in horrid state;
But, not to humble Gallia's pride,
And on the rear of *victory* wait;
She comes the *humbled* to subdue,
And twine round *fading* wreaths, death's baleful yew.
She comes to Britain!—at the thought,
Winter! thy scene with horrors fraught,
Fades from my sight—the present ill
Appears to lose its power to kill:
To *future* scenes pale Fancy flies,
Lifts her dim tearful eyes to heaven, and dies.

(1795)

101 STANZAS WRITTEN UNDER AEOLUS'S HARP

Come, ye whose hearts the tyrant sorrows wound;
Come, ye whose breasts the tyrant passions tear,
And seek this harp,... in whose still-varying sound
Each woe its own appropriate plaint may hear.

Solemn and slow yon murmuring cadence rolls,
Till on the attentive ear it dies away,...
To your fond griefs responsive, ye, whose souls
O'er loved lost friends regret's sad tribute pay.

AMELIA ALDERSON

But hark! in regular progression move
Yon silver sounds, and mingle as they fail,...
Do they not wake thy trembling nerves, O Love,
And into warmer life thy feelings call?

Again it speaks,... but, shrill and swift, the tones
In wild disorder strike upon the ear:
Pale Frenzy listens,... kindred wildness owns,
And starts appalled the well known sounds to hear:

Lo! e'en the gay, the giddy and the vain
In deep delight these vocal wires attend,...
Silent and breathless watch the varying strain,
And pleased the vacant toils of mirth suspend.

So, when the lute on Memnon's statue hung
At day's first rising strains melodious poured
Untouched by mortal hands, the gathering throng
In silent wonder listened and adored.

But the wild cadence of these trembling strings
The enchantress Fancy with most rapture hears;
At the sweet sound to grasp her wand she springs,
And lo! her band of airy shapes appears!

She, rapt enthusiast, thinks the melting strains
A choir of angels breathe, in bright array
Bearing on radiant clouds to yon blue plains
A soul just parted from its silent clay.

And oft at eve her wild creative eye
Sees to the gale their silken pinions stream,
While in the quivering trees soft zephyrs sigh,
And through the leaves disclose the moon's pale beam.

O breathing instrument! be ever near
While to the pensive muse my vows I pay;
Thy softest call the inmost soul can hear,
Thy faintest breath can Fancy's pinions play.

And when art's laboured strains my feelings tire,
To seek thy simple music shall be mine;
I'll strive to win its graces to my lyre,
And make my plaintive lays enchant like thine.

(1795, rev. and repr. 1802)

JANE WEST (née ILIFFE) (1758 – 1852)

She was born in London but moved to Desborough, Northamptonshire when she was about eleven. She had married Thomas West by 1783 and lived at Little Bowden. She wrote verse from early youth and published *Miscellaneous Poetry*..., (1786), *Miscellaneous Poems*..., York 1791, and *Poems and Plays*, 4 vols (1799–1805), *The Mother*... (1809). She published verse in the *Gentleman's Magazine* in 1800. She also wrote novels, *The Advantages of Education*..., 2 vols (1793), *A Gossip's Story*..., 2 vols (1796), *A Tale of the Times*..., 3 vols (1799). (For her possible influence on Jane Austen, see J.M.S. Tomkins, *Review of English Studies*, 16 (1940), pp.33–43, M. Melander, *Studia Neophilologica* 22 (1950), pp.146–70, K.L. Moler, *Review of English Studies*, new series, 17 (1966), pp.413–19. She also published two conduct works, *Letters Addressed to a Young Man*..., 3 vols (1801) and *Letters to a Young Lady*..., 3 vols (1806). She corresponded with Bishop Percy (whose wife came from Desborough) and visited him in Dromore in 1810. She died at Little Bowden in 1852.

102 ODE TO THE IMAGINATIONS

Ye pleasing phantoms, soothing forms,
   Who people Fancy's sunny beam,
When Hope the buoyant bosom warms,
   And Joy inspires the raptured dream;
Ye who the fancied laurels wreathe,
   Which animate the brave to dare;
Ye who the soft enchantments breathe,
   Which spreads perfection round the fair;
Ye echoes of the world's acclaim,
Ye visionary shades of unsubstantial fame!

Deluders of the mind! I own
   Life owes to you its happiest hours;
High seated on your elfin throne,
   Ye rival Nature's plastic powers;
For ye can o'er creation throw
   Charms which reality denies;
And boast, amid the polar snow,
   Arcadian groves, Hesperian skies;
Oh crown me with your thornless rose,
Oh waft me to those isles, where joy's full current flows.

Benignant to a wretch distressed,
   For me your magic simples cull;
And when Remembrance stings this breast,
   With opiate charms my feelings lull:
Bid these dim eyes no longer mourn
   The faithless friend, or lover, lost;
And to its hopeless, joyless urn
   Confine Affection's wailing ghost;
Bid Memory drop her useless hoard
Of vows that could not bind, of looks in vain adored.

Oh from a heart too much deceived,
   Banish the hill, the lawn, the grove,
Where fond Credulity believed,
   Where Falsehood wore the mask of Love.
Nor let it paint the form divine,
   Where every virtue seemed to dwell;
Or tell how from his lips benign
   The honeyed accents graceful fell:
Oh let not his idea reign,
E'en if my vacant heart no other form retain!

Come—bid the sense of honour rise;
   Let female pride and female shame
Disperse in air those guilty sighs,
   That heave but at a traitor's name.
Who all my confidence and truth
   With undeserved wrong repaid
Who for my unsuspicious youth
   The artful snare of ruin laid:
Oh bid me a just vengeance take,
Bid this heart cease to love, or in the struggle break!

(1793)

103 SONNET

Her hair dishevelled, and her robe untied,
   Cassandra rushed amongst the festal train,
   What time young Paris sang his nuptial strain,
And led to Priam's roof the Spartan bride:
Of certain woes that must that crime betide
   The holy virgin prophesied in vain;
   Her warning voice could no attention gain
Till Pyrrhus levelled Ilium's towering pride.
   Ah! in the horrors of that night aghast,
   What shrieks, prophetic maid, thy truth declared!
And thus when youth beholds Misfortune's blast
   O'erturn the fairy bowers by Fancy reared,
Too late it muses on the precepts sage
Of cool experience, and predictive age.

(1796)

104 SONNET TO MAY

Come May, the empire of the earth assume,
Be crowned with flowers as universal queen;
Take from fresh budded groves their tender green,
Bespangled with Pomona's richest bloom,
And form thy vesture. Let the sun illume
The dew-drops glittering in the blue serene,
And let them hang, like orient pearls, between
Thy locks besprent with Flora's best perfume.
Attend your sovereign's steps, ye balmy gales!
O'er her ambrosial floods of fragrance pour;
Let livelier verdure animate the vales,
And brighter hues embellish every flower;
And hark, the concert of the woodland hails,
All gracious May! thy presence, and thy power.

(1799)

ANNA MARIA PORTER (1780 – 1832)

She was born in Durham and went to school in Edinburgh. By 1793 she was in London and published *Artless Tales*. That year she also contributed a poem 'To Night', heavily indebted to Radcliffe, to the *Lady's Magazine*, XXIV (1793), pp.381–2. She also contributed 'Address to Summer', to the *Universal Magazine* (1795), i.369, and many poems to *The Monthly Visitor*, which were later collected in *The Parnassian Garland*. . . , London 1797. She also published *Ballad Romances, and Other Poems*, London 1811. R.A. Davenport, who had also been a contributor to *The Monthly Visitor*, printed further poems, in his *Elegant Extracts*, 12 vols in 6, Chiswick 1827. She also contributed to several annuals. She was, however, mostly known for her novels, which were highly successful. She died of typhus in 1832. Her sister, Jane Porter (1776–1850), also wrote novels and poems.

105 ADDRESS TO POESY

Hail, heavenly maid! thou source of thousand joys!
Say, can a humble suppliant's untaught voice
Be heard by thee, where throned in vernal bowers
Of living laurel, near Pierian fount,
O'er the immortal chords that string thy lyre,
Thy fingers sweep, and a whole world resounds
To the vibrations of thy tuneful song?
Ah! if thine ear can lift a mortal harp,
Bend now to mine, and with benignant eye
Smile on my fond request.—Ambitious wish!—

I ask to catch thy thought-inspiring breath,
To warble trancing lays resembling thine,
The soul of love to melt along my line,
Sigh in each word, and tremble through the song:
I seek the power to touch the gentle heart,
With bleeding sympathy, and kind concern.—
O! for such strains as in the early days
Sighing you breathed into the listening ear
Of widowed Orpheus, on the Thracian shore.
When on his lost Eurydice he called
In sounds, which had they floated on the air
To Pluto's mansions, had once more recalled
Her fleeting spirit! ne'er again to fly!
O! for such lays, as hopeless Petrarch sung
In latter times; when on his darkened soul
The sun of rapture, and of beauty, set
In Laura's grave: when 'neath the pitying moon,
And sighing trees, along the dreary shore,
He strayed alone, and poured upon the cold,
The lifeless urn of her, whom *still* he loved,
The burning gush of agonizing tears!—
Vain, vain the wish; this heart perhaps may feel
As many woes, as the fond bosoms tore
Of Orpheus, and of Petrarch; but it ne'er
Shall sigh its sick soul on the saddened wind,
In tones so touching, so dissolving sweet:
It ne'er shall call a world's unbounded tear,
With sudden grief, and sympathy refined.—
Queen of the human heart, the human mind!
Wilt thou not hear a youthful votary's voice?—
Ah, no! away she turns her frowning face,
And scatters to the wind my useless prayers.
Leave, leave me not for ever sacred muse!
But O! inspire the verse, that sings thy praise;
O! deign to shed upon my lifeless page,
One radiant sparkle from thy kindling eye;
I will no longer ask its *sun* of beams—
No—keep such transport for the happy few
Who at thy side in tender friendship rove,
Through wilds romantic, fairy-painted scenes,
Where never yet has foot unhallowed trod,
Where Philomel for ever weeps her griefs
Soft on the woodland's ear; where, never still,
For ever murmurs the poetic stream;
Where youthful zephyr leans his airy head
On summer's musky breast, or leads her o'er
(With flying footsteps) the blue mountain's top—
Where Fame, a huntress clad in sylvan green,
Calls thy loved train to speed the noble chase,

Herself the inviter, and herself the game:—
Where amid labyrinths of dewy rose,
Of fragrant myrtles, and of blushing vine,
Young Love! encircled by his fairy band,
His light hair waving on his purple cheek,
His waxen bosom bare, his bow unstrung,
His eye all softness, and his breath all balm,
Leads through the mazes of the Lydian dance
The gold-tressed Psyche, and the Graces three,
With looks in dangerous languor sweetly dressed,
And voice tuned only to deceive and please.
Ah! I shall ne'er be with such friendship blessed,
Nor rove through shades that hallow every form—
Yet, while some scanty favours thou wilt grant,
With Fancy I may trace these flowery wilds;
For, at *her* word, what magic pageants rise!
Unnumbered as the light-illumined clouds
That float beneath the sun's effulgent ray;
At *her* command along the rushy moor,
The broad lake spreads, and o'er its twilight edge,
Wave the young poplar, and the willow pale,—
Here, rocks ascend, in grand confusion mixed,
O'er whose bold tops, in flowering cistus clad,
Hang bending firs, and firmly-rooted pines;
Where high in air, the godlike eagle sits,
The Agamemnon of the feathered world
There as the smiling sorceress waves her wing,
Flows out the smooth Savannah's sunny vest,
Robed in such hues as are alternate seen
On the young turtle's gaily-shifting neck.
Here, from the orb of day, meek-flushing, turns
The radiant rose, and bashful hides her charms
In other graces, moss, and vivid leaves—
There, lifts the lily its resplendent head
With conscious dignity, a maiden queen,
She neither seeks, nor shuns, the eye of day.
Fancy can bid the softest zephyr's blow,
Fancy can load them with ten thousand scents,
More sweet than all the spicy breath of Inde;
Her word can make a new creation rise,
And mid deep glooms, and sullen-roaring waves,
(When o'er the scene her magic robe is flung)
She can on sight, on smell, and on the ear,
Pour beauty, balm, and liquid-lulling sounds.
But, ah! the enchantress wants for me the power
To make me dream, I hear *thy* dulcet voice
When prompted by the whispers of my soul,
And sighing love, I wake my simple reed.

(1797)

106 SONNET TO A SEA-GULL WRITTEN ON THE SEA SHORE

Now rave the wild winds o'er the watery waste,
And, springing from the wave, the Sea-gull's form
Flushes its whiteness on the darkening storm.—
Ah, happy bird! where do your pinions haste?
To some strong isle by deathless rocks embraced.
Dauntless you soar, and on some warlike tower,
Or awful height, upon the rude beach place
You sit, and listen to the ocean's roar.
For then, escaped from its destructive power
Sublime in air, the angry winds you hear;
But I, alas! in life's tempestuous hour
See no kind land, no lofty turret near:
Shoreless my sea, and endless is its rage—
O! when will death's dread calm its potent wrath assuage?

(1797)

MARY TIGHE (née BLACHFORD) (1772 – 1810)

She was born in Dublin where she was strictly brought up by her Methodist mother. She married Henry Tighe, a cousin, in 1793. She wrote early verse but it is unlikely that she began *Psyche* in 1795 as has been suggested. It was probably written 1801–03 and was published in a limited edition in 1805. A third edition, London 1811, published after her death, contained previously unpublished poems. Another posthumous work, *Mary, a Series of Reflections during Twenty Years* [ed. William Tighe], Roundwood 1811, contains other poems and is very rare. (The only North American copy is at Harvard.) Her last years were spent in ill health in Dublin and Rosanna, County Wicklow, where the Tighe family had property. There are unpublished Mss. in the National Library of Ireland. Her ill health combined with the erotic subject matter and the Spenserian form of *Psyche* probably added to Keats's interest in her. Felicia Hemans's 'Grave of a Poetess' (*Poems*, copyright edition, Edinburgh 1872, p.411) and Thomas Moore's 'I Saw thy Form in Youthful Prime' (*Poetical Works*, ed. A.D. Godley, London 1910, p.197) similarly testify to the effect of her death on other poets, constituting a possible female counterpart to the fates of Otway, Chatterton and Burns. Linguistically, *Psyche* is important as a significant development in a tradition which used the Spenserian stanza to deal with erotic subjects but mitigated the effects by the use of obsolete vocabulary. In her 'Preface', Mary Tighe states that she deliberately avoided this. The most famous examples of Spenserian 'imitation'—Glocester Ridley, 'Psyche: or, The Great Metamorphosis…', *The Museum*, 3 vols (1746–47), iii.80–97; Thomson's *Castle of Indolence* (1748), Shenstone's *The Schoolmistress* (1742), Beattie's *The Minstrel* (1771–74), and Gavin Turnbull's, 'The Bard', *Poetical Essays*, Glasgow 1788, pp.137–48—had carefully observed archaic poetic usage. For a list of Spenserian imitations in the eighteenth century, see W.L. Phelps, *The Beginnings of the English Romantic Movement*, Boston 1893, pp.175–6. Possible 'English sources' for the poem are Thomas Taylor,

The Fable of Cupid and Psyche..., London 1795, Hudson Gurney, *Cupid and Psyche: A Mythological Tale*..., London 1799. On the significance of the fable for the romantics see Marilyn Butler, *Romantics, Rebels and Reactionaries*, Oxford 1981, pp.132–7. However, by the end of the eighteenth century, it was quite possible to acquire a knowledge of Greco-Roman myth from a wide variety of synopses, compendiums and other source books. (The development of these roughly parallels the development of 'extracts' of English classics—providing a rapid reference, without the boring bits, of Classical and English culture.) In addition, there is considerable evidence that some poets were 'skimmed' by readers in the eighteenth century—Thomson and Akenside certainly were—and any view of sources should take 'extracts' and 'skimming' into account.

107 WRITTEN AT SCARBOROUGH

As musing pensive in my silent home
 I hear far off the sullen ocean's roar,
 Where the rude wave just sweeps the level shore,
Or bursts upon the rocks with whitening foam,
I think upon the scenes my life has known;
 On days of sorrow, and some hours of joy;
 Both which alike time could so soon destroy!
And now they seem a busy dream alone;
While on the earth exists no single trace
 Of all that shook my agitated soul,
 As on the beach new waves for ever roll
And fill their past forgotten brother's place:
 But I, like the worn sand, exposed remain
 To each new storm which frets the angry main.

(Wr. 1796, pub. 1811)

108 SONNET

For me would Fancy now her chaplet twine
 Of Hope's bright blossoms, and Joy's fairy flowers,
 As she was wont to do in gayer hours;
Ill would it suit this brow, where many a line
Declares the spring-time of my life gone by,
 And summer far advanced; what now remain
 Of waining years, should own staid Wisdom's reign.
Shall my distempered heart still idly sigh
For those gay phantoms, chased by sober truth?
 Those forms tumultuous which sick visions bring,
 That lightly flitting on the transient wing
Disturbed the fevered slumbers of my youth?
 Ah, no! my suffering soul at length restored,
 Shall taste the calm repose so oft in vain implored.

(Wr. 1799, pub. 1811)

109 SONNET

Ye dear associates of my gayer hours,
   Ah! whither are you gone? on what light wing
   Is Fancy fled? Mute is the dulcet string
Of long-lost Hope? No more her magic powers
Scatter o'er my lorn path fallacious flowers,
   As she was wont with glowing hand to fling
   Loading with fragrance the soft gales of Spring,
While fondly pointing to fresh blooming bowers,
Now faded, with each dazzling view of bright,
   Delusive pleasure; never more return,
Ye vain, ideal visions of delight!
   For in your absence I have learned to mourn;
To bear the torch of Truth with steady sight,
   And weave the cypress for my future urn.

(Wr. 1800, pub. 1811)

110 *from* PSYCHE, CANTO I [THE ISLAND OF PLEASURE]

   When lo! a gentle breeze began to rise,
   Breathed by obedient Zephyrs round the maid,
   Fanning her bosom with its softest sighs
   Awhile among her fluttering robes it strayed,
   And boldly sportive latent charms displayed:
   And then, as Cupid willed, with tenderest care
   From the tall rock, where weeping she was laid,
   With gliding motion through the yielding air
To Pleasure's blooming isle their lovely charge they bear.

   On the green bosom of the turf reclined,
   They lightly now the astonished virgin lay,
   To placid rest they sooth her troubled mind;
   Around her still with watchful care they stay,
   Around her still in quiet whispers play;
   Till lulling slumbers bid her eyelids close,
   Veiling with silky fringe each brilliant ray,
   While soft tranquillity divinely flows
O'er all her soul serene, in visions of repose.

   Refreshed she rose, and all enchanted gazed
   On the rare beauties of the pleasant scene.
   Conspicuous far a lofty palace blazed
   Upon a sloping bank of softest green;
   A fairer edifice was never seen;
   The high ranged columns own no mortal hand,

But seem a temple meet for Beauty's queen.
Like polished snow the marble pillars stand
In grace attempered majesty sublimely grand.

Gently ascending from a silvery flood,
Above the palace rose the shaded hill,
The lofty eminence was crowned with wood,
And the rich lawns, adorned by nature's skill,
The passing breezes with their odours fill;
Here ever blooming groves of orange glow,
And here all flowers which from their leaves distil
Ambrosial dew in sweet succession blow,
And trees of matchless size a fragrant shade bestow.

The sun looks glorious mid a sky serene,
And bids bright lustre sparkle o'er the tide;
The clear blue ocean at a distance seen
Bounds the gay landscape on the western side,
While closing round it with majestic pride,
The lofty rocks mid citron groves arise;
'Sure some divinity must here reside,'
As tranced in some bright vision, Psyche cries,
And scarce believes the bliss, or trusts her charmed eyes.

When lo! a voice divinely sweet she hears,
From unseen lips proceeds the heavenly sound;
'Psyche approach, dismiss thy timid fears,
At length his bride thy longing spouse has found,
And bids for thee immortal joys abound;
For thee the palace rose at his command,
For thee his love a bridal banquet crowned;
He bids attendant nymphs around thee stand
Prompt every wish to serve, a fond obedient band.'

Increasing wonder filled her ravished soul,
For now the pompous portals opened wide,
There, pausing oft, with timid foot she stole
Through halls high domed, enriched with sculptured pride,
While gay saloons appeared on either side
In splendid vista opening to her sight;
And all with precious gems so beautified,
And furnished with such exquisite delight,
That scarce the beams of heaven emit such lustre bright.

The amethyst was there of violet hue,
And there the topaz shed its golden ray,
The chrysoberyl, and the sapphire blue
As the clear azure of a sunny day,
Or the mild eyes where amorous glances play;

The snow white jasper, and the opal's flame,
The blushing ruby, and the agate grey,
And there the gem which bears his luckless name
Whose death by Phoebus mourned ensured him deathless fame.

There the green emerald, there cornelians glow,
And rich carbuncles pour eternal light,
With all that India and Peru can show,
Or Labrador can give so flaming bright
To the charmed mariner's half dazzled sight:
The coral paved baths with diamonds blaze:
And all that can the female heart delight
Of fair attire, the last recess displays,
And all that Luxury can ask, her eye surveys.

Now through the hall melodious music stole,
And self-prepared the splendid banquet stands,
Self-poured the nectar sparkles in the bowl,
The lute and viol touched by unseen hands
Aid the soft voices of the choral bands;
O'er the full board a brighter lustre beams
Than Persia's monarch at his feast commands:
For sweet refreshment all inviting seems
To taste celestial food, and pure ambrosial streams.

But when meek Eve hung out her dewy star,
And gently veiled with gradual hand the sky,
Lo! the bright folding doors retiring far,
Display to Psyche's captivated eye
All that voluptuous ease could e'er supply
To sooth the spirits in serene repose:
Beneath the velvet's purple canopy
Divinely formed a downy couch arose,
While alabaster lamps a milky light disclose.

Once more she hears the hymeneal strain;
Far other voices now attune the lay;
The swelling sounds approach, awhile remain,
And then retiring faint dissolved away:
The expiring lamps emit a feebler ray,
And soon in fragrant death extinguished lie:
Then virgin terrors Psyche's soul dismay,
When through the obscuring gloom she nought can spy,
But softly rustling sounds declare some Being nigh.

Oh, you for whom I write! whose hearts can melt
At the soft thrilling voice whose power you prove,
You know what charm, unutterably felt,
Attends the unexpected voice of Love:

Above the lyre, the lute's soft notes above,
With sweet enchantment to the soul it steals
And bears it to Elysium's happy grove;
You best can tell the rapture Psyche feels
When Love's ambrosial lip the vows of Hymen seals.

''Tis he, 'tis my deliverer! deep imprest
Upon my heart those sounds I well recal,'
The blushing maid exclaimed, and on his breast
A tear of trembling ecstasy let fall.
But, ere the breezes of the morning call
Aurora from her purple, humid bed,
Psyche in vain explores the vacant hall,
Her tender lover from her arms is fled,
While sleep his downy wings had o'er her eye-lids spread.

(Wr. 1801–1803, pub. 1805)

111 *from* PSYCHE, CANTO II [CUPID ASLEEP]

Allowed to settle on celestial eyes
Soft Sleep exulting now exerts his sway,
From Psyche's anxious pillow gladly flies
To veil those orbs, whose pure and lambent ray
The powers of heaven submissively obey.
Trembling and breathless then she softly rose,
And seized the lamp, where it obscurely lay,
With hand too rashly daring to disclose
The sacred veil which hung mysterious o'er her woes.

Twice, as with agitated step she went,
The lamp expiring shone with doubtful gleam,
As though it warned her from her rash intent:
And twice she paused, and on its trembling beam
Gazed with suspended breath, while voices seem
With murmuring sound along the roof to sigh;
As one just waking from a troublous dream,
With palpitating heart and straining eye,
Still fixed with fear remains, still thinks the danger nigh.

Oh, daring Muse! wilt thou indeed essay
To paint the wonders which that lamp could shew?
And canst thou hope in living words to say
The dazzling glories of that heavenly view?
Ah! well I ween, that if with pencil true
That splendid vision could be well expressed,
The fearful awe imprudent Psyche knew
Would seize with rapture every wondering breast,
When Love's all-potent charms divinely stood confessed.

All imperceptible to human touch,
His wings display celestial essence light,
The clear effulgence of the blaze is such,
The brilliant plumage shines so heavenly bright
That mortal eyes turn dazzled from the sight;
A youth he seems in manhood's freshest years;
Round his fair neck, as clinging with delight,
Each golden curl resplendently appears,
Or shades his darker brow, which grace majestic wears.

Or o'er his guileless front the ringlets bright
Their rays of sunny lustre seem to throw,
That front than polished ivory more white!
His blooming cheeks with deeper blushes glow
Than roses scattered o'er a bed of snow:
While on his lips, distilled in balmy dews,
(Those lips divine that even in silence know
The heart to touch) persuasion to infuse
Still hangs a rosy charm that never vainly sues.

The friendly curtain of indulgent sleep
Disclosed not yet his eyes' resistless sway,
But from their silky veil there seemed to peep
Some brilliant glances with a softened ray,
Which o'er his features exquisitely play,
And all his polished limbs suffuse with light.
Thus through some narrow space the azure day
Sudden its cheerful rays diffusing bright,
Wide darts its lucid beams, to gild the brow of night.

His fatal arrows and celestial bow
Beside the couch were negligently thrown,
Nor needs the god his dazzling arms, to show
His glorious birth, such beauty round him shone
As sure could spring from Beauty's self alone;
The gloom which glowed o'er all of soft desire,
Could well proclaim him Beauty's cherished son;
And Beauty's self will oft these charms admire,
And steal his witching smile, his glance's living fire.

Speechless with awe, in transport strangely lost
Long Psyche stood with fixed adoring eye;
Her limbs immoveable, her senses tossed
Between amazement, fear, and ecstasy,
She hangs enamoured o'er the Deity.
Till from her trembling hand extinguished falls
The fatal lamp—He starts—and suddenly
Tremendous thunders echo through the halls,
While ruin's hideous crash bursts o'er the affrighted walls.

Dread horror seizes on her sinking heart,
A mortal chillness shudders at her breast,
Her soul shrinks fainting from death's icy dart,
The groan scarce uttered dies but half expressed,
And down she sinks in deadly swoon oppressed:
But when at length, awaking from her trance,
The terrors of her fate stand all confessed,
In vain she casts around her timid glance,
The rudely frowning scenes her former joys enhance.

No traces of those joys, alas, remain!
A desert solitude alone appears.
No verdant shade relieves the sandy plain,
The wide-spread waste no gentle fountain cheers,
One barren face the dreary prospect wears;
Nought through the vast horizon meets her eye
To calm the dismal tumult of her fears,
No trace of human habitation nigh,
A sandy wild beneath, above a threatening sky.

(Wr. 1801–1803, pub. 1805)

112 *from* PSYCHE, CANTO III [THE BOWER OF LOOSE DELIGHT]

Quick through the trees a thousand torches blazed
The gloom to banish, and the scene disclose
To Psyche all irresolute, amazed:
A bridge with stately arch at distance rose,
Thither at once the gay assembly goes,
Not unattended by the charmed knight,
Inviting Psyche to partake repose,
Pointing where shone their bower illumined bright,
Their bower so passing fair, the bower of loose Delight.

At length with timid foot the bridge she past,
And to her guardian knight clung fearfully,
While many a doubting glance around she cast,
If still her watchful dove she might espy;
Feebly it seemed on labouring wing to fly,
Till, dazzled by the sudden glare around,
In painful trance is closed its dizzy eye,
And had it not fair Psyche's bosom found,
Its drooping pinion soon had touched the unhallowed ground.

Hence there arose within her heart sore dread
Which no alluring pleasure could dispel;
The splendid hall with luscious banquet spread,
The soft-breathed flutes which in sweet concert swell,

With melody of song unspeakable;
Nor the light dancing troop in roses dressed,
Could chase the terrors which she dared not tell,
While fondly cherished in her anxious breast
She strove in vain to sooth the fluttering bird to rest.

On a soft downy couch the guests are placed,
And close behind them stands their watchful page,
But much his strict attendance there disgraced,
And much was scorned his green and tender age,
His calm fixed eye, and steady aspect sage:
But him nor rude disdain, nor mockery,
Nor soothing blandishments could e'er engage
The wanton mazes of their sports to try,
Or from his lord to turn his firm adhering eye.

White bosomed nymphs around with loosened zones
All on the guests obsequiously tend,
Some sing of love with soft expiring tones,
While Psyche's melting eyes the strain commend;
Some o'er their heads the canopy suspend,
Some hold the sparkling bowl, while some with skill
Ambrosial showers and balmy juices blend,
Or the gay lamps with liquid odours fill
Whose many coloured fires divinest sweets distil.

And now a softer light they seemed to shed,
And sweetest music ushered in their queen:
Her languid steps by winged boys are led,
Who in their semblance might have Cupids been;
Close wrapt in veils her following train was seen;
Herself looked lovely in her loose attire,
Her smiling eyes gave lustre to the scene,
And still, where'er they turned their wanton fire,
Each thrilling nerve confessed the rapture they inspire.

The stranger guests she viewed with welcome glad,
And crowned the banquet with reception sweet,
To fill the glowing bowl her nymphs she bad,
And graceful rising from her splendid seat
She would herself present the sparkling treat;
When lo! the dove alarmed with sudden start,
Spurned the bright cup and dashed it at her feet,
For well he knew 'twas mixed with treacherous art
To sting his Psyche's breast with agonizing smart.

Regardless of her supplicating tears
Each eye with vengeful rage the insult sees,
Her knight's protection now in vain appears;

The offended sovereign anxious to appease,
A thousand hands prepare the dove to seize:
Nor was this all, for as the tumult rose,
Sudden more thick than swarm of summer bees,
The secret dens their venomed hoards disclose,
And horror at the sight her vital spirits froze.

Hissing aloud with undulations dire,
Their forked tongues unnumbered serpents show,
Their tainted breath emitting poisonous fire,
All turn on Psyche as their mortal foe;
But he, whose arm was never weak or slow,
Now rushed before her with resistless spring,
On either side the oft-repeated blow
Repulsed the malice of their deadly sting,
While sparks of wrathful fire from their fierce jaws they fling.

'Fly, Psyche! these are slander's hellish brood!
Contest I know is vain,' her champion cried.
Her passage now the opposing train withstood;
Struck with disgust their hideous forms she spied,
For lo! each silken veil is thrown aside,
And foul deformity, and filth obscene,
With monstrous shapes appear on every side;
But vanished is their fair and treacherous queen,
And with her every charm that decked the enchanted scene.

(Wr. 1801–1803, pub. 1805)

113 *from* PSYCHE, CANTO V [THE CHARM OF POETRY]

Delightful visions of my lonely hours!
Charm of my life and solace of my care!
Oh! would the muse but lend proportioned powers,
And give me language, equal to declare
The wonders which she bids my fancy share,
When rapt in her to other worlds I fly,
See angel forms unutterably fair,
And hear the inexpressive harmony
That seems to float on air, and warble through the sky.

Might I the swiftly glancing scenes recal!
Bright as the roseate clouds of summer's eve,
The dreams which hold my soul in willing thrall,
And half my visionary days deceive,
Communicable shape might then receive,
And other hearts be ravished with the strain:

But scarce I seek the airy threads to weave,
When quick confusion mocks the fruitless pain,
And all the fairy forms are vanished from my brain.

Fond dreamer! meditate thine idle song!
But let thine idle song remain unknown:
The verse, which cheers thy solitude, prolong;
What, though it charm no moments but thine own,
Though thy loved Psyche smile for thee alone,
Still shall it yield thee pleasure, if not fame,
And when, escaped from tumult, thou hast flown
To thy dear silent hearth's enlivening flame,
There shall the tranquil muse her happy votary claim!

My Psyche's wanderings then she loves to trace;
Unrolls the glowing canvas to my sight;
Her chaste calm eye, her soft attractive grace,
The lightning of her heavenly smile so bright,
All yield me strange and unconceived delight:
Even now entranced her journey I pursue,
And gaze enraptured on her matchless knight;
Visions of love, pure, innocent and true!
Oh! may your graceful forms for ever bless my view!

(Wr. 1801–1803, pub. 1805)

BARBARA HOOLE (née WREAKS, later HOFLAND) (1770 – 1844)
She was born in Sheffield, the daughter of a local manufacturer, Robert Wreaks. In 1796, she married Thomas Bradshawe Hoole who died in 1798, leaving her with a young son and daughter and no means of support. She published *Poems*, Sheffield [1805] with two thousand subscribers and thereafter she continued to write to support herself. She also opened a school in Harrogate. In 1808, she married the landscape painter Thomas Hofland, an acquaintance of Wordsworth's. After her marriage, she published voluminously, but *The Son of a Genius* (1812), *Iwanowna* (1813), and *The Captives in India*, 3 vols (1834) are still of interest.

114 CUMBERLAND ROCKS

Scenes of magnificence! your powerful charms,
That burst stupendous on mine aching sight,
Now thrill the trembling vein with wild alarms,
Now wrap the exulting soul in high delight!

From Alpine mountains gush the maddening streams,
That sweep with snow-tipped wave the verdant vale,
Catch with pellucid drops light's quivering beams,
The gay foam sparkling in the gusty gale:—

While on the hoary rock, whose rugged breast
Hath braved the pelting storms of many a year,
Eve's brilliant sunbeams sink in lovely rest,
And tinge the purple clouds that linger near.

Sweet scenes of wonder, scenes of beauty cease;
Ye charm the eye, but can your powers impart
The long-lost vision of returning peace,
The long-lost raptures of a widowed heart?

Ah! no in vain your mighty rocks arise,
Your soft streams murmur in the pensive ear;
Like them my drooping heart more deeply sighs,
Like them dissolves in many an anxious tear.

(1805)

115 SONNET, COMPOSED ON THE BANKS OF ULLSWATER

Ah scenes! beloved by Fancy's beaming eye,
  Enthusiast sweet, that o'er the mountain wild
Breathes in soft ecstasy the rapturous sigh,
  Or sings exulting through the smiling vale;
Now through the dark glen wandering sadly mild,
  Or slowly sauntering through the flowery dale:
In each kind breeze that curls the dimpling lake,
  Each orient beam that gilds the rock's bold brow,
She feels young Genius in her bosom wake,
  And mental morn's resplendent beauties glow.
Blessed ray of heaven, which bids the soul inhale
  Whate'er of good delighted sense portrays,
Pours from each rill and wafts from every gale
  Imagination's intellectual blaze!

(1805)

116 SONNET, COMPOSED IN A CELL (COMMONLY CALLED THE GIANT'S CAVE) ON THE BANKS OF THE EIMONT, IN CUMBERLAND

Hail holy glooms! and thou mysterious cell,
  Washed by the gurgling Eimont's wildest flood,
Where for unnumbered ages thou hast stood
  A hermit-cavern in the rocky dell,
Sheltered amid the close embowering wood,
  And shaded by the dimly distant fell:
Unseen save where the eye of fear surveys
  Sad spectres roving round thy drear domain,
And shrieking o'er the woes of other days,
  Pour on the frighted stream a direful strain;
What time the moon recalls her feeble rays,
  And night, and death, and desolation reign,
Till morn returns, whose first soft-streaming light
  In thy deep dungeon chains the wearied sprite.

(1805)

117 LINES, COMPOSED WHILST CLIMBING SOME ROCKS IN DERBYSHIRE

Ye hoary rocks, primeval turrets, hail!
That scowling crown the mighty mountain's brow,
Tremendous contrast to the smiling vale,
Where dimpling Derwent laves the meads below;
I love your rugged tops, your battered sides,
Snow-covered glens, and unfrequented dells,
Where many a winding streamlet gurgling slides,
And o'er the moss-clad stones meandering swells:
Still would my feet your pathless tracks explore,
Climb the rude crags, and dare the threatening height,
Till Sol's last rays illume the western shore
And tinge the empurpled clouds with golden light;
Feel your dread powers exalt my placid mind,
And leave to care the trifling world behind.

(1805)

JANE TAYLOR (1783 – 1824)

She was born in London, but lived in several places before finally settling in Ongar in 1811 when her father, Isaac Taylor, became the Dissenting minister at the Meeting House. She wrote verse in early childhood with her sister, Ann, some of which was public and some of a private role-playing nature, which has increased significance given the more intense private worlds later created by the Brontë sisters. Her father was an engraver, and both sisters were taught and worked as engravers. They published *Original Poems for Infant Minds*, 2 vols (1804–05), beginning a long succession of such works, which may initially have been influenced by Anna Laetitia Barbauld's activities in this sphere. Taylor's *Essays in Rhyme* (1816) contain her major social and satirical poems, and *Contributions of Q.Q.*, 2 vols (1824) contain her highly popular prose pieces. In later life, like so many women of the period, she became increasingly religious and evangelical. After her death, Isaac Taylor published *Memoirs and Poetical Remains of the Late Jane Taylor*, London 1825.

118 A TOWN

A busy town mid Britain's isle,
   Behold in fancy's eye;
With tower, and spire, and civic pile,
   Beneath a summer sky:

And orchard, garden, field, and park,
   And grove, and sunny wall;
And ranging buildings, light and dark,
   As evening shadows fall.

Then listen to the ceaseless din
   Of hammer, saw, and crane;
And traffic passing out and in,
   From alley, street, and lane.

The sound, without a pause between,
   Of foot, and wheel, and hoof;
The manufacture's loud machine
   From yonder lengthened roof.

And children at their evening sports,
   Parading to and fro;
Assembled in the quiet courts
   Of yonder cottage row.

Gay streets display their shining wares
   To every roving eye,
As, eager in their own affairs,
   The busy tribes go by.

And ah! what varied forms of woe,
What hope and fear are found;
What passions rise, what scandals grow,
Within this narrow bound!

To pass the peaceful dwellings by,
No stranger eye might guess
Those scenes of joy and agony,
Of discord and distress.

Pain writhes within those stately walls;
Here pallid want hath been;
That casement where the curtain falls
Shows death has entered in.

The dwelling, ranging next to this,
A youthful group displays;
Elate they seem with present bliss,
And hope of distant days.

There, at her chamber-window high,
A lonely maiden sits;
Its casement fronts the western sky,
And balmy air admits:

And while her thoughts have wandered far
From all she hears and sees,
She gazes on the evening star
That twinkles through the trees.

Is it to watch the setting sun
She does that seat prefer?—
Alas! the maiden thinks of one
Who never thinks of her.

But lively is the street below,
And ceaseless is the hum,
As some intent on pleasure go,
On schemes of profit some.

Now widening seems the stream to be,
As evening stretches o'er;
Plebeian tribes from toil set free
Pour forth from every door.

A school, arranged in order due,
(Before the sun goes down)
Lady and lady, two and two,
Comes winding through the town.

And what drives up to yonder door
   The gaping crowd among?
A wedding train of chaises four,
   And all the bells are rung.

The laden wagon tinkles by,
   The post is going out,
The lights are lit, the coaches ply
   To tavern, ball, and rout.

Thus closed that merry summer's day;
   And would you ask me how
You might the busy scene survey,
   And see those faces now?—

Then hither turn—yon waving grass
   And mouldering stones will show;
For these transactions came to pass
   A hundred years ago.

(1816)

119 *from* A PAIR

Down a close street, whose darksome shops display
Old clothes and iron on both sides the way;
Loathsome and wretched, whence the eye in pain,
Averted turns, nor seeks to view again;
Where lowest dregs of human nature dwell,
More loathsome than the rags and rust they sell;—
A pale mechanic rents an attic floor,
By many a shattered stair you gain the door:
'Tis one poor room, whose blackened walls are hung
With dust that settled there when he was young.
The rusty grate two massy bricks displays,
To fill the sides and make a frugal blaze.
The door unhinged, the window patched and broke,
The panes obscured by half a century's smoke:
There stands the bench at which his life is spent,
Worn, grooved, and bored, and worm-devoured, and bent,
Where daily, undisturbed by foes or friends,
In one unvaried attitude he bends.
His tools, long practised, seem to understand
Scarce less their functions, than his own right hand.
With these he drives his craft with patient skill;
Year after year would find him at it still:
The noisy world around is changing all,

War follows peace, and kingdoms rise and fall;
France rages now, and Spain, and now the Turk;
Now victory sounds;—but there he sits at work!
A man might see him so, then bid adieu,—
Make a long voyage to China or Peru;
There traffic, settle, build; at length might come,
Altered, and old, and weather-beaten home,
And find him on the same square foot of floor
On which he left him twenty years before.
—The self same bench, and attitude, and stool,
The same quick movements of his cunning tool;
The very distance 'twixt his knees and chin,
As though he had but stepped just out and in.

Such is his fate—and yet you might descry
A latent spark of meaning in his eye.
—That crowded shelf, beside his bench, contains
One old, worn, volume that employs his brains:
With algebraic lore its page is spread,
Where *a* and *b* contend with *x* and *z*:
Sold by some *student* from an Oxford hall,
—Bought by the pound upon a broker's stall.
On this it is his sole delight to pore,
Early and late, when working time is o'er:
But oft he stops, bewildered and perplexed,
At some hard problem in the learned text;
Pressing his hand upon his puzzled brain,
At what the dullest school-boy could explain.

From needful sleep the precious hour he saves,
To give his thirsty mind the stream it craves:
There, with his slender rush beside him placed,
He drinks the knowledge in with greedy haste.
At early morning, when the frosty air
Brightens Orion and the northern Bear,
His distant window mid the dusky row,
Holds a dim light to passenger below.
—A light more dim is flashing on his mind,
That shows its darkness, and its views confined.
Had science shone around his early days,
How had his soul expanded in the blaze!
But penury bound him, and his mind in vain
Struggles and writhes beneath her iron chain.

—At length the taper fades, and distant cry
Of early sweep bespeaks the morning nigh;
Slowly it breaks,—and that rejoicing ray
That wakes the healthful country into day,
Tips the green hills, slants o'er the level plain,

Reddens the pool, and stream, and cottage pane,
And field, and garden, park, and stately hall,—
Now darts obliquely on his wretched wall.
He knows the wonted signal; shuts his book,
Slowly consigns it to its dusty nook;
Looks out awhile, with fixed and absent stare,
On crowded roofs, seen through the foggy air;
Stirs up the embers, takes his sickly draught,
Sighs at his fortunes, and resumes his craft.

(1816)

120 *from* **THE WORLD IN THE HOUSE**

The rage for competition, show, and style,
Is London's plague, and spreads for many a mile.
No rank, nor age, escapes that vulgar sin,
Breathed in its nurseries,—in its schools worked in:
And thus the mania, in maturer years,
In every form of pride and pomp appears,
As each were striving for a near approach—
Climax of grandeur!—to the lord mayor's coach.
—How short the triumph, many a prison cell,
And many a pining family could tell.—
The bridal equipage, in half a year
Brought to the hammer of the auctioneer,
Suffices not to liquidate the debt,
And fame's last bugle sounds in the *Gazette*.

Regions of intellect! serenely fair,
Hence let us rise, and breathe your purer air.
—There shine the stars! one intellectual glance
At that bright host,—on yon sublime expanse,
Might prove a cure;—well, say they, let them shine
With all our hearts,—but let *us* dress and dine.

There are, above the petty influence placed,
By human science and a mental taste.
The man who feels the dignity of thought,
By culture much refined, by science taught,
To loved pursuits devoted, looks below
With true contempt upon the paltry show:
Compared with those in pleasure's vortex hurled,
He loves it not, and lives above the world.

But happier he, who views the toys of time
From loftier heights, from regions more sublime;
Who walks with God while yet he sojourns here;

His hopes still climbing to a brighter sphere.
—Is he of wealth and earthly good possessed?
He takes Heaven's bounty with a cheerful zest.
His quarrel with the world you might not note
From texture, cut, or colour of his coat;
For *studied* plainness, whether dress or speech,
Defeats the very end it aims to reach.
And yet, on all he has there stands impressed
One truth conspicuous—'This is not my rest.'—
From that divine remembrance, ever springs
A moderated care for other things;
—Pilgrim and stranger in a desert spot,
He holds them all as though he held them not.

(1816)

FELICIA DOROTHEA HEMANS (née BROWNE) (1793–1835)

She was born in Liverpool but from 1800 she was brought up in North Wales. She published three precocious collections, *Poems*, Liverpool 1808, *England and Spain*... (1808), *The Domestic Affections, and Other Poems* (1812). In 1812, she married Captain Alfred Hemans. She had five sons but the marriage proved unhappy and he left her in 1818. During the marriage she wrote verse of high technical quality, *The Restoration of the Works of Art to Italy* (1816) and *Modern Greece* (1817), but their lyrical content combined uneasily with the extended form. She continued in this manner for some years, producing *The Sceptic* (1820), *Dartmoor* (1821), *The Vespers of Palermo* (1823), *The Siege of Valencia* (1823). Thereafter she retained an interest in dramatic subjects but produced many more lyrics of greater power. Her major mature verse is contained in *The Forest Sanctuary* (1825), (enlarged second edition, 1829), *Lays of Many Lands* (1825), *Records of Woman* (1828), *Songs of the Affections* (1830), her periodical contributions to *Blackwoods, New Monthly Magazine*, numerous annuals and the post-humous collection edited by David Moir, *Poetical Remains* (1836). She returned to Liverpool in 1828, moved to Dublin in 1831 and died there. She was vigorously promoted by *Blackwoods* and the *New Monthly Magazine* and her facility for producing occasional verse gave her a prominent place in the annuals. Increasingly, her sweetness and melancholy, together with her religious concerns and celebrations of nature, seemed to embody an appealing ideal of tender womanhood and constituted the territory of the true 'poetess'. The rise in her reputation, and the demarcation of female poetic activity from male, coincides with the rapid eclipse of the 'unsexed' radicals of the 1790s. However, the complexities of her responses to distant lands just as the Empire rapidly expanded reveal a hitherto little explored area of literary history between the deaths of Keats, Byron and Shelley and the emergence of Tennyson. She was widely admired in America and had numerous imitators. By mid-century the canon of the major male romantics had to a large extent been established and the demarcation of female territory, though it did little to diminish her popularity, separated her out of the 'romantics' and her verse has received little serious attention.

Nevertheless, when in 1874 'The Lansdowne Poets' collection of English verse appeared, it contained *The Laurel and the Lyre: Fugitive Poetry of the Nineteenth Century*, an expanded anthology of Alaric Alexander Watts (who had been active in the promotion of annuals). The number of poems by the following poets is of interest: Coleridge (1), Byron (5), Keats (3), Shelley (1), Worsdsworth (2), Southey (2), Rogers (1), Hemans (13), Landon (15).

121 THE VOICE OF SPRING

I come, I come! ye have called me long,
I come o'er the mountains with light and song!
Ye may trace my step o'er the wakening earth,
By the winds which tell of the violet's birth,
By the primrose-stars in the shadowy grass,
By the green leaves opening as I pass.

I have breathed on the South, and the chestnut-flowers
By thousands have burst from the forest-bowers,
And the ancient graves, and the fallen fanes,
Are veiled with wreaths on Italian plains.
—But it is not for me, in my hour of bloom,
To speak of the ruin or the tomb!

I have passed o'er the hills of the stormy North,
And the larch has hung all his tassels forth,
The fisher is out on the sunny sea,
And the rein-deer bounds through the pasture free,
And the pine has a fringe of softer green,
And the moss looks bright where my step has been.

I have sent through the wood-paths a gentle sigh,
And called out each voice of the deep blue sky,
From the night-bird's lay through the starry time,
In the groves of the soft Hesperian clime,
To the swan's wild note by the Iceland lakes,
When the dark fir-bough into verdure breaks.

From the streams and founts I have loosed the chain;
They are sweeping on to the silvery main,
They are flashing down from the mountain-brows,
They are flinging spray on the forest boughs,
They are bursting fresh from their sparry caves,
And the earth resounds with the joy of waves.

Come forth, O ye children of gladness, come!
Where the violets lie may be now your home.
Ye of the rose-cheek and dew-bright eye,
And the bounding footstep, to meet me fly,
With the lyre, and the wreath, and the joyous lay,
Come forth to the sunshine, I may not stay!

Away from the dwellings of care-worn men,
The waters are sparkling in wood and glen,
Away from the chamber and dusky hearth,
The young leaves are dancing in breezy mirth,
Their light stems thrill to the wild-wood strains,
And Youth is abroad in my green domains.

But ye!—ye are changed since ye met me last;
A shade of earth has been round you cast!
There is that come over your brow and eye
Which speaks of a world where the flowers must die!
Ye smile!—but your smile hath a dimness yet—
—Oh! what have ye looked on since last we met?

Ye are changed, ye are changed!—and I see not here
All whom I saw in the vanished year!
There were graceful heads, with their ringlets bright,
Which tossed in the breeze with a play of light;
There were eyes, in whose glistening laughter lay,
No faint remembrance of dull decay.

There were steps, that flew o'er the cowslip's head,
As if for a banquet all earth were spread;
There were voices that rung through the sapphire sky,
And had not a sound of mortality!
—Are they gone?—is their mirth from the green hills passed?
—Ye have looked on Death since ye met me last!

I know whence the shadow comes o'er ye now,
Ye have strewn the dust on the sunny brow!
Ye have given the lovely to the earth's embrace,
She hath taken the fairest of Beauty's race!
With their laughing eyes and their festal crown,
They are gone from amongst you in silence down.

They are gone from amongst you, the bright and fair,
Ye have lost the gleam of their shining hair!
—But I know of a world where there falls no blight,
I shall find them there, with their eyes of light!
Where Death 'midst the blooms of the morn may dwell,
I tarry no longer,—farewell, farewell!

The summer is hastening, on soft winds borne,
Ye may press the grape, ye may bind the corn!
For me, I depart to a brighter shore,
Ye are marked by care, ye are mine no more.
I go where the loved who have left you dwell,
And the flowers are not Death's;—fare ye well, farewell!

(1823)

122 THE TREASURES OF THE DEEP

What hid'st thou in thy treasure-caves and cells?
Thou hollow-sounding and mysterious Main!
—Pale glistening pearls, and rainbow-coloured shells,
Bright things which gleam unrecked of, and in vain.
—Keep, keep thy riches, melancholy sea!
We ask not such from thee.

Yet more, the Depths have more!—What wealth untold
Far down, and shining through their stillness lies!
Thou hast the starry gems, the burning gold,
Won from ten thousand royal Argosies.
—Sweep o'er thy spoils, thou wild and wrathful Main!
Earth claims not these again!

Yet more, the Depths have more!—Thy waves have rolled
Above the cities of a world gone by!
Sand hath filled up the palaces of old,
Sea-weed o'ergrown the halls of revelry!
—Dash o'er them, Ocean! in thy scornful play,
Man yields them to decay!

Yet more! the Billows and the Depths have more!
High hearts and brave are gathered to thy breast!
They hear not now the booming waters roar,
The battle-thunders will not break their rest.
—Keep thy red gold and gems, thou stormy grave—
Give back the true and brave!

Give back the lost and lovely!—those for whom
The place was kept at board and hearth so long;
The prayer went up through midnight's breathless gloom,
And the vain yearning woke 'midst festal song!
Hold fast thy buried isles, thy towers o'erthrown,
—But all is not thine own!

To thee the love of woman hath gone down,
Dark flow thy tides o'er manhood's noble head,
O'er youth's bright locks and beauty's flowery crown;
—Yet must thou hear a voice—Restore the dead!
Earth shall reclaim her precious things from thee,
—Restore the Dead, thou Sea!

(1823)

123 THE HEBREW MOTHER

The rose was in rich bloom on Sharon's plain,
When a young mother, with her First-born, thence
Went up to Zion; for the boy was vowed
Unto the Temple-service. By the hand
She led him, and her silent soul, the while,
Oft as the dewy laughter of his eye
Met her sweet serious glance, rejoiced to think
That aught so pure, so beautiful, was hers,
To bring before her God.
So passed they on,
O'er Judah's hills; and wheresoe'er the leaves
Of the broad sycamore made sounds at noon,
Like lulling rain-drops, or the olive-boughs,
With their cool dimness, crossed the sultry blue
Of Syria's heaven, she paused, that he might rest;
Yet from her own meek eyelids chased the sleep
That weighed their dark fringe down, to sit and watch
The crimson deepening o'er his cheek's repose,
As at a red flower's heart: and where a fount
Lay, like a twilight star, midst palmy shades,
Making its banks green gems along the wild,
There too she lingered, from the diamond wave
Drawing clear water for his rosy lips,
And softly parting clusters of jet curls
To bathe his brow.
At last the Fane was reached,
The earth's One Sanctuary; and rapture hushed
Her bosom, as before her, through the day
It rose, a mountain of white marble, steeped
In light like floating gold.—But when that hour
Waned to the farewell moment, when the boy
Lifted, through rainbow-gleaming tears, his eye
Beseechingly to hers, and, half in fear,
Turned from the white-robed priest, and round her arm
Clung e'en as ivy clings; the deep spring-tide
Of nature then swelled high; and o'er her child
Bending, her soul brake forth, in mingled sounds
Of weeping and sad song.—'Alas!' she cried,

'Alas, my boy! thy gentle grasp is on me,
The bright tears quiver in thy pleading eyes,
And now fond thoughts arise,
And silver cords again to earth have won me,
And like a vine thou claspest my full heart—
How shall I hence depart?—

'How the lone paths retrace, where thou wert playing
So late along the mountains at my side?
        And I, in joyous pride,
By every place of flowers my course delaying,
Wove, e'en as pearls, the lilies round thy hair,
        Beholding thee so fair!

'And, oh! the home whence thy bright smile hath parted!
Will it not seem as if the sunny day
        Turned from its door away,
While, through its chambers wandering weary-hearted,
I languish for thy voice, which past me still,
        Went like a singing rill?

'Under the palm-trees, thou no more shalt meet me,
When from the fount at evening I return,
        With the full water-urn!
Nor will thy sleep's low, dove-like murmurs greet me,
As midst the silence of the stars I wake,
        And watch for thy dear sake.

'And thou, will slumber's dewy cloud fall round thee
Without thy mother's hand to smooth thy bed?
        Wilt thou not vainly spread
Thine arms, when darkness as a veil hath wound thee,
To fold my neck; and lift up, in thy fear,
        A cry which none shall hear?

'What have I said, my child?—will He not hear thee
Who the young ravens heareth from their nest?
        Will He not guard thy rest,
And, in the hush of holy midnight near thee,
Breathe o'er thy soul, and fill its dreams with joy?
        Thou shalt sleep soft, my boy!

'I give thee to thy God!—the God that gave thee,
A well-spring of deep gladness to my heart!
        And precious as thou art,
And pure as dew of Hermon, He shall have thee,
My own, my beautiful, my undefiled!
        And thou shalt be His child!

'Therefore, farewell!—I go; my soul may fail me,
As the stag panteth for the water-brooks,
        Yearning for thy sweet looks!
But thou, my First-born! droop not, nor bewail me,
Thou in the shadow of the Rock shalt dwell,
        The Rock of Strength—farewell!'

(1826)

124 THE HOMES OF ENGLAND

-------------- A land of peace,
Where yellow fields unspoiled, and pastures green,
Mottled with herds and flocks, who crop secure
Their native herbage, nor have ever known
A stranger's stall, smile gladly.
See through its tufted alleys to Heaven's roof
The curling smoke of quiet dwellings rise. [Joanna Baillie]

The stately Homes of England,
How beautiful they stand!
Amidst their tall ancestral trees,
O'er all the pleasant land!
The deer across their green-sward bound,
Through shade and sunny gleam;
And the swan glides past them with the sound
Of some rejoicing stream.

The merry Homes of England!
Around their hearths by night
What gladsome looks of household love
Meet in the ruddy light!
There woman's voice flows forth in song,
Or childhood's tale is told;
Or lips move tunefully along
Some glorious page of old.

The blessed Homes of England!
How softly on their bowers
Is laid the holy quietness
That breathes from Sabbath-hours!
Solemn, yet sweet, the church-bell's chime
Floats through their woods at morn;
All other sounds, in that still time,
Of breeze and leaf are born.

The Cottage-Homes of England!
By thousands, on her plains,
They are smiling o'er the silvery brooks,
And round the hamlet-fanes.
Through glowing orchards forth they peep,
Each from its nook of leaves,
And fearless there they lowly sleep,
As the bird beneath their eaves.

The free, fair Homes of England!
Long, long, in hut and hall,
May hearts of native proof be reared,
To guard each hallowed wall!
And green for ever be the groves,
And bright the flowery sod,
Where first the child's glad spirit loves
Its Country and its God!

(1827)

125 THE BETTER LAND

'I hear thee speak of the better land,
Thou call'st its children a happy band;
Mother! oh, where is that radiant shore?—
Shall we not seek it, and weep no more?—
Is it where the flower of the orange blows,
And the fire-flies glance through the myrtle-boughs?'
—'Not there, not there, my child!'

'Is it where the feathery palm-trees rise,
And the date grows ripe under sunny skies?—
Or 'midst the green islands of glittering seas,
Where fragrant forests perfume the breeze,
And strange, bright birds, on their starry wings,
Bear the rich hues of all glorious things?'
—'Not there, not there, my child?'

'Is it far away, in some region old,
Where the rivers wander o'er sands of gold?—
Where the burning rays of the ruby shine,
And the diamond lights up the secret mine,
And the pearl gleams forth from the coral strand—
Is it there, sweet mother, that better land?'
—'Not there, not there, my child!

'Eye hath not seen it, my gentle boy!
Ear hath not heard its deep songs of joy;
Dreams cannot picture a world so fair—
Sorrow and death may not enter there;
Time doth not breathe on its fadeless bloom,
For beyond the clouds, and beyond the tomb,
It is there, it is there, my child!'

(1827)

126 THE VOICE OF THE WIND

There is nothing in the wide world so like the voice of a spirit. [Gray's Letters]

Oh! many a voice is thine, thou Wind! full many a voice is thine,
From every scene thy wing o'ersweeps, thou bear'st a sound and sign.
A minstrel wild, and strong thou art, with a mastery all thine own;
And the Spirit is thy harp, O Wind! that gives the answering tone.

Thou hast been across red fields of war, where shivered helmets lie,
And thou bringest thence the thrilling note of a Clarion in the sky;
A rustling of proud banner-folds, a peal of stormy drums—
All these are in thy music met, as when a leader comes.

Thou hast been o'er solitary seas, and from their wastes brought back
Each noise of waters that awoke in the mystery of thy track;
The chime of low soft southern waves on some green palmy shore,
The hollow roll of distant surge, the gathered billows' roar.

Thou art come from forests dark and deep, thou mighty rushing
Wind!
And thou bearest all their unisons in one full swell combined;
The restless pines, the moaning stream, all hidden things and free,
Of the dim old sounding wilderness, have lent their soul to thee.

Thou art come from cities lighted up for the conqueror passing by,
Thou art wafting from their streets a sound of haughty revelry;
The rolling of triumphant wheels, the harpings in the hall,
The far-off shout of multitudes, are in thy rise and fall.

Thou art come from kingly tombs and shrines, from ancient
minsters vast,
Through the dark aisles of a thousand years thy lonely wing hath
passed;
Thou hast caught the Anthem's billowy swell, the stately Dirge's
tone,
For a Chief with sword, and shield, and helm, to his place of
slumber gone.

Thou art come from long-forsaken homes, wherein our young days
flew,
Thou hast found sweet voices lingering there, the loved, the kind,
the true;
Thou callest back those melodies, though now all changed and
fled—
Be still, be still, and haunt us not with music from the dead!

Are all these notes in *thee*, wild Wind? these many notes in *thee*?
Far in our own unfathomed souls their fount must surely be;
Yes! buried but unsleeping *there*, Thought watches, Memory lies,
From whose deep Urn the tones are poured through all earth's
harmonies!

(1828)

127 PROPERZIA ROSSI

Properzia Rossi, a celebrated female sculptor of Bologna, possessed also of talents for poetry and music, died in consequence of an unrequited attachment. —A painting by Ducis, represents her showing her last work, a basso-relievo of Ariadne, to a Roman Knight, the object of her affection, who regards it with indifference.

——Tell me no more, no more
Of my soul's lofty gifts! Are they not vain
To quench its haunting thirst for happiness?
Have I not loved, and striven, and failed to bind
One true heart unto me, whereon my own
Might find a resting-place, a home for all
Its burden of affections? I depart,
Unknown, though Fame goes with me; I must leave
The earth unknown. Yet it may be that death
Shall give my name a power to win such tears
As would have made life precious.

One dream of passion and of beauty more!
And in its bright fulfilment let me pour
My soul away! Let earth retain a trace
Of that which lit my being, though its race
Might have been loftier far.—Yet one more dream!
From my deep spirit one victorious gleam
Ere I depart! For thee alone, for thee!
May this last work, this farewell triumph be,—
Thou, loved so vainly! I would leave enshrined
Something immortal of my heart and mind,
That yet may speak to thee when I am gone,
Shaking thine inmost bosom with a tone
Of lost affection;—something that may prove
What she hath been, whose melancholy love
On thee was lavished; silent pang and tear,
And fervent song, that gushed when none were near,
And dream by night, and weary thought by day,
Stealing the brightness from her life away,—
While thou—Awake! not yet within me die,
Under the burden and the agony
Of this vain tenderness,—my spirit, wake!
Even for thy sorrowful affection's sake,
Live! in thy work breathe out!—that he may yet,
Feeling sad mastery there, perchance regret
Thine unrequited gift.

It comes,—the power
Within me born, flows back; my fruitless dower
That could not win me love. Yet once again
I greet it proudly, with its rushing train
Of glorious images:—they throng—they press—
A sudden joy lights up my loneliness,—
I shall not perish all!

The bright work grows
Beneath my hand, unfolding, as a rose,
Leaf after leaf, to beauty; line by line,
I fix my thought, heart, soul, to burn, to shine,
Through the pale marble's veins. It grows—and now
I give my own life's history to thy brow,
Forsaken Ariadne! thou shalt wear
My form, my lineaments; but oh! more fair,
Touched into lovelier being by the glow
Which in me dwells, as by the summer-light
All things are glorified. From thee my woe
Shall yet look beautiful to meet his sight,
When I am passed away. Thou art the mould
Wherein I pour the fervent thoughts, the untold,
The self-consuming! Speak to him of me,
Thou, the deserted by the lonely sea,
With the soft sadness of thine earnest eye,
Speak to him, lorn one, deeply, mournfully,
Of all my love and grief! Oh! could I throw
Into thy frame a voice, a sweet, and low,
And thrilling voice of song!—when he came nigh,
To send the passion of its melody
Through his pierced bosom—on its tones to bear
My life's deep feeling, as the southern air
Wafts the faint myrtle's breath,—to rise, to swell,
To sink away in accents of farewell,
Winning but one, *one* gush of tears, whose flow
Surely my parted spirit yet might know,
If love be strong as death!

Now fair thou art,
Thou form, whose life is of my burning heart!
Yet all the vision that within me wrought,
I cannot make thee! Oh! I might have given
Birth to creations of far nobler thought,
I might have kindled, with the fire of heaven,
Things not of such as die! But I have been
Too much alone; a heart, whereon to lean,
With all these deep affections that o'erflow
My aching soul, and find no shore below,
An eye to be my star, a voice to bring
Hope o'er my path, like sounds that breathe of spring,
These are denied me—dreamt of still in vain,—
Therefore my brief aspirings from the chain,
Are ever but as some wild fitful song,
Rising triumphantly, to die ere long
In dirge-like echoes.

Yet the world will see
Little of this, my parting work in thee,

Thou shalt have fame! Oh, mockery! give the reed
From storms a shelter,—give the drooping vine
Something round which its tendrils may entwine,—
Give the parched flower a rain-drop, and the meed
Of love's kind words to woman! Worthless fame!
That in *his* bosom wins not for my name
The abiding place it asked! Yet how my heart,
In its own fairy world of song and art,
Once beat for praise!—Are those high longings o'er?
That which I have been can I be no more?—
Never, oh! never more; though still thy sky
Be blue as then, my glorious Italy!
And though the music, whose rich breathings fill
Thine air with soul, be wandering past me still,
And though the mantle of thy sunlight streams
Unchanged on forms instinct with poet-dreams;
Never, oh! never more! Where'er I move,
The shadow of this broken-hearted love
Is on me and around! Too well *they* know,
Whose life is all within, too soon and well,
When there the blight hath settled;—but I go
Under the silent wings of Peace to dwell;
From the slow wasting, from the lonely pain,
The inward burning of those words—'*in vain*,'
Seared on the heart—I go. 'Twill soon be past.
Sunshine, and song, and bright Italian heaven,
And thou, oh! thou, on whom my spirit cast
Unvalued wealth,—who know'st not what was given
In that devotedness,—the sad, and deep,
And unrepaid—farewell! If I could weep
Once, only once, beloved one! on thy breast,
Pouring my heart forth ere I sink to rest!
But that were happiness, and unto me
Earth's gift is *fame*. Yet I was formed to be
So richly blest! With thee to watch the sky,
Speaking not, feeling but that thou wert nigh;
With thee to listen, while the tones of song
Swept even as part of our sweet air along,
To listen silently;—with thee to gaze
On forms, the deified of olden days,—
This had been joy enough;—and hour by hour,
From its glad well-springs drinking life and power,
How had my spirit soared, and made its fame
A glory for thy brow!—Dreams, dreams!—the fire
Burns faint within me. Yet I leave my name—
As a deep thrill may linger on the lyre
When its full chords are hushed—awhile to live,
And one day haply in thy heart revive
Sad thoughts of me:—I leave it with a sound,

A spell o'er memory, mournfully profound,
I leave it, on my country's air to dwell,—
Say proudly yet—"*Twas hers who love me well!*'

(1828)

128 INDIAN WOMAN'S DEATH-SONG

[An Indian woman, driven to despair by her husband's desertion of her for another wife, entered a canoe with her children, and rowed it down the Mississippi towards a cataract. Her voice was heard from the shore singing a mournful death-song, until overpowered by the sound of the waters in which she perished. The tale is related in Long's *Expedition to the Source of St Peter's River*.]

> Non, je ne puis vivre avec un coeur brisé. Il faut que je retrouve la joie, et que je m'unisse aux esprits de l'air. [Schiller's] *Bride of Messina*, translated by Madame de Staël.

> Let not my child be a girl, for very sad is the life of a woman. [Fennimore Cooper's] *The Prairie*

Down a broad river of the western wilds,
Piercing thick forest glooms, a light canoe
Swept with the current: fearful was the speed
Of the frail bark, as by a tempest's wing
Borne leaf-like on to where the mist of spray
Rose with the cataract's thunder.—Yet within,
Proudly, and dauntlessly, and all alone,
Save that a babe lay sleeping at her breast,
A woman stood. Upon her Indian brow
Sat a strange gladness, and her dark hair waved
As if triumphantly. She pressed her child,
In its bright slumber, to her beating heart,
And lifted her sweet voice, that rose awhile
Above the sound of waters, high and clear,
Wafting a wild proud strain, her Song of Death.

Roll swiftly to the Spirit's land, thou mighty stream and free!
Father of ancient waters, roll! and bear our lives with thee!
The weary bird that storms have tossed, would seek the sunshine's calm,
And the deer that hath the arrow's hurt, flies to the woods of balm.

Roll on!—my warrior's eye hath looked upon another's face,
And mine hath faded from his soul, as fades a moonbeam's trace;
My shadow comes not o'er his path, my whisper to his dream,
He flings away the broken reed—roll swifter yet, thou stream!

The voice that spoke of other days is hushed within *his* breast,
But *mine* its lonely music haunts, and will not let me rest;

It sings a low and mournful song of gladness that is gone,—
I cannot live without that light—Father of waves! roll on!

Will he not miss the bounding step that met him from the chase?
The heart of love that made his home an ever sunny place?
The hand that spread the hunter's board, and decked his couch of
yore?—
He will not!—roll, dark foaming stream, on to the better shore!

Some blessed fount amidst the woods of that bright land must flow,
Whose waters from my soul may lave the memory of this woe;
Some gentle wind must whisper there, whose breath may waft away
The burden of the heavy night, the sadness of the day.

And thou, my babe! though born, like me, for woman's weary lot,
Smile!—to that wasting of the heart, my own! I leave thee not;
Too bright a thing art *thou* to pine in aching love away,
Thy mother bears thee far, young Fawn! from sorrow and decay.

She bears thee to the glorious bowers where none are heard to weep,
And where the unkind one hath no power again to trouble sleep;
And where the soul shall find its youth, as wakening from a dream,—
One moment, and that realm is ours.—On, on, dark rolling stream!

(1828)

129 THE SPIRIT'S MYSTERIES

And slight, withal, may be the things which bring
Back on the heart the weight which it would fling
Aside for ever; – it may be a sound –
A tone of music – summer's breath, or spring –
A flower – a leaf – the ocean – which may wound –
Striking the electric chain wherewith we are darkly bound. [Byron],
Childe Harold

The power that dwelleth in sweet sounds to waken
Vague yearnings, like the sailor's for the shore,
And dim remembrances, whose hue seems taken
From some bright former state, our own no more;
Is not this all a mystery?—Who shall say
Whence are those thoughts, and whither tends their way?

The sudden images of vanished things,
That o'er the spirit flash, we know not why;
Tones from some broken harp's deserted strings,
Warm sunset hues of summers long gone by,
A rippling wave—the dashing of an oar—
A flower scent floating past our parents' door;

A word—scarce noted in its hour perchance,
Yet back returning with a plaintive tone;
A smile—a sunny or a mournful glance,

Full of sweet meanings now from this world flown;
Are not these mysteries when to life they start,
And press vain tears in gushes from the heart?

And the far wanderings of the soul in dreams,
Calling up shrouded faces from the dead,
And with them bringing soft or solemn gleams,
Familiar objects brightly to o'erspread;
And wakening buried love, or joy, or fear,—
These are night's mysteries—who shall make them clear?

And the strange inborn sense of coming ill,
That ofttimes whispers to the haunted breast,
In a low tone which nought can drown or still,
Midst feasts and melodies a secret guest;
Whence doth that murmur wake, that shadow fall?
Why shakes the spirit thus?—'tis mystery all!

Darkly we move—we press upon the brink
Haply of viewless worlds, and know it not;
Yes! it may be, that nearer than we think,
Are those whom death has parted from our lot!
Fearfully, wondrously, our souls are made—
Let us walk humbly on, but undismayed!

Humbly—for knowledge strives in vain to feel
Her way amidst these marvels of the mind;
Yet undismayed—for do they not reveal
The immortal being with our dust entwined?—
So let us deem! and e'en the tears they wake
Shall then be blest, for that high nature's sake.

(1828)

130 THE TRAVELLER AT THE SOURCE OF THE NILE

In sunset's light, o'er Afric thrown,
A wanderer proudly stood
Beside the well-spring, deep and lone,
Of Egypt's awful flood;
The cradle of that mighty birth,
So long a hidden thing to earth!

He heard its life's first murmuring sound,
A low mysterious tone;
A music sought, but never found,
By kings and warriors gone;
He listened—and his heart beat high—
That was the song of victory!

The rapture of a conqueror's mood
Rushed burning through his frame,—
The depths of that green solitude
Its torrents could not tame;
Though stillness lay, with eve's last smile—
Round those far fountains of the Nile.

Night came with stars:—across his soul
There swept a sudden change,
E'en at the pilgrim's glorious goal
A shadow dark and strange
Breathed from the thought, so swift to fall
O'er triumph's hour—*and is this all?*

No more than this!—what seem'd it *now*
First by that spring to stand?
A thousand streams of lovelier flow
Bathed his own mountain land!
Whence far o'er waste and ocean track,
Their wild, sweet voices called him back.

They called him back to many a glade,
His childhood's haunt of play,
Where brightly through the beechen shade
Their waters glanced away;
They called him, with their sounding waves,
Back to his fathers' hills and graves.

But darkly mingling with the thought
Of each familiar scene,
Rose up a fearful vision, fraught
With all that lay between;
The Arab's lance, the desert's gloom,
The whirling sands, the red simoom!

Where was the glow of power and pride?
The spirit born to roam?
His altered heart within him died
With yearnings for his home!
All vainly struggling to repress
That gush of painful tenderness.

He wept—the stars of Afric's heaven
Behold his bursting tears,
E'en on that spot where fate had given
The meed of toiling years!—
Oh, happiness! how far we flee
Thine own sweet paths in search of thee!

(1829)

FELICIA DOROTHEA HEMANS

131 THE MIRROR IN THE DESERTED HALL

O dim, forsaken Mirror!
How many a stately throng
Hath o'er thee gleamed, in vanished hours
Of the wine-cup and the song!

The song hath left no echo,
The bright wine hath been quaffed,
And hushed is every silvery voice
That lightly here hath laughed.

O Mirror, lonely Mirror,
Thou of the silent Hall!
Thou hast been flushed with beauty's bloom—
Is this too vanished all?

It is, with the scattered garlands
Of triumphs long ago,
With the melodies of buried lyres,
With the faded rainbow's glow.

And for all the gorgeous pageants,
For the glance of gem and plume,
For lamp, and harp, and rosy wreath,
And vase of rich perfume;

Now, dim, forsaken Mirror,
Thou giv'st but faintly back
The quiet stars and the sailing moon,
On her solitary track.

And thus with man's proud spirit
Thou tellest me 't will be,
When the forms and hues of this world fade
From his memory as from thee:

And his heart's long-troubled waters
At last in stillness lie,
Reflecting but the images
Of the solemn world on high.

(1830)

> What is Poesy, but to create
> From overfeeling, good or ill, and aim
> At an external life beyond our fate?
> Bestowing fire from Heaven, and then, too late,
> Finding the pleasure given repaid with pain!
> And vultures to the heart of the bestower,
> Who, having lavished his high gift in vain,
> Lies chained to his lone rock by the sea shore. [Byron], *Prophecy of Dante*

Sound on, thou dark unslumbering sea!
My dirge is in thy moan;
My spirit finds response in thee,
To its own ceaseless cry—'Alone, alone!'

Yet send me back one other word,
Ye tones that never cease!
Oh! let your hidden leaves be stirred,
And say, deep waters! can you give me peace?

Away!—my weary soul hath sought
In vain one echoing sigh,
One answer to consuming thought
In human breasts—and will the *wave* reply?

Sound on, thou dark unslumbering sea!
Sound in thy scorn and pride!
I ask not, alien world! from *thee*,
What my own kindred earth hath still denied!

And yet I loved that earth so well,
With all its lovely things!
Was it for *this* the death-wind fell
On my rich lyre, and quenched its living strings?

Let them lie silent at my feet!
Since, broken even as they,
The heart, whose music made them sweet,
Hath poured on desert sands its wealth away.

Yet glory's light hath touched my name,
The laurel wreath is mine—
With a worn heart, a weary frame,
O! restless Deep! I come to make them thine!

Give to that crown, that burning crown,
Place in thy darkest hold!
Bury my anguish, my renown,
With hidden wrecks, lost gems, and wasted gold!

Thou sea-bird, on the billow's crest,
Thou hast thy love, thy home!
They wait thee in the quiet nest—
And I—unsought, unwatched for—I too come!

I, with this winged nature fraught,
These visions, brightly free,
This boundless love, this fiery thought—
Alone, I come! O! give me peace, dark Sea!

(1831)

133 THE ROCK OF CADER-IDRIS: A LEGEND OF WALES

[It is an ancient tradition of Wales, that whoever should pass a night alone on the summit of the Mountain Cader-Idris, would be found in the morning either dead, in a state of frenzy, or endowed with the highest poetical inspiration.]

I lay on that rock where the storms have their dwelling,
The birthplace of phantoms, the home of the cloud;
Around it for ever deep music is swelling,
The voice of the Mountain-wind, solemn and loud.
'Twas a midnight of shadows, all fitfully streaming,
Of wild gusts and torrents that mingled their moan,
Of dim-shrouded stars, as through gulfs faintly gleaming,
And my strife with stern nature was darksome and lone.

I lay there in silence:—a spirit came o'er me;
Man's tongue hath no language to speak what I saw!
Things glorious, unearthly, passed floating before me,
And my heart almost fainted with rapture and awe!
I viewed the dread Beings around us that hover,
Though veiled by the mists of Mortality's breath;
And I called upon Darkness the vision to cover,
For within me was battling of madness and death!

I saw them—the Powers of the Wind and the Ocean,
The rush of whose pinion bears onward the storm;
Like the sweep of the white-rolling wave was their motion,
I felt their dread presence, but knew not their form.
I saw them—the mighty of ages departed—
The dead were around me that night on the hill;
From their eyes, as they passed, a cold radiance they darted;
There was light on my soul, but my heart's blood was chill.

I saw what man looks on, and dies!—but my spirit
Was strong, and triumphantly lived through that hour,
And as from the grave I awoke, to inherit
A flame all immortal, a voice and a power!
Day burst on that Rock with the purple cloud crested,
And high Cader-Idris rejoiced in the sun;
But oh! what new glory all nature invested,
When the sense which gives *soul* to her beauty was won!

(1834)

134 DESPONDENCY AND ASPIRATION

Per correr miglior acqua aiza le vele,
Omai la navicella del mio Intelletto. [Dante]

My soul was mantled with dark shadows, born
Of lonely Fear, disquieted in vain;
Its phantoms hung around the star of morn,
A cloud-like weeping train;
Through the long day they dimmed the autumn-gold
On all the glistening leaves; and wildly rolled,
When the last farewell flush of light was glowing,
Across the sunset sky;
O'er its rich isles of vaporous glory throwing
One melancholy dye.

And when the solemn Night
Came rushing with her might
Of stormy oracles from caves unknown,
Then with each fitful blast
Prophetic murmurs passed,
Wakening or answering some deep Sybil tone,
Far buried in my breast, yet prompt to rise
With every gusty wail that o'er the wind-harp flies.

'Fold, fold thy wings,' they cried, 'and strive no more,
Faint spirit, strive no more!—for thee too strong
Are outward ill and wrong,
And inward wasting fires!—Thou canst not soar
Free on a starry way
Beyond their blighting sway,
At Heaven's high gate serenely to adore!
How shouldst *thou* hope Earth's fetters to unbind?
O passionate, yet weak! O trembler to the wind!

'Never shall aught but broken music flow
From joy of thine, deep love, or tearful woe;
Such homeless notes as through the forest sigh,
From the reed's hollow shaken,
When sudden breezes waken
Their vague wild symphony:
No power is theirs, and no abiding-place
In human hearts; their sweetness leaves no trace,—
Born only so to die!

'Never shall aught but perfume, faint and vain,
On the fleet pinion of the changeful hour,
From thy bruised life again
A moment's essence breathe;
Thy life, whose trampled flower
Into the blessed wreath
Of household charities no longer bound,
Lies pale and withering on the barren ground.

'So fade, fade on! thy gift of love shall cling,
A coiling sadness, round thy heart and brain,
A silent, fruitless, yet undying thing,
All sensitive to pain!
And still the shadow of vain dreams shall fall
O'er thy mind's world, a daily darkening pall.
Fold, then, thy wounded wing, and sink subdued,
In cold and unrepining quietude!'

Then my soul yielded; spells of numbing breath
Crept o'er it heavy with a dew of death,
Its powers, like leaves before the night-rain, closing;
And, as by conflict of wild sea-waves tossed
On the chill bosom of some desert coast,
Mutely and hopelessly I lay reposing.

When silently it seemed
As if a soft mist gleamed
Before my passive sight, and, slowly curling,
To many a shape and hue
Of visioned beauty grew,
Like a wrought banner, fold by fold unfurling.
Oh! the rich scenes that o'er mind inward eye
Unrolling, then swept by,
With dreamy motion! Silvery seas were there
Lit by large dazzling stars, and arched by skies
Of Southern midnight's most transparent dyes,
And gemmed with many an island, wildly fair,
Which floated past me into orient day,
Still gathering lustre on the illumined way,
Till its high groves of wondrous flowering trees
Coloured the silvery seas.

And then a glorious mountain-chain uprose,
Height above spiry height!
A soaring solitude of woods and snows,
All steeped in golden light!
While as it passed, those regal peaks unveiling,
I heard, methought, a waving of dread wings
And mighty sounds, as if the vision hailing,
From lyres that quivered through ten thousand strings:
Or as if waters forth to music leaping.

From many a cave, the Alpine Echo's hall,
On their bold way victoriously were sweeping,
Linked in majestic anthems; while through all
That billowy swell and fall,
Voices, like ringing crystal, filled the air
With inarticulate melody, that stirred

My being's core; then, moulding into word
Their piercing sweetness, bade me rise and bear
In that great choral strain my trembling part
Of tones, by Love and Faith struck from a human heart.

Return no more, vain bodings of the night!
A happier oracle within my soul
Hath swelled to power;—a clear unwavering light
Mounts through the battling clouds that round me roll,
And to a new control
Nature's full harp gives forth rejoicing tones,
Wherein my glad sense owns
The accordant rush of elemental sound
To one consummate harmony profound;
One grand Creation-Hymn,
Whose notes the Seraphim
Lift to the glorious height of music winged and crowned.

Shall not those notes find echoes in my lyre,
Faithful though faint?—Shall not my spirit's fire,
If slowly, yet unswervingly, ascend
Now to its fount and end?
Shall not my earthly love, all purified,
Shine forth a heavenward guide?
An angel of bright power?—and strongly bear
My being upward into holier air,
Where fiery passion-clouds have no abode,
And the sky's temple-arch o'erflows with God?
The radiant hope new-born
Expands like rising morn
In my life's life: and as a ripening rose,
The crimson shadow of its glory throws
More vivid, hour by hour, on some pure stream
So from that hope are spreading
Rich hues, o'er nature shedding,
Each day, a clearer, spiritual gleam.

Let not those rays fade from me;—once enjoyed,
Father of spirits! let them not depart!
Leaving the chilled earth, without form and void,
Darkened by mine own heart!
Lift, aid, sustain me! Thou, by whom alone
All lovely gifts and pure
In the soul's grasp endure;—
Thou, to the steps of whose eternal throne
All knowledge flows—a sea for evermore
Breaking its crested waves on that sole shore—
O consecrate my life! that I may sing
Of Thee with joy that hath a living spring

In a full heart of music!—Let my lays
Through the resounding mountains waft thy praise,
And with that theme the wood's green cloisters fill,
And make their quivering leafy dimness thrill
To the rich breeze of song! O! let me wake
        The deep religion, which hath dwelt from yore,
Silently brooding by lone cliff and lake,
        And wildest river shore!
And let me summon all the voices dwelling
Where eagles build, and caverned rills are welling,
And where the cataract's organ-peal is swelling,
        In that one spirit gathered to adore!

Forgive, O Father! if presumptuous thought
    Too daringly in aspiration rise!
Let not thy child all vainly have been taught
    By weakness, and by wanderings, and by sighs
Of sad confession!—lowly be my heart,
    And on its penitential altar spread
The offerings worthless, till Thy grace impart
    The fire from heaven, whose touch alone can shed
Life, radiance, virtue!—let that vital spark
Pierce my whole being, wildered else and dark!
Thine are all holy things—O make *me* Thine,
So shall I too be pure—a living shrine
Unto that spirit, which goes forth from Thee,
            Strong and divinely free,
Bearing thy gifts of wisdom on its flight,
And brooding o'er them with a dove-like wing,
Till thought, word, song, to Thee in worship spring,
Immortally endowed for liberty and light.

(1835)

MARIA JANE JEWSBURY (later FLETCHER) (1800 – 33)

She was born at Measham in Derbyshire. The family moved to Manchester in 1818 where she contributed verse to the *Manchester Gazette* which attracted the attention of Alaric A. Watts. Thereafter she became a prolific contributor to many annuals. In 1825, she published *Phantasmagoria, or, Sketches of Life and Literature*..., 2 vols (1825), with a dedication to Wordsworth. In 1829, she published *Lays of Leisure Hours* (1829), with a dedication to Felicia Hemans. She was a close friend of Dora Wordsworth and stayed several times at Rydal Mount from 1825 to 1829. Wordsworth and his daughter also visited her in Manchester where she had a house in Grosvenor Street, off Oxford Road. Wordsworth had a high opinion of her talents and addressed 'Liberty' (1829) to her. In a note to its publication in 1835, he recalled 'In one quality, viz. quickness in the motions of her mind, she had, within the range of the Author's acquaintance, no equal' (*Poetical Works*, iv,157). Her quickness and intellectual vigour also struck other contemporaries. Although close to, and deeply sympathetic to, Hemans and Landon, she is perhaps, along with Emma Roberts, the most tough-minded and independent of the women poets in the 1820s and 1830s. She perhaps recognised this and in a review of Joanna Baillie (*Athenaeum*, no. 187, 28 May 1831) she distinguished the newer from the previous generation of women writers, who were 'in the spirit of their intellect, more essentially masculine; our younger ones are integrally feminine'. Again, together with Emma Roberts, she represents a lost strain of women's culture, combining the 'masculinine' intellect of the 1790s with strong attachments to female friendship. (Jewsbury was close to Hemans, Roberts close to Landon.) Hemans's sister, Harriet Hughes, similarly drew a gender distinction between Jewsbury and Hemans—'the one so intensely feminine, so susceptible and imaginative, so devoted to the tender and beautiful; the other endowed with masculine energies, with a spirit that seemed born for ascendancy, with strong powers of reasoning, fathomless profundity of thought' (*The Works of Felicia Hemans*, ed. Harriet Hughes, 7 vols, Edinburgh 1839, i,142). (The 'masculinity' of Jewsbury appears not to have been based on her appearance—portraits of her reveal a rather beautiful woman—but on her intellectual activity.) Her prose, particularly the literary criticism, is unjustly neglected. Her essay 'Woman's Love' is a subtle and energetic treatment of a difficult theme which Hemans, Landon and Abdy handled with less understanding of the implications. Her review of Shelley in 1831 accurately demarcates those aspects of Shelley which ensured his entry into the canon in the 1840s—'The very cadence of his verse, the structure of his language, seems the struggle of a spirit with sound and form, manifests a yearning after immateriality—a desire to make mere words etherial essences, impersonations of beauty—melody woke by the wind, drank by the dew, heard by the heart, and giving birth to dreams of things not earthly...', (*Athenaeum*, no. 194 (16 July 1831), p.457). *The Three Histories* (1830) takes up central themes of the cost of knowledge to women, its value, and its dangers, first articulated by Wollstonecraft and Hays, with the significant displacement of Rousseau by Madame de Staël as the reading scene which leads to the thirst for knowledge and experience, thereby releasing concepts of gender and the idea of the female artist with a female geneaology. From 1830 to 1833, she contributed numerous articles and verse to *The Athenaeum Journal* and lived in London, in Charlotte Street, off Fitzroy Square where Sara Coleridge visited her. A series of articles in *The Athenaeum* in 1832, 'On Modern Female Cultivation' (nos 222, 223, 224, 226, 250), is probably by her. She married in 1832 the Rev. William Kew Fletcher, a chaplain to the East India Company, and travelled with him to India. She died of cholera in 1833 at Poona, where Emma Roberts was also to die in 1840. They are buried close to each other. Wordsworth's letter to Edward Quillinan (11 June 1834) on hearing of her death underlines the dangers of women accompanying their husbands to posts in the Empire—'from the first we had a fore-feeling that it would be so' (WW *CL*, v. p.719).

135 THE GLORY OF THE HEIGHTS

Fame is the spur that the clear spirit doth raise,
To scorn delights and live laborious days. [Milton]

O mockery to dream of genius wed
To quiet happiness! The vale may wear
The sunlight, like a garment, rich and fair;
But the bold mountains towering overhead,
Must robe in mist and cloud,
Be girt with stormy shroud,
And when awhile in partial verdure dressed,
Must hide unmelted snows for ever in their breast.

Yet have they beauty gorgeous and divine,
And precious, even for its fitful stay;
Morn's blushing welcome, sunset's golden ray,
Can make their summits seem a glittering mine:—
Where, as with jewels strewn,
Cavern and crag unhewn,
Glow with the varied and effulgent hues,
That sapphires, amethysts, and pearls suffuse.

Yet have the mountains glory;—not repose
The bright monotony of cloudless days,
Living and dying in a sunny haze,—
Their glory is the storm;—the storm that throws
Its kindling power around,
Till passive things rebound,
And weaker elements arise, and share
The lofty strife, that else they might not dare.

Yet have the mountains glory;—they remain
The earth's eternal tenants; while the vale
Changing and changing like tradition's tale,
May scarcely one old lineament retain,—
They from their solitude
Oft see the world renewed,
The history of each age—power—pomp—decay—
And then oblivion:—not so their sway.

O mockery to dream of genius wed
To quiet happiness!—Promethean Power
Survey, and be content thy state and dower;—
A name when kings are nameless; life, when dead

Are countless generations;
A record among nations
That never knew thy being or thy birth;—
An immortality bestowed on earth!

Yet, art thou sad Magician? canst thou give
The thrilling joy thou hast no power to feel?
Yet, o'er thy spirit do the shadows steal,
Till the charmed life 'tis weariness to live?
Look from thy cloudy throne;
Heed not thy chilling zone;
To Heaven aspire;—not *there*, thy soul shall fail
To blend with mountain-power the quiet of the vale!

(1829)

136 TO MY OWN HEART

I am a little world made cunningly. [Donne]

Come, let me sound thy depths, unquiet sea
Of thought and passion; let thy wild waves be
Calm for a moment. Thou mysterious mind—
No human eye may see, no fetters bind;
Within me, ever near me as a friend
That whilst I know I fail to comprehend;
Fountain, whence sweet and bitter waters flow,
The source of happiness, the cause of woe,—
Of all that spreads o'er life enchantment's spell,
Or bids it be anticipated hell;—
Come let me talk with thee, allotted part
Of immortality—my own deep heart!
Yes, deep and hidden now, but soon unsealed,
Must thou thy deepest thoughts and secrets yield:
Like the old sea, put off the shrouding gloom
That makes thee now a prison-house and tomb;
Spectres and sins that undisturbed have lain,
Must hear the judgment-voice and live again.
Then woe or bliss for thee:—thy ocean-mate,
Material only in its birth and fate,
Its rage rebuked, its captive hosts set free,
And homage paid, shall shrink away, and be
With all the mutinous billows o'er it hurled,
Less than a dew-drop on a rose impearled!
But thou—but thou—or darker, or more fair
The sentence and the doom that waits thee there.
No rock will hide thee in its friendly breast,
No death dismiss thee to eternal rest;
The solid earth thrilled by the trumpet's call,

Like a sere leaf shall tremble ere it fall,—
From heaven to hell one Eye extend and shine,
That can forgotten deeds and thoughts divine—
How wilt thou brook that day, that glance, frail heart of mine?

Spirit within me, speak; and through the veil
That hides thee from my vision, tell thy tale;
That so the present and the past may be
Guardians and prophets to futurity.
Spirit by which I live, thou art not dumb,
I hear thy voice; I called and thou art come;
I hear thy still and whispering voice of thought
Thus speak, with memories and musings fraught:—

'Mortal, Immortal, would desires like these
Had claimed thy prime, employed thine hours of ease!
But then, within thee burned the enthusiast's fire,
Wild love of freedom, longings for the lyre;—
And ardent visions of romantic youth,
Too fair for time, and oh! too frail for truth!
Aspirings nursed by solitude and pride,
Worlds to the dreamer, dreams to all beside;
Bright vague imaginings of bliss to be,
None ever saw, yet none despaired to see,
And aimless energies that bade the mind
Launch like a ship and leave the world behind.
But duty disregarded, reason spurned,
Knowledge despised, and wisdom all unlearned,
Punished the rebel who refused to bow,
And stamped Self-Torturer on the enthusiast's brow.

'No earthly happiness exists for such,
They shrink like insects from the gentlest touch;
A breath can raise them, but a breath can kill,
And such wert thou—how sad the memory still!
Without a single real grief to own,
Yet ever mourning fancied joys o'erthrown;—
Viewing mankind with delicate disdain,
Unshared their pleasures, unrelieved their pain;
Self, thy sole object, interest, aim, end, view,
The circle's centre, oft the circle too.

''Tis past! 'tis past!—and never more may rise
The wasted hours I now have learned to prize;
Youth, like a summer sun, hath sunk to rest,
But left no glory lingering in its west.
Maturer life hath real sorrows brought,
And made me blush for those that such once thought;
Fancy is bankrupt of her golden schemes,

Tried in the world they proved but glittering dreams;
Remembrance views with unavailing tears,
The accusing phantoms of departed years,
While Hope too often lays her anchor by,
Or only lifts to heaven a troubled eye;
Too oft forebodings agonize the soul,
As lamentation filled the prophet's roll.

'Why do I speak of this? though sad, though true,
I know a calmer mood, a brighter view:
The restless ocean hath its hours of rest,
And sleep may visit those by pain oppressed;
More shade than sunlight o'er his heart may sweep,
Who yet is cheerful, nay, may seldom weep;
And he may learn, though late, and by degrees,
To love his neighbour and desire to please;
Rejoice o'er those who never go astray,
And those who do, assist to find their way:
Life he may look on with a sobered eye,
And how to live, think less than how to die;
Love all that's fair on earth, or near or far,
Yet deem the fairest but a shooting star,
And strive to point his spirit's inward sight,
To orbs for ever fixed, for ever bright;
Mourn countless sins, yet trust to be forgiven,
And feel a hesitating hope of heaven!'

(1829)

137 OCEANIDES, NO. I: THE OUTWARD-BOUND SHIP

She is on her way, a goodly ship,
With her tacklings loosed, her pilot gone;
Behind, beneath, around, the deep,
And far the land where she beareth on:
Fading, fast fading, yonder lie
The last of her home, the hills of Devon,
And the brightness and calm of a Sabbath sky
Have made them shine like the gates of heaven.

To those who watch her from the strand,
She is but a cloud 'mid sea and air!
And having gazed, perchance the band
Move onward with a languid prayer.
Yet is she vast from deck to keel,
A city moving on the waters,
Freighted with business, woe and weal,
Freighted with England's sons and daughters.

The sea is round them: many a week
They o'er that deep salt sea must roam,
And yet the sounds of land will break
The spell, and send their spirits home;
The cry of prisoned household bird,
Shrill mingling with the boatswain's call;
With surge and sail, the lowing herd,
And hark—street music over all!

'Arouse thee,' from the bugle's mouth,
And with the merry viol's aid,
Tunes gathered from the north and south,
For dance and dinner signals made:
Harsh music to the gifted ear,
Teasing, perhaps, heard day by day,
Yet often precious, often dear,
As waking dreams of—Far away.

Alas! the sea itself wakes more!
With its briny smell and heaving breast,
With its length and breadth without a shore,
With its circling line from east to west,
Telleth it not of home, of *earth*,
With her rills, and flowers, and steadfastness,
Till sick thoughts in the soul have birth,
And loathed is the foaming wilderness?

No more, no more: we are on our way:
The tropics are gained, and who would pine
For the pallid sun of an English day?
For the glittering cold of its night's moonshine?
No more, no more—why pine for flowers,
If Duty our Indian amaranth be?
If we look to the land that shall soon be ours,
A land where is 'no more sea'!

(1832)

138 OCEANIDES, NO. III: THE BURDEN OF THE SEA

Isaiah xxiii

The sea hath spoken! Hear, O Earth!
Where everlasting hills arise;
And all the host of heaven, stand forth;
Together with the crystal skies;—
And thou—world's curse and blessing—Man,
Creating, desolating all
That mind may gather in its span—
Stand forth, and bear a mightier thrall!

'I am thy prophet—puny world,
'Tis God himself that speaks by me!
By me, his wrath is oftenest hurled;
Hear, then, the vision of the sea:
Ye talk of kingdoms and of kings,
Of fleets to triumph o'er me, born,
Know—that my weeds are mightier things,
And laugh you in my depths to scorn.

'Famed cities with their harbours strong:
Where now is Tyre? and Sidon where?
I made their power, and I have rung
Their knell, upon the mountains bare:
The merchant and the mariner,
In purple clothed, and sage with skill,
Looked on me as their Servitor—
They found I had a master's will.

'Old Ninus never dared my frown;
Nor Belus, gorgeous power and bold;
Wise Egypt dared—and, overthrown,
Her hosts lie gathered in my fold.
As ocean, or as inland sea,
By golden Ind or Grecian isle,
I mock at man—the same to me
The royal fleet, the pirate vile.

'I bear them to their port of rest—
How loud their vaunts of lordly pride!
Like foam I dash them from my breast—
How cruel then my waters wide!
Yet am I one, or calm or heaving,
The changing, yet the changeless sea;
And victor, vanquished—joyous, grieving—
But one, is mortal man to me.

'The billows that engulf a fleet
And desolate a thousand homes,
The sea-bird skims with careless feet;
The nautilus securely roams;
I know not little, know not great—
Earth hath for me nor friend nor foe:
To me God never gave a mate;
The hollow of his hand I know.

'I work his will—a spirit bland,
A gentle minister of good;—
Or scatter death from land to land,
And make a burial place my flood.

Of myriad navies, myriad hosts,
I have the wrecks beneath my waves;—
Call ye them trophies?—idle boasts!
They match the coral of my caves.

'Vaunt on, proud creatures, formed of clay,
Subdue, and build, and desolate;
And grave in brass from day to day
Your strength, your glory, and your state:
March through your lands from east to west,
And be like Lucifer's your will;
But I am God's—and on my breast
Veil that high look—be meek—be still.'

(1833)

139 OCEANIDES, NO VI: THE VOYAGER'S REGRET

They are thinking far away
Of their loved ones on the water;
The mother of her son,
The father of his daughter;
And a theme of awe and wonder,
If little ones there be,
Are those parted far asunder
By the wide and unknown sea.

The hoarse roar of the billow
Is ever in my ear,
For close, close lies my pillow
To the watery desert drear;
Yet distant tones are nearer,
The greeting, song, or sigh,
Of those than empires dearer;
And tears rush to my eye.

A prisoner on the ocean,
How oft my cabin-room
On this wilderness of motion,
Reminds me of a tomb!
Yet through its windows streaming,
Flash daybreaks rich as noon;
And on my couch comes gleaming
Full oft a sunlike moon.

And stars the night-sky brighten,
Unseen, unknown before;
Alas! regret they heighten
For those beheld no more!

For constellations vanished
Though lovelier come on,
The heart's star of the banished,
The Polar Star, is gone.

Strange birds the blue air cleaving
Attract the wanderer's sight,
And stranger creatures weaving
Their path, through waves as bright;—
But I, grown sick with pining
After the things that *were*,
Over the deep reclining
But see 'mid strange or fair,
My sister's sweet face shining!—
My father's thin grey hair!

(1833)

140 OCEANIDES, NO. VII: THE SPIRIT OF THE CAPE

Change the vision. Now no more
   Gorgeous smile both sea and sky;
Sunset mimics now no shore
   Where bright domes and gardens lie;
Past are Ocean's gentle forms;
Now he breathes but cold and storms.

Seek no longer that sweet blue
   Mirrored lately in his breast;
Love and peace are gone; now view
   Death, with terror for his crest;
Briny hills in horrid show,
Heaving, boiling, to and fro.

Look not for the pearl-like spray
   Scattered late with playful hand,
Then, 'twas Ocean's holiday;
   Now, he wars with trump and brand;
Asking aid but from one other;
The old wind, his stronger twin-brother.

Hark the summons! they are greeting;
   Dire their friendship, wind and wave;
Sayst thou, man, but two are meeting?
   Mock them on, and find thy grave;
Mock with mind and fiery will;
They have mightier power and skill.

They are meeting—they are met—
Where is now the gallant ship?
Down on her side—all bruised her pride—
Her topmast on the deep—
And her strongest—amplest sail,
Shred in tatters by the gale.

Lo, they grapple! beast and prey;
Blast and billow; shroud and hull;
Grim destruction hath its way,
Till the vessel beautiful
As with woman's nerve and heart,
Downward sinks with groan and start.

Hail to thee, thou surging foam!
Hail to thee, thou screaming blast!
And hail the drowner's thought of home,
His saddest, fondest, last!
And a few more days and leagues a few,
Hail to *thee*, Ocean, calm and blue!

(1833)

141 OCEANIDES, NO. XII: THE HAVEN GAINED

And we are parting, glorious Sea!
And thou art anchored, gallant ship!
Strange, that the hour which makes me free,
Should be the one that tempts to weep;
Strange, strange that through my heart should flow
Regrets, I never dreamed to know.

How often, in a wayward mood,
Upon our thronged and sultry deck,
I've sat and longed for solitude
And silence—fondly tracing back
The fresh and stilly evening air,
All that made England dear and fair.

How often have I looked with scorn
On what I deemed my prison home;
Sick of the vastness daily born
In ocean's circle, heaven's high dome,—
Turned from the sun with evil eye,
Nay, greeted moonlight with a sigh!

But this is over: long relieved,
I have rejoiced in Night and Day;
Loved our sea-life, and only grieved
That Time, like waters, lapsed away;
Not lately, Discontent, old Sea,
Hath bent a wrinkled brow on thee.

My cabin, that I thought a tomb,
Despite its neat and bright array,
Seems now a smiling summer room
Where only Peace hath leave to stay;
And Occupation's Eden-state,
Light, mirthful, earnest, and elate.

And I have learned to read the face
Of many a rude yet kindly tar;
So loves the human eye to trace
The lines of brotherhood afar;
So longs the human heart to love
Something, beneath, around, above.

But hark, that sound!—the boat is lowered,
I never thought 'twould vex mine ear;
I thought not when I came on board
To leave at last with sigh and tear;—
But then, I did not dream to find
Such friendship as I leave behind.

(1833)

LETITIA ELIZABETH LANDON (later MACLEAN) (1802 – 38)
She was born in London and went to the same school in Chelsea as Lady Caroline Lamb and Mary Russell Mitford. She lived in Chelsea for most of her life, first at Old Brompton, where William Jerdan was a neighbour, and later in Hans Place off Sloane Street. Jerdan was shown some of her adolescent verse and encouraged her. She caused a sensation in 1820 with her first poems, contributed to Jerdan's *Literary Gazette*, with many people wondering who she was. She continued her association with the magazine until 1836, also contributing reviews. She also contributed to the *New Monthly Magazine*, particularly after 1833 and to almost every annual, editing *Fisher's Drawing-Room Scrapbook* from 1830. She published longer poems in separate volumes, *The Fate of Adelaide* (1821), *The Improvisatrice* (1824), *The Troubadour* (1825), *The Golden Violet* (1827), *The Venetian Bracelet* (1828), *The Vow of the Peacock* (1835). Emma Roberts, a friend with whom she lived for a time, published a posthumous collection with a memoir, *The Zenana and Minor Poems* (1839), as did Laman Blanchard, *Life and Literary Remains*, 2 vols (1841). W.B. Scott edited *The Poetical Works* (1873). (An

earlier *Poetical Works*, 2 vols (1850) is very incomplete.) Landon's novels included *Romance and Reality*, 3 vols (1831), and *Ethel Churchill*, 3 vols (1837). She was subject to much rumour of indiscretion, infidelity and possibly abortion. As early as 1824, Mary Howitt remarked that she was 'a most thoughtless girl in company, doing strangely extravagant things'. Some, however, thought that the rumours of an affair with Dr Maginn were the scurrilous efforts of a minor group associated with *Blackwood's* who had earlier feted her. An engagement to John Forster was broken off and in June 1838 she married George Maclean, the Governor of Cape Coast Castle. This may have been due to the increasing rumours but Lord Lytton, who knew her well, thought that the romance of the far-away had got the better of her. However, the Countess of Blessington recalled in 1839 that the rumours, though untrue, had caused her great suffering, and she could not sleep without narcotics. (Her generosity in supporting relatives from the profits of her writings did little to redeem her.) She returned with Maclean, and two of her last poems were probably written on the voyage to the Gold Coast. She died in mysterious circumstances four months later from prussic acid poisoning. There were rumours at the time that she had been poisoned by the negro daughter of a king who had four or five children by Maclean but suicide was widely accepted and accidental death the most polite version.

142 ST GEORGE'S HOSPITAL, HYDE-PARK CORNER

These are familiar things, and yet how few
Think of this misery! –

I left the crowded street and the fresh day,
And entered the dark dwelling, where Death was
A daily visitant,—where sickness shed
Its weary langour o'er each fevered couch.
There was a sickly light, whose glimmer showed
Many a shape of misery: there lay
The victims of disease, writhing with pain;
And low faint groans, and breathings short and deep,
Each gasp a heartfelt agony, were all
That broke the stillness.—There was one, whose brow
Dark with hot climates, and gashed o'er with scars,
Told of the toiling march, the battle-rush,
Where sabres flashed, the red shots flew, and not
One ball or blow but did Destruction's work:
But then his heart was high, and his pulse beat
Proudly and fearlessly:—now he was worn
With many a long day's suffering,—and death's
A fearful thing when we must count its steps!
And was this, then, the end of those sweet dreams
Of home, of happiness, of quiet years
Spent in the little valley which had been
So long his land of promise? Farewell all
Gentle remembrances and cherished hopes!
His race was run, but its goal was the grave.—
I looked upon another, wasted, pale,
With eyes all heavy in the sleep of death;

Yet she was lovely still,—the cold damps hung
Upon a brow like marble, and her eyes,
Though dim, had yet their beautiful blue tinge.
Neglected as it was, her long fair hair
Was like the plumage of the dove, and spread
Its waving curls like gold upon her pillow;
Her face was a sweet ruin. She had loved,
Trusted, and been betrayed! In other days,
Had but her cheek looked pale, how tenderly
Fond hearts had watched it! They were far away,—
She was a stranger in her loneliness,
And sinking to the grave of that worst ill,
A broken heart.—And there was one whose cheek
Was flushed with fever—'twas a face that seemed
Familiar to my memory,—'twas one
Whom I had loved in youth. In days long past,
How many glorious structures we had raised
Upon Hope's sandy basis! Genius gave
To him its golden treasures: he could pour
His own impassioned soul upon the lyre;
Or, with a painter's skill, create such shapes
Of loveliness, they were more like the hues
Of the rich evening shadows, than the work
Of human touch. But he was wayward, wild;
And hopes that in his heart's warm summer clime
Flourished, were quickly withered in the cold
And dull realities of life;... he was
Too proud, too visionary, for this world;
And feelings which, like waters unconfined,
Had carried with them freshness and green beauty,
Thrown back upon themselves, spread desolation
On their own banks. He was a sacrifice,
And sank beneath neglect; his glowing thoughts
Were fires that preyed upon himself. Perhaps,
For he has left some high memorials, Fame
Will pour its sunlight o'er the picture, when
The artist's hand is mouldering in the dust,
And fling the laurel o'er a harp whose chords
Are dumb for ever. But his eyes he raised
Mutely to mine—he knew my voice again,
And every vision of his boyhood rushed
Over his soul; his lip was deadly pale,
But pride was yet upon its haughty curve;...
He raised one hand contemptuously, and seemed
As he would bid me mark his fallen state,
And that it was unheeded. So he died
Without one struggle, and his brow in death
Wore its pale marble look of cold defiance.

(1822)

143 [RUINS OF IDEAL PRESENCE]

Is there not a far people, who possess
Mysterious oracles of olden time,
Who say that this earth labours with a curse,
That it is fallen from its first estate,
And is now but the shade of what it was?
I do believe the tale. I feel its truth
In my vain aspirations, in the dreams
That are revealings of another world,
More pure, more perfect than our weary one,
Where day is darkness to the starry soul.

O heart of mine! my once sweet paradise
Of love and hope! how changed thou art to me!
I cannot count thy changes: thou hast lost
Interest in the once idols of thy being;
They have departed, even as if wings
Had borne away their morning; they have left
Weariness, turning pleasure into pain,
And too sure knowledge of their hollowness.

And that too is gone from me; that which was
My solitude's delight! I can no more
Make real existence of a shadowy world.
Time was, the poet's song, the ancient tale,
Were to me fountains of deep happiness,
For they grew visible in my lonely hours,
As things in which I had a deed and part;
Their actual presence had not been more true:
But these are bubbling sparkles, that are found
But at the spring's first souce. Ah! years may bring
The mind to its perfection, but no more
Will those young visions live in their own light;
Life's troubles stir life's waters all too much,
Passions chase fancies, and though still we dream,
The colouring is from reality....

(1827)

144 [INTIMATIONS OF PREVIOUS EXISTENCE]

Methinks we must have known some former state
More glorious than our present, and the heart
Is haunted with dim memories, shadows left
By past magnificence; and hence we pine
With vain aspirings, hopes that fill the eyes
With bitter tears for their own vanity.

Remembrance makes the poet: 'tis the past
Lingering within him, with a keener sense
Than is upon the thoughts of common men
Of what has been, that fills the actual world
With unreal likenesses of lovely shapes,
That were and are not; and the fairer they,
The more their contrast with existing things;
The more his power, the greater is his grief.
—Are we then fallen from some noble star,
Whose consciousness is an unknown curse,
And we feel capable of happiness
Only to know it is not of our sphere?

(1829)

145 THE FACTORY

'Tis an accursed thing! –

There rests a shade above yon town,
  A dark funereal shroud:
'Tis not the tempest hurrying down,
  'Tis not a summer cloud.

The smoke that rises on the air
  Is as a type and sign;
A shadow flung by the despair
  Within those streets of thine.

That smoke shuts out the cheerful day,
  The sunset's purple hues,
The moonlight's pure and tranquil ray,
  The morning's pearly dews.

Such is the moral atmosphere
  Around thy daily life;
Heavy with care, and pale with fear,
  With future tumult rife.

There rises on the morning wind
  A low appealing cry,
A thousand children are resigned
  To sicken and to die!

We read of Moloch's sacrifice,
  We sicken at the name,
And seem to hear the infant cries—
  And yet we do the same;—

And worse—'twas but a moment's pain
   The heathen altar gave,
But we give years,—our idol, Gain,
   Demands a living grave!

How precious is the little one,
   Before his mother's sight,
With bright hair dancing in the sun,
   And eyes of azure light!

He sleeps as rosy as the south,
   For summer days are long;
A prayer upon the little mouth,
   Lulled by his nurse's song.

Love is around him, and his hours
   Are innocent and free;
His mind essays its early powers
   Beside his mother's knee.

When after-years of trouble come,
   Such as await man's prime,
How will he think of that dear home,
   And childhood's lovely time!

And such should childhood ever be,
   The fairy well; to bring
To life's worn, weary memory
   The freshness of its spring.

But here the order is reversed,
   And infancy, like age,
Knows of existence but its worst,
   One dull and darkened page;—

Written with tears, and stamped with toil,
   Crushed from the earliest hour,
Weeds darkening on the bitter soil
   That never knew a flower.

Look on yon child, it droops the head,
   Its knees are bowed with pain;
It mutters from its wretched bed,
   'Oh, let me sleep again!'

Alas! 'tis time, the mother's eyes
   Turn mournfully away;
Alas! 'tis time, the child must rise,
   And yet it is not day.

The lantern's lit—she hurries forth,
  The spare cloak's scanty fold
Scarce screens her from the snowy north,
  The child is pale and cold.

And wearily the little hands
  Their task accustomed ply;
While daily, some mid those pale bands,
  Droop, sicken, pine, and die.

Good God! to think upon a child
  That has no childish days,
No careless play, no frolics wild,
  No words of prayer and praise!

Man from the cradle—'tis too soon
  To earn their daily bread,
And heap the heat and toil of noon
  Upon an infant's head.

To labour ere their strength be come,
  Or starve,—is such the doom
That makes of many an English home
  One long and living tomb?

Is there no pity from above,—
  No mercy in those skies;
Hath then the heart of man no love,
  To spare such sacrifice?

Oh, England! though thy tribute waves
  Proclaim thee great and free,
While those small children pine like slaves,
  There is a curse on thee!

(1835)

146 [INFLUENCE OF POETRY]

This is the charm of poetry: it comes
On sad perturbed moments; and its thoughts,
Like pearls amid the troubled waters, gleam.
That which we garnered in our eager youth,
Becomes a long delight in after years:
The mind is strengthened and the heart refreshed
By some old memory of gifted words,
That bring sweet feelings, answering to our own,
Or dreams that waken some more lofty mood
Than dwelleth with the common-place of life.

(1837)

147 THREE EXTRACTS FROM THE DIARY OF A WEEK

A record of the inward world, whose facts
Are thoughts—and feelings—fears, and hopes, and dreams.
There are some days that might outmeasure years—
Days that obliterate the past, and make
The future of the colour which they cast.
A day may be a destiny: for life
Lives in but little—but that little teems
With some one chance, the balance of all time:
A look—a word—and we are wholly changed.
We marvel at ourselves—we would deny
That which is working in the hidden soul;
But the heart knows and trembles at the truth:
On such these records linger.

WE MIGHT HAVE BEEN!

We might have been!—these are but common words,
   And yet they make the sum of life's bewailing;
They are the echo of those finer chords,
   Whose music life deplores when unavailing.
         We might have been!

We might have been so happy! says the child,
   Pent in the weary school-room during summer,
When the green rushes 'mid the marshes wild,
   And rosy fruits, attend the radiant comer.
         We might have been!

It is the thought that darkens on our youth,
   When first experience—sad experience—teaches
What fallacies we have believed for truth,
   And what few truths endeavour ever reaches.
         We might have been!

Alas! how different from what we are
   Had we but known the bitter path before us;
But feelings, hopes, and fancies left afar,
   What in the wide bleak world can e'er restore us?
         We might have been!

It is the motto of all human things,
   The end of all that waits on mortal seeking;
The weary weight upon Hope's flagging wings,
   It is the cry of the worn heart while breaking.
         We might have been!

And when, warm with the heaven that gave it birth,
   Dawns on our world-worn way Love's hour Elysian,
The last fair angel lingering on our earth,
   The shadow of what thought obscures the vision?
         We might have been!

A cold fatality attends on love,
Too soon or else too late the heart-beat quickens;
The star which is our fate springs up above,
And we but say—while round the vapour thickens—
We might have been!

Life knoweth no like misery; the rest
Are single sorrows,—but in this are blended
All sweet emotions that disturb the breast;
The light that was our loveliest is ended.
We might have been!

Henceforth, how much of the full heart must be
A sealèd book at whose contents we tremble?
A still voice mutters 'mid our misery,
The worst to hear, because it must dissemble—
We might have been!

Life is made up of miserable hours,
And all of which we craved a brief possessing,
For which we wasted wishes, hopes, and powers,
Comes with some fatal drawback on the blessing.
We might have been!

The future never renders to the past
The young beliefs intrusted to its keeping;
Inscribe one sentence—life's first truth and last—
On the pale marble where our dust is sleeping—
We might have been.

NECESSITY

In the ancestral presence of the dead
Sits a lone power—a veil upon the head,
Stern with the terror of an unseen dread.

It sitteth cold, immutable, and still,
Girt with eternal consciousness of ill,
And strong and silent as its own dark will.

We are the victims of its iron rule,
The warm and beating human heart its tool;
And man, immortal, godlike, but its fool.

We know not of its presence, though its power
Be on the gradual round of every hour,
Now flinging down an empire, now a flower.

And all things small and careless are its own,
Unwittingly the seed minute is sown,—
The tree of evil out of it is grown.

At times we see and struggle with our chain,
And dream that somewhat we are freed, in vain;
The mighty fetters close on us again.

We mock our actual strength with lofty thought,
And towers that look into the heavens are wrought,—
But after all our toil the task is nought.

Down comes the stately fabric, and the sands
Are scattered with the work of myriad hands,
High o'er whose pride the fragile wild-flower stands.

Such are the wrecks of nations and of kings,
Far in the desert, where the palm-tree springs;
'Tis the same story in all meaner things.

The heart builds up its hopes, though not addrest
To meet the sunset glories of the west,
But garnered in some still, sweet-singing nest.

But the dark power is on its noiseless way,
The song is silent so sweet yesterday,
And not a green leaf lingers on the spray.

We mock ourselves with freedom, and with hope,
The while our feet glide down life's faithless slope;
One has no strength, the other has no scope.

So we are flung on Time's tumultuous wave,
Force there to struggle, but denied to save,
Till the stern tide ebbs—and there is the grave.

MEMORY

I do not say bequeath unto my soul
   Thy memory,—I rather ask forgetting;
Withdraw, I pray, from me thy strong control,
   Leave something in the wide world worth regretting.

I need my thoughts for other things than thee,
   I dare not let thine image fill them only;
The hurried happiness it wakes in me
   Will leave the hours that are to come more lonely.

I live not like the many of my kind;
   Mine is a world of feelings and of fancies,
Fancies whose rainbow-empire is the mind,
   Feelings that realize their own romances.

To dream and to create has been my fate,
   Alone, apart from life's more busy scheming;
I fear to think that I may find too late
   Vain was the toil, and idle was the dreaming.

Have I upreared my glorious pyre of thought,
   Up to the heavens, but for my own entombing?
The fair and fragrant things that years have brought
   Must they be gathered for my own consuming?

Oh! give me back the past that took no part
   In the existence it was but surveying;
That knew not then of the awakened heart
   Amid the life of other lives decaying.

Why should such be mine own? I sought it not:
   More than content to live apart and lonely,
The feverish tumult of a loving lot,
   Is what I wished, and thought to picture only.

Surely the spirit is its own free will;
   What should o'ermaster mine to vain complying
With hopes that call down what they bring of ill,
   With fears to their own questioning replying?

In vain, in vain! Fate is above us all;
   We struggle, but what matters our endeavour?
Our doom is gone beyond our own recall,
   May we deny or mitigate it?—never!

And what art thou to me,—thou who dost wake
   The mind's still depths with trouble and repining?
Nothing;—though all things now thy likeness take;
   Nothing,—and life has nothing worth resigning.

Ah, yes! one thing, thy memory; though grief
   Watching the expiring beam of hope's last ember;
Life had one hour,—bright, beautiful, and brief,
   And now its only task is to remember.

(1837)

148 FELICIA HEMANS

No more, no more—oh, never more returning,
   Will thy beloved presence gladden earth;
No more wilt thou with sad, yet anxious yearning
   Cling to those hopes which have no mortal birth.
Though art gone from us, and with thee departed,
   How many lovely things have vanished too;
Deep thoughts that at thy will to being started,
   And feelings, teach us our own were true.
Thou hast been round us, like a viewless spirit,
   Known only by the music on the air;
The leaf or flowers which thou hast named inherit
   A beauty known but from thy breathing there:
For thou didst on them fling thy strong emotion,
   The likeness from itself the fond heart gave;
As planets from afar look down on ocean,
   And give their own sweet image to the wave.

And thou didst bring from foreign lands their treasures,
   As floats thy various melody along;
We know the softness of Italian measures,
   And the grave cadence of Castilian song.
A general bond of union is the poet,
   By its immortal verse is language known,
And for the sake of song do others know it—
   One glorious poet makes the world his own.
And thou—how far thy gentle sway extended!
   The heart's sweet empire over land and sea;
Many a stranger and far flower was blended
   In the soft wreath that glory bound for thee.
The echoes of the Susquehanna's waters
   Paused in the pine-woods words of thine to hear;
And to the wide Atlantic's younger daughters
   Thy name was lovely, and thy song was dear.

Was not this purchased all too dearly?—never
   Can fame atone for all that fame hath cost.
We see the goal, but know not the endeavour,
   Nor what fond hopes have on the way been lost.
What do we know of the unquiet pillow,
   By the worn cheek and tearful eyelid pressed,
When thoughts chased thoughts, like the tumultuous billow,
   Whose very light and foam reveals unrest?
We say, the song is sorrowful, but know not
   What may have left that sorrow on the song;
However mournful words may be, they show not
   The whole extent of wretchedness and wrong
They cannot paint the long sad hours, passed only

In vain regrets o'er what we feel we are.
Alas! the kingdom of the lute is lonely—
Cold is the worship coming from afar.

Yet what is mind in woman, but revealing
In sweet clear light the hidden world below,
By quicker fancies and a keener feeling
Than those around, the cold and careless, know?
What is to feed such feeling, but to culture
A soil whence pain will never more depart?
The fable of Prometheus and the vulture
Reveals the poet's and the woman's heart.
Unkindly are they judged—unkindly treated—
By careless tongues and by ungenerous words;
While cruel sneer, and hard reproach, repeated,
Jar the fine music of the spirit's chords.
Wert thou not weary—thou whose soothing numbers
Gave other lips the joy thine own had not?
Didst thou not welcome thankfully the slumbers
Which closed around thy mourning human lot?

What on this earth could answer thy requiring,
For earnest faith—for love, the deep and true,
The beautiful, which was thy soul's desiring,
But only from thyself its being drew.
How is the warm and loving heart requited
In this harsh world, where it awhile must dwell.
Its best affections wronged, betrayed, and slighted—
Such is the doom of those who love too well.
Better the weary dove should close its pinion,
Fold up its golden wings and be at peace:
Enter, O ladye, that serene dominion
Where earthly cares and earthly sorrows cease.
Fame's troubled hour has cleared, and now replying,
A thousand hearts their music ask of thine.
Sleep with a light, the lovely and undying
Around thy grave—a grave which is a shrine.

(1838)

149 NIGHT AT SEA

The lovely purple of the noon's bestowing
   Has vanished from the waters, where it flung
A royal colour, such as gems are throwing
   Tyrian or regal garniture among.
'Tis night, and overhead the sky is gleaming,
   Through the slight vapour trembles each dim star;
I turn away—my heart is sadly dreaming
   Of scenes they do not light, of scenes afar.
            My friends, my absent friends!
               Do you think of me, as I think of you?

By each dark wave around the vessel sweeping,
   Farther am I from old dear friends removed,
Till the lone vigil that I now am keeping,
   I did not know how much you were beloved.
How many acts of kindness little heeded,
   Kind looks, kind words, rise half reproachful now!
Hurried and anxious, my vexed life has speeded,
   And memory wears a soft accusing brow.
            My friends, my absent friends!
               Do you think of me, as I think of you?

The very stars are strangers, as I catch them
   Athwart the shadowy sails that swell above;
I cannot hope that other eyes will watch them
   At the same moment with a mutual love.
They shine not there, as here they now are shining,
   The very hours are changed.—Ah, do ye sleep?
O'er each home pillow, midnight is declining,
   May some kind dream at least my image keep!
            My friends, my absent friends!
               Do you think of me, as I think of you?

Yesterday has a charm, to-day could never
   Fling o'er the mind, which knows not till it parts
How it turns back with tenderest endeavour
   To fix the past within the heart of hearts.
Absence is full of memory, it teaches
   The value of all old familiar things;
The strengthener of affection, while it reaches
   O'er the dark parting, with an angel's wings.
            My friends, my absent friends!
               Do you think of me, as I think of you?

The world with one vast element omitted—
   Man's own especial element, the earth,
Yet, o'er the waters is his rule transmitted
   By that great knowledge whence has power its birth.

How oft on some strange loveliness while gazing
  Have I wished for you,—beautiful as new,
The purple waves like some wild army raising
  Their snowy banners as the ship cuts through.
    My friends, my absent friends!
      Do you think of me, as I think of you?

Bearing upon its wing the hues of morning,
  Up springs the flying fish, like life's false joy,
Which of the sunshine asks that frail adorning
  Whose very light is fated to destroy.
Ah, so doth genius on its rainbow pinion,
  Spring from the depths of an unkindly world;
So spring sweet fancies from the heart's dominion,—
  Too soon in death the scorched up wing is furled.
    My friends, my absent friends!
      Whate'er I see is linked with thoughts of you.

No life is in the air, but in the waters
  Are creatures, huge and terrible and strong,
The sword-fish and the shark pursue their slaughters,
  War universal reigns these depths along.
Like some new island on the ocean springing,
  Floats on the surface some gigantic whale,
From its vast head a silver fountain flinging
  Bright as the fountain in a fairy tale.
    My friends, my absent friends!
      I read such fairy legends while with you.

Light is amid the gloomy canvass spreading,
  The moon is whitening the dusky sails,
From the thick bank of clouds she masters, shedding
  The softest influence that o'er night prevails.
Pale is she like a young queen pale with splendour,
  Hunted with passionate thoughts too fond, too deep,
The very glory that she wears is tender,
  The eyes that watch her beauty fain would weep.
    My friends, my absent friends!
      Do you think of me, as I think of you?

Sunshine is ever cheerful, when the morning
    Wakens the world with cloud-dispelling eyes;
The spirits mount to glad endeavour, scorning
  What toil upon a path so sunny lies.
Sunshine and hope are comrades, and their weather
  Calls into life the energies of earth;
But memory and moonlight go together,
  Reflected in the light that either brings.
    My friends, my absent friends!
      Do you think of me then? I think of you.

The busy deck is hushed, no sounds are waking
   But the watch pacing silently and slow;
The waves against the sides incessant breaking,
   And rope and canvass swaying to and fro.
The topmast sail seems some dim pinnacle
   Cresting a shadowy tower amid the air;
While red and fitful gleams come from the binnacle,
   The only light on board to guide us—where?
            My friends, my absent friends!
               Far from my native land, and far from you.

On one side of the ship the moonbeams shimmer
   Inluminous vibration sweeps the sea,
But where the shadow falls, a strange pale glimmer
   Seems glow-worm like amid the waves to be.
All that the spirit keeps of thought and feeling,
   Takes visionary hues from such an hour;
But while some fantasy is o'er me stealing,
   I start, remembrance has a keener power.
            My friends, my absent friends,
               From the fair dream I start to think of you!

A dusk line in the moonlight I discover,
   What all day long vainly I sought to catch;
Or is it but the varying clouds that hover
   Thick in the air, to mock the eyes that watch?
No! well the sailor knows each speck appearing.
   Upon the tossing waves, the far-off strand
To that dusk line our eager ship is steering.
   Her voyage done—to-morrow we shall land.

(Wr. 1838, pub. 1839)

MARIA ABDY (née SMITH) (*c.* 1797 – 1867)

She was born in London and was writing verse by the age of nine. At an early age she married the Rev. John Channing Abdy. She contributed to *The New Monthly Magazine* and various annuals. She published *Poetry* (1834) and seven more privately printed volumes.

150 THE DREAM OF THE POETESS

She smiles in her slumber—what visions arise
Beneath the closed lids of those beautiful eyes!
Does she feel inspiration vast, mighty, and deep?
Does the light of her mind sparkle forth in her sleep?

Does she tread the gay hall? does she hear the soft strain
Of eager and earnest devotion again?
Does she gather fresh laurels to bind on her brow?
No; quelled is the pride of the Poetess now!

She dreams of the home where in childhood she strayed:
Once more she reclines in the sycamore shade;
Before her, the river glides gaily along,
And she hears the sweet tones of the nightingale's song.

The bright, varied flowers of her garden she tends,
She roams through the woodlands with dear valued friends;
She sits with her kindred at evening's calm hour,
And touches the lute in her jessamine bower.

She wakes—she goes forth to the multitude's gaze,
They greet her with murmurs of pleasure and praise!
She is courted by dames in the trappings of pride,
And nobles contend for a place at her side.

But her dark eye is dimmed by a sorrowing tear,
The voice of the stranger sounds harsh in her ear;
She thinks on her home, on the pleasures long fled,
On the friends and the parents, changed, absent, or dead.

Oh! thus turns the heart with unvarying truth
To the scenes and the thoughts of its earliest youth;
And we feel when life's gaudiest gifts are possessed,
Our simplest enjoyments have still been our best.

'Tis true, when the banner of Fame is unfurled,
Man finds his reward in the smiles of the world;
But Woman, though raised by that world to a throne,
Will languish, if destined to fill it alone.

Though her path be illumined by intellect's ray,
She sighs for companions to gladden her way;
And this feeling her proudest renown must attend—
In an equal alone we can hope for a friend.

The region of fancy faint bliss can impart
To her who has lived in the world of the heart;
And the thoughts of the Poetess ever are cast
To the friends of her youth, to the home of the past.

(1836)

MARY BROWNE (later GRAY) (1812 – 45)

She was born in Maidenhead and wrote verse from an early age. She published *Mont Blanc* (1827), *Ada* (1828), *Repentance* (1829), *The Coronal* (1833), *The Birth-day Gift* (1834), *Ignatia* (1838). She moved to Liverpool in 1836 and Dublin in 1839, marrying James Gray in 1842. Although rumoured to be Felicia Hemans's sister, she was not, and lived in some poverty.

151 THE POETESS

She was a worshipped one!
   Wreathed with a poet's crown;
And o'er her path the sun
   Of fame shone down.

And in the glittering crowd,
   None were more praised than she;
And idly flatterers bowed
   To her the knee.

And when the wine was poured,
   To her the cup was crowned;
And, at the festal board,
   Her name went round.

Yet, was her young heart shut,
   And to their flattery chill;
For, oh! her heart was but
   A woman's still,

Oh! haughtier man may turn,
   To search for fame afar,
And on his brow may burn
   Glory's false star.

But woman soonest sees
   How fading is its light!
How soon its beauty flees,
   And leaves but night.

Sweeter than bard ere sung,
   Are the dear words that come
Warm from the heart and tongue
   Of those at home!

Oh! woman's heart is like
   The silent ocean cave,
Where sunbeams never strike
   Through the pure wave.

Yet in its treasure cells,
   Far from the tempest's power,
Affection fondly dwells,
   Like the sea-flower.

And countless, priceless heaps
   Of gem-like feelings bright,
Hidden within its deeps,
   Are all its light.

The glow of fame may play
   Awhile upon its face,
But soon will pass away,
   And have no place.

And, as the sunshine ne'er
   Down to the sea cave came,
So never pierceth there
   The light of fame.

(1828)

152 THOUGHTS ON THE SEA SHORE IN AN AUTUMN EVENING

Lonely I wander forth—
Evening is coming down with floating wing
Noiselessly through the sky, and over earth
      No wind is murmuring;
The giant shadows of the rocks no more
Fall darkly on the bed of shining sand,
      That bounds the ocean hoar;
The sun hath set behind them, and unfanned
By a single breath, e'en on their very tops,
Bend the tall sea-weeds, looking down below
Upon the narrow ridge, where the goat crops
The short wild plants that in their fissures grow—
So high as they, no human foot can go;
And higher than they the birds have made their nests,
And the eagle sitteth on their craggy crests;
And higher than birds can soar we know is heaven.
Oh! man should gaze, and feel his littleness!
Vainly to reach those summits he has striven,
And yet, compared to the birds, is powerless.
The quiet mists rise from the sleeping sea,
And wrap it in their curtain silently:
A mother could not gentlier veil her child,
Or hold her breath more stilly than the air;

Look up! the very clouds are resting there
Unstirred, between the faint stars—dewy, mild.
And there is but one sound—the low soft fret
Of the incoming tide,—the midmost sea
Is voiceless as the heavens,—not yet—not yet,
But soon shall all its lucid beauty be
Revealed,—for lo! afar the moon's bright face
Is raised above the eastern mountain's cover,
And the far sea hath one long line of light;
Oh! she is peering from her resting-place,
Like some fond princess on her whispering lover,
When her proud sovereign sire is out of sight!

Up, up in heaven! look, look! at last—at last—
She is careering—not through ether clear
As in a summer's night; around her cast
Is a dim cloudy halo—it does appear
As if from the sea's mantling mist 'twere formed,
But into life and perfect beauty warmed,
By her it circleth with its graceful curl;
Call it a royal chariot of pure pearl,
For is she not a queen? the queen of night!
Lo! the bold foreheads of the rocks rejoice,
And their lone weeds look silvery in her light;
And the king eagle greets her with his voice,
In one long shriek, as, turning in his nest,
His eye half opening catches her pure light:
'Tis not the light he loves of all the best,
But it is grateful to him, 'tis so bright:
His eye is shut again—his plumes are still,
Save where the beatings of his savage heart
Move them like the deep ocean down below;
Who knows but he may dream? and even now,
Visions of his day conquests up may start,
    And through his spirit thrill,
But softened by the potency of sleep,
The moonlight, and the murmuring of the deep.

'Tis strange, I can remember some years past,
When I was yet a child, unknowing sorrow,
My heart, from such a scene as this, did borrow
Merely a sense of something vague, grand, vast;
I could not have described it for the world;
Like the mist o'er yon waters it so curled
Around my heart, it shut out all things, save
A feeling—many feelings—deep—intense,
But as unlinked with any thing of sense,
    As the stars with the wave,
Whose bosom in its distant swell seems heaving

Close to the heavens, but when we are near it seems
Still the horizon stretching onwards—leaving
The spirit nought but dreams
Of an eternity of sea and sky.
Oh, feeling then was all my poesy!
I had no power to speak it, or my powers
Were lazy in luxuriance; in those hours
My heart slept 'midst its wealth of pure affection,
And bowed beneath its influence (like a tree
Bending with its own blossoms); cold reflection,
Like the wind, came not near, so rich, and free,
My love shed incense on the atmosphere
Of my sweet home,—alas! the blossoms died!
The breath of autumn winds is sighing near!
My heart hath brought itself to poverty,
By squandering upon worthless hearts its store
Of hope and passion—confidence and pride!
Alas, alas! it is a leafless tree!
It shall not bow beneath its blossoms more.
But its bare stem can catch each passing wind
Of passion, and re-echo it—its bough
Rustles and tells of feelings, undefined
In happy days, but named and measured now.

(1833)

153 MIDNIGHT MUSINGS

Solemn midnight's tingling silentness. [Shelley]

To sit alone at midnight hour,
To gaze upon the poet's page,
And with some still, mysterious power,
That o'er the throbbing heart may lower,
The war with reason's dart to wage;
To watch the quivering, glimmering lamp,
Or, on the uncurtained window pane,
To see the cold and misty rain
From darkness creep with glistening damp;
To listen even for a breath,
Yet on the quickened sense to feel
Only the stilliness of death,
So heavy, that the thunder peal
And lightning flash, rending at once
The veil of silence and of gloom,
That o'er the world in broad expanse
Hangs, like some giant raven's plume,
Would be relief;—oh! hours like these,
How often have I courted them,

They brought such calmness on my soul,—
The soul, that, even as the seas,
Held shrouded many a precious gem
Of thought, that in the waters' roll
Was hidden, but shone clearly through
When quiet did its strength renew.

Strange thoughts—deep thoughts—mysterious thoughts,
In hours like these have haunted me,
Sometimes as numerous as the motes
In sunshine, and as rapidly
Changing and circling, all confused;
And sometimes, stately visions came,
Built as it were of living flame;
And sometimes, calmly I have mused,
And thought of days and hours past by,
Of things that pleased me as a child;
And in my solitude have smiled,
At memories of my free and wild
Delights; and sometimes heaved a sigh
For wasted love, and hope's deceiving,
For all the dreams that came and went,
Like clouds across the firmament,
And still rebuked my fond believing.

And then, awhile forgetting self,
(That pivot upon which the mind
Still turns, and turns, and turns again,
Although our thoughts for other men
Wave round it still, as in the wind
Weeds quiver, though upon the shelf
Of some firm rock their roots are set;)
Forgetting self, I say, awhile,
Forgetting fear, and grief, and guile,
In council calm, my thoughts have met;
And in its orb, even as an eye
Dilating o'er some prospect wide,
My soul has spread, as o'er the tide
Of human hopes, and fears, and ways,
It fixed its clear and earnest gaze.

And then it seems as if my heart
And spirit, near the crowd of men,
Stood watching them, alone—apart—
And unallied to mortals then;—
And Time!—methinks it well may seem
Even as an everflowing river,
That men are breasting still, for ever,
And striving onwards 'gainst the stream

That bears all hopes and joys,—all save
Themselves, and even themselves at last,
When weak with struggling with the wave,—
Down to the ocean of the past.
And human hopes! oh! they resemble
The flowers upon the orchard trees,
That in the April breezes tremble
And fall, some leaving fruit behind,
In summer to be perfected,
But mostly scattered in the wind
Of disappointment, that doth seize
So many dreams by fancy bred.
And sometimes, in more cheerful moods,
Cheerful, yet grave, I think of all
The blessedness, that still doth fall
Upon earth's varied multitudes;
Of all the hearts where love is dwelling,
As in a temple,—of the springs
Of happiness around them welling—
And of the fervent faith, that clings
To woman's heart; of mothers, blessing
Their little children as they sleep;
Of fathers, who, again caressing
The prodigal, for gladness weep;
Of all the holy household spells,
Laid on our hearts in early days,—
Our mother's smile, our father's praise,
To be to us as pleasant wells
In memory's paths, on whose green brink
In safety we may sit and drink.

Thoughts of the glorious outer world,
Dreams of the mountain and the river,
And clouds on clouds, at sunset curled,
And of the moonlight's silver quiver
Upon the sea—and oftener still
Sweet fantasies of garden bowers,
With a low wind-like creeping thrill,
Whispering amongst the quiet flowers,
As though in unknown tongues they held
Converse, too pure and too refined
To fill the grosser earthly mind,
Which, in the chilly atmosphere
Of worldly thoughts grown hard and dull,
The subtle influences repelled
Of those low voices beautiful,
Which it imperfectly did hear.

MARY
BROWNE

Queen lily! and thou, crimson rose!
Blushing as if with passion, but
So pure, with such a deep repose
Around thee, and the leaves so shut
About thy heart, thou canst but be
An image made for youthful love
In its first unsunned purity,
Flowing like starlight from above.
And thou, rich dewy violet!
A gem of light in darkness set.
And blessed primrose! that dost bring,
Thoughts of the purest virgin, Spring!
Oh! often in my midnight thought,
Have ye amidst my visions wrought;
And Memory, with her power intense,
Hath your own freshest fragrance brought
Almost upon my very sense,
Leaving an aching at my heart,
A longing to be out again
Into the woodland and the plain,
Or in the garden where sweet art
Worketh with nature.—Flowers! ye are,
Of all my dreams, the fairest far.
But be my thoughts of what they will,
Still do they always merge in one,—
As many various pathways run
Unto one point, all tending still,—
The thought—Of all this world below,
How little doth the wisest know,
How less of all the thoughts that start
To life in one poor human heart,
Of which so few e'er find a word,
And fewer still are registered.
And humbled do I turn at length,
With lowly heart, and tearful eyes,
To that One Mind, whose endless strength
Around us as a girdle lies;
From whom we borrow all the light
That through our weary darkness shines,
To whom we look through life's long night,
While the impatient spirit pines
For day and knowledge. We are blind,
We stumble in an unknown path,
And faith alone may be the clue
That power, and strength, and safety hath,
To guide us the dark valley through;
And then our strength He will renew,
And from our eyes the veil unbind.
Oh, thinking on my littleness,

And on my ignorance, and sin,
On all the wayward thoughts within,
Rising like tyrants to oppress,
Kneeling, and humbled to the dust,
Thus have I prayed in faith and trust.—

The merciful art Thou,
   Spirit! who dwellest in the heaven above;
   Now, in thy boundless love,
Unto the creature of thy framing, bow.

I pray not to be taught
   The mysteries that none have fathomed here;
   I pray not 'gainst the fear
Upon my spirit by thy glory brought;

I pray not for revealings
   Of future days—not for an earthly gift
   My hands and heart I lift,
In the impassioned glow of earthly feelings;

I pray for patient faith,
   That I may still the longings of my soul,
   And its strong gasps control,
Until thou raisest up the veil of death.

I pray for holiness,
   For calm, pure thoughts, untouched by passion's stain,
   Like flowers, before the rain
Hath drooped their gentle heads in meek distress.

I pray that I may feel
   My own unworthiness—my helpless weakness;
   Oh! keep my soul in meekness,
And full of patient hope, and trustful zeal.

And teach me to submit
   Unto all earthly sorrow cheerfully—
   Knowing that none shall be,
But what thy holy wisdom seeth fit.

And passing death's dark stream,
   That flows between my spirit and its rest,
   Oh! let my path be blest
With the pure radiance of hope's placid beam.

And breasting the cold wave,
   Oh! let me feel Thou art my God indeed,
   My God in utmost need,
Mighty to shield, to strengthen, and to save!

(1833)

154 THE FEVER OF THE MIND

A burning brow, a throbbing heart,
Starting with uncalled-for start,
At some imagined sound or sight,—
The vague fancy of some foot,
Stepping lightly near;
Or the imagining that an eye,
With a wild, uncertain light,
Gleamed strangely for a moment nigh,
And stirred the voice of fear,
Ever awake, though sometimes mute;
And the inward sudden shiver,
And the faint heart's sick, low quiver,
These are signs of the spirit's fever.

And the vague, mysterious dreams,
Of stormy skies, and troubled streams.
Mingled with flashes of soft light,
And gleams of scenes intensely bright;
Sounds that, ever and anon,
(But like phantoms of sweet sounds)
Come and go, now heard, now gone;
The strange unreason that confounds
Dreamy things with things of earth,—
Earth's beings with those of mental birth,
And casts o'er all a mist, half dark,
Half light, so that the world looks dim,
And the heart heaves like a labouring bark,
And there's unrest in every limb;
These have been, will be for ever,
Tokens of the spirit's fever.

And the impatience of the day,
The longing for the night,
The sleepless couch, the taper's ray,
Watched with a still affright;
The fretting at the shadows tall,
Of the curtains on the wall;
The wishing the dark hours away,
The praying for the light.
Oh wretchedness! yet this is so,
In spite of each endeavour,
How many gifted bosoms know
The spirit's restless fever!

Look on the brows of aged men,
Or on the face of many a one
Who has not reached threescore and ten,

Yet says his task is nearly done.
Many would deem that mouldering grief
Had written its records, dark and brief,
In the furrows on the brow,
In the hair's untimely snow;
Ask them—they will tell thee, though
They have had friends, and earthly treasure,
And wandered through each path of pleasure;
Yet feelings quick, and restless mind,
Have worn them, as the roving wind
Tosses unseen the bough, and tears
And scatters the rich leaves it bears:
And till the soul from clay shall sever,
These must feel the spirit's fever.

(1833)

155 IMAGINARY LANDS

Were they but visions of the olden time,
Those sunny lands, whereon our childhood mused?
Were their undying flowers, their summer prime,
But from some poet's glowing heart, transfused
Into the deathless page? Had they no place
In the cold bounds of earth? Were all their streams,
Their myrtle forests, and their glorious race
Of nymphs and swains, but phantasies and dreams?

Were they but visions? 'Araby the Blest,'
Though hidden now beneath the burning sand,
Have not our spirits, with thy fame possessed,
Longed to behold thee, oh, thou lovely land!
Have we not almost felt the spicy gales
That flung their influence o'er the pathless sea,
And envied those of old whose swelling sails
Caught the rich odour, breathing all of thee?

And thou, Arcadia, with thy chiming waters,
Thy sloping lawns, thy broad and glassy glades,
And more than those, thy fair and flower-crowned daughters,
Gliding like spirits through thy leafy shades;
While the sweet flutes breathed softly on the breeze,
And the delicious voices gushed in song—
Are *these* but visions? do not scenes like these
Unto the weary paths of earth belong?

And El Dorado! who hath trod thy shores?
   Are there no sands that sparkle so with gold?
Are there no rivers over hidden stores
   Of pearls and diamonds to the ocean rolled?
All the strange blossoms, with their rich perfumes,
   And giant bells, and urns, and splendid dyes,
All the bright nameless birds with gorgeous plumes,
   Are *these* but of the poet's phantasies?

They may be dreams; yet by the magic claim
   They had upon our love in early days,
And by the minds that could such visions frame,
   And things so radiant from their musings raise,
And by the deep response the elder heart
   Gives to the tales of their unreal bowers,
We feel and know that our immortal part
   Longs for a fairer, purer sphere than ours!

(1838)

CATHERINE GRACE GODWIN (née GARNETT) (1798 – 1845)

She was born in Glasgow, the second daughter of Dr Thomas Garnett, an eminent chemist and first holder of the Chair of Chemistry at the Royal Institution. Her mother died in childbirth, and her sister died in a fire while on honeymoon in Italy. She lived for much of her life in the village of Barbon in Westmorland and knew Southey and Wordsworth. She dedicated 'The Wanderer's Legacy' (1828) to Wordsworth and he replied with a significant letter on the Spenserian stanza. She married Thomas Godwin in 1824. She contributed to the annuals, *Literary Gazette* and *Blackwood's*, and published several volumes of verse.

156 *from* THE WANDERER'S LEGACY

May not the mind, whose purer element
Springs from that great Ethereal Fount which flows
In countless streams of vital intellect,
Or pre-ordained, or chance-directed, free
From every law prescribed by human will,
Alike to all, of high or low estate,—
May not the mind, with ray instinct, condensed,
And centred on itself, some fruits produce
Not all unworthy the inquirer's note?
Count not as valueless the moments given
To meditation by the midnight lamp;—
One virtuous feeling fathomed to its source

Is as important in the scale of life
As river tracked o'er Afric's burning sands,
Or loftiest peak of Himalay attained.
Yea, all are good, whatever tends to move
Man's latent energies to high emprize,
Or mental, or corporeal, all are good,
Contributing to work the general weal;
Blending as do the bright and varied dyes
Of some fair tissue, each hue still distinct,
Imbued with its own separate excellence,
Contrasting, yet in pleasant unity,
Forming, conjoined, an admirable whole.

My youth hath been in quiet musings spent,
My very childhood garbed itself in thoughts
That were of riper years. My whole life since
Hath been a maze of marvel and delight
In all the gifts wherewith the hand divine
Hath decked this mortal dwelling-place of man.
I well remember me, ere language flowed
In unison with the mind's eloquence,
How my heart, labouring with its feelings deep,
Seeking in words some utterance of its joy,
Rejected always with a vexed disdain
The guise uncouth in which the precious ore
Was issued from the mine; for harmony,
Though unattained, was in my heart instinct:
I felt her presence in the haunts I loved,
She floated round me in the summer's gales,
I saw her impress on the mountain peaks,
The groves, the glades, with her voice resonant,
Whispered her accents to the murmuring brooks.
The poetry of Nature then was felt,
Albeit not yet distinctly understood.
I only knew that my aspirings soared
Far, far above this earth's corporeal things;
That my conceptions were beyond the scope
Of my untaught and wild philosophy;
That all was mystery. Mine own sense of being—
The restless, the resistless tide of thought
Rolling for ever through my inmost soul,
Was an enigma I could not resolve....

(1829)

CATHERINE GRACE GODWIN

157 THE VOICE OF THE WATERFALL

Look back!
Lo! where it comes like an eternity! [Byron]

Voice of the Waterfall! thy booming sound
Rules like a spell of power the glens around;
We list thee from afar, and pause to dream
Of the near rushing of the mighty stream:
We seek thee near, e'en where thy rugged throne,
And all thy rude magnificence, are shown,
And hear, in thy stern music, tones that rise
Like oracles of Nature's mysteries.
How oft have I, amid the solemn woods,
When twilight's mantle drooped o'er fells and floods,
Sat hearkening thee, the while thy clarion-call
Waked drowsy Echo in her sylvan hall;
And seen, for thou, wild spirit, hast a form
Majestic as the genius of the storm.
Thy white crest tossed aloft in proud disdain,
Like some sea-lion's crisped and hoary mane!

Hours of romance—yes, I have mused away
The lavish glories of a summer day,
Full oft beneath the forest's whispering shade,
Rocked by the thunders of the near cascade:
Or, more remote, have sought a gentler scene.
Where all around was fragrant, cool, and green;
Where flowerets oped their petals to emboss
With richer hues the dew-bespangled moss;
Where still the roar of neighbouring waters came,
By distance tempered, but in mood the same.
Yet thou, O Waterfall! that seem'st to be
A symbol meet of perpetuity,
E'en thou obey'st at times a loftier power,
Like some magician in his feeble hour.
Bleak Winter issues from his arctic caves,
And chains thy strength and curbs thy headlong waves;
Mute as the grave, thy rolling thunders cease,
And where the tumult maddened—there is peace.

(1832)

158 A DREAMER

She was the child of dreams—through life's dull paths
She roved with mind enchanted. Earth to her
O'erflowed with beauty. Never Asian princess,
The heroine of lays wild and wonderful,
In Peri-bower or sea-nymph's grot beheld
Visions more bright than she. Hours of romance

Were hers, beneath the forest's green arcades
When scarce a leaf stirred round her mossy couch,
And all was stilled in summer's breathless noon.
The softened light which through the umbrage stole
In gem-like radiance—the low-warbled notes
Of birds amid the branches—the faint scents
Exhaled by wilding blossoms, and the noise
Of brooklet tinkling 'midst adjacent rocks
Fell on her spirit like a potent charm,
And she became herself a voice of nature
Pouring forth then, (even as those harps whose strings
Touched by the winds, give out melodious tones,)
Spontaneous minstrelsy.
Oh how she loved
To sit at eve upon some lonely shore,
Watching the waves that, like dusk Indian kings,
Crested with emerald, ruby, gold and pearl,
Came riding up in triumph, canopied
By sunset's crimson banner. Nor less joy
Felt she when Ocean, taunted by rude gales,
Roused him indignant from his ancient lair,
And shook aloft his white and angry mane,
Daring the skies to combat. Nature then
The image seemed of an impassioned soul
Stirred to its inmost depths.
In solitude,
Well pleased, would she her midnight vigil keep
Amid the russet shades of those same woods
Stripped of their summer pride; yet glorious still,
And solemnly beautiful, when through their boughs,
Leafless, but clothed with mosses many-hued,
The moon-beams glinting made their mazes long
The fitting scene for goblins' eerie revels,
Or necromancy wild. No mood assumed
By changeful nature, that her mood as changeful
Found not congenial, for she was one
To whom the gift of feelings finely stringed,
Of strong perceptions, and in brief, of all
That makes or mars the happiness of mortals
Heaven lavishly had awarded. She too cherished
Ambition that would grasp eternity—
Hope, dazzling as the lightnings; but alas!
Like to that fabled bird of Eastern climes,
Doomed still to soar, and find on earth no home.

Yet she was blest. Thick coming fantasies,
Thoughts that were in themselves Elysium, thronged
Her active brain. A keener sense of being—
A tranced existence—moments that condensed

Ages of glory—these, these all were hers!
And oft, beneath their fascination, she
Would sit all day upon some green hill's side,
Gazing into the azure arch—perchance
Some isolated cloud she there might note,
Sailing along, in semblance, so she deemed,
Of a heaven-bound and heaven-constructed bark;
Or it might be, did see in it the emblem
Of her own fleeting solitary life,
Flinging a transient shadow on the earth,
Then melting viewless in the realms of air.

(Wr. *c.* 1830 – 1833, pub. 1854)

CAROLINE NORTON (née SHERIDAN, later STIRLING-MAXWELL) (1808 – 77)

She was born in London. Her father Thomas Sheridan was the son of Richard Brinsley Sheridan, the famous playwright. In 1809, they experienced financial disaster when the Drury Lane Theatre was ruined by fire. She was left with relatives in Scotland and grew up there. She returned to England and married George Norton in June 1827. The marriage had failed by 1836 and she later fought for the custody of her three sons, which she won, setting an important precedent and paving the way for the Infant Custody Act 1839. There were numerous rumours about her and Lord Melbourne but at the end of the criminal conversation trial in 1836 the judge summed up the position: 'As a wife her conduct has been irreproachable; as a mother she has set a bright example to her sex.' Her fate contrasts starkly with that of Letitia Landon. Both were thought to be the female equivalent of Byron. However, although she and Melbourne suffered briefly, they had powerful friends and the rumour was not widely believed. She published *The Sorrows of Rosalie* (1829), *The Undying One* (1830), *Poems*, Boston 1833, *A Voice from the Factories* (1836), *The Dream* (1840), and *The Child of the Islands* (1845). She also wrote on a number of social issues, including custody and divorce. Her *English Laws for Women in the Nineteenth Century* (1854) is still of value. Her husband died in 1875 and she married Sir William Stirling-Maxwell in 1877. She died three months later. H.N. Coleridge, in his important 'Modern English poetesses', *Quarterly Review*, LXVI (1840), p.376, described her as 'the Byron of our modern poetesses', but R.H. Horne's contrast of her with Elizabeth Barrett is perhaps closer: 'The imagination of Mrs Norton is chiefly occupied with domestic feelings and images, and breathes melodious plaints, or indignations over the desecrations of her sex's loveliness; that of Miss Barrett often wanders amidst the supernatural darkness of Calvary, sometimes with anguish and tears of blood. . . . The one is all womanhood; the other all wings' (*A New Spirit of the Age*, London 1844, ii.139–40). She was thought to have been the model for George Meredith's *Diana of the Crossways*, 3 vols (1885).

159 THE HEART'S WRECK

CAROLINE NORTON

The lulling winds may still the sea,
All beautiful in its repose;
And with a soft tranquillity
The rippling water ebbs and flows.

But when the tempests wildly blow,
Its bosom heaves with many a wreck
Which, till that moment, slept below,
Nor dimmed its surface with a speck.

So *I* can talk, and laugh, and seem
All that the happiest souls could be;
Lulled for a moment, by some dream,
Soft as the sunset on the sea.

But when a word, a tone, reminds
My bosom of its perished love,
Oh! fearful are the stormy winds
Which dash the *heart's* wild wrecks above!

One after one they rise again,
And o'er dark memory's ocean steal,
Floating along, through years of pain—
Such as the heart-struck only feel!

(1829)

160 BABEL

Know ye in ages past that tower
By human hands build strong and high?
Arch over arch, with magic power,
Rose proudly each successive hour,
To reach the happy sky.

It rose, till human pride was crushed—
Quick came the unexpected change;
A moment every tone was hushed,
And then again they freely gushed,
But sounded wild and strange.

Loud, quick, and clear, each voice was heard,
Calling for lime, and stone, and wood,
All uttered words—but not one word;
More than the carol of a bird,
Their fellows understood.

CAROLINE NORTON

Is there no Babel but that one,
The storied tower of other days?—
Where, round the giant pile of stone,
Pausing they stood—their labour done,
To listen in amaze.

Fair springs the tower of hope and fame,
When all our life is fairy land;
Till, scarcely knowing what to blame,
Our fellows cease to feel the same—
We cease to understand.

Then, when they coldly smile to hear
The burning dreams of earlier days;
The rapid fall from hope to fear,
When eyes whose every glance was dear,
Seem changing as they gaze:

Then, when we feel 'twere vain to speak
Of fervent hopes—aspirings high—
Of thoughts for which all words are weak—
Of wild far dreams, wherein we seek
Knowledge of earth and sky:

Of communings with nature's God,
When impulse deep the soul hath moved—
Of tears which sink within the sod,
Where, mingling with the valley clod,
Lies something we have loved:

Then cometh ours;—and better theirs—
Of stranger tongues together brought,
Than that in which we all have shares,
A Babel in a world of cares—
Of feeling and of thought!

(1830)

161 THE CHILD OF EARTH

Fainter her slow step falls from day to day,
Death's hand is heavy on her darkening brow;
Yet doth she fondly cling to earth, and say,
'I am content to die—but, oh! not now!—
Not while the blossoms of the joyous spring
Make the warm air such luxury to breathe—
Not while the birds such lays of gladness sing—
Not while bright flowers around my footsteps wreathe.

Spare me, great God! lift up my drooping brow—
I am content to die—but, oh! not now!'

The spring hath ripened into summer-time;
   The season's viewless boundary is past;
The glorious sun hath reached his burning prime:
   Oh! must this glimpse of beauty be the last?
'Let me not perish while o'er land and lea,
   With silent steps, the Lord of light moves on;
Not while the murmur of the mountain-bee
   Greets my dull ear with music in its tone!
Pale sickness dims my eye and clouds my brow—
I am content to die—but, oh! not now!'

Summer is gone: and autumn's soberer hues
   Tint the ripe fruits, and gild the waving corn;—
The huntsman swift the flying game pursues,
   Shouts the halloo! and winds his eager horn.
'Spare me awhile, to wander forth and gaze
   On the broad meadows, and the quiet stream,
To watch in silence while the evening rays
   Slant through the fading trees with ruddy gleam!
Cooler the breezes play around my brow—
I am content to die—but, oh! not now!'

The bleak wind whistles: snow-showers far and near
   Drift without echo to the whitening ground;
Autumn hath passed away, and, cold and drear,
   Winter stalks on with frozen mantle bound:
Yet still that prayer ascends. 'Oh! laughingly
   My little brothers round the warm hearth crowd,
Our home-fire blazes broad, and bright, and high,
   And the roof rings with voices light and loud:
Spare me awhile! raise up my drooping brow!
I am content to die—but, oh! not now!'

The spring is come again—the joyful spring!
   Again the banks with clustering flowers are spread;
The wild bird dips upon its wanton wing:—
   The child of earth is numbered with the dead!
'Thee never more the sunshine shall awake,
   Beaming all redly through the lattice-pane;
The steps of friends thy slumbers may not break,
   Nor fond familiar voice arouse again!
Death's silent shadow veils thy darkened brow—
Why didst thou linger?—thou art happier now!'

(1832)

When first thou camest, gentle, shy, and fond,
My eldest-born, first hope, and dearest treasure,
My heart received thee with a joy beyond
All that it yet had felt of earthly pleasure;
Nor thought that *any* love again might be
So deep and strong as that I felt for thee.

Faithful and fond, with sense beyond thy years,
And natural piety that leaned to Heaven;
Wrung by a harsh word suddenly to tears,
Yet patient of rebuke when justly given—
Obedient—easy to be reconciled—
And meekly-cheerful—such wert thou, my child!

Not willing to be left; still by my side
Haunting my walks, while summer-day was dying;—
Nor leaving in thy turn; but pleased to glide
Through the dark room where I was sadly lying,
Or by the couch of pain, a sitter meek,
Watch the dim eye, and kiss the feverish cheek.

Oh! boy, of such as thou are oftenest made
Earth's fragile idols; like a tender flower,
No strength in all thy freshness,—prone to fade,—
And bending weakly to the thunder-shower,—
Still, round the loved, thy heart found force to bind,
And clung, like woodbine shaken in the wind!

Then Thou, my merry love;—bold in thy glee,
Under the bough, or by the firelight dancing,
With thy sweet temper, and thy spirit free,
Didst come, as restless as a bird's wing glancing,
Full of a wild and irrepressible mirth,
Like a young sunbeam to the gladdened earth!

Thine was the shout! the song! the burst of joy!
Which sweet from childhood's rosy lip resoundeth;
Thine was the eager spirit nought could cloy,
And the glad heart from which all grief reboundeth;
And many a mirthful jest and mock reply,
Lurked in the laughter of thy dark-blue eye!

And thine was many an art to win and bless,
The cold and stern to joy and fondness warming;
The coaxing smile;—the frequent soft caress;—
The earnest tearful prayer all wrath disarming!
Again my heart a new affection found,
But thought that love with *thee* had reached its bound.

At length Thou camest; thou, the last and least;
Nick-named 'The Emperor' by thy laughing brothers,
Because a haughty spirit swelled thy breast,
And thou didst seek to rule and sway the others;
Mingling with every playful infant wile
A mimic majesty that made us smile:—

And oh! most like a regal child wert thou!
An eye of resolute and successful scheming;
Fair shoulders—curling lip—and dauntless brow—
Fit for the world's strife, not for Poet's dreaming:
And proud the lifting of thy stately head,
And the firm bearing of thy conscious tread.

Different from both! Yet each succeeding claim,
I, that all other love had been forswearing,
Forthwith admitted, equal and the same;
Nor injured either, by this love's comparing,
Nor stole a fraction for the newer call—
But in the Mother's heart, found room for All!

(1837)

EMMA ROBERTS (*c.* **1794 – 1840)**

She was born at Methley, near Leeds, but was brought up by her mother in Bath. She was a friend of Letitia Landon's and lived with her briefly in London. In 1828, she accompanied her married sister to India and in 1831, following her sister's death, moved to Calcutta, where she edited *The Oriental Observer*. She returned to England in 1832, and in December she began to contribute a series of articles on India and Anglo-Indian society to the *Asiatic Journal* and later published them as *Scenes and Characteristics of Hindostan, with Sketches of Anglo-Indian Society*, 3 vols (1835). Her insights and observations on the status and condition of women in the Empire, and the difficulties of their lives abroad and on return, deserve to be better known. See especially ch. ii, 'Bengal Bridals and Bridal Candidates', i.18–44, and ch. iv, 'Feminine Employments, Amusements, and Domestic Economy', i.73–104. In 1839 she returned to India but died in Poona in 1840 and was buried near Maria Jane Jewsbury who had also died there in 1833. Her considerable literary activity in India and contributions to numerous expatriate journals have not been fully investigated. She also contributed to most of the annuals and collected much of her verse in *Oriental Scenes* (1830). She edited Landon's *The Zenana* (1839), and *Notes of an Overland Journey through France and Egypt to Bombay*. . . . (1841) appeared posthumously.

EMMA ROBERTS

163 NIGHT ON THE GANGES

How calm, how lovely is the soft repose
Of nature sleeping in the summer night;
How sweet, how lullingly the current flows
Beneath the stream of melted chrysolite,
Where Ganges spreads its floods,—reflecting o'er
Its silvery surface, with those countless stars
The ingot gems of Heaven's cerulean floor,
Mosques, groves, and cliffs, and pinnacled minars.

The air is fresh, and yet the evening breeze
Has died away; so hushed, 'tis scarcely heard
To breathe amid the clustering lemon trees,
Whose snowy blossoms, by its faint sighs stirred,
Give out their perfume; and the bulbul's notes
Awake the echoes of the balmy clime;
While from yon marble-domed pagoda floats
The music of its bell's soft, silvery chime.

Mildly, yet with resplendent beauty, shines
The scene around, although the stars alone,
From the bright treasures of their gleaming mines
A tender radiance o'er the earth have thrown.
Oh! far more lovely are those gentle rays
With their undazzling lustre, than the beam
The sun pours down in his meridian blaze,
Lighting with diamond pomp the sparkling stream.

Each tint its vivid colouring receives:
There is the glossy peepul—the bamboo
Flings down its rich redundancy of leaves,
And trailing plants their wandering course pursue,
In hues as bright as if the sun revealed
The mantling foliage of the woody glade;
Nor is yon lone sequestered hut concealed
Sleeping within the green hill's deepest shade.

With snowy vases crowned, the lily springs
In queen-like beauty by the river's brink;
And o'er the wave the broad-leaved lotus flings
Its roseate flowers in many a knotted link.
Oh! when the sultry sun has sunk to rest,
When evening's soft and tender shadows rise,
How sweet the scene upon the river's breast,
Beneath the starlight of these tropic skies!

(1830)

CAROLINE BOWLES (later SOUTHEY) (1786 – 1854)

She was born in Buckland, Hampshire, the daughter of Captain Charles Bowles (and not William Lisle Bowles, as was sometimes thought, possibly as a result of her long acquaintance with Robert Southey). She published in *Blackwood's* and published separately *Ellen Fitzarthur* (1820), *The Widow's Tale* (1822), *Solitary Hours* (1826), *Tales of the Factories* (1833), and *The Birth-day* (1836). Her correspondence with Southey, extending over twenty years, was published by Edward Dowden, Dublin 1881. She married Southey in 1839 when he was already senile. *The Birth-day* (1836) retains considerable interest as an autobiographical poem, consciously eschewing the sublime elements of Wordsworth.

164 [MARTYRS OF SENSIBILITY]

I despise and loathe
The affected whine of canting sentiment,
That loves to expatiate on its own fine frame
Of exquisite perception—nerve all o'er—
Too tremblingly alive for the mind's peace
To every shade of delicate distress.
Such sensitives there are, whose melting souls
Dissolve in tender pity, or flame out
With generous indignation, if they see
A dog chastised, or noxious reptile crushed:—
Does a fly tease you, and with impulse quick
Your dexterous hand destroys the buzzing pest—
Prepare ye for an eloquent appeal
On the sweet duties of humanity,
And all the tender charities we owe
To the poor, pretty, little helpless things
'That float in ether.' Then some hackneyed verse—
Your sensitive must doat on poetry—
She quotes to illustrate the touching theme,
How 'the poor beetle that we tread upon
In corporal sufferance feels a pang as great
As when a giant dies.' 'Tis odious thus
To hear the thing one venerates profaned
By sickly affectation: to my ear
Doubly distasteful, for I heard the words
First from her lips whose heart was pity's throne.
That voice maternal taught my infant tongue
To speak the sentence, and my youthful heart
To feel and cherish, while its pulses beat,
Mercy and kindness for all living things.

Go where you will, the sensitive finds out
Whereon to expatiate largely—to pour forth
The flood of her pathetic eloquence.

CAROLINE
BOWLES

A plodding clown to market drives along
His swine obstreperous: right and left they run
In sheer perversity: so right and left
Resounds the whip, but scarcely reaches them,
Whate'er their horrid dissonance implies.
No matter—feeling's champion cannot hear
Unmoved the cry of innocence oppressed;
So forth she steps, and speaks, with hand on heart,
Tender remonstrance to the boor, who stands
Scratching his bushy pate, with hat pushed up,
And eyes and mouth distended with surprise,
Vented at last, when the oration ends,
In one expressive expletive—'Anan!'

A cart comes by—ah! painful sight indeed,
For it conveys, bound fast with cruel cords,
To the red slaughter-house a bleating load
Of fleecy victims. Now the impassioned soul
Of sensibility finds ample scope
To excruciate its own feelings, and their hearts
Condemned to hear, while she minutely dwells
On things revolting—'How the murderous knife
Shall stop those bleating throats, and dye with gore
Those milk-white fleeces.'
Thus expatiates she,
While feeling turns aside, and hurries on.

But vulgar sufferings, 'mongst the vulgar part
Of our own species, often fail to excite
Those tender feelings that evaporate half
O'er flies and earwigs, and expend themselves
In picturesque affliction.
'Ah!' cries one,
'How happy is the simple peasant's lot,
Exempt from polished life's heart-riving woes.
And elegant distresses!'
Bid them turn—
Those sentimental chymics, who extract
The essence of imaginary griefs
From overwrought refinement,—bid them turn
To some poor cottage—not a bower of sweets
Where woodbines cluster o'er the neat warm thatch,
And mad Marias sing fantastic ditties,
But to some wretched hut, whose crazy walls,
Crumbling with age and dripping damps, scarce prop
The rotten roof, all verdant with decay;
Unlatch the door, those starting planks that ill
Keep out the wind and rain, and bid them look
At the *home-comforts* of the scene within.

There on the hearth a few fresh-gathered sticks,
Or smouldering sods, diffuse a feeble warmth,
Fanned by that kneeling woman's labouring breath
Into a transient flame, o'erhanging which
Cowers close, with outspread palms, a haggard form,
But yesterday raised up from the sick-bed
Of wasting fever, yet to-night returned
From the resumption of his daily toil.
'Too hastily resumed—imprudent man!'
Ay, but his famished infants cried for bread;
So he went forth and strove, till nature failed,
And the faint dews of weakness gathered thick
In the dark hollows of his sallow cheek,
And round his white-parched lips. Then home he crawled
To the cold comforts of that cheerless hearth,
And of a meal whose dainties are set out
Invitingly—a cup of coarse black tea,
With milk unmingled, and a crust of bread.
No infant voices welcome his return
With joyous clamour, but the piteous wail,
'Father! I'm hungry—father! give me bread!'
Salutes him from the little huddled group
Beside that smoky flame, where one poor babe,
Shaking with ague-chills, creeps shuddering in
Between its mother's knees—that most forlorn,
Most wretched mother, with sad lullaby
Hushing the sickly infant at her breast,
Whose scanty nourishment yet drains her life.

Martyrs of sensibility! look there!
Relieve in acts of charity to those
The exuberance of your feelings.
'Ay, but those
Are horrid objects—squalid, filthy, low
Disgusting creatures—sentiment turns sick
In such an atmosphere at such a sight.
True cottage children are delightful things,
With rosy dimpled cheeks, and clustering curls;
It were an interesting task to dress
Such pretty creatures in straw cottage-bonnets,
And green stuff gowns, with little bibs and aprons
So neat and nice! and every now and then,
When visitors attend the Sunday school,
To hear them say their catechism and creed.
But those!—oh heaven! what feelings could endure
Approach or contact with those dirty things?
True—they *seem* starving; but 'tis also true
The parish sees to all those vulgar wants;
And when it does not, doubtless there must be—

Alas! too common in this wicked world—
Some artful imposition in the case.'

Martyrs of sensibility! farewell!
I leave ye to your earwigs and your flies....

(1836)

165 [LONDON SPARROWS]

How I hate
Those London Sparrows! Vile, pert, noisy things!
Whose ceaseless clamour at the window-sill—
The back-room window opening on some mews—
Reminds one of the country just so far
As to bemock its wild and blithesome sounds,
And press upon the heart our pent-up state
In the great Babylon;—oppressed, engulfed
By crowds, and smoke, and vapour: where one sees,
For laughing vales fair winding in the sun,
And hill-tops gleaming in his golden light,
The dingy red of roofs and chimneys tall
On which a leaden orb looks dimly down!
For limpid rills, the kennel's stream impure;
For primrose banks, the rifled, scentless things
Tied up for sale, held out by venal hands;
For lowing herds and bleating flocks, the cries
Of noisy venders threading every key
From bass to treble, of discordant sound;
For trees, unnatural stinted mockeries
At windows, and on balconies stuck up
Fir-trees in vases!—picturesque conceit!—
Whereon, to represent the woodland choir,
Perch those sweet songsters of the sooty wing....

(1836)

SARA COLERIDGE (née COLERIDGE) (1802 – 52)

She was born at Greta Hall, Keswick, in the Lake District. Her father was Samuel Taylor Coleridge. Her mother was Sarah Fricker. See Molly Lefebure, *The Bondage of Love: A Life of Mrs Samuel Taylor Coleridge*, London 1986. As a result of her father's difficulties, she lived for many years with her uncle, Robert Southey. In 1829, she married her cousin, Henry Nelson Coleridge, with whom she later collaborated in editing her father's works. *Phantasmion* (1837), an extended fairy-tale, never achieved popularity, although a number of the poems have often been anthologised.

166 'O SLEEP, MY BABE, HEAR NOT THE RIPPLING WAVE'

O sleep, my babe, hear not the rippling wave,
Nor feel the breeze that round thee lingering strays
To drink thy balmy breath,
And sigh one long farewell.

Soon shall it mourn above thy watery bed,
And whisper to me, on the wave-beat shore,
Deep murmuring in reproach,
Thy sad untimely fate.

Ere those dear eyes had opened on the light,
In vain to plead, thy coming life was sold,
O! wakened but to sleep,
Whence it can wake no more!

A thousand and a thousand silken leaves
The tufted beech unfolds in early spring,
All clad in tenderest green,
All of the self same shape:

A thousand infant faces, soft and sweet,
Each year sends forth, yet every mother views
Her last not least beloved
Like its dear self alone.

No musing mind hath ever yet foreshaped
The face to-morrow's sun shall first reveal,
No heart hath e'er conceived
What love that face will bring.

O sleep, my babe, nor heed how mourns the gale
To part with thy soft locks and fragrant breath,
As when it deeply sighs
O'er autumn's latest bloom.

(1837)

167 'I TREMBLE WHEN WITH LOOK BENIGN'

I tremble when with look benign
Thou tak'st my offered hand in thine,
Lest passion-breathing words of mine
The charm should break:
And friendly smiles be forced to fly,
Like soft reflections of the sky,
Which, when rude gales are sweeping by,
Desert the lake.

Of late I saw thee in a dream;
The day-star poured his hottest beam,
And thou, a cool refreshing stream,
Did'st brightly run:
The trees where thou wert pleased to flow,
Threw out their flowers, a glorious show,
While I, too distant doomed to grow,
Pined in the sun.

By no life-giving moisture fed,
A wasted tree, I bowed my head,
My sallow leaves and blossoms shed
On earth's green breast:
And silent prayed the slumbering wind,
The lake, thy tarrying place, might find,
And waft my leaves, with breathings kind,
There, there, to rest.

(1837)

168 'I WAS A BROOK IN STRAITEST CHANNEL PENT'

I was a brook in straitest channel pent,
Forcing 'mid rocks and stones my toilsome way,
A scanty brook in wandering well-nigh spent;
But now with thee, rich stream, conjoined I stray,
Through golden meads the river sweeps along,
Murmuring its deep full joy in gentlest undersong.

I crept through desert moor and gloomy glade,
My waters ever vexed, yet sad and slow,
My waters ever steeped in baleful shade:
But, whilst with thee, rich stream, conjoined I flow,
E'en in swift course the river seems to rest,
Blue sky, bright bloom and verdure imaged on its breast.

And, whilst with thee I roam through regions bright,
Beneath kind love's serene and gladsome sky,
A thousand happy things that seek the light,
Till now in darkest shadow forced to lie,
Up through the illumined waters nimbly run,
To show their forms and hues in the all revealing sun.

(1837)

169 'BLEST IS THE TARN WHICH TOWERING CLIFFS O'ERSHADE'

Blest is the tarn which towering cliffs o'ershade,
Which, cradled deep within the mountain's breast
Nor voices loud, nor dashing oars invade:
Yet e'en the tarn enjoys no perfect rest,
For oft the angry skies her peace molest,
With them she frowns, gives back the lightning's glare,
Then rages wildly in the troubled air.

This calmer lake, which potent spells protect,
Lies dimly slumbering through the fires of day,
And when yon skies, with chaste resplendence decked,
Shine forth in all their stateliest array,
O then she wakes to glitter bright as they,
And view the face of heaven's benignant queen
Still looking down on hers with smile serene!

What cruel cares the maiden's heart assail,
Who loves, but fears no deep-felt love to gain,
Or, having gained it, fears that love will fail!
My power can soothe to rest her wakeful pain,
Till none but calm delicious dreams remain,
And, while sweet tears her easy pillow steep,
She yields that dream of bliss to ever welcome sleep.

(1837)

EMILY BRONTË (1818 – 48)

She was born at Hartshead-cum-Clifton, near Leeds, in 1818. In 1820, the family moved to Haworth, where their father, Patrick Brontë, became curate. In 1825 two elder sisters, Maria and Elizabeth, died. She lived at Haworth throughout her life except for a short period as a governess at Law Hill, near Halifax, and a stay in Brussels. The Brontë children, Anne, Charlotte, Emily and Branwell, often wrote collaboratively, establishing the complex fictional worlds of Gondal (in the South Pacific) and Angria (in Africa). Under the name Ellis Bell she published *Wuthering Heights*, 2 vols (1847) and poems in the collection, *Poems by Currer, Ellis, and Acton Bell* (1846). She died after having caught a cold at her brother's funeral.

170 'HIGH WAVING HEATHER, 'NEATH STORMY BLASTS BENDING'

High waving heather, 'neath stormy blasts bending,
Midnight and moonlight and bright shining stars;
Darkness and glory rejoicingly blending,
Earth rising to heaven and heaven descending,
Man's spirit away from its drear dungeon sending,
Bursting the fetters and breaking the bars.

All down the mountain sides, wild forests lending
One might voice to the life-giving wind;
Rivers their banks in the jubilee rending,
Fast through the valleys a reckless course wending,
Wider and deeper their waters extending,
Leaving a desolate desert behind.

Shining and lowering and swelling and dying,
Changing for ever from midnight to noon;
Roaring like thunder, like soft music sighing,
Shadows on shadows advancing and flying,
Lightning-bright flashes the deep gloom defying,
Coming as swiftly and fading as soon.

(13 November 1836)

171 'O GOD OF HEAVEN! THE DREAM OF HORROR'

O God of heaven! the dream of horror,
The frightful dream is over now;
The sickened heart, the blasting sorrow,
The ghastly night, the ghastlier morrow,
The aching sense of utter woe;

The burning tears that would keep welling,
The groans that mocked at every tear
That burst from out their dreary dwelling

As if each gasp were life expelling,
But life was nourished by despair;

The tossing and the anguished pining;
The grinding teeth and staring eye;
The agony of still repining,
When not a spark of hope was shining
From gloomy fate's relentless sky;

The impatient rage, the useless shrinking
From thoughts that yet could not be borne;
The soul that was for ever thinking,
Till nature, maddened, tortured, sinking,
At last refused to mourn—

It's over now—and I am free,
And the ocean wind is caressing me,
The wild wind from that wavy main
I never thought to see again.

Bless thee, Bright Sea—and glorious dome,
And my own world, my spirit's home;
Bless thee, Bless all—I can not speak:
My voice is choked, but not with grief;
And salt drops from my haggard cheek
Descend, like rain upon the heath.

How long they've wet a dungeon floor,
Falling on flag-stones damp and grey!
I used to weep even in my sleep;
The night was dreadful, like the day.

I used to weep when winter's snow
Whirled through the grating stormily,
But then it was a calmer woe
For everything was drear as me.

The bitterest time, the worst of all,
Was that in which the summer sheen
Cast a green lustre on the wall
That told of fields of lovelier green.

Often I've sat down on the ground,
Gazing up to that flush scarce seen,
Till, heedless of the darkness round,
My soul has sought a land serene.

It sought the arch of heaven divine,
The pure blue heaven with clouds of gold;
It sought thy father's home and mine
As I remembered it of old.

O even now too horribly
Come back the feelings that would swell,
When with my face hid on my knee
I strove the bursting groans to quell.

I flung myself upon the stone,
I howled and tore my tangled hair,
And then, when the first gush had flown,
Lay in unspeakable despair.

Sometimes a curse, sometimes a prayer
Would quiver on my parchèd tongue;
But both without a murmur there
Died in the breast from whence they sprung.

And so the day would fade on high,
And darkness quench that lonely beam,
And slumber mould my misery
Into some strange and spectral dream
Whose phantom horrors made me know
The worst extent of human woe—

But this is past, and why return
O'er such a past to brood and mourn?
Shake off the fetters, break the chain,
And live and love and smile again.

The waste of youth, the waste of years,
Departed in that dungeon's thrall;
The gnawing grief, the hopeless tears,
Forget them—O forget them all.

(7 August 1837)

172 'ALONE I SAT; THE SUMMER DAY'

Alone I sat; the summer day
Had died in smiling light away;
I saw it die, I watched it fade
From misty hill and breezeless glade;

And thoughts in my soul were rushing,
And my heart bowed beneath their power;
And tears within my eyes were gushing
Because I could not speak the feeling,
The solemn joy around me stealing
In that divine, untroubled hour.

I asked myself, 'O why has heaven
Denied the precious gift to me,
The glorious gift to many given
To speak their thoughts in poetry?

'Dreams have encircled me,' I said,
'From careless childhood's sunny time;
Visions by ardent fancy fed
Since life was in its morning prime.'

But now, when I had hoped to sing,
My fingers strike a tuneless string;
And still the burden of the strain
Is 'Strive no more; 'tis all in vain.'

(August 1837)

173 'SLEEP BRINGS NO JOY TO ME'

Sleep brings no joy to me,
Remembrance never dies;
My soul is given to misery
And lives in sighs.

Sleep brings no rest to me;
The shadows of the dead
My waking eyes may never see
Surround my bed.

Sleep brings no hope to me;
In soundest sleep they come,
And with their doleful imagery
Deepen the gloom.

Sleep brings no strength to me,
No power renewed to brave,
I only sail a wilder sea,
A darker wave.

Sleep brings no friend to me
To soothe and aid to bear;
They all gaze, oh, how scornfully,
And I despair.

Sleep brings no wish to knit
My harassed heart beneath;
My only wish is to forget
In the sleep of death.

(November 1837)

174 'THE NIGHT IS DARKENING ROUND ME'

The night is darkening round me,
The wild winds coldly blow;
But a tyrant spell has bound me
And I cannot, cannot go.

The giant trees are bending
Their bare boughs weighed with snow,
And the storm is fast descending
And yet I cannot go.

Clouds beyond clouds above me,
Wastes beyond wastes below;
But nothing drear can move me;
I will not, cannot go.

(November 1837)

175 'O DREAM, WHERE ART THOU NOW?'

O Dream, where art thou now?
Long years have past away
Since last, from off thine angel brow
I saw the light decay.

Alas, alas for me
Thou wert so bright and fair,
I could not think thy memory
Would yield me nought but care!

The sun-beam and the storm,
The summer-eve divine,
The silent night of solemn calm,
The full moon's cloudless shine,

Were once entwined with thee,
But now with weary pain,
Lost vision! 'tis enough for me—
Thou canst not shine again.

(5 November 1838)

Loud without the wind was roaring
Through the waned autumnal sky;
Drenching wet, the cold rain pouring
Spoke of stormy winters nigh.

All too like that dreary eve
Sighed within repining grief;
Sighed at first, but sighed not long—
Sweet—How softly sweet it came!
Wild words of an ancient song,
Undefined, without a name.

'It was spring, for the skylark was singing.'
Those words, they awakened a spell—
They unlocked a deep fountain whose springing
Nor Absence nor Distance can quell.

In the gloom of a cloudy November,
They uttered the music of May;
They kindled the perishing ember
Into fervour that could not decay.

Awaken on all my dear moorlands
The wind in its glory and pride!
O call me from valleys and highlands
To walk by the hill-river's side!

It is swelled with the first snowy weather;
The rocks they are icy and hoar
And darker waves round the long heather
And the fern-leaves are sunny no more.

There are no yellow-stars on the mountain,
The blue-bells have long died away
From the brink of the moss-bedded fountain,
From the side of the wintery brae—

But lovelier than corn-fields all waving
In emerald and scarlet and gold
Are the slopes where the north-wind is raving,
And the glens where I wandered of old.

'It was morning; the bright sun was beaming.'
How sweetly that brought back to me
The time when nor labour nor dreaming
Broke the sleep of the happy and free.

But blithely we rose as the dusk heaven
Was melting to amber and blue;
And swift were the wings to our feet given
While we traversed the meadows of dew,

For the moors, for the moors where the short grass
Like velvet beneath us should lie!
For the moors, for the moors where each high pass
Rose sunny against the clear sky!

For the moors where the linnet was trilling
Its song on the old granite stone;
Where the lark—the wild skylark was filling
Every breast with delight like its own.

What language can utter the feeling
That rose when, in exile afar,
On the brow of a lonely hill kneeling
I saw the brown heath growing there.

It was scattered and stunted, and told me
That soon even that would be gone;
Its whispered, 'The grim walls enfold me;
I have bloomed in my last summer's sun.'

But not the loved music whose waking
Makes the soul of the Swiss die away
Has a spell more adored and heart-breaking
Than in its half-blighted bells lay.

The spirit that bent 'neath its power,
How it longed, how it burned to be free!
If I could have wept in that hour
Those tears had been heaven to me.

Well, well, the sad minutes are moving
Though loaded with trouble and pain;
And sometime the loved and the loving
Shall meet on the mountains again.

(11 November 1838)

CHARLOTTE BRONTË (later NICHOLLS) (1816 – 55)

She went to school with Emily at The Clergy Daughters' School at Cowan Bridge where the elder sisters Maria and Elizabeth had already gone. Their ill health, weakened by the strict regime, led to their removal but they died shortly afterwards in 1825. Emily and Charlotte were also removed and the four remaining children stayed at home. After Branwell was given a box of toy soldiers, they invented worlds for them, beginning the Glasstown sagas. The stories took different directions, Charlotte and Branwell writing about Angria in Africa and Anne and Emily about Gondal in the South Pacific. Charlotte returned to a different school in 1831 and was later invited back as a governess. In 1837 she sent some of her verse to Southey whose reply was polite but discouraging. In 1842 Emily and Charlotte went to a school in Brussels for six months with Charlotte later returning. *Jane Eyre*, 3 vols (1847) was an instant success and was followed by *Shirley*, 3 vols (1849) and *Villette*, 3 vols (1853). *The Professor*, 2 vols (1857) was written earlier but published posthumously. Unlike Emily, Charlotte made friends easily both at school and much later in the 1850s in literary London. She married the Rev. Arthur Bell Nicholls in 1854 but she died the following year, her health weakened by the strain of pregnancy.

177 *from* RETROSPECTION

We wove a web in childhood,
   A web of sunny air;
We dug a spring in infancy
   Of water pure and fair;

We sowed in youth a mustard seed,
   We cut an almond rod;
We are now grown up to riper age—
   Are they withered in the sod?

Are they blighted, failed and faded,
   Are they mouldered back to clay?
For life is darkly shaded;
   And its joys fleet fast away.

Faded! the web is still of air,
   But how its folds are spread,
And from its tints of crimson clear
   How deep a glow is shed.
The light of an Italian sky
Where clouds of sunset lingering lie
   Is not more ruby-red.

But the spring was under a mossy stone,
   Its jet may gush no more.
Hark! sceptic bid thy doubts be gone,
   Is that a feeble roar
Rushing around thee? Lo! the tide
Of waves where armèd fleets may ride

Sinking and swelling, frowns and smiles
An ocean with a thousand isles
  And scarce a glimpse of shore.

The mustard-seed in distant land
  Bends down a mighty tree,
The dry unbudding almond-wand
  Has touched eternity.
There came a second miracle
Such as on Aaron's sceptre fell,
And sapless grew like life from heath,
Bud, bloom and fruit in mingling wreath
All twined the shrivelled off-shoot round
As flowers lie on the lone grave-mound.

Dream that stole o'er us in the time
When life was in its vernal clime,
Dream that still faster o'er us steals
  As the mild star of spring declining
The advent of that day reveals,
  That glows in Sirius' fiery shining:
Oh! as thou swellest, and as the scenes
  Cover this cold world's darkest features,
Stronger each change my spirit weans
  To bow before thy god-like creatures.

When I sat 'neath a strange roof-tree
With nought I knew or loved round me,
Oh how my heart shrank back to thee,
Then I felt how fast thy ties had bound me.

That hour, that bleak hour when the day
  Closed in the cold autumn's gloaming,
When the clouds hung so bleak and drear and grey
  And a bitter wind through their folds was roaming.

There shone no fire on the cheerless hearth,
  In the chamber there gleamed no taper's twinkle.
Within, neither sight nor sound of mirth,
  Without, but the blast, and the sleet's chill sprinkle.

Then sadly I longed for my own dear home
  For a sight of the old familiar faces,
I drew near the casement and sat in its gloom
  And looked forth on the tempest's desolate traces.

Ever anon that wolfish breeze
  The dead leaves and sere from their boughs was shaking,
And I gazed on the hills through the leafless trees
  And felt as if my heart was breaking. . .

(19 December 1835)

178 THE LONELY LADY

She was alone that evening—and alone
She had been all that heavenly summer day.
She scarce had seen a face, or heard a tone
And quietly the hours had slipped away,
Their passage through the silence hardly known
Save when the clock with silver chime did say
The number of the hour, and all in peace
Listened to hear its own vibration cease.

Wearied with airy task, with tracing flowers
Of snow on lace, with singing hymn or song
With trying all her harp's symphonious powers
By striking full its quivering strings along,
And drawing out deep chords, and shaking showers
Of brilliant sound, from shell and wires among,
Wearied with reading books, weary with weeping,
Heart-sick of Life, she sought for death in sleeping.

She lay down on her couch—but could she sleep?
Could she forget existence in a dream
That blotting out reality might sweep
Over her weariness, the healing stream
Of hope and hope's fruition?—Lo the deep
And amber glow of that departing beam
Shot from that blood-red sun—points to her brow
Straight like a silent index, mark it now

Kindling her perfect features, bringing bloom
Into the living marble, smooth and bright
As sculptured effigy on hallowed tomb
Glimmering amid the dimmed and solemn light
Native to Gothic pile—so wan, so white
In shadow gleamed that face, in rosy flush
Of setting sun, rich with a living blush.

Up rose the lonely lady, and her eyes
Instinctive raised their fringe of raven shade
And fixed upon those vast and glorious skies
Their lustre that in death alone might fade.
Skies fired with crimson clouds, burning with dyes
Intense as blood—they arched above and rayed
The firmament with broad and vivid beams
That seemed to bend towards her all their gleams.

It was the arc of battle, leagues away
In the direction of that setting sun
An army saw that livid summer day

Closing their serried ranks and squared upon,
Saw it with awe, so deeply was the ray,
The last ray tinged with blood—so wild it shone,
So strange the semblance gory, burning, given
To pool and stream and sea by that red heaven.

(probably May 1837)

179 MY DREAMS

Again I find myself alone, and ever
The same voice like an oracle begins
Its vague and mystic strain, forgetting never
Reproaches for a hundred hidden sins,
And setting mournful penances in sight,
Terrors and tears for many a watchful night.

Fast change the scenes upon me all the same,
In hue and drift the regions of a land
Peopled with phantoms, and how dark their aim
As each dim guest lifts up its shadowy hand
And parts its veil to show one withering look,
That mortal eye may scarce unblighted brook.

I try to find a pleasant path to guide
To fairer scenes—but still they end in gloom;
The wilderness will open dark and wide
As the sole vista to a vale of bloom,
Of rose and elm and verdure—as these fade
Their sere leaves fall on yonder sandy shade.

My dreams, the Gods of my religion, linger
In foreign lands, each sundered from his own,
And there has passed a cold destroying finger
O'er every image, and each sacred tone
Sounds low and at a distance, sometimes dying
Like an uncertain sob, or smothered sighing.

Sea-locked, a cliff surrounded, or afar
Asleep upon a fountain's marble brim—
Asleep in heart, though yonder early star,
The first that lit its taper soft and dim
By the great shrine of heaven, has fixed his eye
Unsmiling though unsealed on that blue sky.

Left by the sun, as he is left by hope:
Bowed in dark, placid cloudlessness above,
As silent as the Island's palmy slope,

All beach untrodden, all unpeopled grove,
A spot to catch each moonbeam as it smiled
Towards that thankless deep so wide and wild.

Thankless he too looks up, no grateful bliss
Stirs him to feel the twilight-breeze diffuse
Its balm that bears in every spicy kiss
The mingled breath of southern flowers and dews,
Cool and delicious as the fountain's spray
Showered on the shining pavement where he lay.

(probably May or June 1837)

180 'WHAT DOES SHE DREAM OF, LINGERING ALL ALONE'

What does she dream of, lingering all alone
On the vast terrace, o'er that stream impending?
Through all the dim, still night no life-like tone
With the soft rush of wind and wave is blending.
Her fairy step upon the marble falls
With startling echo through those silent halls.

Chill is the night, though glorious, and she folds
Her robe upon her breast to meet that blast
Coming down from the barren Northern wolds.
There, how she shuddered as the breeze blew past
And died on yonder track of foam, with shiver
Of giant reed and flag fringing the river.

Full, brilliant shines the moon—lifted on high
O'er noble land and nobler river flowing,
Through parting hills that swell upon that sky
Still with the hue of dying daylight glowing,
Swell with their plumy woods and dewy glades,
Opening to moonlight in the deepest shades.

Turn lady to thy halls, for singing shrill
Again the gust descends—again the river
Frets into foam—I see thy dark eyes fill
With large and bitter tears—thy sweet lips quiver.

(probably November 1837 or January 1838)

181 REMEMBRANCE

The human heart has hidden treasures,
  In secret kept, in silence sealed;—
The thoughts, the hopes, the dreams, the pleasures,
  Whose charms were broken if revealed.
And days may pass in gay profusion,
  And nights in rosy riot fly,
While, lost in Fame's or Wealth's illusion,
  The memory of the past may die.

But there are hours of lonely musing,
  Such as in evening silence come,
When, soft as birds their pinions closing,
  The heart's best feelings gather home.
When around our heart there seems to languish
  A tender grief that is not woe;
And thoughts that once wrung groans of anguish,
  Now cause but some mild tears to flow.

And feelings, once as strong as passions,
  Come softly back—a faded dream;
Our own sharp griefs and wild sensations,
  The tale of others' sufferings seem.
Oh! when the heart is freshly bleeding,
  How longs it for that time to be,
When, through the mist of years receding,
  Its woes but live in reverie!

And it can dwell on moonlight glimmer,
  On evening shade and loneliness;
And, while the sky grows dim and dimmer,
  Feel no untold and strange distress—
Only a deeper impulse given
  By lonely hour and darkened room,
To solemn thoughts that rise to heaven,
  Seeking a life and world to come.

(probably late 1837 or before 29 January 1838)

ELIZABETH BARRETT (later BROWNING) (1806 – 61)

She was born Elizabeth Barrett Moulton-Barrett at Coxhoe, Co. Durham. In 1809 the family moved to Hope End in Hertfordshire where she sustained a spinal injury in her teens although this does not fully account for her semi-invalid status throughout much of her life. She displayed great precocity in learning Latin and Greek. She published *An Essay on Mind* (1826), *Prometheus Unbound* (1833), and *The Seraphim* (1838). Her reputation was firmly established by *Poems*, 2 vols (1844) which led to a correspondence with Robert Browning, whom she married in 1846 and lived with abroad for long periods. Her later poetry (which lies outside the scope of this volume) is more widely available but there is still no modern scholarly edition. See Charlotte Porter and Helen A. Clarke (eds), *The Complete Works of Elizabeth Barrett Browning*, 6 vols (1900). repr. 6 vols New York 1973, [H. Buxton Forman] (ed.), *Hitherto Unpublished Poems and Stories: With an Inedited Autobiography*, 2 vols, Boston 1914, W. Barnes, '"The sorrows of the muses": an early poem by Elizabeth Barrett', *Books at Iowa*, 4 (1966), pp.19–35.

182 THE TEMPEST: A FRAGMENT

Mors erat ante occulos [Lucan] *lib. ix.*

*   *   *   *   *   *   *   *

The forest made my home—the voiceful streams
My minstrel throng: the everlasting hills,—
Which marry with the firmament, and cry
Unto the brazen thunder, 'Come away,
Come from thy secret place, and try our strength,—'
Enwrapped me with their solemn arms. Here, light
Grew pale as darkness, scarëd by the shade
O' the forest Titans. Here, in piny state,
Reigned Night, the Aethiopian queen, and crowned
The charmëd brow of Solitude, her spouse.

*   *   *   *   *   *   *   *
*   *   *   *   *   *   *   *
*   *   *   *   *   *   *   *

A sign was on creation. You beheld
All things encoloured in a sulphurous hue,
As day were sick with fear. The haggard clouds
O'erhung the utter lifelessness of air;
The top boughs of the forest all aghast
Stared in the face of Heaven; the deep-mouthed wind,
That hath a voice to bay the armëd sea,
Fled with a low cry like a beaten hound;
And only that askance the shadows, flew
Some open-beakëd birds in wilderment,
Naught stirred abroad. All dumb did Nature seem,
In expectation of the coming storm.

It came in power. You soon might hear afar
The footsteps of the martial thunder sound
Over the mountain battlements; the sky

Being deep-stained with hues fantastical,
Red like to blood, and yellow like to fire,
And black like plumes at funerals; overhead
You might behold the lightning faintly gleam
Amid the clouds which thrill and gape aside,
And straight again shut up their solemn jaws,
As if to interpose between Heaven's wrath
And Earth's despair. Interposition brief!
Darkness is gathering out her mighty pall
Above us, and the pent-up rain is loosed,
Down trampling in its fierce delirium.

Was not my spirit gladdened, as with wine,
To hear the iron rain, and view the mark
Of battle on the banner of the clouds?
Did I not hearken for the battle-cry,
And rush along the bowing woods to meet
The riding Tempest—skyey cataracts
Hissing around him with rebellion vain?
Yea! and I lifted up my glorying voice
In an 'All hail;' when, wildly resonant,
As brazen chariots rushing from the war,
As passioned waters gushing from the rock,
As thousand crashëd woods, the thunder cried:
And at his cry the forest tops were shook
As by the woodman's axe; and far and near
Staggered the mountains with a muttered dread.

All hail unto the lightning! hurriedly
His lurid arms are glaring through the air,
Making the face of heaven to show like hell!
Let him go breathe his sulphur stench about,
And, pale with death's own mission, lord the storm!
Again the gleam—the glare: I turned to hail
Death's mission: at my feet there lay the dead!
The dead—the dead lay there! I could not view
(For Night espoused the storm, and made all dark)
Its features, but the lightning in his course
Shivered above a white and corpse-like heap,
Stretched in the path, as if to show his prey,
And have a triumph ere he passed. Then I
Crouched down upon the ground, and groped about
Until I touched that thing of flesh, rain-drenched,
And chill, and soft. Nathless, I did refrain
My soul from natural horror! I did lift
The heavy head, half-bedded in the clay,
Unto my knee; and passed my fingers o'er
The wet face, touching every lineament,
Until I found the brow; and chafed its chill,

To know if life yet lingered in its pulse.
And while I was so busied, there did leap
From out the entrails of the firmament,
The lightning, who his white unblenching breath
Blew in the dead man's face, discovering it
As by a staring day. I knew that face—
His, who did hate me—his, whom I did hate!

I shrunk not—spake not—sprang not from the ground!
But felt my lips shake without cry or breath,
And mine heart wrestle in my breast to still
The tossing of its pulses; and a cold,
Instead of living blood, o'ercreep my brow.
Albeit such darkness brooded all around,
I had dread knowledge that the open eyes
Of that dead man were glaring up to mine,
With their unwinking, unexpressive stare;
And mine I could not shut nor turn away.
The man was my familiar. I had borne
Those eyes to scowl on me their living hate,
Better than I could bear their deadliness:
I had endured the curses of those lips,
Far better than their silence. Oh constrained
And awful silence!—awful peace of death!

There is an answer to all questioning,
That one word—*death*. Our bitterness can throw
No look upon the face of death, and live.
The burning thoughts that erst my soul illumed,
Were quenched at once; as tapers in a pit
Wherein the vapour-witches weirdly reign
In charge of darkness. Farewell all the past!
It was out-blotted from my memory's eyes,
When clay's cold silence pleaded for its sin.

Farewell the elemental war! farewell
The clashing of the shielded clouds—the cry
Of scathëd echoes! I no longer knew
Silence from sound, but wandered far away
Into the deep Eleusis of mine heart,
To learn its secret things. When armëd foes
Meet on one deck with impulse violent,
The vessel quakes through all her oaken ribs,
And shivers in the sea; so with mine heart:
For there had battled in her solitudes,
Contrary spirits; sympathy with power,
And stooping unto power;—the energy
And passiveness,—the thunder and the death!

Within me was a nameless thought: it closed
The Janus of my soul on echoing hinge,
And said 'Peace!' with a voice like War's. I bowed,
And trembled at its voice: it gave a key,
Empowered to open out all mysteries
Of soul and flesh; of man, who doth begin,
But endeth not; of life, and *after life*.

* * * * * * * *

Day came at last: her light showed grey and sad,
As hatched by tempest, and could scarce prevail
Over the shaggy forest to imprint
Its outline on the sky—expressionless,
Almost sans shadow as sans radiance:
An idiocy of light. I wakened from
My deep unslumbering dream, but uttered naught.
My living I uncoupled from the dead,
And looked out, 'mid the swart and sluggish air,
For place to make a grave. A mighty tree
Above me, his gigantic arms outstretched,
Poising the clouds. A thousand muttered spells
Of every ancient wind and thunderous storm,
Had been off-shaken from his scathless bark.
He had heard distant years sweet concord yield,
And go to silence; having firmly kept
Majestical companionship with Time.
Anon his strength waxed proud: his tusky roots
Forced for themselves a path on every side,
Riving the earth; and, in their savage scorn,
Casting it from them like a thing unclean,
Which might impede his naked clambering
Unto the heavens. Now blasted, peeled, he stood,
By the gone night, whose lightning had come in
And rent him, even as it rent the man
Beneath his shade: and there the strong and weak
Communion joined in deathly agony.

There, underneath, I lent my feverish strength,
To scoop a lodgement for the traveller's corse.
I gave it to the silence and the pit,
And strewed the heavy earth on all: and then—
I—I, whose hands had formed that silent house,—
I could not look thereon, but turned and wept!

* * * * * * * *

* * * * * * * *

Oh Death—oh crownëd Death—pale-steedëd Death!
Whose name doth make our respiration brief,
Muffling the spirit's drum! Thou, whom men know
Alone by charnel-houses, and the dark
Sweeping of funeral feathers, and the scath

Of happy days,—love deemed inviolate!—.
Thou of the shrouded face, which to have seen
Is to be very awful, like thyself!—
Thou, whom all flesh shall see!—thou, who dost call,
And there is none to answer!—thou, whose call
Changeth all beauty into what we fear,
Changeth all glory into what we tread,
Genius to silence, wrath to nothingness,
And love—not love!—thou hast no change for love!
Thou, who art Life's betrothed, and bear'st her forth
To scare her with sad sights,—who hast thy joy
Where'er the peopled towns are dumb with plague,—
Where'er the battle and the vulture meet,—
Where'er the deep sea writhes like Laocoon
Beneath the serpent winds, and vessels split
On secret rocks, and men go gurgling down,
Down, down, to lose their shriekings in the depth!
Oh universal thou! who comest aye
Among the minstrels, and their tongue is tied;—
Among the sophists, and their brain is still;—
Among the mourners, and their wail is done;—
Among the dancers, and their tinkling feet
No more make echoes on the tombing earth;—
Among the wassail rout, and all the lamps
Are quenched; and withered the wine-pouring hands!

Mine heart is armëd not in panoply
Of the old Roman iron, nor assumes
The Stoic valour. 'Tis a human heart,
And so confesses, with a human fear;—
That only for the hope the cross inspires,
That only for the Man who died and lives,
'Twould crouch beneath thy sceptre's royalty,
With faintness of the pulse, and backward cling
To life. But knowing what I soothly know,
High-seeming Death, I dare thee! and have hope,
In God's good time, of showing to thy face
An unsuccumbing spirit, which sublime
May cast away the low anxieties
That wait upon the flesh—the reptile moods;
And enter that eternity to come,
Where live the dead, and only Death shall die.

(1833)

ELIZABETH BARRETT

183 A SEA-SIDE MEDITATION

Ut per aquas quae nunc rerum simulacra videmus. [Lucretius] *lib. i.*

Go, travel 'mid the hills! The summer's hand
Hath shaken pleasant freshness o'er them all.
Go, travel 'mid the hills! There, tuneful streams
Are touching myriad stops, invisible;
And winds, and leaves, and birds, and your own thoughts,
(Not the least glad) in wordless chorus, crowd
Around the thymele of Nature.

Go,
And travel onward. Soon shall leaf and bird,
Wind, stream, no longer sound. Thou shalt behold
Only the pathless sky, and houseless sward;
O'er which anon are spied innumerous sails
Of fisher vessels like the wings o' the hill,
And white as gulls above them, and as fast.—
But sink they—sink they out of sight. And now
The wind is springing upward in your face;
And, with its fresh-toned gushings, you may hear
Continuous sound which is not of the wind,
Nor of the thunder, nor o' the cataract's
Deep passion, nor o' the earthquake's wilder pulse;
But which rolls on in stern tranquillity,
As memories of evil o'er the soul;—
Boweth the bare broad Heaven.—What view you? sea—and sea!

The sea—the glorious sea! from side to side,
Swinging the grandeur of his foamy strength,
And undersweeping the horizon,—on—
On—with his life and voice inscrutable.
Pause: sit you down in silence! I have read
Of that Athenian, who, when ocean raged,
Unchained the prisoned music of his lips,
By shouting to the billows, sound for sound.
I marvel how his mind would let his tongue
Affront thereby the ocean's solemness.
Are we not mute, or speak restrainedly,
When overhead the trampling tempests go,
Dashing their lightning from their hoofs? and when
We stand beside the bier? and when we see
The strong bow down to weep—and stray among
Places which dust or mind hath sanctified?
Yea! for such sights and acts do tear apart
The close and subtle clasping of a chain,
Formed not of gold, but of corroded brass,
Whose links are furnished from the common mine
Of every day's event, and want, and wish;
From work-times, diet-times, and sleeping-times:

And thence constructed, mean and heavy links
Within the pandemonic walls of sense,
Enchain our deathless part, constrain our strength,
And waste the goodly stature of our soul.

Howbeit, we love this bondage; we do cleave
Unto the sordid and unholy thing,
Fearing the sudden wrench required to break
Those claspëd links. Behold! all sights and sounds
In air, and sea, and earth, and under earth,
All flesh, all life, all ends, are mysteries;
And all that is mysterious dreadful seems,
And all we cannot understand we fear.
Ourselves do scare ourselves: we hide our sight
In artificial nature from the true,
And throw sensation's veil associative
On God's creation, man's intelligence;
Bowing our high imaginings to eat
Dust, like the serpent, once erect as they;
Binding conspicuous on our reason's brow
Phylacteries of shame; learning to feel
By rote, and act by rule, (man's rule, not God's!)
Until our words grow echoes, and our thoughts
A mechanism of spirit.

Can this last?
No! not for aye. We cannot subject aye
The heaven-born spirit to the earth-born flesh.
Tame lions *will* scent blood, and appetite
Carnivorous glare from out their restless eyes.
Passions, emotions, sudden changes, throw
Our nature back upon us, till we burn.
What warmed Cyrene's fount? As poets sing,
The *change* from light to dark, from dark to light.

All that doth force this nature back on us,
All that doth force the mind to view the mind,
Engendereth what is named by men, *sublime*.
Thus when, our wonted valley left, we gain
The mountain's horrent brow, and mark from thence
The sweep of lands extending with the sky;
Or view the spanless plain; or turn our sight
Upon yon deep's immensity;—we breathe
As if our breath were marble: to and fro
Do reel our pulses, and our words are mute.
We cannot mete by parts, but grapple all:
We cannot measure with our eye, but soul;
And fear is on us. The extent unused,
Our spirit, sends, to spirit's element,

To seize upon abstractions: first on space,
The which *eternity in place* I deem;
And then upon eternity; till thought
Hath formed a mirror from their secret sense,
Wherein we view ourselves, and back recoil
At our own awful likeness; ne'ertheless,
Cling to that likeness with a wonder wild,
And while we tremble, glory—proud in fear.

So ends the prose of life: and so shall be
Unlocked her poetry's magnific store.
And so, thou pathless and perpetual sea,
So, o'er thy deeps, I brooded and must brood,
Whether I view thee in thy dreadful peace,
Like a spent warrior hanging in the sun
His glittering arms, and meditating death;
Or whether thy wild visage gathereth shades,
What time thou marshall'st forth thy waves who hold
A covenant of storms, then roar and wind
Under the racking rocks; as martyrs lie
Wheel-bound; and, dying, utter lofty words!
Whether the strength of day is young and high,
Or whether, weary of the watch, he sits
Pale on thy wave, and weeps himself to death;—
In storm and calm, at morn and eventide,
Still have I stood beside thee, and out-thrown
My spirit onward on thine element,—
Beyond thine element,—to tremble low
Before those feet which trod thee as they trod
Earth,—to the holy, happy, peopled place,
Where there is no more sea. Yea, and my soul,
Having put on thy vast similitude,
Hath wildly moanëd at her proper death,
Echoed her proper musings, veiled in shade
Her secrets of decay, and exercised
An elemental strength, in casting up
Rare gems and things of death on fancy's shore,
Till Nature said, 'Enough.'
                                        Who longest dreams,
Dreams not for ever; seeing day and night
And corporal feebleness divide his dreams,
And, on his elevate creations weigh
With hunger, cold, heat, darkness, weariness:
Else should we be like gods; else would the course
Of thought's free wheels, increased in speed and might
By an eterne volution, oversweep
The heights of wisdom, and invade her depths:
So, knowing all things, should we have all power;
For is not knowledge power? But mighty spells

Our operation sear: the Babel must,
Or ere it touch the sky, fall down to earth:
The web, half formed, must tumble from our hands,
And, ere they can resume it, lie decayed.
Mind struggles vainly from the flesh. E'en so,
Hell's angel (saith a scroll apocryphal)
Shall, when the latter days of earth have shrunk
Before the blast of God, affect his heaven;
Lift his scarred brow, confirm his rebel heart,
Shoot his strong wings, and darken pole and pole,—
Till day be blotted into night; and shake
The fevered clouds, as if a thousand storms
Throbbed into life! Vain hope—vain strength—vain flight!
God's arm shall meet God's foe, and hurl him back!

(1833)

184 TO A POET'S CHILD

A far harp swept the sea above;
A far voice said thy name in love:
Then silence on the harp was cast;
The voice was chained—the love went last!

And as I heard the melodie,
Sweet-voicëd Fancy spake of thee:
And as the silence o'er it came,
Mine heart, in silence, sighed thy name.

I thought there was one only place,
Where thou couldst lift thine orphaned face;
A little home for prayer and woe;—
A stone above—a shroud below;—

That evermore, that stone beside,
Thy withered joys would form thy pride;
As palm-trees, on their south sea bed,
Make islands with the flowers they shed.

Child of the Dead! my dream of thee
Was sad to tell, and dark to see;
And vain as many a brighter dream;
Since thou canst sing by Babel's stream!

For here, amid the worldly crowd,
'Mid common brows, and laughter loud,
And hollow words, and feelings sere,
Child of the Dead! I meet thee here!

And is thy step so fast and light?
And is thy smile so gay and bright?
And *canst* thou smile, with cheek undim,
Upon a world that frowned on *him*?

The minstrel's harp is on his bier;
What doth the minstrel's orphan here?
The loving moulders in the clay;
The loved,—she keepeth holyday!

'Tis well! I would not doom thy years
Of golden prime, to only tears.
Fair girl! 'twere better that thine eyes
Should find a joy in summer skies,

As if their sun were on thy fate.
Be happy; strive not to be great;
And go not, from thy kind apart,
With lofty soul and stricken heart.

Think not too deeply: shallow thought,
Like open rills, is ever sought
By light and flowers; while fountains deep
Amid the rocks and shadows sleep.

Feel not too warmly: lest thou be
Too like Cyrene's waters free,
Which burn at night, when all around
In darkness and in chill is found.

Touch not the harp to win the wreath:
Its tone is fame, its echo death!
The wreath may like the laurel grow,
Yet turns to cypress on the brow!

And, as a flame springs clear and bright,
Yet leaveth ashes 'stead of light;
So genius (fatal gift!) is doomed
To leave the heart it fired, consumed.

For thee, for thee, thou orphaned one,
I make an humble orison!
Love all the world; and ever dream
That all are true who truly seem.

Forget! for, so, 'twill move thee not,
Or lightly move; to be forgot!
Be streams thy music; hills, thy mirth;
Thy chiefest light, the household hearth.

So, when grief plays her natural part,
And visiteth thy quiet heart;
Shall all the clouds of grief be seen
To show a sky of hope between.

So, when thy beauty senseless lies,
No sculptured urn shall o'er thee rise;
But gentle eyes shall weep at will,
Such tears as hearts like thine distil.

(1833)

185 THE ROMAUNT OF MARGRET

I plant a tree, whose leaf
   The cypress leaf will suit,
But when its shade is o'er you laid,
   Turn ye, and pluck the fruit.
Now reach my minstrel harp,
   Which hangeth on the wall,
And hearken loving hearts and bold,
   To a wild madrigal.
         Margret, Margret!

Sitteth the fair ladye
   Close to the river side,
Which runneth on with a merry tone,
   Her merry thoughts to guide.
It runneth through the trees,
   It runneth by the hill—
Pathless the ladye's thoughts have found
   A way more pleasant still.—
         Margret, Margret!

The night is in her hair,
   And giveth shade to shade,
And the pale moonlight on her forehead white,
   Like a spirit's hand is laid.
Her lips part with a smile
   Instead of speakings done:
I ween she thinketh of a voice,
   Albeit, uttering none.
         Margret, Margret!

All little birds do sit
   With heads beneath their wings,
And nature doth seem in a mystic dream,
   Apart from her living things.

That dream by that ladye,
   I ween, is unpartook;
For she looketh to the high, cold stars
   With a tender human look.
                  Margret, Margret!

The ladye's shadow lies
   Upon the running river;
It lieth no less in its quietness,
   For that which resteth never:
Most like a trusting heart
   Upon a passing faith—
Or as, upon the course of life,
   The steadfast doom of death.
                  Margret, Margret!

The ladye doth not move—
   The ladye doth not dream—
Yet she seeth her shade no longer laid
   In rest upon the stream.
It shaketh without wind—
   It parteth from the tide—
It standeth upright in the cleft moonlight—
   It sitteth at her side!
                  Margret, Margret!

Look in its face, ladye,
   And keep thee from thy swound;
With a spirit bold thy pulses hold,
   And hear its voice's sound.
For so will sound thy voice,
   When thy face is to the wall!
And so will look thy face, ladye,
   When the maidens work thy pall.
                  Margret, Margret!

'Am I not like to thee?'
   The voice was calm and low;
And between each word you might have heard
   The silent grasses grow!
'The like may sway the like,'
   By which mysterious law,
Mine eyes from thine, and my lips from thine,
   The light and breath may draw.
                  Margret, Margret!

My lips do need thy breath—
   My lips do need thy smile—
And my pale deep eyne, that light in thine,
   Which met the stars ere while.

Yet go with light and life,
If that thou lovest one
In all the earth, who loveth thee
More truly than the sun,
Margret, Margret!

Her cheek had waxen white,
Like cloud, at fall of snow:
Here like to one, at set of sun,
It waxed red alsò.
For love's name maketh bold,
As if the loved were near,
And sighed she the deep, long sigh
Which cometh after fear.
Margret, Margret!

'Now, sooth, I fear thee not—-
Shall never fear thee now.'
(And a noble sight, was the sudden light
Which lit her lifted brow).
'Can earth be dry of streams,
Or hearts of love?'—she said;
'Who doubteth love—knoweth not love—
Already is he dead!'
Margret, Margret!

'I have'—and then her lips
Some word in pause did keep;
And gave, the while, a quiet smile,
As if she smiled in sleep—
'I have—a brother dear,
A knight of knightly fame—
And I broidered him a knightly scarf
With letters of my name;'
Margret, Margret.

'I fed his gay goss-hawk—
I kissed his fierce blood-hound—
I sate at home when he might come,
To hear his horn's far sound.
I sang him songs of old—
I poured him the red wine;
And looked he from the cup and said—
I love thee, sister mine:
Margret, Margret.'

It trembled on the grass
With a low shadowy laughter—
And the sounding river which rolléd ever,
Stood dumb and stagnant after.

'Brave knight thy brother is,
   But better loveth he
Thy pouréd wine than thy chantéd song—
   And better both, than thee!
                  Margret, Margret!'

The ladye did not heed
   The river's pause—the while
Her own thoughts still ran at their will,
   And calm was still her smile—
'My little sister wears
   The look our mother wore;
I smooth her locks with a golden comb,
   I bless her evermore.'
                  Margret, Margret.

'I gave her my first bird,
   When first my voice it knew;
I made her share my posies rare,
   And told her where they grew.
I taught her God's high words—
   God's worthy praise, to tell:
She looked from heaven into my face,
   And said, "I love thee well,
                  Margret, Margret!"'

It trembled on the grass
   With a low shadowy laughter—
And each glass-eyed bird awoke and stared
   Through the shrivelled tree-leaves after.
'Fair child thy sister is,
   But better loveth she
Thy golden comb than posied flowers—
   And better both, than thee!
                  Margret, Margret!'

The ladye did not heed
   The withering on the bough;
Still calm her smile, albeit the while,
   A little pale her brow.
'I have a father old,
   The lord of ancient halls;
An hundred friends are in the court,
   Yet only me, he calls'—
                  Margret, Margret.

'An hundred knights are there;
   Yet read I by his knee—
And when forth they go to the tourney show,
   I rise not up to see.

'Tis a weary book to read—
   My trysts at set of sun—
Yet dear and loving neath the stars
   Is his blessing, when I've done.'
            Margret, Margret.

It trembled on the grass
   With a low shadowy laughter—
And moon and star, most bright and far,
   Did shrink and darken, after.
'High lord thy father is,
   And better loveth he
His ancient halls than hundred friends—
   His ancient halls, than thee,
            Margret, Margret!'

The ladye did not heed
   That the high stars did fail;
Still calm her smile, albeit the while—
   Nay! *but she is not pale*.
'I have a more than friend
   Across the mountains dim;
No other's voice is soft to me,
   Unless it nameth *him*.'
            Margret, Margret.

'Though louder treads mine heart,
   I know his step again—
And his far plume aye, unless *turned away*,
   For tears do blind me *then*.
We brake no gold, a sign
   Of stronger faith to be—
But I wear his last look in my soul;
   It said "I love but thee!
            Margret, Margret!"'

It trembled on the grass
   With a low shadowy laughter—
And the wind did toll, as a passing soul
   Were sped by church-bell, after.
And shadows, 'stead of light,
   Fell from the stars above,
In flakes of darkness on her face
   All bright with trusting love,—
            Margret, Margret!

'He loveth none but thee?—
   That love is ended too:—
The black crow's bill doth dabble still
   I' the mouth that vowed thee true.

Will he open his dull eyes,
  When tears fall on his brow?
Behold! the death-worm, to his heart,
  Is a nearer thing than thou,
    Margret, Margret!'

Her face was on the ground,—
  None saw the agony:
But the men at sea, did that night agree
  They heard a drowning cry.
And when the morning brake,
  Fast rolled the river's tide—
With the green trees waving overhead,
  And a white corse lain beside!
    Margret, Margret!

A knight's blood-hound, and he,
  The funeral watch did keep—
And he turnéd round, to stroke the hound,
  Which howled to see him weep.
A fair child kissed the dead,
  And started from its cold,—
And alone, yet proudly, in his hall,
  Did stand a baron old!
    Margret, Margret!

Hang up mine harp again,
  I have no voice for song;
Not song, but wail—and mourners pale,
  Not bards, to *love* belong.
Oh! failing human love,
  Oh! light, by darkness known!
Oh! false, the while thou treadest earth,
  Oh! deaf, beneath the stone!
    Margret, Margret!

No friends! no name but *His*,
  Whose name, as *Love* appears,—
Look up to heaven, as God's forgiven,
  And see it not for tears!
Yet see with spirit-sight
  The eternal Friend, undim—
Who died for love, and joins above
  All friends who love in *Him*.
And, with his piercéd hands, may He
The guardian of your clasped ones be!
Which prayer doth end my lay of thee,
    Margret, Margret!

(1836)

ELIZABETH BARRETT

We walkèd by the sea,
After a day which perished silently
Of its own glory—like the princess weird,
Who, combating the Genius, scorched and seared,
Uttered with burning breath, 'Ho, victory!'
And sank adown, an heap of ashes pale.
So runs the Arab tale.

The sky above us showed
An universal and unmoving cloud;
Athwart the which, yon cliffs did let us see
Only the outline of their majesty;
As master-minds, when gazed at by the crowd:
And, shining with a gloominess, the water
Swang as the moon had taught her.

Nor moon, nor stars were out;
They did not dare to tread so soon about,
Though trembling, in the footsteps of the sun.
The light was neither night's nor day's, but one
Which, life-like, had a beauty in its doubt;
And silence's impassioned breathings round,
Seemed wandering into sound.

Oh solemn-beating heart
Of Nature! I have knowledge that thou art,
Bound unto man's, by cords he cannot sever—
And, what time they are slackened by him ever,
So to attest his own supernal part,
Still runneth thy vibration fast and strong,
The slackened cord along.

For though we never spoke
Of water colourless and shaded rock,
Dark wave and stone, unconsciously, were fused
Into the plaintive speaking that we used,
Of absent friends and memories unforsook;
Then, had we seen each other's face, we had
Seen, haply, each was sad.

(1836)

187 L.E.L.'s LAST QUESTION

Do you think of me as I think of you?
— From her poem written during the voyage to the Cape.

'Do you think of me as I think of you,
My friends, my friends?' She said it from the sea,
The English minstrel in her minstrelsy—
While under brighter skies than erst she knew,
Her heart grew dark, and gropëd as the blind,
To touch, across the waves, friends left behind—
'Do you think of me as I think of you?'

It seemed not much to ask—*as I of you*—
We all do ask the same—no eyelids cover
Within the meekest eyes that question over—
And little in this world the loving do,
But sit (among the rocks?) and listen for
The echo of their own love evermore—
Do you think or me as I think of you?

Love-learnëd, she had sung of only love—
And as a child asleep (with weary head
Dropped on the fairy-book he lately read),
Whatever household noises round him move,
Hears in his dream some elfin turbulence—
Even so, suggestive to her inward sense,
All sounds of life assumed one tune of love.

And when the glory of her dream withdrew,
When knightly gestes and courtly pageantries
Were broken in her visionary eyes
By tears, the solemn seas attested true—
Forgetting that sweet lute beside her hand,
She asked not 'Do you praise me, O my land,'
But, 'Think ye of me, friends, as I of you?'

True heart to love, that pourëd many a year
Love's oracles for England, smooth and well,—
Would God, thou hadst an inward oracle
In that lone moment, to confirm thee dear!
For when thy questioned friends in agony
Made passionate response, 'We think of thee,'
Thy place was in the dust—too deep to hear!

Could she not wait to catch the answering breath?—
Was she content with that drear ocean's sound,
Dashing his mocking infinite around
The craver of a little love?—beneath

Those stars, content—where last her song had gone?
They, mute and cold in radiant life, as soon
Their singer was to be, in darksome death!

Bring your vain answers—cry, 'We think of thee!'
How think ye of her?—in the long ago
Delights!—or crowned by new bays?—not so—
None smile, and none are crowned where lyeth she—
With all her visions unfulfilled, save one,
Her childhood's, of the palm-trees in the sun—
And lo!—their shadow on her sepulchre!

Do you think of me as I think of you?—
O friends, O kindred, O dear brotherhood
Of the whole world—what are we that we should
For covenants of long affection sue?—
Why press so near each other, when the touch
Is barred by graves? Not much, and yet too much,
This, 'Think upon me as I think of you.'

But, while on mortal lips I shape anew
A sigh to mortal issues, verily
Above the unshaken stars that see us die,
A vocal pathos rolls—and He who drew
All life from dust, and *for* all, tasted death,
By death, and life, and love appealing, saith,
Do you think of me as I think of you?

(1839)

Notes

ABBREVIATIONS

Athenaeum *The Athenaeum Journal, 1828–.*

Aubin Robert A. Aubin, *Topographical Poetry in XVIII-century England*, New York: MLA 1936.

Backscheider *et al.* *An Annotated Bibliography of Twentieth-century Critical Studies of Women and Literature, 1660–1800*, eds Paula Backscheider, Felicity Nussbaum and Philip B. Anderson, New York: Garland 1977.

BDMBR *Biographical Dictionary of Modern British Radicals*, vol. I: *1770–1830*, eds Joseph O. Baylen and Norbert J. Gossman, Brighton: Harvester Press 1979.

Boyle Andrew Boyle, *An Index to the Annuals (1820–1850)*, Worcester: Andrew Boyle 1967.

Courtney J. E. Courtney, *The Adventurous Thirties: A Chapter in the Women's Movement*, London: Oxford University Press 1933.

De Quincey *CW* *The Collected Writings of Thomas De Quincey*, ed. David Mason, 14 vols, Edinburgh 1889–90.

DNB *The Dictionary of National Biography*, ed. Leslie Stephen and Sidney Lee, 63 vols, London 1885–1900.

Elwood Anne Katherine Elwood, *Memoirs of the Literary Ladies of England, from the Commencement of the Last Century*, 2 vols, London 1843.

ER *European Magazine and London Review*, 1782–.

FC *The Feminist Companion to English Literature*, eds Virginia Blain, Patricia Clements, Isobel Grundy, London: Batsford 1990.

Fullard *British Women Poets 1660–1800: An Anthology*, ed. Joyce Fullard, Troy, New York: Whitston 1990.

GM *Gentleman's Magazine; or Monthly Intelligencer*, 1731–.

Hazlitt *CW* *The Complete Works of William Hazlitt*, ed. P. P. Howe, 21 vols, London: J. M. Dent & Sons, 1930–34.

HNC H. N. Coleridge, 'Modern English poetesses', *Quarterly Review*, LXVI (1840), 374–418.

Jackson *Romantic Poetry by Women: A Bibliography, 1770–1835*, Oxford: Clarendon Press 1993.

LG *Literary Gazette, 1817–*.

LLC *The Library of Literary Criticism*, ed. C. W. Moulton, 8 vols, New York: Moulton 1901–05.

Lonsdale *Eighteenth Century Women Poets: An Oxford Anthology*, ed Roger Lonsdale, Oxford: Oxford University Press 1989.

LR *Location Register of English Literary Manuscripts and Letters*, ed. David C. Sutton, 2 vols, London: The British Library 1995.

MM *Monthly Magazine, and British Register*, 1796–.

MP *Morning Post and Daily Advertiser*, 1772–.

NCBEL *New Cambridge Bibliography of English Literature*, vols 2–3, ed. George Watson, Cambridge: Cambridge University Press 1969–71.

NMM *New Monthly Magazine*, new series, 1821–.

Schlueter *Encyclopaedia of British Women Writers*, ed. Paul Schlueter and June Schlueter, Chicago: St James Press 1988.

STC *CL* *Collected Letters of Samuel Taylor Coleridge* [1785–1836], ed. E. L. Griggs, 6 vols, Oxford: Clarendon Press 1956–71.

Todd *A Dictionary of British and American Women Writers, 1660–1800*, ed. Janet Todd, London: Methuen 1987.

Watt *Bibliotheca Britannica or a General Index to British and Foreign Literature*, ed. Robert Watt, 4 vols, Edinburgh 1824.

WW *CL* *The Letters of William and Dorothy Wordsworth*, [1787–1853], eds E. de Selincourt, second edition, rev. C. L. Shaver, Mary Moorman, A. G. Hill, 7 vols, Oxford: Clarendon Press 1967–88.

For texts published separately, the period 1701–50 has been covered by D. F. Foxon, *English Verse 1701–1750*, 2 vols, Cambridge 1975. The period 1770–1835 has been covered by J. R. de J. Jackson, *Annals of English Verse 1770–1835*, New York 1985, and *Romantic Poetry by Women: A Bibliography, 1770–1835*, Oxford 1993. See also R. C. Alston, *A Checklist of Women Writers 1801–1900*, London 1990, Gwen Davis and Beverly A. Joyce, *Poetry by Women to 1900: A Bibliography of American and British Writers*, London 1991. Several volumes of romantic poetry were reprinted in a subsequently discontinued series, *The*

Romantic Context: Poetry 1789–1830, ed. Donald H. Reiman, 128 vols, New York, 1976–. See also the series of reprints, *Revolution and Romanticism*, 1789–1834 ed. Jonathan Wordsworth, Oxford: 1989–. I have been unable to locate the following: Susanna Rowson, *Poems on Various Subjects*, London 1788, Jane Smith, *Select Poems on Various Subjects*, London 1790, Mrs M. Strickland, *Miscellaneous Poems, and Other Compositions*, [Exeter?] 1790. For poems published in America, see the bibliography by Oscar Wegelin, *Early American Poetry, 1650–1799*, second edition, Gloucester, Mass. 1965. For information on the 'Annuals', see F. W. Faxan, *Literary Annuals and Gift-books: A Bibliography, 1823–1903*, Boston 1912, A. Bose, 'The verse of the English annuals', *RES*, new series, IV (1953), 38–51. For American 'Annuals', see R. Thompson, *American Literary Annuals and Gift-books, 1825–1865*, New York 1936. Many women poets are also included in Chadwyck-Healey's *The English Poetry Full-Text Database*, Cambridge 1992–.

For reviews of particular works, consult William S. Ward, *Literary Reviews in British Periodicals, 1789–1797, 1798–1820* (2 vols), *1821–1826: A Bibliography*, 4 vols, New York 1972–79. For information on the periodicals themselves, see Alvin Sullivan (ed.) *British Literary Magazines: . . . 1698–1788, 1789–1836*, 2 vols, Westport, Conn. 1983.

For loco-descriptive poems in the period, see the lists compiled by Aubin: Hill-poems, pp.298–314; Mine- and Cave-poems, p.314; Sea-poems, pp.314–15; Estate-poems, pp.316–33; Town-poems, pp.333–50; Building-poems, pp.350–64; Region-poems, pp.365–77; River-poems, pp.377–85; Journey-poems, pp.385–91. For poems on or about the throne of melancholy, see John F. Sena, *A Bibliography of Melancholy 1660-1800*, London 1970, pp.23–43. For political and war poetry, see the texts in *British War Poetry in the Age of Romanticism: 1793–1815*, ed. Betty T. Bennett, New York 1976.

For criticism, see Backscheider *et al.* See also *The Eighteenth Century: A Current Bibliography*, new series, 1–12 (1975-86), *The Romantic Movement: A Selected and Critical Bibliography, ELH, 1937–1949, PQ, 1950–1964, ELN, 1965–1978, 1979–*, ed. D. Erdman *et al.*, New York 1980-, *Bibliographies of Studies in Victorian Literature* (for 1932–44, ed. W. D. Templeman; for 1945–54, ed. A. Wright; for 1955–64, ed. R. C. Slack; for 1965–74, ed. R. E. Freeman; for 1975–84, ed. R. C. Tobias). See also the *Annual Bibliography of Victorian Studies*, ed. B. Chaudhuri *et al.*, 1976–. See also the Gale Research guides: *English Poetry, 1600–1800*, ed. Donald C. Mell; *English Romantic Poetry, 1800–1835*, ed. Donald H. Reiman.

For individual authors, see T. H. Howard-Hill, *Bibliography of Literary Bibliographies* (*Index to British Literary Bibliography*, I), second edition, revised and enlarged, Oxford 1987, *British Bibliography and Textual Criticism* (*Index to British Literary Bibliography*, V), Oxford 1979 and the individual entries in the criticism bibliographies previously mentioned.

For manuscripts, those located in British repositories can be traced through *LR*. For manuscripts held in North America, the OCLC and ARLIN databases are useful though incomplete, and it is still necessary to consult *NUC* and *American Literary Manuscripts*. Sale catalogues, such as Sotheby's, also contain important information on manuscript material.

In addition to Lonsdale and Fullard, a number of nineteenth-century anthologies are still worth consulting: Alexander Dyce, *Specimens of British Poetesses; Selected and Chronologically Arranged*, London 1825; George Washington Bethune, *The British Female Poets; with Biographical and Critical Notes*, Philadelphia 1848; Jane Williams, *The Literary Women of England, Including a Biographical Epitome of all the Most Eminent to the Year 1700; and Sketches of the Poetesses to the Year 1850*, London 1861; Eric S. Robertson, *English Poetesses: A Series of Critical Biographies, with Illustrative Extracts*, London 1883; Elizabeth Amelia Sharp, *Women's Voices*, London 1887, *Women Poets of the Victorian Era*, London [1890]. Other useful collections include A. H. Miles (ed.), *The Poets and the Poetry of the Century*, vol. 7, *Joanna Baillie to Mathilde Blind*, London [1892]; J. C. Squire, *A Book of Women's Verse*, London 1921; Clifford Bax and Meum Stewart, *The Distaff Muse*, London 1949. For American women poets, see Pattie Cowell (ed.), *Women Poets in Prerevolutionary America, 1650–1775*, Troy, New York 1981 and Rufus Wilmot Griswold, *The Female Poets of America*, Philadelphia 1849.

Of more than passing interest is Stainforth's *[A Collection of] Portraits of English Poetesses. With some Autograph Letters*, 2 vols unpublished, in the British Library (1876.f.22).

For writings by women other than poetry, see G. Davis and B. A. Joyce, *Personal Writings by Women to 1900: A Bibliography of American and British Writers*, London 1989, and Cheryl Cline, *Women's Diaries, Journals, and Letters: An Annotated Bibliography*, New York 1989.

ANNA SEWARD (1742-1809)

DNB; *LR*, ii.849–51; *NCBEL*, 2. 682-8; *FC*, 967; Lonsdale, 311–13, 530; Schlueter, 405–6; *LLC*, iv.541–4; Elwood, i.241–58; *Letters*, 6 vols, Edinburgh 1811; R. A. Hesselgrave, *Lady Miller and the Batheaston Literary Circle*, New Haven 1927; M. Ashmun, *The Singing Swan: An Account of Anna Seward . . .*, New Haven 1931; S. H. Monk, 'Anna Seward and the romantic poets: a study in taste', in E. L. Griggs (ed.), *Wordsworth and Coleridge: Studies in Honour of G. M. Harper*, Princeton 1939, pp.118–34. Untraced Mss: *Catalogue of the Extraordinary Library . . . Formed by the late Rev. F. J. Stainforth, Consisting Entirely of Works of British and American Poetesses, and Female Dramatic Writers . . .*, London: Sotheby, Wilkinson & Hodge 1867, p.164: *Songs and Other Poems*, 1790 by Honora Sneyd, *Sonnets by Anna Seward and Others* 1788. 2 vols.

1–5, 7. Texts: *Original Sonnets on Various Subjects . . .*, London 1799, pp. 9, 20, 39, 65, 73, 97.

1. See Aubin, 377–85. For other river poems by women see Ann Radcliffe, 'To the River Dove', in *Gaston de Blondville . . .*, 4 vols, London

1826, iv.236–9, Mary Robinson, 'To the Wild Brook', in *The Poetical Works*, 3 vols, London 1806, ii.264–5 (first pub. *MP*, 6 August 1799). Compare also 'Ode Written on the River Derwent, in a Romantic Valley Near its Source', by Seward's friend Erasmus Darwin (*GM* (1783), LV. ii.641), William Lisle Bowles, 'Monody Written at Matlock . . .' (1791), Eyles Irwin, 'Elegy to the River Derwent, at Matlock Bath, 9th September 1802', *EM*, XLIII (1803), 147–8.

4. See note to **11**.

5. On the significance of poppies and the derivative opium in romanticism, see M. H. Adams, *The Milk of Paradise*, Cambridge, Mass. 1934, Elizabeth Schneider, *Coleridge. Opium and Kubla Khan*, Chicago 1953, Alethea Hayter, *Opium and the Romantic Imagination*, London 1968. For other poems on this subject by women, see Maria Logan, 'To Opium' in *Poems on Several Occasions*, York 1793, pp.17–21, Henrietta O'Neill, 'Ode on the Poppy', in Charlotte Smith, *Desmond* . . . , 3 vols, London 1792, iii.165–6 (reprinted in Lonsdale, pp.458–9, Fullard, pp.271–2), Mary Robinson, 'The Poet's Garret', *Morning Post*, 27 August 1800, reprinted in *The Poetical Works*, 3 vols, London 1806, iii.233–5. For prose works on opium, see Watt, vol. 4.

6. Text: *GM*, 1789, ii, August, p.743. This poem was not reprinted in *Original Sonnets* (1799), presumably because of its political content. It was one of the earliest responses to the French Revolution.

8–9. Texts: from *Louisa, a Poetical Novel, in Four Epistles* . . . , third edition, Lichfield 1784, pp.2–4, 66–7.

8. In the Preface, Seward claimed that the opening 156 lines had been written when she was nineteen (1761–62).

8–9. Louisa's 'application of the beautiful scenic objects, by which she was at that interval surrounded, to her own, and to her Lover's situation; and the passing suddenly to their present altered appearance, contrasts the charms, and bloom of the first, with the chill dreariness of the second. There it was that the Author had in view that striking letter in the 3rd Vol. of the Nouvelle-Heloise, which describes St. Preaux accompanying Mrs. Wolmar to the rocks of Meillerie, then covered with the richness of Summer-luxuriance, and painting to her the situation of that very Scene, when he had visited it alone, amidst the horrors of Winter, and found those horrors congenial to the temper of his Soul' (Anna Seward, Preface, [ii]).

It would be difficult to underestimate the powerful effect and formative power the *Nouvelle Héloïse* had on a number of eighteenth-century readers and how it released autobiographical modes of thinking and seemed to reveal their destinies. Mary Hays notes how the pleasure approached the limits of pain and was 'productive of a long chain of consequences, that will continue till the day of my death' (*Memoirs of Emma Courtney*, 2 vols (1796), i.41) and for Mary Wollstonecraft's Maria it seemed to open a new world to her—the only one worth inhabiting' ('The

Wrongs of Woman', in *Mary and the Wrongs of Woman*, ed. Gary Kelly, Oxford 1980, p.88). Jane Baillie Welsh (later Carlyle) was similarly struck by the work—'This book this fatal book has given me an idea of a love so *pure* . . . so constant, so disinterested, so exalted—that no love the men of this world can offer me will ever fill up the picture my imagination has drawn with the help of Rousseau—No lover will Jane Welsh ever find like St. Preux—no husband like Wolmar . . . O Lord O Lord! where is the St. Preux? Where is the Wolmar?—Bess I am in earnest—I shall never marry . . .' (Letter to Eliza Stodart, January 1822, *The Collected Letters of Thomas and Jane Welsh Carlyle*, Duke-Edinburgh Edition, ed. C. R. Sanders *et al.*, ii.17, North Carolina 1970). Wollstonecraft's fierce attack on Rousseau in *Vindication of the Rights of Woman* (1792), concentrates on other areas in Rousseau's works, and is not representative of the full range of Dissenting responses to the *Nouvelle Héloïse*. In a complicated set of emotional experiences, Hazlitt begins reading it on his birthday, walks to Llangollen vale and reads Coleridge's 'Ode to the Departing Year' and ends up in 'the cradle of a new existence . . . baptised in the waters of Helicon'. At other times, he recalled that the work revealed his 'glassy essence' or had the same effect on him as the sight of Marie Antoinette on Burke (Hazlitt, *CW*, 8.186, 12.224, 12.304, 17.115, 20.405).

10. Text. Scots Magazine, XLVII (1785), pp.90–1, where it was entitled 'Verses written by Miss Anna Sward in the Blank Leaves of her Poems . . .'. It was later retitled (with additional notes), 'Independent Industry True Virtue . . .' in *The Poetical Works* . . . , ed. Walter Scott, 3 vols, Edinburgh 1810, ii.320–9.

11. Text: *The Poetical Works* . . . , ed. Walter Scott, 3 vols, Edinburgh 1810, ii.314-19. Bodley, Ms. Pigott d. 12. f. 13–17. See also **4**. Coalbrookdale was famed for its iron furnaces and the area was one of the centres of the industrial revolution. Between 1779 and 1781 the famous Iron Bridge over the Severn was built. In 1796 Trevithick and Telford moved there and the first locomotive to be run on rails was constructed in 1802. Coalbrookdale was also important for its brilliant night fires which lit up the area and was frequently seen as an apocalyptic emblem of the horrors of industry set in an idyllic pastoral landscape: 'Colebrook Dale itself is a very romantic spot, it is a winding glen between two immense hills which break into various forms, and all thickly covered with wood, forming the most beautiful sheets of hanging wood. Indeed too beautiful to be much in unison with that variety of horrors art has spread at the bottom: the noise of the forges, mills, &c. with their vast machinery, the flames bursting from the furnaces with the burning of the coal and the smoak of the lime kilns, are altogether sublime, and would unite well with craggy and bare rocks, like St. Vincent's at Bristol.' Arthur Young (ed.), *Annals of Agriculture*, IV, London, 1785, p.168. 'The large ironworks carried on there, where the roaring of the blast furnaces, the long beds of glowing coke, the jets of flame and showers of sparks, and the stalwart forms of the various forger men, mingled with the woods, the rocks, and caverns, or reflected in the broad waters of the Severn, give it a peculiarity of appearance which I have never seen elsewhere.' Mary Anne Schimmelpenninck, c.1790, in Christiana H. Hankin (ed.), *The Life of Mary Anne Schimmelpenninck*, 2 vols, London 1848, i.231. It was frequently painted, most notably by Robertson, de Loutherbourg and Turner. See Christine Vialls, *Coalbrookdale and the Iron Revolution*, Cambridge 1976, Arthur Raistrick, *The Coalbrookdale Ironworks: A Short History*, Ironbridge 1975. See also 'Coalbrookdale and the sublime', in F. D. Klingender, *Art and the Industrial Revolution* (1968) rev. Arthur Elton, London 1972, pp.75-80.

Plutus] In Greek myth, the personification of wealth.

Naiads] Nymphs who presided over rivers, springs, wells and fountains.

Sabrina] The river Severn.

Cyclops] One-eyed giants in Homer but Seward refers to the tradition which treats them as workmen.

Mithra] Indo-Persian god of light, frequently represented as the sun.

Mercian] The ancient English kingdom, south of the Humber, encompassing most of the present Midlands.

Her famed Triumphirate] 'Messrs Boulton, Watt, and Kier' (AS). Matthew Boulton (1728–1809) and James Watt (1736–1819) collaborated on the development of the steam engine. James Keir (1735–1820), a distinguished chemist and geologist, managed their engineering works at Soho, Birmingham, while they worked on the steam engine. All three were members of the Lunar Society.

The rapt sage] Joseph Priestley (1733–1804), scientist, educationalist and radical Dissenter, whose house was later attacked by a mob in Birmingham in 1791 owing to his radical sympathies. He later emigrated to America.

dusky sister, Ketley yields] 'Wolverhampton has the greatest part of her iron from Ketley, a dreary and barren wold in her vicinity' (AS).

Sheffield's arid moor] 'The East-moor, near Sheffield, which is dreary, though the rest of the country surrounding that town, is very fine' (AS)

Erebus] In Greek mythology, the son of Chaos and hence the personification of darkness.

ANNA LAETITIA BARBAULD (née AIKIN) (1743–1825)

William McCarthy and Elizabeth Kraft (eds) *The Poems of Anna Laetitia Barbauld*, Athens, Georgia: University of Georgia Press 1994, is definitive with fine notes and an indispensable bibliography.

DNB; *LR*, i.38; *NCBEL*, 2, 639–40; *FC*, 58–9, Lonsdale, 299–300, Schlueter, 20–1; *LLC*, v.22–6; Elwood, i.224–40; Lucy Aikin, 'Memoir', in *The Works*, 2 vols (1825); A. L. Le Breton, *Memoir of Mrs Barbauld*, London 1874, B. Rodgers, *Georgian Chronicle: Mrs Barbauld and her Family*, London 1958, C. E. Moore, *The Literary Career of Anna Laetitia Barbauld*, Ph.D. University of North Carolina 1969, S. M. Clarke, *A Bibliography of Mrs Barbauld*, unpub. dissertation London University,

School of Librarianship 1949, Edith J. Morley (ed.), *Henry Crabb Robinson on Books and their Writers*, 3 vols, London 1938, i.8, i.74.

12–14. Texts: *Poems*, London 1773, pp.3–6, 97–100, 131–8.

12. The cause of Corsican liberty and its leader, General Pasquale Paoli, who later fled to England, were championed by James Boswell. See his *An Account of Corsica* . . . , Glasgow 1768 and the collection he edited, *British Essays in Favour of the Brave Corsicans* . . .', London 1769.

Cyrnus] A Roman term for Corsica, after Cyrnus, the son of Hercules.

Liberty / The mountain Goddess] Compare a similar association of mountains and liberty in Mary Robinson, 'Sonnet: "Oh! Liberty! transcendent and sublime!" (**83**) and 'Hail, Liberty sublime! . . .' (**86**). Throughout most of the eighteenth century, the association linked personal and national liberty, and has often been seen as an element of Whig ideology. After the French Revolution, however, the binding process becomes complicated. The genealogy of liberty remains unchanged but the site of liberty (mountains) often changes to a scene and symbol of tyranny, mirroring the development and corruption of human institutions. Mountains can be images of unalterable authority, an unchanging (political) landscape and the instruments of human change, catalysts of human resurrection from political ruins. Mary Robinson, for example, sometimes saw mountains as emblems of tyranny. See *Vacenza; or The Dangers of Credulity*, third edition, 2 vols (1792), i.35–7. Compare Charlotte Dacre, *The Passions*, 4 vols (1806), i.1–4, 35–7. The positions of the male romantics is equally complicated. On mountains as 'Characters of the great apocalypse, / The types and symbols of eternity', see Wordsworth, *The Prelude* (1805), bk vi.593ff. On mountains and the voice which can 'repeal / Large codes of fraud and woe', see Shelley, 'Mont Blanc' (1816). For Mont Blanc as the 'dread ambassador from earth to heaven', see Coleridge 'Hymn before Sunrise in the Vale of Chamouni' (1802). The mountain–liberty theme was restated by Wordsworth in his 'Thought of a Briton on the Subjugation of Switzerland' (1806–07). The connection between mountains and liberty was judiciously examined by Peacock in 'Melancourt' (1817), chapter xxxvii, 'Mountains': 'What have the mountains done for freedom and mankind? When have the mountains, to speak in the cant of the new school of poetry, "sent forth a voice of power" [Wordsworth] to awe the oppressors of the world? . . . The only source of freedom is intellectual light.' Yet 'those who seek the mountains in a proper frame of feeling, will find in them images of energy and liberty, harmonizing most aptly with the loftiness of an unprejudiced mind, and nerving the arm of resistance to every variety of impression and imposture, that winds the chains of power round the free-born spirit of man.' Mary Shelley restated an amalgam of complex ideas of mountains as 'the habitation of another race of beings', 'a glorious presence chamber of imperial nature', and the 'silent working of immutable laws' in chapter 9 of *Frankenstein; or, The Modern Prometheus* (1818). See also **135** for mountains as the 'earth's eternal tenants' and **176n**. for Charlotte Brontë's linkage of the moors, liberty and personality. See also Anne Brontë, 'The North Wind', in *The Poems of Anne Brontë*, ed. Edward Chitham, London 1979, pp.63–4. On mountain rivers, the destiny of man, mysterious tendencies written hieroglyphically, and the great alphabet of Nature, see De Quincey, 'Literary and Lake Reminiscences' (De Quincey, *CW*, ii.400ff.). On mountains/valleys and 'inward characters of Liberty, Genius, Love and Virtue' and 'the cradle of a new existence', see Hazlitt, 'On Going on a Journey' (Hazlitt, *CW* viii.186–7), and 'My First Acquaintance with Poets' (*ibid*. xvii.115). For poetic responses earlier in the century, see S. H. Monk, *The Sublime* (1935), Ann Arbor 1960 and M. H. Nicolson, *Mountain Gloom and Mountain Glory*, Ithaca 1959.

Tyrrhene] Etruscan.

13. 'Hope waits upon the flowery prime.'] Edmund Waller, 'To my young lady. Lucy Sidney.' Poems, &c., London 1645, p.19.

Hazlitt read the 'Ode to Spring' in William Enfield's *The Speaker* (1774) (eleven editions by 1800), an influential anthology, particularly in Dissenting academies, such as the one he attended at Hackney, and remembered 'being much divided in my opinion at that time, between her Ode to Spring and Collins's Ode to Evening' (Hazlitt, *CW*, v.147). However, the remark is revisionist and refers to his youthful not mature appreciation. Hazlitt's lecture 'On the Living Poets' updates the English canon after Anderson, but consigns the female poets to being novel or prose writers.

14. 'One sun by day, by night ten thousand shine'] Edward Young, *The Complaint: or, Death, and Immortality. The Consolation* [Night the ninth], London 1745, line 748.

Dian's bright crescent] The moon. Diana was variously a moon goddess, goddess of hunting, woodlands and fertility in Roman mythology.

Hesperian gardens] Italy. The Greeks called Italy 'the western land'.

Sinai] Mount Sinai where Moses received the ten commandments (Exodus, 19: 20–5, 20: 1–21).

15–18. Text: *The Works . . . With a Memoir by Lucy Aikin*, 2 vols, London 1825, i.159–60, i.180–2, i.185–7, i.188–9.

16. First published as 'To a great nation', *Cambridge Intelligencer*, 2 November 1793.

Briareus-like] one of the hundred-armed giants who fought with Zeus against the Titans.

17. Compare Susanna Rowson, 'Rights of Woman', in *Miscellaneous Poems . . .*, Boston 1804, pp.98–104, Rachel Prescott, 'Stanzas to the Late Mrs Godwin, on Reading her "Rights of Woman"', *Poems*, London 1799, pp.51–2, Robert Burns, 'The Rights of Woman', *Poems and Songs*, ed. James Kinsley, Oxford 1978, pp.527–8, Robert Southey, 'The Triumph of Woman' (1793), in *The Poetical Works . . .*, 10 vols (1837–38), ii.1–19. For prose works on this subject, see *The Feminist Controversy* *in England, 1788-1810*, ed. Gina Luria, 44 vols, New York: Garland 1974–, and, in particular, Mary Wollstonecraft, *Vindication of the Rights of Woman* . . . , London 1792, and [Mary Robinson], *A Letter to the Women of England, on the Injustice of Mental Subordination*, London 1799.

19. Text: *MM*, IV (1797), p.452.

———And their voice, . . .] Shakespeare, *As You Like It*. II.vii. 161–3, (Jacques' 'All the world's a stage' speech).

the buskined step] Buskins were high shoes worn by actors in Ancient Greece.

linen-horse] clothes-horse.

Montezuma] emperor of Mexico, tortured and killed by Cortez. In *The Works*, ed. Lucy Aikin, 2 vols (1825), i.204, Montezuma is replaced by Guatimozin, his nephew. The source for most of the information on the Spanish Conquest was probably William Robertson's *The History of America*, 2 vols, London 1777.

Erebus] the son of Chaos. His name was given to the underground cavern leading to Hades. Hence darkness.

Montgolfier, thy silken ball] The Montgolfier brothers, inventors of the hot-air balloon, which was made out of silk and filled with hydrogen. The first human ascents took place in 1783 and excited great interest. See Mary Alcock, 'The Air Balloon', *Poems* [ed. Joanna Hughes], London 1799, pp.107–11.

20. Text: *MM*, VII (1799), pp.231–2.

the hill of science] See Barbauld's prose allegory, 'The Hill of Science: A Vision', *Miscellaneous Pieces in Prose*, London 1773, pp.27–38.

Circe] In Homer, the sorceress who turned Odysseus' men into swine.

Coleridge visited Barbauld in August 1797 (STC *CL*, i.341n.).

21–3. Texts: from *Eighteen Hundred and Eleven, a Poem*, London 1812, pp.4–10, 12–17, 23–5. For other responses to urban life, see M. Byrd, *London Transformed: Images of the City in the Eighteenth-Century*, New Haven 1978, R. Williams, *The Country and the City*, London 1973, M. Vicinus, *The Industrial Muse: A Study of Nineteenth Century British Working-class Literature*, New York 1974, W. B. Thesing, *The London Muse: Victorian Poetic Responses to the City*, Athens, Georgia, 1982, pp.1–33.

21. Midas] Phrygian King who requested of the gods that everything he might touch should turn to gold. When his food turned to gold, he begged to be released from his request.

Platan's] Plane-tree.

Thy Lockes, thy Paleys] John Locke (1632–1704): to Dissenters, Locke was as important for his defence of religious tolerance and the 1688 settlement, as for *An Essay Concerning Human Understanding*. William Paley (1743–1805): author of *Principles of Moral and Political Philosophy* (1785) and *Natural Theology* (1802) which developed a theological utilitarianism much admired in Dissenting circles (Paley himself was not a Dissenter).

Hagley's woods] Hagley, the seat of Lord Lyttelton, was famous for its beautiful park, woods and views into Wales.

Thomson] James Thomson (1700–48), poet. His poem *The Seasons* was one of the earliest and most significant landscape-descriptive poems in English. His political views were also admired by Dissenters.

loved Joanna] Joanna Baillie (1762–1851), poet and friend of Barbauld. She was much better known for her psychological drama than her poetry. But see **65–72**.

Basil, . . . Ethwald] Characters in Joanna Baillie's tragedies.

22. Johnson's form] Samuel Johnson (1709–84), critic and moralist.

Howard's sainted feet] John Howard (1725–90), prison reformer, author of *The State of the Prisons in England and Wales*, Warrington 1777.

Chatham's eloquence] William Pitt, 1st Earl of Chatham (1708–78). Whig politician and orator whose foreign policy is often credited with the successful prosecution of the Seven Years War, the prosperity which ensued and the beginning of the Empire when Britain gained European hegemony in Canada and India. He opposed the war against the American colonies and was generally thought to have acquired power from popularity, rather than from the King, which has sometimes been seen as a fundamental shift in power towards more democratic government. 'His lips were cloathed, with inspiration and prophecy. Sublimity, upon his tongue, sat, so enveloped in beauty, that it seemed, unconscious of itself. It fell upon us unexpectedly, it took us by surprise, and, like the fearful whirlpool, it drew every understanding, and every heart, into its vortex' (William Godwin, *The History of the Life of William Pitt, Earl of Chatham*, London 1783, p.301).

Fox] Charles James Fox (1749–1806) dominated Whig opposition politics from the American War of Independence to his death. Although many radicals doubted his idealism, he was an energetic defender of parliamentary liberties, and his last major speech was in support of the abolition of the Slave Trade.

Garrick] David Garrick (1717–79). The most famous actor of Barbauld's youth.

loftiest tone] 'Every reader will recollect the sublime telegraphic despatch, "England expects every man to do his duty"' (ALB). Reported to be Nelson's words at the Battle of Trafalgar.

gallant Moore] '"I hope England will be satisfied," were the last words of General Moore' (ALB). Sir John Moore (1761–1809) was killed defending the Peninsula retreat at Corunna in 1809.

Davy] Sir Humphry Davy (1778–1829) chemist and natural philosopher, whose electrical and other discoveries gained him an international reputation. He played an important role in the development of the Royal Institution where he lectured from 1801.

Franklin] Benjamin Franklin (1706–90), American printer, scientist and diplomat who signed all four major documents of the founding of the

United States. He was equally famous in France and England. He wrote part of his *Autobiography* at the Shipley family home at Twyford Moors in 1771 where Anna Maria Jones then lived.

Priestley's injured name] Joseph Priestley (1733–1804), scientist, educationalist, and radical. Barbauld had known him since his time as a tutor in Warrington. His house was attacked and burned by a Birmingham mob in 1791. He then took up a post at Hackney College but emigrated to America in 1794.

Reynolds] Sir Joshua Reynolds (1723–92), the leading portrait and history painter and President of the Royal Academy.

23. Chimborazo . . . La Plata . . . Potosi] Refers not so much to the specific places in Ecuador, Argentina and Bolivia but to the freedom of South America itself.

24. Text: from *The Works . . . with a Memoir by Lucy Aikin*, 2 vols, London 1825, i.261–2. The poem was admired by Wordsworth, who believed, on unknown authority, that it had been written when Barbauld 'was not less than 80 years of age' (WW *CL*, v.529), a dating which conflicts with Lucy Aikin's primarily chronological arrangement of 1825 and Crabbe Robinson's report of 1805, that Wordsworth had remarked 'I wish I had written those lines' (Henry Crabbe Robinson, *op. cit.* i.8.)

'Animula, vagula blandula'] 'Ah! gentle, fleeting, wav'ring sprite'. The motto is the first line of a poem by the Emperor Hadrian, translated by Byron in 1804, as 'Adrian's address to his soul when dying'. See *Poetical Works*, ed. F. Page, London 1970, p.4. Barbauld would probably have known it through Pope's translation or the unsigned translation in MM, 1796, p.567.

HANNAH MORE (1745–1833)

DNB; *LR* ii.666–9; *NCBEL*, 2, 1598–1600; *FC*, 760–1; Lonsdale, 323–5, 531; Schlueter, 335–6; *LLC* v.190–6; Elwood, i.259–83; W. Roberts, *Memoirs of . . . Hannah More*, 4 vols, London 1834; H. Thompson, *Life of Hannah More . . .*, London 1838; M. A. Hopkins, *Hannah More and her circle*, New York, 1947; M. G. Jones, *Hannah More*, Cambridge 1952.

25–6. Texts: from *The Search after Happiness: A Pastoral Drama. The Second Edition, with Additions*, Bristol 1773, pp.17–18, 18–20.

25. Newton, and Halley] Sir Isaac Newton (1642–1727), mathematician and astronomer whose *Principia* (1687) and *Opticks* (1704) revolutionised science and, in many respects, the arts. For his influence on literature, see M. H. Nicolson, *Newton Demands a Muse: Newton's 'Opticks' and the Eighteenth-Century Poets*, Princeton 1946. Edmond Halley (1656–1742), mathematician and astronomer, discoverer of the comet named after him, who promoted and defended Newton.

Descartes, and Euclid] More means here studies of geometry. At the time Descartes was as well known for advances in geometry as for the method of doubt in the philosophical works.

Locke] John Locke (1632–1704), author of *An Essay Concerning*

Human Understanding (1690) who effectively established the primacy of empirical observation over metaphysical speculation.

Boyle] Robert Boyle (1627–91) chemist, experimental philosopher and leading member of the Royal Society.

MARY HAYS (1760–1843)

LR, i.442; *FC*, 503–4; *BDMBR*, i.215–17; M. Ray Adams, 'Mary Hays, disciple of William Godwin', in *Studies in the Backgrounds of English Radicalism*, Pennsylvania 1947, pp.82–103; J. M. S. Tompkins, 'Mary Hays, philosophess', in *The Polite Marriage*, Cambridge 1938, pp.150–90; Gina Luria, *Mary Hays: A Critical Biography*, Ph.D., New York University, 1972. Mss, including early poems, in the Pforzheimer Library, New York Public Library.

27. Text: from *Letters and Essays, Moral and Miscellaneous* . . . , London 1793, pp.253–5. First published in *The Lady's Poetical Magazine, or Beauties of British Poetry*, 4 vols, London 1781–82, ii.464–5.

'Lydian measures'] 'Lap me in soft Lydian airs, / Married to immortal verse' Milton, *L'Allegro*, lines 136–7.

28. Text: from *Universal Magazine*, LXXV (1784), p.333. Not republished.

29. Text: from *Letters and Essays, Moral and Miscellaneous*, London 1793, p.257. First published in *Universal Magazine*, LXXVII (1785), p.329.

CHARLOTTE SMITH (née TURNER) (1749–1806)

DNB; *LR*, ii.878; *NCBEL*, 2, 683–4; *FC*, 996; Lonsdale, 365–7, 533; Schlueter, 417–19; *LLC*, iv.496–8; Elwood, i.284–309; F. M. A Hilbish, *Charlotte Smith, Poet and Novelist*, Philadelphia 1941; Stuart Curran (ed.) *The Poems of Charlotte Smith*, Oxford 1993; R. F. Turner, *Charlotte Smith (1749–1806): Some New Light on her Life and Literary Career*, Ph.D. University of Southern California 1966; D. J. McNutt, *The Eighteenth-century Gothic Novel; An Annotated Bibliography* . . . , Folkestone 1975, pp.173–85, P. W. Gledhill, *The Sonnets of Charlotte Smith*, Ph.D. University of Oregon 1976, Bishop C. Hunt, 'Wordsworth and Charlotte Smith', *Wordsworth Circle*, i (1970), pp.85–103.

Note: Charlotte Smith's own notes (CS), have been adapted and modified for reasons of space.

30. Text: *Elegaic Sonnets: The Third Edition. With Twenty Additional Sonnets*, London [1786], p.4. See B. R. Pollin, 'Keats, Charlotte Smith, and the nightingale', *N&Q* 211 (1966), pp.180–1, G. W. Whiting, 'Charlotte Smith, Keats, and the nightingale', *Keats-Shelley Journal*, 12 (1963), pp.4–8.

Poor melancholy bird] The idea is from the 43rd Sonnet of Petrarch, Secondo Parte, 'Quel rosigniuol, che si soave piagne' (CS) (That nightingale that so sweetly weeps).

31. Text: *Ibid.*, p.6. First published *ER*, ii (1782), p.311. Ms. Bodl. Montague. 14. f.26.

your turf, your flowers among] 'Whose turf, whose shade, whose flowers among' Gray, 'Ode on a Distant Prospect of Eton College' (CS).

Aruna!] The river Arun (CS).

32. Text: *Ibid*,m p.8. First published as 'On the Farewell to the Nightingale', *ER*, ii (1782). p.235.

night's dull ear] Shakespeare, *Henry V*, IV.Prol. (CS).

Whether on spring] Alludes to the supposed migration of the nightingale (CS).

The pensive muse shall own thee for her mate] 'Whether the Muse or Love call thee for his mate, / Both them I serve, and of their train am I' Milton's First Sonnet (CS).

33. Text: *Elegaic Sonnets . . . The Fifth Edition, with Additional Sonnets and Other Poems*, London 1789, p.42.

night-jar] Omen of misfortune for travellers (CS).

34–5. Texts: *The Young Philosopher* . . . , 4 vols, London 1798, iii.52, iii.75. Reprinted, *Elegaic Sonnets, and Other Poems*, vol. II, second edition, London 1800, p.26, p.27.

34. runnels] 'Bubbling runnels joined the sound'—Collins, 'The Passions. An Ode for Music' (CS).

36–7. Texts: from *The Emigrants, a Poem, in Two Books*, London 1793, pp.1-5, pp.39–44. The 'emigrants' are French refugees who came to England after the execution of Louis XVI in January 1793.

36. Brighthelmstone] Brighton.

day star] the sun.

Beach] Beech?

the fabled Danaïds] The fifty daughters of Danaus, King of Argos, who married the sons of Aegyptus. All except Hypermnestra murdered their husbands on their wedding night. They were punished in Hades by having to draw water from a well in sieves.

the wretch] Sisyphus, who cheated death and was punished in the Underworld by having to push up to the top of a hill a rock which always rolled down again.

37. Hope still waits . . .] Waller. See **13n**.

'Famine, and Sword, and Fire . . .'] Shakespeare, *Henry V*. Prolo 7–8.

38. Text: *Conversations Introducing Poetry: Chiefly on Subjects of Natural History. For the Use of Children and Young Persons*, 2 vols, London 1804, ii.151–6. Reprinted in *Beachy Head* . . . , London 1807, pp.100–9.

day's bright star] the sun.

diamond bow] crescent moon.

Boreal climes] arctic regions.

ling] common heath.

frith] firth.

Orcades] The Roman name for the Orkneys.

39–40. Texts: from *Beachy Head: With Other Poems . . .*, London 1807, pp.79–83, 1–51.

39. Compare Lady Charlotte Campbell, 'On the Swallow', *Poems on Several Occasions*, London 1797, pp.13–18.

Her nuptials] Alluding to the Ovidian fable of the Metamorphosis of Procne and Philomela into the Swallow and the Nightingale (CS).

linger torpid] hibernating.

40. The poem was left unfinished at CS's death.

Of vast concussion] Alluding to the theory that England and France were separated by a convulsion of nature (CS).

tarrocks] young kittiwakes.

Bursts from its pod the vegetable down] cotton (CS).

The beamy adamant] diamonds (CS).

Neustria] The western part of the ancient Frankish kingdom, corresponding to north-western France, i.e. Normandy (CS).

O'er which that mass of ruin frowns] Pevensey Castle (CS).

Dogon, Fier-a-bras, and Humfroi] Paladins or knights-errant of the Emperor Charlemagne who later ruled Sicily.

Trinacria] Sicily.

Parthenope] One of the Greek Sirens.

Taillefer] The Northern French court poet who accompanied William the Conqueror in 1066. During the invasion he rode ahead of the other horsemen, singing of Charlemagne and Roland.

Roland] The most famous of Charlemagne's paladins, the subject of the medieval romance, *Le Chanson de Roland* and Ariosto's *Orlando Furioso*.

Saxon heptarchy] The seven English kingdoms of the sixth to eighth century; Kent, Sussex, Essex, Wessex, East Anglia, Mercia and Northumbria.

Then the holy pile] Battle Abbey (CS).

Gallia] France.

Batavian] of the ancient kingdom of Batavi, now part of Holland. Alluding to the Anglo-Dutch navies defeat by the French in 1690 and the subsequent invasion threat (CS).

Of one, who sometimes watches on the heights] smugglers' lookout.

Or turbary] Turbary is the right to dig turf or peat, usually on common or other people's ground.

charlock] field mustard.

'Unprofitably gay'] 'With blossomed furze, unprofitably gay', Goldsmith, *The Deserted Village* (CS).

Vecta] The Isle of Wight.

vetch] plant of the pea family often used for forage.

bittersweet] woody nightshade.

bryony] white bryony, or English Mandrake.

bindweed] kinds of climbing plants.

pagil] paigle, or cowslip.

tumps] hillock, mound or mole-hill.

Elephant] The remains of an elephant had been discovered in Burton Park in 1740. They were probably brought over by the Romans (CS).

robbery, fire and sword] See the final note to **37**.

hermit life] A hermit was reputed to have lived in a cave near Beachy Head.

'close the eye of day'] 'And liquid notes that close the eye of day', Milton (CS), 'close the eye of anguish', *King Lear*, IV.iv.14.

feelingly alive] 'What then is taste, but these internal powers / Active, and strong, and feelingly alive / To each fine impulse?' Mark Akenside, *The Pleasures of Imagination* (1744), p.135.

ELIA KNIPE (later CLARKE, later COBBOLD) (1767–1824)

LR, i.214; *FC*, 219–20; Mss. BL and a large collection at Ipswich & Suffolk Record Office, HA, 231.3.

41–2. Texts: from *Poems on Various Subjects*, Manchester 1783, pp.47–51, 51–4. See *Thematic Index* for other women's responses to Lake or Welsh scenery. See also Isabella Lickbarrow, 'On Esthwaite Water', 'On Underbarrow Scar', *Poetical Effusions*, Kendal, 1814, pp.67–8, 94–6, Hannah Cowley, 'Edwinna' ('Skiddaw! I climb thy high uplifted form'), in William Hutchinson, *The History of the County of Cumberland*, 2 vols, Carlisle 1794, ii.5.

41. Thaumantia's bow] a rainbow. Thaumantia, better known as Iris, was the goddess of the rainbow, along which she could travel.

Claude] The English form for the French landscape painter, Claude Gelée (Claude Lorraine) (1600–82), who was widely admired in England throughout the eighteenth century.

42. Dodonean tree] The oracular shrine of Zeus at Dodona.

Aeolus] the god of the winds.

ANNE HUNTER (née HOME) (1742–1821)

DNB; *LR*, i.498; *NCBEL*, 2. 2026–7; *FC*, 552, Lonsdale, 363, 532.

43. Text: *Poems*, London 1802, pp.1–5. First published anonymously in Charles Moore, *A Full Inquiry into the Subject of Suicide . . .*, 2 vols, London 1790, i.352–4, as 'The Progress of November'.

Far from the madding crowd,] Gray's Elegy, line 73.

Hyem] Winter.

44. Text: *Poems*, London 1802, pp.35–6.

DNB; *LR*, ii. 1000–1; *NCBEL*, 2, 693–4; *FC*, 1169; Lonsdale, 413–14, 535; *LLC*, v.74–5; *BDMBR*, i.539–42; L. D. Woodward, *Une Adhérente anglaise de la Révolution française: Hélène-Maria Williams et ses amis*, Paris 1930; M. Ray Adams, 'Helen Maria Williams and the French revolution', in *Wordsworth and Coleridge: Studies in Honor of G. M. Harper*, ed. E. L. Griggs, Princeton 1939, pp.87–117; Julie Ellison, 'Redoubled feeling: politics, sentiment, and the sublime in Williams and Wollstonecraft', in L. E. Brown and P. Craddock (eds.), *Studies in Eighteenth-century Culture*, xx (1990), pp.197–215.

45–6. Texts: from *Poems*, 2 vols, London 1786, i.17–18, ii.201–2. Both first published, *Universal Magazine*, LXXV September (1784), pp.351–2.

46. 'Of him the Muses loved] Thomas Chatterton (1752–70), the poet whose suicide, like Gray's *Bard*, became an emblem of the fate of poets in society. He was the subject of numerous poems. Other women also wrote poems on the subject. See Ann Yearsley, 'Elegy on Mr Chatterton' in *A Second Book of Poems in Various Subjects*, London 1787, pp.145–9, Hannah Cowley, 'Monody on the Death of Chatterton', in *Scots Magazine*, LI (1789), pp.444–5, Mary Robinson, 'Monody to the Memory of Chatterton', in *Poems*, London 1791, pp.75–9, Anne Hunter, 'To the Memory of Thomas Chatterton', in *Poems*, London 1802, pp.21–2. Compare Coleridge, 'Monody on the Death of Chatterton', in *Rowley Poems*, ed. Lancelot Sharpe, Cambridge 1794, pp.xxv–xxviii, and the two versions in *Poetical Works* (second edition), ed. F. de Selincourt, Oxford 1952, pp.235–40.

47–8. Texts: from *Julia a Novel: Interspersed with some Poetical Pieces*, 2 vols, London 1790, i.15–24, i.204.

47. Ye southern isles, emerged so late] 'The songs of the bards or minstrels of Otaheite [Tahiti] were unpremeditated, and accompanied with music. They were continually going about from place to place; and they were rewarded by the master of the house with such things as the one wanted, and the other could spare.—Cook's *Voyage*' (HMW). The idea of the poet, as spontaneous, lyrical, itinerant, politically significant, and socially welcome, had first been applied to Homer by Thomas Blackwell in his *Enquiry into the Life and Writings of Homer*, London 1735. By the 1760s, the idea had encompassed Provençal troubadours, Welsh bards, and Ossian. The interest in 'primitive' poetry was partly antiquarian, partly motivated by a desire to create literary history, and partly political.

'At times, between the rushing blast', 'of other years', 'the joy of tears'] Referring to James Macpherson's collections of Ossian's poems. The quotations are not necessarily specific and such phrases are common throughout the text. The repetition of such phrases, the sublimity of scenery and the tenderness of sentiment was first discussed by Hugh Blair in *A Critical Dissertation on the Poems of Ossian* (1763, rev. 1765).

'Kiss with cold lips the sacred veil, / And drop with every bead too soft a tear!'] Pope, 'Eloisa to Abelard' (misquoted).

'melancholy marked her own'] Gray, 'Elegy Written in a Country Churchyard' (misquoted).

Or let me o'er old Conway's flood / Hang on the frowning rock . . .] Referring to Gray's Bard.

'ratify thy doom'] Gray, 'The Bard: A Pindaric Ode' (misquoted).

48. In *Poems on Various Subjects* . . . , London 1823, p.203n., Williams remarked 'I commence the sonnets with that to HOPE, from a predilection in its favour, for which I have proud reason; it is that of Mr Wordsworth, who lately honoured me with his visits while at Paris, having repeated it to me from memory, after a lapse of many years.' Wordsworth had visited her in October 1820. Much earlier, in 1791, on his way to France, he had asked Charlotte Smith in Brighton for a letter of introduction.

49. Text: *Letters from France* . . . , vol. II, second edition, London 1792, pp.10–13.

50–7. Texts: from *Paul and Virginia: Translated from the French of Bernardin Saint-Pierre*, [Paris] 1795, pp.33, 53, 78, 91, 105, 113, 200, 202. These sonnets 'written at Paris, amidst the horrors of Robespierre's tyranny' appear not to be complete. Williams noted that a few sonnets were seized by the French authorities 'and are not likely to be restored to my possession'. A search of the Paris archives has not produced them.

58. Text: from *A Tour in Switzerland* . . . , 2 vols, London 1798, ii.16–19. Compare Georgiana Cavendish, Duchess of Devonshire, 'The Passage of the Mountain of St Gothard', [London] [1799], reprinted in Lonsdale, pp.511–14.

MARY HUNT (1764–1834)

59. Text: from *Poems, Chiefly by Gentlemen of Devonshire and Cornwall* . . . , ed. Richard Polwhele, 2 vols, Bath 1792, i.134–6. First published anonymously as 'On Visiting the Ruins of an Ancient Abbey, in Devonshire. By a Lady', *ER*, X (1786), pp.384–5. Compare Mary Whateley, 'Elegy to the Ruins of Kenilworth Castle', in *Poems on Several Occasions*, 2 vols, Walsall 1794, i.1–7, Barbara Hoole, 'Elegaic Lines Composed in the Ruins of Roche Abbey', in *Poems*, Sheffield [1805], pp.13–17. For other poems on abbeys and ruins, see Aubin, pp.350–64.

ANN YEARSLEY (née CROMARTIE) (1752–1806)

DNB; *LR*, ii. 1031; *NCBEL*, 2, 298; *FC*, 1197; Lonsdale, 392–5, 534; Schlueter, 492–3; W. Roberts, *Memoirs of Mrs Hannah More*, 4 vols (1834), i.361–75, 383–91; Robert Southey, *The Lives and Works of the Uneducated Poets*, ed. J. S. Childers, Oxford 1925; Joseph Cottle, *Reminiscences of Coleridge and Southey* (1847), pp.47–51; J. M. S. Tompkins, 'The Bristol Milk-woman', in *The Polite Marriage*, Cambridge 1938, pp.58–102; M. Ferguson, 'Resistance and power in the life and writings of Ann Yearsley', *The Eighteenth Century*, 27 (1986), pp.247–68; Donna Landry, *The Muses of Resistance: Laboring-Class Women's Poetry in Britain, 1739–1796*, Cambridge 1990, pp.120–85.

60. Text: *A Second Book of Poems on Various Subjects*, London 1787, pp.77–82.

fabled Nine] The Muses, the nine daughters of Zeus and Mnemosyne.

Castalian spring] a fountain of Mount Parnassus, sacred to the Muses, with the power of imparting the gift of poetry to those who drank from it.

Zoroaster] Persian king and philosopher and, according to some classical sources, the founder of magic.

Ormazes] Ahuramazda. A similar variant spelling was used by Shelley in 'The Revolt of Islam', X.xxxi, 'Oromaze'. In Zoroastrian belief the world was ruled by two conflicting spirits of good and evil, Ahuramazda and Angramainyu.

61–3. Texts: from *The Royal Captives* . . . , 4 vols, London 1796, iv.68–9, iv.70, iv.105–12. Compare Helen Maria Williams, 'Sonnet to Peace', in *Julia* . . . , 2 vols, London 1790, ii.159. Compare Mary Robinson, 'The Horrors of Anarchy', *Morning Post*, 25 April 1798, and later republished as part of *The Progress of Liberty*.

63. Persian King] Xerxes.

Cassandra's fire] See **103n**.

MARY O'BRIEN (fl. 1785–90)

FC, 806–7; Todd, 236.

64. Text: from *The Political Monitor; or Regent's Friend* . . . , Dublin 1790, pp.49–51.

JOANNA BAILLIE (1762–1851)

DNB; *LR*, i.31–2; *NCBEL*, 3, 363–4; *FC*, 50–1; Lonsdale, 429–30, 536; Schlueter, 15–16; *LLC*, v.689–95; M. S. Carhart, *The Life and Works of Joanna Baillie*, New Haven 1923.

65–9. Texts: *Poems: Wherein it is Attempted to Describe Certain Views of Nature and of Rustic Manners* . . . , London 1790, pp.10–16, 27–33, 73–81, 108–11, 115–19, 122–4.

67. driven] In poetry we have only to do with appearances; and the zig-zag lightning, commonly thought to be the thunder-bolt, is certainly firm and embodied, compared to the ordinary lightning, which takes no distinct shape at all' (JB).

70–1. Texts: *Fugitive Verses*, London 1840, pp.140–2, 237–44.

72. Text: *A Collection of Poems, Chiefly Manuscript, and from Living Authors*, London 1823, pp.259–64.

'in populous city pent'] Milton, *Paradise Lost*, ix.445.

ANNA MARIA JONES (née SHIPLEY) (1748–1829)

DNB, Jonathan and William Shipley, William Augustus Hare, Francis Hare-Naylor; Augustus J. C. Hare, *The Story of my Life*, 6 vols (1896–1900), i.13, 16, 20, 35, ii.144, vi.5, *Memorials of a Quiet Life*, 3 vols (1872–76), i.87–206, containing some correspondence; *BDMBR* 273–4, G. H. Cannon, 2 vols, Oxford 1970, *Bengal Past and Present*, 25 (1921), p.148, 28 (1924), p.140, India Office Library Mss (Executors' effects, 16 November 1829), Twyford Church, Shipley family papers at Hampshire Record Office.

73–6. Texts: *The Poems of Anna Maria . . .* , Calcutta 1793, pp.22, 49–52, 61–4, 65–8.

73. Echo was in love with Narcissus but punished by Hera never to speak except to repeat what was said to her. Unable to express herself, she was ignored by Narcissus and eventually wasted away until only her voice remained.

74. Compare Mary Robinson, 'Marie Antoinette's Lamentation', in *Poems*, vol. II, London 1793, pp.89–92. For other examples of this genre, see Betty T. Bennett (ed.) *British War Poetry in the Age of Romanticism, 1793–1815*, New York 1976.

76. Et vix sustinuit dicere Lingua – vale!] And my tongue could scarcely bear to say 'Farewell!'. Ovid, Heroides, v.52. Slightly misquoted.

MARY ROBINSON (née DARBY) (1758–1800)

DNB; *LR*, ii.803; *NCBEL*, 2. 680–1; *FC*, 916–17; Lonsdale, 468–70, 537; Schlueter, 391–2; *LLC*, iv.411–12; STC *CL*, 322, 333, 349, 355, 361, 377, 479; *A Biographical Dictionary of Actors, Actresses, Musicians, Dancers, Managers & Other Stage Personnel in London 1660–1800*, vol. 13, ed. P. H. Highfill, K. A. Burnim and E. A. Langhans, Carbondale, 1991; M. Steen, *The Lost One: A Biography of Mary Robinson*, London 1937; R.D. Bass, *The Green Dragon: The Lives of Banastre Tarleton and Mary Robinson*, New York 1957; M. Ray Adams, 'Mrs. Mary Robinson: a study of her later career', in *Studies in the Literary Backgrounds of English Radicalism*, Pennsylvania 1947, pp.104–29; L. W. Koengeter, *Mrs Mary Robinson: A Biographical and Critical Appraisal*, Ph.D. Harvard University 1975; For Della Cruscan connections, see W. N. Hargreave-Mawdsley, *The English Della Cruscans and their Time, 1783–1828*, The Hague 1967, and *NCBEL*, 2, 698. For reviews, see Ward, i.202–3.

77. Text: *Poems*, London 1791, pp.29–32. See also her 'Second Ode to the Nightingale, *ibid.* pp.33–7. There was no shortage of poems to nightingales in the eighteenth century although their significance is a neglected area in Keats scholarship given the canonical status of his 'Ode to a Nightingale'. William Ashburnham, Anne Bannerman, Peter Courtier, Sarah Dixon, George Dyer, Anne Finch, Henry Headley, Charles Hoyland, Mary Hays, Anne Hunter, Samuel Oram, Cuthbert Shaw, Christopher Smart, Charlotte Smith, James Thomson and many others wrote on the subject.

78–9. Texts: *Poems*, vol. II, London 1793, pp.70–3, 62–4. First published *The Oracle*, 3 August 1792 and 30 November 1792 respectively.

78. ********] Banastre Tarleton.

80. Text: *The Poetical Works* . . . , 3 vols 1806, i.193–6. First published *GM*, LXIV (1794), ii.1033.

81. Text: *The Poetical Works* . . . , iii.274–6. First published *MP*, 29 January 1795.

82–3. Texts: *Angelina: A Novel* . . . , 3 vols, London 1796, i.227–32, iii.30, 90. Reprinted *The Poetical Works* . . . , 3 vols, London 1806, i.43–8. For poems on melancholy, see Sena, pp.23–43.

84. Text: *The Poetical Works* . . . , i.123–4. First published *Walsingham: or, The Pupil of Nature* . . . , 4 vols, London 1797, i.53–5. Reprinted *MP*, 26 December 1797. For Coleridge's response to this poem, see *PW*, i.356–8, *CL*, I.361.

85. Text: *GM* (1797), i.62–3.

86–7. Texts from 'The Progress of Liberty', in *Memoirs of the Late Mrs Robinson, Written by Herself. With Some Posthumous Pieces* [ed. Maria Elizabeth Robinson], 4 vols, London 1801, iv.5–9, iv.92–5. 'The Progress of Liberty' appeared in a different form in *MP*, 17 April 1798 to 30 August 1800. On mountains and liberty, see note to **13**.

88. Text: *The Poetical Works* . . . , 3 vols, London 1806, iii.223–4. First published *MP*, 23 August 1800.
coopers] cask-makers.

89. Text: *Memoirs of the Late Mrs Robinson, Written by Herself. With Some Posthumous Pieces* [ed. Maria Elizabeth Robinson], 4 vols, London 1801, iv.145–9. Reprinted, *The Poetical Works* . . . , 3 vols, London 1806, i.226–9. On the quotations from 'Kubla Khan' ('sunny dome', 'caves of ice'), see James Dykes Campbell (ed.), *The Poetical Works of Samuel Taylor Coleridge*, London 1907, p.593; J. L. Lowes, *The Road to Xanadu* (revised edition), Boston 1930, p.355; Norman Fruman, *Coleridge, the Damaged Archangel*, London 1972, pp.539, 541.

90. Text: *The Poetical Works* . . . , 3 vols, London 1806, i.221–5. First published *MP*, 17 October 1800. On the pedagogic function of mountains in the education of children, see *Thematic Index*, Coleridge, 'Frost at Midnight', Mary Howitt, 'Mountain Children', *Winter's Wreath* (1829), pp.397–8, Maria Jane Jewsbury, 'To a Poet's Infant Child', *Literary Souvenir* (1826), pp.78–80.

91. Text: *Lyrical Tales*, London 1800, pp.72–6. First published *MP*, 26 February 1800. Coleridge recommended the poem to Southey for inclusion in the second volume of the *Annual Anthology*, remarking on its 'fascinating Metre' (STC, *CL*, i.L322).

92. Text: *The Wild Wreath* [ed. Maria Elizabeth Robinson], London 1804, pp.160–2, where it carries the signature (for reasons unknown) of the daughter (M.E.R.). First published, as 'The Camp', *MP*, 1 August 1800.

Suttling houses] Run by camp-followers, they sold provisions to troops and other camp-followers.

sociables] open carriages with facing side-seats.

ANN RADCLIFFE (née WARD) (1764–1823)

DNB; *LR*, ii.786; *NCBEL*, 3. 758–60; *FC*, 884; Lonsdale, 448–9, 536; Schlueter, 373–4; *LLC*, iv.717–21; Elwood, ii.155–73; T. N. Taulford, *Memoir*, prefixed to *Gaston de Blondville* . . . , 4 vols, London 1826; [T. N. Taulford?], Obituary Notice, *NMM*, IX (1823), p.232; D. J. McNutt, *The Eighteenth-century Gothic Novel: An Annotated Bibliography* . . . , Folkestone 1975, pp.116–35, 186–225; A. A. S. Wieten, *Mrs Radcliffe: Her Relation toward Romanticism*, Amsterdam 1926; M. Ware, *Sublimity in the Novels of Ann Radcliffe* . . . , Upsala 1963. See also T. N. Taulford (ed.), 'On the Supernatural in Poetry. By the Late Mrs Radcliffe', *NMM*, xvi. part i (1826), pp.145–52. For her possible influence on Keats and Shelley, see W. E. Peck, 'Keats, Shelley, and Mrs Radcliffe', *MLN*, XXXIX (1924), 251–2.

93–5. Texts: *The Romance of the Forest: Interspersed with Some Pieces of Poetry* . . . , 3 vols, London 1791, i.86–7, ii.129–31, iii.160–2. A few of the poems included in the novel had previously been published in the *Gazeteer and New Daily Advertiser*.

93. Compare Joseph Warton, 'Ode to Fancy', *Odes on Various Subjects*, London 1746, pp.5–11; John Langhorne, *The Visions of Fancy: In Four Elegies*, London 1762, Thomas Walley, 'Irregular Ode on the Power of Fancy' (*c.* 1788), *Journals and Correspondence*, ed. H. Wickham, 2 vols (1863), i.239–43; John Scott, 'Ode to Fancy' (*c.* 1783), *ER*, XXXVI (1799), p.46.

94. First published *The Gazeteer and New Daily Advertiser*, 28 January 1791.

95. yellow sands] Ariel's Song, *The Tempest*, I.ii.377.

sweet sprites!] Ariel's Song, *The Tempest*, I.ii.382.

O fairy forms! . . . to poets only shown] 'fairy forms', 'fairy ground', and the 'fairy way of writing' were key elements in critical theory from Addison to Joseph Warton and had first been hinted at by Dryden. Warton, particularly, was fond of quoting *The Faerie Queene, A Midsummer Night's Dream* and *The Tempest* non-contextually, making quotations as mottoes for critical activity. Radcliffe's combination of elements from *A Midsummer Night's Dream* and *The Tempest* was not therefore new critically, though poetically the otherworldliness in a present situation had not received such sustained treatment. There were, of course, other routes to 'fairy forms', most obviously through Ossian, but it would be hard to see why a woman would opt for a gender-restricted 'sublime' poet such as Ossian when access was much easier through the two Shakespeare plays.

96. Text: *The Mysteries of Udolpho, a Romance: Interspersed with Some Pieces of Poetry*, 4 vols, London 1794, ii.59–60.

97. Text: *Gaston de Blondville . . . with Some Poetical Pieces . . .*, 4 vols, London 1826, iv.240–8.

Compare Elizabeth Barrett, 'The Sea-Mew', in *The Seraphim, and other Poems*, London 1838, pp.293–6.

AMELIA ALDERSON (later OPIE) (1769–1853)

DNB (Amelia Opie); *LR*, ii.719–22; *NCBEL*, 3, 753–4; *FC*, 815–16; Todd, 236–7; Schlueter, 353–4; *LLC*, v.741–4; Boyle, 215–16; C. L. Brightwell, *Memorials of . . . Amelia Opie*, London 1854; M. E. MacGregor, 'Amelia Opie: wordling and friend', *Smith College Studies in Modern Languages*, xiv, nos 1–2, 1932–33. A large portion of unpublished literary remains, used by Brightwell and MacGregor, was sold at Sotheby's, 22 June 1953, and remains untraced. It contains several unpublished early poems, including 'A Sonnet Written in Cumberland' (1790), 'At the Sight of the Tricolour', the novel *The Painter and his Wife*, portraits and Godwin Mss.

98. Text: *The Annual Anthology*, 2 vols, Bristol 1799–1800, i.202–4. Reprinted in *Poems*, London 1802, pp.161–5. In the 1790s, 'Twilight' increasingly became an object of attention, receiving authority from popular Gothic sources such as Ann Radcliffe's novels and philosophical sources promoting the picturesque, such as Uvedale Price, *An Essay on the Picturesque, as Compared with the Sublime and the Beautiful . . .*, London 1794.

99. Text: *The Warrior's Return, and Other Poems*, London 1808, pp.57–65.

100. Text: *The Cabinet*, 3 vols, Norwich 1795, ii.92–5. Alderson lived in Norwich, a famous centre of radicalism and unitarianism in the 1790s. See C. B. Jewson, *The Jacobin City: A Portrait of Norwich in its Reaction to the French Revolution, 1788–1802*, London 1975, Peter H. Marshall,

William Godwin, New Haven 1984, pp.17–31. William Enfield, the former Warrington tutor and friend of the Aikin family, was minister at the dissenting Octagon Chapel 1785–97.

Famine] The harvest failed frequently in the 1790s with exports of wheat and wheat flour at their lowest levels since the beginning of the century. Imports reached their highest ever level, almost three times the level of the 1780s.

101. Text: *Poems*, London 1802, pp.121–4. First published *The Cabinet*, 3 vols, Norwich 1795, iii.128–30. Mary Wollstonecraft notes that 'Nature is the nurse of sentiment—the true source of taste;—yet what misery, as well as rapture, is produced by a quick perception of the beautiful and sublime, when it is exercised in observing animated nature, when every beauteous feeling and emotion excites responsive sympathy, and the harmonized soul sinks into melancholy, or rises to ecstasy, just as the chords are touched like the aeolian harp agitated by the changing wind' (*A Short Residence in Sweden, Norway and Denmark* . . . , ed. Richard Holmes, Harmondsworth 1987, p.99). On the significance of the aeolian harp in romanticism, see Georges Kastner, *La Harpe d'Eole*, Paris 1856, Geoffrey Grigson, *The Harp of Aeolus*, London 1948, George Dekker, *Coleridge and the Literature of Sensibility*, London 1978, pp.101–41.

Memnon] Killed by Achilles in the Trojan War. His statue at Thebes was said to have produced a musical chord when struck by the rising sun.

JANE WEST (née ILIFFE) (1758–1852)

DNB; *LR*, ii.991–2; *NCBEL*, 3, 772; *FC*, 1151; Lonsdale, 379–80, 533; Schlueter, 472–3; P. L. Simmons, *N&Q* 229 (1984), pp.469–70.

102. Text: from *The Advantages of Education, or, The History of Maria Williams* . . . , 2 vols, London 1793, ii. 84–6. See Charlotte Seymour, *The Works of the Imagination* . . . , London 1803, Emily Brontë, 'To Imagination', *Poems by Currer, Ellis, and Acton Bell*, London 1846, pp.96–7, and *Thematic Index*.

103. Text: *A Gossip's Story* . . . , 2 vols, London 1796, ii.140.

Cassandra] The prophetic daughter of Priam, who foretold the Fall of Troy but was never believed. Raped by Ajax and later given to Agamemnon.

Paris] Cassandra's brother whose 'abduction' of Helen caused the Trojan War.

Priam] King of Troy, killed by Pyrrhus.

Pyrrhus] Son of Achilles who killed Priam on the Fall of Troy.

104. Text: *A Tale of the Times* . . . , 3 vols, London 1799, ii.139–40.

Pomona] The Roman goddess of fruit.

Flora] Roman goddess of flowers and spring.

ANNA MARIA PORTER (1780–1832)

DNB; *LR*, ii.774; *NCBEL*, 3, 757; *FC*, 865–6; Boyle, 227; Elwood, ii. 276–303; Mss. variously dispersed in Britain and North America after the sale of the Ker-Porter papers at Sotheby's, 28 June 1966.

105–6. Texts: *The Parnassian Garland; Forming the Poetry of the Monthly Visitor* . . . , London 1797, pp.3–5, 32.

105. Pierian] The birthplace of the muses and Orpheus, on the northern slopes of Mount Olympus.

Thracian] Thrace was the most northern area of Greece.

MARY TIGHE (née BLACHFORD) (1772–1810)

DNB; *LR*, ii.950–1; *NCBEL*, 3, 405; *FC*, 1081; *LLC*, iv.550–2; P. Henchy, *The Works of Mary Tighe: Published and Unpublished*. Bibliographical Society of Ireland Publication 6, no. 6, Dublin 1957; E. V. Weller, *Keats and Mary Tighe* . . . , New York 1928.

107–9. Texts: *Psyche, with Other Poems* . . . , second edition, London 1811, pp.220, 225, 228.

107. Dated August 1796.

109. Dated 1800, in *Mary, a series of reflections during twenty years*, [Roundwood] 1811.

110–13. Texts: *Psyche, or the Legend of Love*, London 1805, pp.27–34, 53–7, 83–7, 145–7.

BARBARA HOOLE (née WREAKS, later HOFLAND) (1770–1844)

DNB; *LR*, i.459–60; *NCBEL*, 3, 733–5; *FC*, 530; Thomas Ramsay (ed.), *The Life and Literary Remains of Barbara Hofland* . . . , London 1849.

114–17. Texts: *Poems*, Sheffield 1805, pp.28–9, 69, 70, 99.

JANE TAYLOR (1783–1824)

DNB; *LR*, ii.926; *NCBEL*, 3, 1087; *FC*, 1058; Elwood, ii.262–75; D. M. Armitage, *The Taylors of Ongar*, Cambridge 1939; Christina Duff Stewart, *The Taylors of Ongar: An Analytical Bio-bibliography*, 2 vols, New York 1978.

118. Text: *Essays in Rhyme, on Morals and Manners*, London 1816, pp.123–8.

119. Text: from 'A pair', *ibid.*, pp.134–9.

120. Text: from 'The world in the house', *ibid.*, pp.148–50.

FELICIA DOROTHEA HEMANS (née BROWNE) (1793–1835)

DNB; *LR*, i.452–4; *NCBEL*, 3, 383–4; *FC*, 510–11; Schlueter, 226–7; *LLC*, v.254–62; Boyle, 120–3; Elwood, ii.225–61; *Memoir* by D. M. Moir, prefixed to *Political Remains*, Edinburgh 1836; H. F. Chorley, *Memorials of Mrs Hemans*, 2 vols, London 1836, Harriet Hughes (ed.), *The Poetical Works of Mrs Hemans, with a Memoir of her Life*, 7 vols, Edinburgh 1839; F. Espinasse, *Lancashire Worthies: Second Series* (1877), pp.286–95; E. Dumeril, *Une Femme poète au déclin du romantisme anglais; Felicia Hemans*, Toulouse 1929; Courtney, pp.20–32; Letitia Elizabeth Landon, 'On the Character of Mrs Hemans' Writings', *NMM*, xliv (1835), pp.425–33 (reprinted in Felicia Hemans, *Poems*, copyright edition, Edinburgh 1872); M. I. Leslie, *Felicia Hemans; The Basis of a Biography*, Ph.D. University of London 1943; E. G. Wilson, *Felicia Hemans*, Ph.D. Harvard University 1952; M. B. Ross, *The Contours of Masculine Desire*, Oxford 1989; Norma Clarke, *Ambitious Heights: Writing, Friendship, Love—the Jewsbury Sisters, Felicia Hemans, and Jane Welsh Carlyle*, London 1990.

121. Text: *NMM*, new series, VII.i (1823), pp.439–40. For Hemans's comments on this poem, see *Poetical Remains of the Late Mrs Hemans . . . [with a Memoir]*, ed. D. M. Moir, Edinburgh, pp.66–8.

122. Text: *NMM*, new series, VIII.ii (1823), p.160. Reprinted in *The Forest Sanctuary: and Other Poems*, London 1825, pp.187–8.

123. Text: from *The Amulet* (1826), pp.1–4.

124. Text: from *Blackwood's Edinburgh Magazine*, XXI (April 1827), p.392. Reprinted in *Records of Woman: with Other Poems*, Edinburgh 1828, pp.169–71.

A land of peace] Joanna Baillie, *Ethwald: a tragedy*, Part Second, 1.ii. Hemans replaced the motto by Joanna Baillie with one from Walter Scott—'Where's the coward that would not dare / To fight for such a land?' (*Marmion*).

125. Text: *The Literary Souvenir* (1827), pp.65–6. Reprinted in *Songs of the Affections, with Other Poems*, Edinburgh 1830, pp.225–6.

126. Text: *Blackwood's Edinburgh Magazine*, XXIV (November 1828), p.639. Reprinted in *Songs of the Affections, with Other Poems*, Edinburgh 1830, pp.196–200.

There is nothing in the wide world] Possibly a misquotation of Gray's famous letter to West (16 November 1739), on the Grande Chartreuse: 'not a precipice, not a torrent, not a cliff, but is pregnant with religion and poetry. There are certain scenes that would awe an atheist into belief, without the help of other argument. One need not have a very fantastic imagination to see spirits there at noon-day . . . . You seemed to call me from the other side of the precipice, but the noise of the river below was so great, that I could not distinguish what you said; it seemed to have a cadence like verse.'

127. Text: *Records of Woman: with Other Poems*, Edinburgh 1828, pp.45–54.

Prosperzia Rossi] The main source for information on her life is Giorgio Vasari, *Lives of the Most Eminent Painters, Sculptors, and Architects* (1568), 10 vols, London: Warner 1912, v.123–8.

Tell me no more] Probably by Hemans herself.

128. Text: *Records of Woman: with Other Poems*, Edinburgh 1828, pp.103–8.

Non, je ne puis vivre] *Trans*, No, I cannot live with a broken heart. I must rediscover joy and join the free spirits of the air.

The Bride of Messina] *Die Braut von Messina* (1803), a drama by Friedrich Schiller (1759–1805).

The Prairie] *The Prairie* (1827), a novel by James Fenimore Cooper (1789–1851).

129. Text: *Records of Woman: with Other Poems*, Edinburgh 1828, pp.264–6.

And slight, withal] Byron, Childe Harold's Pilgrimage, Canto iv, St.xxiii.

130. Text: *The Forest Sanctuary: with Other Poems. The Second Edition with Additions*, Edinburgh 1829, pp.239–42.

and is this all?] 'A remarkable description of feelings thus fluctuating from triumph to despondency, is given in Bruce's *Abyssinian Travels*. The buoyant exultation of his spirits on arriving at the source of the Nile, was almost immediately succeeded by a gloom, which he thus portrays: "I was, at that very moment, in possession of what had for many years been the principal object of my ambition and wishes; indifference, which, from the usual infirmity of human nature, follows, at least for a time, complete enjoyment, had taken place of it. The marsh and the fountains of the Nile, upon comparison with the rise of many of our rivers, became now a trifling object in my sight. I remembered that magnificent scene in my own native country, where the Tweed, Clyde, and Annan, rise in one hill. I began, in my sorrow, to treat the inquiry about the source of the Nile as a violent effort of a distempered fancy' (FDH). James Bruce traced the course of the shorter Blue Nile from its source in Khartoum in the 1770s. See James Bruce, *Travels to Discover the Source of the Nile* . . . [1768–73], second edition, 8 vols, Edinburgh 1805. Compare Hemans, 'The Stranger in Louisiana', *NMM*, xiii (1825), p.496, 'A Voyager's Dream of Land', *ibid.*, xiv (1825), pp.77–8.

Simoom] hot, dry, suffocating, desert wind.

131. Text: *The Literary Souvenir* (1830), pp.356–7. Reprinted in *Songs of the Affections, with Other Poems*, Edinburgh 1830, pp.257–9.

132. Text: *Blackwood's Edinburgh Magazine*, XXIX (January 1831), p.129. Reprinted in *National Lyrics, and Songs for Music*, Dublin 1834, pp.61–4. See also Mary Robinson, *Sappho and Phaon* . . . , London 1796, Catherine Grace Godwin, 'Sappho: A Dramatic Sketch', *The Night before the Bridal* . . . , London 1824, pp.113–86.

What is Poesy, but to create] Byron, *The Prophecy of Dante*, Canto IV, lines 11–19. Hemans misquotes, omitting 'And be the new Prometheus of new men,' which follows '. . . beyond our fate'.

[Suggested by a beautiful sketch, the design of the younger Westmacott. It represents Sappho sitting on a rock above the sea, with her lyre cast at her feet.

There is a desolate grace about the whole figure, which seems penetrated with the feeling of utter abandonment.] (FDH)

133. Text: *NMM*, XL.i (1834), p.365. Reprinted in *National Lyrics, and Songs for Music*, Dublin 1834, pp.220–3.

134. Text: *Blackwood's Edinburgh Magazine*, XXXVII (May 1835), pp. 793-5. The epigraph is from the opening of Dante's *Purgatorio*, slightly misquoted (Dante uses 'ingegno' not 'intelletto'): 'To course over better waters the little bark of my wit now lifts her sails'. See also Emily Brontë, 'Faith and Despondency', *Poems by Currer, Ellis, and Acton Bell*, London 1846, pp.8–10.

MARIA JANE JEWSBURY (later FLETCHER) (1800–33)

DNB; *LR*, i.516; *FC*, 577–8; Schlueter, 256; Boyle, 152–4; Courtney, 94–5; F. Espinasse, *Lancashire Worthies: Second Series* (1877), pp.323–39; Eric Gillett (ed.), *Maria Jane Jewsbury: Occasional Papers, with a Memoir*, London 1932; Monica Fryckstedt, 'The hidden rill: the life and career of Maria Jane Jewsbury, *Bulletin of the John Rylands University Library of Manchester*, LXVI.2 (1984), pp.177–203, LXVII.1 (1984), pp.450–73; Norma Clarke, *Ambitious Heights: Writing, Friendship, Love—the Jewsbury Sisters, Felicia Hemans, and Jane Welsh Carlyle*, London 1990.

135. Text: *Lays of Leisure Hours* . . . , London 1829, pp.29–32.

Fame is the spur] Milton, *Lycidas*, ll. 70–2, misquoted.

like a garment, rich and fair] '"The city now doth like a garment wear / The beauty of the morning"—Wordsworth' (MJJ).

136. Text: *ibid.*, pp.180–5.

I am a little world] John Donne, *Divine Meditations*, Sonnet 5.

137–41. Texts: *The Athenaeum Journal*, no. 270 (29 December 1832), no. 285 (13 April 1833), no. 288 (4 May 1833), no. 289 (11 May 1833), no. 322 (28 December 1833).

138. Isaiah xxiii] The biblical oracle concerning Tyre and the ships of Tyre.

The sea hath spoken] Isaiah xxiii, v.4.

140. The Spirit of the Cape] 'The Cape of Good Hope was so named by King John of Portugal; the discoverer, Bartholomew Diaz, gave it the more emphatic, and to this day the more deserved, title of the Cape of Tempests' (MJJ).

LETITIA ELIZABETH LANDON (later MACLEAN) (1802–38)

DNB; *LR*, ii.556–7; *NCBEL*, 3, 531–2; *FC*, 623; Schlueter, 280–1; *LLC*, v.322–8; Boyle, 162–6; Elwood, ii.304–32; *Memoir* by Emma Roberts, prefixed to *The Zenana and Minor Poems*, London 1839, L. Blanchard, *Life and Literary Remains*, 2 vols, London 1841; S. Sheppard, *Characteristics of the Genius and Writings of L.E.L.*, London 1841; *The Autobiography of William Jerdan . . .*, 4 vols (1852–54), iii.169–206; D. E. Enfield, *L.E.L.: A Mystery of the Thirties*, London 1928; Courtney, 44–72; H. Ashton, *Letty Landon*, London 1951; L. Stevenson, 'Miss Landon, "The milk-and-watery moon of our darkness", 1824–1830', *MLQ*, VIII (1947), pp.355–63; Germaine Greer, 'The Tulsa Center for the study of women's literature: what we are doing and why we are doing it', *Tulsa Studies in Women's Literature*, 1 (1982), pp.5–26.

142. Text: *Literary Gazette*, no. 279 (25 May 1822), p.331. Reprinted in *The Improvisatrice: and Other Poems*, London 1824, pp.179–84.
These are familiar things] Untraced, probably by Landon herself.

143. Text: from 'Erinna', in *The Golden Violet . . . and Other Poems*, London 1827, pp.263–5. The ideas are probably from Byron, 'a ruin amidst ruins'. See *Childe Harold's Pilgrimage*, canto IV (1818), and the analysis of the Fall in *Don Juan* by G. M. Ridenour, *The Style of Don Juan*, New Haven 1960, pp.19–89. See also Thomas McFarland, *Romanticism and the Ruins of Form: Wordsworth, Coleridge and Modalities of Fragmentation*, Princeton 1981.

144. Text: from 'A History of the Lyre' in *The Venetian Bracelet . . . and Other Poems*, London 1829, pp.106–7. Landon later used part of it as an epigraph in her novel *Ethel Churchill* (1837). The poem is something of a palimpsest—Byronesque ideas of ruin written over Wordsworthian ideas expressed in 'Ode, Intimations of Immortality' and the 'Preface' to *Lyrical Ballads*. Compare Shelley, 'Mont Blanc', *History of a Six Weeks Tour . . .*, London 1817, pp.175–83, esp. ll.50ff, ('Some say that gleams of a remoter world'). Compare Hemans, 'The spirit's mysteries', **129**.

145. Text: *The Vow of the Peacock, and Other Poems*, London 1835, pp. 231–7. The Factory Act 1833 outlawed the work of children under nine. Children between nine and thirteen could still work eight hours a day, and fourteen to eighteen-year-olds 12 hours a day. A number of women poets were proponents of factory reform. See Caroline Bowles, *Tales of the Factories*, Edinburgh 1833, Caroline Norton, *A Voice from the Factories*, London 1836.
'Tis an accursed thing] Untraced, probably by Landon herself.
Moloch's sacrifice] Moloch, or Molech, the god of the Ammonites, to whom children were sacrificed (2 Kings 23:10). 'First Moloch, horrid king besmeared with blood / Of human sacrifice and parents' tears', Milton, *Paradise Lost* 1.392–3.

146. Text: from *Ethel Churchill: or The Two Brides*, 3 vols, London 1837, ii.236.

147. Text: *NMM*, XLIX (1837), pp.478–81.
A record of the inward world] Untraced, probably by Landon herself.

148. Text: *Fisher's Drawing-Room Scrapbook* (1838), pp.10–11. A number of women wrote poems eulogizing Felicia Hemans after her death. See Landon's 'Stanzas on the Death of Mrs Hemans', *NMM*, XLIV (1835), pp.286–8, and her prose criticism 'On the Character of Mrs Hemans' Writings', *ibid.*, pp.265–8. See also Elizabeth Barrett, 'Stanzas on the Death of Mrs Hemans . . .', in *The Seraphim, and Other Poems*, London 1838, pp.271–5, Maria Abdy, 'Lines on the Death of Mrs Hemans', *Poetry*, second series, London 1838, pp.24–7, Catherine Grace Godwin's 'To Felicia Hemans', in *The Poetical Works*, London 1854, pp.438–40.

Prometheus and the vulture] Prometheus, one of the Greek Titans, was assigned by Zeus to make men out of mud. He subsequently stole the gift of fire from the gods for the benefit of his creations and was punished by Zeus on Mount Caucasus where his liver was consumed by a vulture by day and regenerated by night. 'The only imaginary being resembling in any degree Prometheus, is Satan . . . But Prometheus is, as it were, the type of the highest perfection of moral and intellectual nature, impelled by the purest and truest motives to the best and noblest ends' (Shelley, Preface to *Prometheus Unbound* (1820)). For Landon, however, the link with Prometheus is 'woman's heart', a frequent concern of other women poets such as Hemans, Jewsbury and Abdy, and, more personally, her suffering caused by 'careless tongues' and 'ungenerous words'.

149. Text: *NMM*, LV (1839), pp.30–2. The poem was probably written on the voyage to the Gold Coast where she died soon afterwards. The question 'Do you think of me as I think of you?' was quickly taken as her tragic epitaph when the news of her death reached London. See also Elizabeth Barrett, 'L.E.L.'s Last Question', in *Poems*, 2 vols, London 1844, ii.219–22, given here (**187**) in an earlier version. The refrain 'Do you think of me as I think of you?' possibly had its origin in Hemans' 'The Parting Song', *Forest Sanctuary; and Other Poems*, London 1825 ('When will you think of me, my friends?').

MARIA ABDY (née SMITH) (1797–1867)

DNB; *FC*, 1–2; Boyle, 3–6.

150. Text: from *NMM*, XLVI.i (1836), p.343. Reprinted in *Poetry*, second series, London 1838, pp.44–5. Compare, Landon, 'The Prophetess', *Fisher's Drawing-Room Scrapbook* (1838), pp.43–4, Felicia Hemans, 'The Beings of the Mind', *The Forest Sanctuary: and Other Poems*, London 1828, pp.212–16, and of course *Records of Woman* . . . London 1828. For a contemporary discussion, see Mary Ann Stodart, *Female Writers: Thoughts on their Proper Sphere and on their Powers of Usefulness*, London 1842.

MARY ANN BROWNE (later GRAY) (1812–45)

FC, 455; Boyle, 40–1.

151. Text: from *Ada, and Other Poems* . . . , London 1828, pp.182–5.

'There came the aspiring, the unrest, the aching sense of being misunderstood, the consciousness that those a thousand time inferior were yet more beloved. Genius places a woman in an unnatural position; notoriety frightens away every affection; and superiority has for its attendant fear, not love . . . What is poetry, and what is a poetical career? The first is to have an organisation of extreme sensibility, which the second exposes bareheaded to the rudest weather. The original impulse is irresistible—all professions are engrossing when once begun; and, acting with perpetual stimulus, nothing takes more complete possession of its follower than literature. But never can success repay its cost . . . If this be true even of one sex, how much more true of the other! Ah! Fame to a woman is indeed but a royal mourning in purple for happiness,' (Letitia Landon, 'On the Character of Mrs Hemans' Writings', *op. cit.*)

152–4. Texts: from *The Coronal: Original Poems* . . . , London 1833, pp. 67–72, 73–83, 129-31.

153. Solemn midnight's tingling silentness] Shelley, *Alastor* (1816), line 7.

155. Text: from *Ignatia, and Other Poems*, London and Liverpool 1838, pp.150–1.
'Araby the Blest'] Milton, *Paradise Lost*, iv.163.

CATHERINE GRACE GODWIN (née GARNETT) (1798–1845)

LR, i.404; *Memoir* by A. C. Wigan, prefixed to *The Poetical Works* . . . , London, 1854; Boyle, 103–4; WW *CL*, v.57–9.

156. Text: from 'The Wanderer's Early Recollections', in *The Wanderer's Legacy: A Collection of Poems, on Various Subjects*, London 1829, pp.29–32.

157. Text: *Forget-me-not* (1832), pp.241–2. For two important statements on Lakeland waterfalls, see Coleridge, 'Letter to Sara Hutchinson, 25th Aug. 1802', *Letters*, ed. E. L. Griggs, Oxford 1956, ii.852–5, Keats, 'Letter to Tom Keats, 25–27th June, 1818', *Letters*, ed. H. E. Rollins, Cambridge 1958, i.298–301.
Look back!] Byron, *Childe Harold's Pilgrimage*, Canto IV. st.lxxi.

158. Text: from *The Poetical Works* . . . , ed. A. Cleveland Wigan, London 1854, pp. 428–9.

CAROLINE NORTON (née SHERIDAN, later STIRLING-MAXWELL) (1808–77)

DNB; *LR*, ii.708–11; *NCBEL*, 3, 544; *FC*, 799; *LLC*, vii. 101–6; Boyle, 211–12; HNC, 376–82; Courtney, 72–90; R. H. Horne, 'Miss E. B. Barrett and Mrs Norton', in *A New Spirit of the Age*, 2 vols (1844), ii.129–40; J. G. Perkins, *The Life of Mrs Norton*, London 1909; A. S. Acland, *Catherine Norton*, London 1948.

159. Text: *The Sorrows of Rosalie: A Tale. With Other Poems*, London 1829, pp.111–12.

160. Text: *The Undying One, and Other Poems*, London 1830, pp.237–9.

161. Text: *The Amulet*, 1832, pp.209–11.

162. Text: *NMM*, XLIX, i (1837) p.7.

EMMA ROBERTS (*c.* 1794–1840)

DNB; *LR*, ii.801; *FC*, 909–10; Boyle, 242–3; Courtney, 104–13; Elwood, ii.333–47; *Memoir*, prefixed to *Notes of an Overland Journey* . . . (1841); Obituary, *Asiatic Journal*, December 1840.

163. Text: from *Oriental Scenes, Dramatic Sketches and Tales, with Other Poems*, Calcutta 1830, pp.39–41.

With the expansion of the Empire and the aid of prints, India became a significant arena in the English imagination. See Courtney, 91–126, John Barrell, *The Infection of Thomas De Quincey: A Psychopathology of Imperialism*, New Haven 1991, Nigel Leask, *Romanticism and the Interest of Empire*, Cambridge 1993, Mildred Archer and Ronald Lightbown, *India Observed: India as Viewed by British Artists, 1760–1860*, London: Victoria & Albert Museum 1982. Several women had direct experience, notably Maria Jane Jewsbury and Emma Roberts (Boyle, pp.152–5, 242–3), but annuals such as *Fisher's Drawing Room Scrapbook*, edited by Landon from 1833 to 1838, added an extra dimension to the eighteenth-century idea of 'ideal presence' by linking prints and poems, poems operating as both sub-text or gloss and in their own right as dreams ('fairy lands'), social commentary (wife-burning, incarceration, superstition), and escape from domesticity ('better lands'). See Landon's poems.

peepul] Sacred Indian fig-tree.

CAROLINE BOWLES (later SOUTHEY) (1786–1854)

DNB; *LR*, i.83–5; *NCBEL*, 3, 368–9; *FC*, 124; Boyle, 35–6; HNC, 402–4; Courtney, 33–43.

164–5. Text: from *The Birthday: a poem . . . to which are added, Occasional Verses*, Edinburgh and London 1836, pp.64–5, 77–84.

SARA COLERIDGE (née COLERIDGE) (1802–52)

DNB; *LR*, i.226–7; *NCBEL*, 3, 515; *FC*, 224; Schlueter, 119–20; *LLC*, v. 733–5; HNC, 411–16, *Memoir and Letters*, ed. E. Coleridge, 2 vols, London 1873; E. L. Griggs, *Coleridge Fille: A Biography of Sara Coleridge*,

Oxford 1940; Bradford Keys Mudge, *Sara Coleridge: A Victorian Daughter*, New Haven, 1989; Virginia Woolf, 'Sara Coleridge' in *The Death of the Moth and Other Essays*, London 1942, pp.73–7.

166–9. Texts: *Phantasmion . . .*, London 1837, pp.141, 157–8, 248–9, 287.

EMILY JANE BRONTË (1818–48)

DNB; *LR*, i.91–2; *NCBEL*, 3, 866–7; *FC*, 139–41; Schlueter, 58–60; *LLC*, v.521–7; Barbara Rosenbaum and Pamela White (eds), *Index to English literary manuscripts*, iv. (1800–1900), part 1, London 1982; Anne Passel, *Charlotte and Emily Brontë: An Annotated Bibliography*, New York 1979); R. W. Crump, *Charlotte and Emily Brontë, 1846–1915: A Reference Guide*, Boston 1982; Janet M. Barclay, *Emily Brontë Criticism, 1900–1968: An Annotated Checklist*, New York 1974; S. Akiho and T. Fujita, *A Concordance to the Complete Poems of Emily Jane Brontë*, Tokyo 1976; Jacques Blondel, *Emily Brontë: experience spirituelle et création poetique*, Paris 1956; Winifred Gérin, *Emily Brontë: A Biography*, Oxford 1971; Edward Chitham, *A Life of Emily Brontë*, Oxford 1987; Jean-Pierre Petit (ed.), *Emily Brontë: A Critical Anthology*, Harmondsworth 1973; Anne Smith (ed.), *The Art of Emily Brontë*, London 1976; Stevie Davies, *Emily Brontë: The Artist as a Free Woman*, Manchester 1983; Maureen Peeck-O'Toole, *Aspects of the Lyric in the Poetry of Emily Brontë*, Amsterdam 1988; Irene Taylor, *Holy Ghosts: The Male Muses of Emily and Charlotte Brontë*, New York 1990.

170–6. Texts: *The Complete Poems of Emily Jane Brontë*, ed. C. W. Hatfield, New York 1941, pp.31, 40–3, 48–9, 54–5, 56–7, 63, 87, 90–2. Texts **170–5**, were first printed in *Poems of Charlotte, Emily, and Anne Brontë: Now for the First Time Printed*, New York 1902. The dates at the ends of the poems are those in the manuscript.

172. I have transposed the rhymes *gushing / rushing* on the basis of concordance evidence without examining the manuscript. Hatfield's text is conjectural on this point and the rhymes marked by asterisks.

173. Hatfield omitted 'the' in the last line for metrical reasons but records that it is in Ms.

176. First printed (with alterations) in *Wuthering Heights and Agnes Grey . . . a New Edition Revised, with a Biographical Notice of the Authors, a Selection from their Literary Remains, and a Preface* [ed. Charlotte Brontë], London 1850, pp.476–8.

For the moors] 'The scenery of these hills is not grand—it is not romantic; it is scarcely striking. Long low moors, dark with heath, shut in little valleys, where a stream waters, here and there, a fringe of stunted copse. Mills and scattered cottages chase romance from these valleys; it is only higher up, deep in amongst the ridges of the moors, that Imagination can find rest for the whole of her foot; and even if she finds it there, she must be a solitude-loving raven—no gentle dove. If she demand beauty to inspire her, she must bring it inborn; these moors are too stern to yield any product so delicate. The eye of the gazer must *itself* brim with a "purple light", intense enough to perpetuate the brief flower-flush of August on the heather, or the rare sunset-smile of June . . . My sister Emily loved the moors . . . She found in the bleak solitude many and dear delights; and not the least and best loved was—liberty' ([Charlotte Brontë], 'Prefatory Note' to 'Selections from the Poems of Ellis Bell', in *Wuthering Heights* . . . (1850), pp.471–2).

CHARLOTTE BRONTË (later NICHOLLS) (1816–55)

DNB; *LR*, i.90–1; *NCBEL*, 3, 865–6; *FC*, 139–41; Schlueter, 56–8; *LLC*, vi.17–31; Winifred Gerin, *Charlotte Brontë: The Evolution of Genius*, Oxford 1967; Tom Winnifrith, *A New Life of Charlotte Brontë*, Basingstoke 1988; Rebecca Fraser, *Charlotte Brontë*, London 1988; F. E. Ratchford, *The Brontës' Web of Childhood*, New York 1941; Christine Alexander, *The Early Writings of Charlotte Brontë*, Oxford 1983; *An Edition of the Early Writings of Charlotte Brontë*, 2 vols in 3, Oxford 1987–91; Patricia H. Wheat, *The Adytum of the Heart: The Literary Criticism of Charlotte Brontë*, Rutherford, N.J. 1992. See also the above entry for Emily Brontë.

177–81. Texts: *The Poems of Charlotte Brontë: A New Annotated and Enlarged Edition of the Shakespeare Head Brontë*, ed. Tom Winnifrith, Oxford 1984, pp.184–6, 204–5, 202–3, 225–6, 58–9. Texts have been slightly amended from *The Poems of Charlotte Brontë: A New Text and Commentary*, ed. Victor A. Neufeldt, New York 1985, pp.165–6, 240–1, 246–7, 255, 476–7.

177. mustard seed . . . almost rod] Matthew 13.31–2. 'The kingdom of heaven is like a mustard seed . . . it is the smallest of seeds, but when it has grown it is the greatest of shrubs and becomes a tree, so that the birds of the air come and make nests in its branches.' Numbers 17:8. 'and behold, the rod of Aaron for the house of Levi had sprouted and put forth buds, and produced blossoms, and it bore ripe almonds.'

Sirius] the Dog-Star. In Homer, Sirius was the dog of Orion, the hunter.

ELIZABETH BARRETT (later BROWNING) (1806–61)

DNB; *LR*, i.98–101; *NCBEL*, 3. 435–9; *FC*, 151–2; Schlueter, 66–8; *LLC*, vi.228–47; HNC, 382–8; Margaret Foster, *Elizabeth Barrett Browning: A Biography*, London 1988; Dorothy Merwin, *Elizabeth Barrett Browning: The Origins of a New Poetry*, Chicago 1989, G. W. Hudson, *An Elizabeth Barrett Browning Concordance*, 4 vols, Detroit 1973; J. Magoon, *A Bibliography of Writings about the Brownings: Robert Browning and Elizabeth Barrett Browning from 1980 to 1989*, Bournemouth 1990.

182–4. Texts: from *Prometheus Bound: Translated from the Greek of Aeschylus. And Miscellaneous Poems*, London 1833, pp.81–92, 93–101, 117–21.

182. Mors erat . . .] Lucan, *Pharsalia*, Bk ix. *Trans*. Death was before my eyes.

the forest Titans] giant trees. The Titans were giants who fought against Jupiter.

Night, the Aethiopian queen] Ethiopians were dark-skinned.

deep Eleusis] mysteries. Eleusis, in Attica, where mysteries in the worship of Ceres were practised.

Janus of my soul] Janus was two-faced. Hence conflicting feelings in the soul.

Laocoon] Laocoon correctly warned of the dangers of the wooden horse to Troy. Two sea-serpents strangled him and his children and the Trojans took this to be an omen that his warning was false.

183. Ut per aquas . . .] Lucretius, *De Rerum Natura*, Bk. 1. Trans. For over the waters, what phantasms do we see now.

thymele] The central point of the choral movements in the Greek theatre (EBB).

Of that Athenian] Demosthenes, the orator who in order to cure a speech defect declaimed to the ocean with pebbles in his mouth.

Phylacteries of shame] ribands of parchment fixed to Jewish boys on their thirteenth birthday, containing four passages of the law.

Cyrene's fount] Cyrene was a water nymph, daughter of the river Peneus, beloved by Apollo.

Before those feet] Christ walking on water. March 6:48, Matt. 14:25.

Babel] Genesis 11:1–9.

Hell's angel] Revelation 20:7–10 where Satan is released.

184. The child may possibly have been Byron's daughter, Ada Byron.

Cyrene's waters] See note to **183** above.

185. Text: *NMM*, XLVII (1836), pp.316–20. Reprinted in *The Seraphim, and Other Poems*, London 1838, pp.119–35, where an epigraph was added: 'Can my affections find out nothing best, / But still and still remove?'—Quarles. (Francis Quarles, *Emblemes*, London 1635, p.109.)

186. Text: *Athenaeum*, no. 453 (2 July 1836), p.468. Reprinted in *The Seraphim, and Other Poems*, London 1838, pp.290–2, where an epigraph was added, 'If these doe so, can *I* have feeling lesse?'—*Britannia's Pastorals* (William Browne, *Britannia's Pastorals. The Second Booke*, London 1616, p.95.)

the princess weird] In the Continuation to the Tale of the Second Royal Mendication, in the *Arabian Nights*, the Princess and a Sorcerer oppose each other, undergo a series of metamorphoses and are consumed in the process.

187. Text: *Athenaeum*, no. 587 (26 January 1839). Reprinted in *Poems*, 2 vols, London 1844, ii.219–22. See **149**.

Index of first lines

Selected thematic index

Numbers refer to poems, not pagination